ENGLISH DRAMA,
1660-1800

AMERICAN LITERATURE, ENGLISH LITERATURE, AND WORLD LITERATURES IN ENGLISH: AN INFORMATION GUIDE SERIES

Series Editor: Theodore Grieder, Curator, Division of Special Collections, Fales Library, New York University, New York, New York

Associate Editor: Duane DeVries, Assistant Professor, Polytechnic Institute of New York, Brooklyn, New York

Other books on English literature in this series:

ENGLISH DRAMA TO 1660—*Edited by Frieda Elaine Penninger*

ENGLISH DRAMA AND THEATRE, 1800-1900—*Edited by L.W. Conolly and J.P. Wearing**

ENGLISH DRAMA, 1900-1950—*Edited by E.H. Mikhail**

CONTEMPORARY DRAMA IN ENGLAND AND AMERICA, 1950-1970—*Edited by Richard H. Harris***

THE ENGLISH LITERARY JOURNAL TO 1900—*Edited by Robert B. White, Jr.*

ENGLISH-CANADIAN LITERATURE TO 1900—*Edited by R.G. Moyles*

ENGLISH PROSE, PROSE FICTION, AND CRITICISM TO 1660—*Edited by S.K. Heninger, Jr.*

OLD AND MIDDLE ENGLISH POETRY TO 1500—*Edited by Walter H. Beale*

ENGLISH POETRY, 1500-1660—*Edited by S.K. Heninger, Jr.***

ENGLISH POETRY, 1660-1800—*Edited by Christopher Cohane***

ENGLISH POETRY IN THE NINETEENTH CENTURY—*Edited by Donald Reiman***

ENGLISH POETRY, 1900-1950—*Edited by Emily Ann Anderson***

CONTEMPORARY POETRY IN AMERICA AND ENGLAND, 1950-1970—*Edited by Calvin Skaggs***

*in press
**in preparation

The above series is part of the

GALE INFORMATION GUIDE LIBRARY

The Library consists of a number of separate series of guides covering major areas in the social sciences, humanities, and current affairs.

General Editor: Paul Wasserman, Professor and former Dean, School of Library and Information Services, University of Maryland

ENGLISH DRAMA, 1660-1800

A GUIDE TO INFORMATION SOURCES

*Volume 9 in the American Literature, English
Literature, and World Literatures in English
Information Guide Series*

Frederick M. Link

*Professor of English
University of Nebraska*

Gale Research Company
Book Tower, Detroit, Michigan 48226

Library of Congress Cataloging in Publication Data

Link, Frederick M
    English drama, 1660-1800.

    (American literature, English literature, and world
literatures in English ; v. 9) (Gale information guide library)
    Includes index.
    1. English drama--History and criticism--Bibliography.
2. Theatre--Great Britain--Bibliography.   I. Title.
Z2014.D7L55 [PR625]   016.822   73-16984
ISBN 0-8103-1224-7

For Peggy

VITA

Frederick M. Link is presently professor of English at the University of Nebraska-Lincoln. He received his A.B. from Southwestern-at-Memphis and his M.A. and Ph.D. from Boston University. Link is the author of APHRA BEHN and has edited Behn's THE ROVER and John Dryden's AURENG-ZEBE for the Regents Restoration Drama Series. He has also written a number of articles, reviews, and poems for various magazines and has served as acting director of the University of Nebraska Press.

CONTENTS

Contents

Contents

Contents

Contents

PREFACE

This book is a guide to the scholarship on English drama 1660–1800. It is divided into two parts. Part 1 covers reference materials, the stage, theatrical biography, dramatic history, and general criticism; Part 2, individual dramatists. Part 1 is organized topically; within topics the treatment is either chronological or from the general to the more specific. To facilitate cross reference, the sections in Part 1 have been numbered. Part 2 is organized alphabetically. One index provides a guide to authors' names and locates topics in Part 1; another provides page references for all contemporary plays mentioned in the text.

Certain exclusions have been made to keep the length of the volume within reasonable bounds. Book reviews and reviews of productions, theses and dissertations, foreign language editions, ephemera, manuscript materials, books or articles clearly superseded by later scholarship, brief or survey treatments of major authors, and student guides have usually been omitted. Reference sources concerned with some of these areas are, however, discussed in Part 1, Section 1. I have not treated in any detail the philosophy or psychology of drama, literary theory, or criticism not bearing directly on a dramatist active in the period. Studies of performances between 1660 and 1800 of earlier English plays are included only if they contribute substantially to an understanding of Restoration and eighteenth-century theatre. For example, contemporary criticism of Shakespeare is excluded, but not studies of Shakespearian adaptations or productions 1660–1800. Studies of foreign influence on English drama in the period are included, but studies of the reciprocal influence are not. Studies relating the drama of the period to other genres or later periods of literary history are also excluded. Contemporary dramatic history and criticism are selectively treated, especially in the case of pamphlets. I have also been selective in listing nineteenth-century criticism, much of which is superficial appreciation or attack on moral grounds. The bias of this guide is therefore modern; I believe that most useful work on the topic has been done since about 1880, Lamb and Hazlitt notwithstanding.

Since this is a guide to information sources rather than a history of drama in the period, the user should not expect it to be fully self-contained. The author list (Part 2) does not include really minor figures, nor many for whom no information or editions subsequent to the BIOGRAPHIA DRAMATICA of 1812 can be cited. Exceptions to these criteria have been made for those authors whose work is historically or theatrically significant. The nondramatic work of an author is usually ignored. Biographical information is supplied only for minor authors and is kept to a minimum. A list of plays is usually supplied only for authors uncollected since the period, or authors of whose work no good bibliography is easily available; when furnished, such lists ordinarily include only those plays produced in London before the end of the 1799-1800 season. Collected editions of an author are cited, as are separate modern editions of all but the most frequently printed plays, which are treated selectively. For little known or rarely printed plays, modern collections are sometimes cited; for more systematic treatment of plays in collections see Part 1, Sections 2.1 and 2.2.

Despite these exclusions, my aim has been to list every substantial book and article dealing with English drama 1660-1800 published through 1973 and most significant material published in 1974. Throughout, I have made descriptive or evaluative comments on those items the contents or significance of which are not apparent from their titles. I have occasionally listed items, particularly contemporary works, which I have not been able to see. In every such case, I have attempted to verify the accuracy of the entry from at least two independent sources. In evaluating books and articles I have inevitably revealed my own prejudices, but since an author rarely has the opportunity to rebut such judgments, I have tried not to be capricious or idiosyncratic in making them.

It will be clear from my comments throughout that I do not believe a satisfactory history of drama in this period has yet been written. For example, I do not share the common view that the period exhibits progressive decline from Elizabethan and Jacobean heights. Nor do I think its drama will be revalued as generations of critics reveal structural and stylistic complexities in it hitherto undreamed of. My view is that critics and historians alike have been misled by a too narrow perspective. They have dealt with drama 1660-1800 purely as verbal art, almost never with it as theatre. Hence Theodore Spencer can dismiss Nahum Tate's LEAR with contempt, although prior to 1800 its stage success easily rivaled that of Shakespeare's play. Hence the comedy of the eighteenth century is seen as a wasteland, despite the development in the period of new forms of enormous vitality and consequence. It is easy to dismiss ballad opera, comic opera, and burletta if one ignores music and spectacle--even easier to dismiss pantomime and melodrama. Yet few would wish to judge THE MAGIC FLUTE without taking notice of Mozart's music, or "The Gold Rush" without considering the visual and aural dimensions of Chaplin's film. Received dramatic history not only does tend to ignore or undervalue these elements, but also to exhibit an aristocratic bias against theatrical (as opposed to literary) and popular forms.

My debt to earlier scholars, especially bibliographers, is nevertheless great. Without THE LONDON STAGE, the NEW CBEL, Allardyce Nicoll's HISTORY OF ENGLISH DRAMA 1660-1900, the Stratman-Spencer-Devine RESTORATION AND EIGHTEENTH-CENTURY THEATRE RESEARCH: A BIBLIOGRAPHICAL GUIDE, and the annual bibliographies in PMLA, PQ, RECTR, YWES, and SEL, my task would have been far more difficult. I have made an effort to correct such errors as I have found without introducing new ones of my own and to add

material not included in previous bibliographies. If I am as successful as my
predecessors have been, I shall be more than content. My main purpose,
however, has been to organize and present the scholarship on the period so as
best to serve the needs of the serious student.

This is not a descriptive bibliography, and I have therefore taken certain liber-
ties with titles cited, in the interests of consistency and the convenience of the
user. Spelling and punctuation have been modernized and normalized throughout
both in citation and commentary. For example, the phrase eighteenth-century
is regularly hyphenated when adjectival, Isaac Bickerstaffe's name is always spelled
with the final e, British spelling is silently Americanized, and a colon always
separates a scholarly book's title from its subtitle. Omissions in title listings
are indicated by ellipses. The date supplied for a play is the date of first known
production unless otherwise indicated; all dates are given according to the modern
calendar. A play is cited by its production title, which in some cases differs
from the title as given in the printed edition. (Allardyce Nicoll's ALPHA-
BETICAL CATALOGUE, cited in Part 1, Section 6.4, will usually provide any
necessary cross-references.) Production dates and titles are usually given from
THE LONDON STAGE, occasionally altered or indicated as less certain on
the basis of subsequent scholarship. A publication date, when given, is that
of the first edition.

Publishers are listed for books published after 1800, dates alone for those published in London in the period. Authors and dates, where known, are supplied
even if not printed. Since the combination of volume number and date adequately identifies nearly all periodicals cited, no indication is ordinarily given
of series. Only one publisher and place of publication is cited for a given
book; later editions, especially photographic reprints, are indicated by means
of an asterisk following the original date cited. (No systematic effort has
been made to record all such reprints; for fuller information in a particular
case, the user should consult BOOKS IN PRINT and BRITISH BOOKS IN
PRINT.) A number of standard sources discussed in Part 1 are later referred
to by author and short title only, sometimes with date of publication. In all
such cases the full citation may be located by referring to the first (underlined)
page number cited in the appropriate entry in the author-subject index.

ABBREVIATIONS

NOTE: An asterisk precedes the abbreviation for a periodical of particular importance for the study of drama in the period.

AH	AMATEUR HISTORIAN
AIM	ANNALS OF INTERNAL MEDICINE
AN&Q	AMERICAN NOTES AND QUERIES
AR	ARCHITECTURAL REVIEW
ARec	ARCHITECTURAL RECORD
AWR	ANGLO-WELSH REVIEW
BA	BEIBLATT ZUR ANGLIA
BB	BULLETIN OF BIBLIOGRAPHY
BBA	BONNER BEITRAEGE ZUR ANGLISTIK
BC	BOOK COLLECTOR
BJ	BOOKMAN'S JOURNAL
BJRL	BULLETIN OF THE JOHN RYLANDS LIBRARY (Manchester)
BM	BURLINGTON MAGAZINE
BMQ	BRITISH MUSEUM QUARTERLY
BNYPL	BULLETIN OF THE NEW YORK PUBLIC LIBRARY
BSF	BALL STATE UNIVERSITY FORUM
BSFM	BULLETIN DE LA SOCIETE FRANCAISE DE MUSICOLOGIE
BSM	BRITISH STUDIES MONITOR
BUK	BULLETIN OF THE UNIVERSITY OF KANSAS, HUMANISTIC SERIES
CBEL	CAMBRIDGE BIBLIOGRAPHY OF ENGLISH LITERATURE
CD	COMPARATIVE DRAMA
CE	COLLEGE ENGLISH
CH	COMPUTERS AND THE HUMANITIES
CL	COMPARATIVE LITERATURE
CLAJ	COLLEGE LANGUAGE ASSOCIATION JOURNAL
CLC	COLUMBIA LIBRARY COLUMNS
CLS	COMPARATIVE LITERATURE STUDIES (Wales)
CR	CONNECTICUT REVIEW
DC	DRAMA CRITIQUE
DNB	DICTIONARY OF NATIONAL BIOGRAPHY
*DS	DRAMA SURVEY
DUJ	DUBLIN UNIVERSITY JOURNAL
E&S	ESSAYS AND STUDIES
EA	ETUDES ANGLAISES

Abbreviations

EBST	EDINBURGH BIBLIOGRAPHICAL SOCIETY TRANSACTIONS
EC	ESSAYS IN CRITICISM
*ECS	EIGHTEENTH-CENTURY STUDIES
EDH	ESSAYS BY DIVERS HANDS: TRANSACTIONS OF THE ROYAL SOCIETY OF LITERÁTURE
EE	ENLIGHTENMENT ESSAYS
EHR	ENGLISH HISTORICAL REVIEW
ELH	ENGLISH LITERARY HISTORY
ELN	ENGLISH LANGUAGE NOTES
ER	EDINBURGH REVIEW
ES	ENGLISH STUDIES (Amsterdam)
ESA	ENGLISH STUDIES IN AFRICA
ESt	ENGLISCHE STUDIEN
*ETJ	EDUCATIONAL THEATRE JOURNAL
EUQ	EMORY UNIVERSITY QUARTERLY
Exp	EXPLICATOR
GLL	GERMAN LIFE AND LETTERS
HAB	HUMANITIES ASSOCIATION BULLETIN
HLB	HARVARD LIBRARY BULLETIN
HLQ	HUNTINGTON LIBRARY QUARTERLY
HSN	HARVARD STUDIES AND NOTES IN PHILOLOGY AND LITERATURE
IJES	INDIAN JOURNAL OF ENGLISH STUDIES
JDSG	JAHRBUCH DER DEUTSCHEN SHAKESPEARE-GESELLSCHAFT
JEGP	JOURNAL OF ENGLISH AND GERMANIC PHILOLOGY
JGLS	JOURNAL OF THE GIPSY LORE SOCIETY
JHI	JOURNAL OF THE HISTORY OF IDEAS
JHM	JOURNAL OF THE HISTORY OF MEDICINE
JNT	JOURNAL OF NARRATIVE TECHNIQUE
JPC	JOURNAL OF POPULAR CULTURE
JRL	JOURNAL OF THE RUTGERS UNIVERSITY LIBRARY
JRSI	JOURNAL OF THE ROYAL SOCIETY OF ANTIQUARIES OF IRELAND
JWI	JOURNAL OF THE WARBURG AND COURTAULD INSTITUTE
KR	KENYON REVIEW
LC	LIBRARY CHRONICLE (University of Pennsylvania)
LHR	LOCK HAVEN REVIEW
LM	LONDON MERCURY
LN&Q	LINCOLNSHIRE NOTES AND QUERIES
LR	LIBRARY REVIEW
LS	LANGUAGE AND STYLE
MA	MUSICAL ANTIQUARY
MB	MORE BOOKS (Boston Public Library)
MiQ	MILTON QUARTERLY
MK	MASKE UND KOTHURN
ML	MUSIC AND LETTERS
MLA	Modern Language Association of America
MLN	MODERN LANGUAGE NOTES
MLPS	MEMOIRS OF THE LITERARY AND PHILOSOPHICAL SOCIETY OF MANCHESTER
MLQ	MODERN LANGUAGE QUARTERLY
MLR	MODERN LANGUAGE REVIEW
MP	MODERN PHILOLOGY
MQ	MICHIGAN QUARTERLY

MQR	MICHIGAN QUARTERLY REVIEW
MwQ	MIDWEST QUARTERLY
*N&Q	NOTES AND QUERIES
Np	NEOPHILOLOGUS
NM	NEUPHILOLOGISCHE MITTEILUNGEN
OED	OXFORD ENGLISH DICTIONARY
OSTB	OHIO STATE UNIVERSITY THEATRE COLLECTION BULLETIN
P&P	PLAYS AND PLAYERS
PBSA	PUBLICATIONS OF THE BIBLIOGRAPHICAL SOCIETY OF AMERICA
PLL	PAPERS ON LANGUAGE AND LITERATURE
PLS	PROCEEDINGS OF THE LEEDS PHILOSOPHICAL AND LITERARY SOCIETY, LITERARY AND HISTORICAL SECTION
PM	PENNSYLVANIA MAGAZINE OF HISTORY AND BIOGRAPHY
PMA	PROCEEDINGS OF THE MUSICAL ASSOCIATION
PMLA	PUBLICATIONS OF THE MODERN LANGUAGE ASSOCIATION
POBS	PROCEEDINGS AND PAPERS OF THE OXFORD BIBLIOGRAPHICAL SOCIETY
*PQ	PHILOLOGICAL QUARTERLY
PULC	PRINCETON UNIVERSITY LIBRARY CHRONICLE
QJS	QUARTERLY JOURNAL OF SPEECH
QQ	QUEEN'S QUARTERLY
RB	REVUE BELGE DE PHILOSOPHIE ET D'HISTOIRE
RD	RENAISSANCE DRAMA
*RECTR	RESTORATION AND EIGHTEENTH-CENTURY THEATRE RESEARCH
REL	REVIEW OF ENGLISH LITERATURE (Leeds)
RES	REVIEW OF ENGLISH STUDIES
RLC	REVUE DE LA LITTERATURE COMPAREE
RLV	REVUE DES LANGUES VIVANTES (Brussels)
RMS	RENAISSANCE AND MODERN STUDIES
RR	ROMANIC REVIEW
RSW	RESEARCH STUDIES OF THE STATE COLLEGE OF WASHINGTON
RUO	REVUE DE L'UNIVERSITE D'OTTAWA
SAB	SOUTH ATLANTIC BULLETIN
SAQ	SOUTH ATLANTIC QUARTERLY
SB	STUDIES IN BIBLIOGRAPHY
SBT	STUDIES IN BURKE AND HIS TIME
SCBS	SOUTH CENTRAL BULLETIN STUDIES
SEL	STUDIES IN ENGLISH LITERATURE 1500-1900
SET	STUDIES IN ENGLISH, UNIVERSITY OF TEXAS
SFQ	SOUTHERN FOLKLORE QUARTERLY
SH	SCRIPTA HIEROSOLYMITA
ShQ	SHAKESPEARE QUARTERLY
ShS	SHAKESPEARE SURVEY
SIMG	SAMMELBAENDE DER INTERNATIONALEN MUSIKGESELLSCHAFT
SM	SPEECH MONOGRAPHS
SN	STUDIA NEOPHILOLOGICA
SP	STUDIES IN PHILOLOGY
SR	SEWANEE REVIEW
SSJ	SOUTHERN SPEECH JOURNAL
SSL	STUDIES IN SCOTTISH LITERATURE
TBSI	TRANSACTIONS OF THE BIBLIOGRAPHICAL SOCIETY OF IRELAND
TA	THEATRE ANNUAL

Abbreviations

TAM	THEATRE ARTS MONTHLY
TCBS	TRANSACTIONS OF THE CAMBRIDGE BIBLIOGRAPHICAL SOCIETY
*TD	THEATRE DOCUMENTATION
THAS	TRANSACTIONS OF THE HUNTER ARCHEOLOGICAL SOCIETY
*TLS	TIMES LITERARY SUPPLEMENT (London)
*TN	THEATRE NOTEBOOK
*TR	THEATRE RESEARCH
*TS	THEATRE SURVEY
TSE	TULANE STUDIES IN ENGLISH
TSL	TENNESSEE STUDIES IN LITERATURE
TSLL	TEXAS STUDIES IN LANGUAGE AND LITERATURE
UCS	UNIVERSITY OF COLORADO STUDIES, SERIES IN LANGUAGE AND LITERATURE
UIS	UNIVERSITY OF ILLINOIS STUDIES
UMP	UNIVERSITY OF MICHIGAN PUBLICATIONS IN LANGUAGE AND LITERATURE
UNS	UNIVERSITY OF NEVADA STUDIES
UTQ	UNIVERSITY OF TORONTO QUARTERLY
UTS	UNIVERSITY OF TEXAS STUDIES IN ENGLISH
UWR	UNIVERSITY OF WINDSOR REVIEW
UWS	UNIVERSITY OF WISCONSIN STUDIES IN LITERATURE AND LANGUAGE
VC	VIRGINIA CAVALCADE
VQR	VIRGINIA QUARTERLY REVIEW
WRB	WESTERN RESERVE BULLETIN
WS	WESTERN SPEECH
XUS	XAVIER UNIVERSITY STUDIES
YLG	YALE UNIVERSITY LIBRARY GAZETTE
YWES	THE YEAR'S WORK IN ENGLISH STUDIES
ZAA	ZEITSCHRIFT FUER ANGLISTIK UND AMERIKANISTIK

SHORT TITLE ABBREVIATIONS FOR ESSAY COLLECTIONS AND REFERENCE WORKS

Arnott and Robinson's ENGLISH THEATRICAL LITERATURE.

ENGLISH THEATRICAL LITERATURE 1559-1900: A BIBLIOGRAPHY. Ed. James F. Arnott and John W. Robinson. London: Society for Theatre Research, 1970.

BROWN COLLECTION.

RESTORATION THEATRE. Ed. John R. Brown and Bernard Harris. London: Arnold, 1965.

ENTHOVEN COLLECTION.

STUDIES IN ENGLISH THEATRE HISTORY IN MEMORY OF GABRIELLE ENTHOVEN, O.B.E. London: Society for Theatre Research, 1952

GEOFFRIN COLLECTION.

DRAMATURGIE ET SOCIETE: RAPPORTS ENTRE L'OEUVRE THEATRALE, SON INTERPRETATION, ET SON PUBLIC AUX XVIe ET XVIIe SIECLES. Ed. C. Geoffrin et al. 2 vols. Paris: Editions du Centre National de la Recherche Scientifique, 1968.

JAQUOT COLLECTION.

LE LIEU THEATRAL A LA RENAISSANCE. Ed. Jean Jacquot et al. Paris: Editions du Centre National de la Recherche Scientifique, 1964.

LAWRENCE COLLECTION 1 and 2.

Lawrence, William J. THE ELIZABETHAN PLAYHOUSE AND OTHER STUDIES, FIRST [SECOND] SERIES. Straford-on-Avon: Shakespeare Head Press, 1912 [1913].

Short Title Abbreviations

THE LONDON STAGE.

THE LONDON STAGE 1660-1800: A CALENDAR OF PLAYS, ENTERTAIN-
MENTS, AND AFTERPIECES . . .. Ed. William Van Lennep et al. 5 parts
in 11 vols. Carbondale: Southern Illinois Univ. Press, 1960-70.

LOVE COLLECTION.

RESTORATION LITERATURE: CRITICAL APPROACHES. Ed. Harold Love.
London: Methuen, 1972.

NEW CBEL.

THE NEW CAMBRIDGE BIBLIOGRAPHY OF ENGLISH LITERATURE. Ed.
George Watson. 4 vols. Cambridge: Cambridge Univ. Press, 1969-74

Nicoll's HISTORY.

Nicoll, Allardyce. A HISTORY OF ENGLISH DRAMA 1660-1900. 6 vols.
Cambridge: Cambridge Univ. Press, 1952-59.

RICHARDS COLLECTION.

ESSAYS ON THE EIGHTEENTH-CENTURY STAGE. Ed. Kenneth Richards and
Peter Thomson. London: Methuen, 1972.

Stratman's BIBLIOGRAPHICAL GUIDE.

RESTORATION AND EIGHTEENTH-CENTURY THEATRE RESEARCH: A BIBLIO-
GRAPHICAL GUIDE 1900-1968. Ed. Carl. J. Stratman, David G. Spencer,
and Mary E. Devine. Carbondale: Southern Illinois Univ. Press, 1971.

WOODWARD AND MCMANAWAY'S CHECKLIST.

Woodward, Gertrude L., and James G. McManaway. A CHECKLIST OF
ENGLISH PLAYS 1641-1700. Chicago: Newberry Library, 1945.

Part 1

GENERAL BIBLIOGRAPHY

Chapter I

BIBLIOGRAPHY AND REFERENCE

A. BACKGROUND AND SOURCE MATERIAL

Theatre

1.1 GENERAL WORKS ON THEATRE. The specialized nature of this guide permits only brief mention of the hundreds of bibliographies and reference works useful for theatre research generally. Such guides as Blanch M. Baker, THEATRE AND ALLIED ARTS: A GUIDE TO BOOKS DEALING WITH THE HISTORY, CRITICISM, AND TECHNIC OF THE DRAMA AND THEATRE, AND RELATED ARTS AND CRAFTS (New York: Wilson, 1952); Oscar Brockett et al., A BIBLIOGRAPHICAL GUIDE TO RESEARCH IN SPEECH AND DRAMATIC ART (Glenview, Ill.: Scott, Foresman, 1963); and Frederick J. Hunter, DRAMA BIBLIOGRAPHY: A SHORT TITLE GUIDE TO EXTENDED READING FOR THE ENGLISH-SPEAKING AUDIENCE AND STUDENTS IN THEATRE (Boston: Hall, 1971), are good starting points. Many bibliographies are listed in MUSIC AND DRAMA: A BIBLIOGRAPHY OF BIBLIOGRAPHIES (Totowa, N.J.: Rowman & Littlefield, 1971), compiled by the publishers from the fourth edition of Theodore Besterman, A WORLD BIBLIOGRAPHY OF BIBLIOGRAPHIES . . ., 5 vols. (Lausanne: Societas Bibliographica, 1965-66). The most useful and scholarly dictionary is THE OXFORD COMPANION TO THE THEATRE, 3rd ed., ed. Phyllis Hartnoll (Oxford: Oxford Univ. Press, 1967); the best general reference work, unfortunately without parallel in English, is the ENCICLOPEDIA DELLO SPETTACOLO, 9 vols. (Rome: Le Machere, 1954-62). An index to this appeared in 1968; a supplement covering the years 1955-65 was issued in 1966 (both by Unione Editoriale). "A Checklist of Current Performing Arts Periodicals," by James L. Kottwinkel et al., lists the theatrical serials currently being received by the New York Public Library (TD 1, no. 2 [1969], 3-36). PERFORMING ARTS BOOKS IN PRINT, ed. Ralph N. Schoolcraft (New York: Drama Book Specialists, 1973), is a standard annotated guide to the field.

1.2 SPECIAL TOPICS: THEATRE. Theatrical portraits may be looked up in Lillian A. Hall's CATALOGUE OF DRAMATIC PORTRAITS IN THE THEATRE COLLECTION OF THE HARVARD COLLEGE LIBRARY, 4 vols. (Cambridge, Mass.: Harvard Univ. Press, 1930-34), and in J.F. Kerslake's CATALOGUE OF

THEATRICAL PORTRAITS IN LONDON PUBLIC COLLECTIONS (London: Society for Theatre Research, 1961). Theatrical costuming is covered by Hilaire and Meyer Hiler's BIBLIOGRAPHY OF COSTUME: A DICTIONARY CATALOG OF ABOUT EIGHT THOUSAND BOOKS AND PERIODICALS, ed. Helen Cushing and Adah Morris (New York: Wilson, 1939), and by Isabel Monro and Dorothy E. Cook's COSTUME INDEX: A SUBJECT INDEX TO PLATES AND TO ILLUSTRATED TEXT (New York: Wilson, 1937), to which Isabel and Kate Monro later provided a SUPPLEMENT (New York: Wilson, 1957). Bibliographies on acting may be found in The American Educational Theatre Association's A SELECTED BIBLIOGRAPHY AND CRITICAL COMMENT ON THE ART, THEORY, AND TECHNIQUE OF ACTING (Ann Arbor: AETA, 1948), and in Edwin Duerr's THE LENGTH AND DEPTH OF ACTING (New York: Holt, Rinehart, Winston, 1962). William B. Gamble's THE DEVELOPMENT OF SCENIC ART AND STAGE MACHINERY: A LIST OF REFERENCES IN THE NEW YORK PUBLIC LIBRARY, rev. ed. (New York: New York Public Library, 1928), lists more than 3,000 works on this topic. For dramatic theory and criticism one may consult Richard B. Vowles's DRAMATIC THEORY: A BIBLIOGRAPHY (New York: New York Public Library, 1956) and E.H. Mikhail's COMEDY AND TRAGEDY: A BIBLIOGRAPHY OF CRITICAL STUDIES (Troy, N.Y.: Whitston, 1972); both lists are, however, extremely selective. A third source is Helen H. Palmer and Anne J. Dyson's EUROPEAN DRAMA CRITICISM (Hamden, Conn.: Shoe String Press, 1968; Supplement 1, 1970), which includes English authors. Volume 1 of Arthur Coleman and Gary Tyler's DRAMA CRITICISM (Denver: Swallow, 1966) is A CHECKLIST OF INTERPRETATIONS SINCE 1940 OF ENGLISH AND AMERICAN PLAYS.

1.3   SPECIAL THEATRE COLLECTIONS. Many special collections of theatrical and performing arts materials exist. A useful guide is George Freedley's "The Twenty-Six Principal Theatre Collections in American Libraries and Museums," BNYPL 62 (1958), 319-29. More comprehensive guides are Rosamund Gilder and George Freedley's THEATRE COLLECTIONS IN LIBRARIES AND MUSEUMS: AN INTERNATIONAL HANDBOOK (New York: Theatre Arts, 1936), and especially PERFORMING ARTS LIBRARIES AND MUSEUMS OF THE WORLD, ed. André Veinstein, 2nd ed. rev. and enlarged by Cécile Giteau (Paris: Centre National de la Recherche Scientifique, 1967). A useful discussion of one of the best collections in America is Helen D. Willard's "The Harvard Theatre Collection," RECTR 3, no. 1 (1964), 14-22. The superb collection of the Research Libraries of the New York Public Library is largely covered in THE CATALOG OF THE THEATRE AND DRAMA COLLECTIONS, 21 vols. (Boston: Hall, 1967); this is divided into an author listing (6 vols.), a list of works according to cultural origin (6 vols.; Vols. 2 and 3 including English works), and a list of books on the theatre (9 vols.). The Folger library's CATALOG OF PRINTED BOOKS . . ., 28 vols. (Boston: Hall, 1970), is occasionally useful, especially for the Restoration period. A good microfilm collection of British dramatic periodicals is available at Loyola University, Chicago--see RECTR 2, no. 1 (1963), 20-31, and 3, no. 1 (1964), 46-50. Material available from Xerox University Microfilms in Ann Arbor, Michigan, is listed by Vincent L. Angotti in SOURCE MATERIALS IN THE FIELD OF THEATRE: AN ANNOTATED BIBLIOGRAPHY AND SUBJECT INDEX TO THE MICROFILM COLLECTION (1967).

English Literature and Literary Scholarship

1.4   ENGLISH STUDIES: GENERAL. There are several good bibliographical guides to English studies. The most complete and up-to-date is Arthur G. Kennedy and Donald B. Sands's A CONCISE BIBLIOGRAPHY FOR STUDENTS OF ENGLISH, 5th ed., rev. by William E. Colburn (Stanford, Calif.: Stanford Univ. Press, 1972). This work is exceptionally well organized and gives both the Dewey class number and the Library of Congress number for most entries. The SELECTIVE BIBLIOGRAPHY FOR THE STUDY OF ENGLISH AND AMERICAN LITERATURE, by Richard D. Altick and Andrew Wright, 5th ed. (New York: Macmillan, 1975), is also helpful, as is Donald F. Bond's A REFERENCE GUIDE TO ENGLISH STUDIES, 2nd ed. (Chicago: Univ. of Chicago Press, 1971). More selective, but also more fully annotated, are the second edition of Frederick W. Bateson's A GUIDE TO ENGLISH LITERATURE (London: Longman, 1967) and Andrew H. Wright's A READER'S GUIDE TO ENGLISH AND AMERICAN LITERATURE, 4th ed. (Glenview, Ill.: Scott, Foresman, 1970). The most important serial bibliography is the MLA INTERNATIONAL BIBLIOGRAPHY OF BOOKS AND ARTICLES ON THE MODERN LANGUAGES AND LITERATURES, published by the Modern Language Association. Begun in 1922, this work was limited until 1956 to books and articles by American authors; in 1969 it was separated from its parent volume PMLA, and it is now issued as a multivolume work. Volume 1 includes general works and English literature among the categories covered. The ANNUAL BIBLIOGRAPHY OF ENGLISH LANGUAGE AND LITERATURE published by the Modern Humanities Research Association (1921--) is also useful. Volume 46 (1973) covers 1971. THE YEAR'S WORK IN ENGLISH STUDIES is an annual review of research rather than a simple listing; the first volume, covering 1919-20, appeared in 1921. ABSTRACTS OF ENGLISH STUDIES (1958--) prints abstracts of articles appearing in more than a thousand periodicals. The newest and potentially most comprehensive work of this sort is MLA ABSTRACTS (1970--).

The most important bibliographies for English Literature generally are THE NEW CAMBRIDGE BIBLIOGRAPHY OF ENGLISH LITERATURE, 4 vols., ed. George Watson (Cambridge: Cambridge Univ. Press, 1969-74) and Trevor H. Howard-Hill's BIBLIOGRAPHY OF BRITISH LITERARY BIBLIOGRAPHIES (Oxford: Clarendon Press, 1969). Volume 2 of the former covers 1660-1800, but one may also consult Volume 2 of the original edition, ed. Frederick W. Bateson (Cambridge: Cambridge Univ. Press, 1940), which is more complete in its listing of scholarship prior to World War II on the social and political background of the period. The bibliographies at the end of James R. Sutherland's ENGLISH LITERATURE OF THE LATE SEVENTEENTH CENTURY (1969), Bonamy Dobrée's ENGLISH LITERATURE IN THE EARLY EIGHTEENTH CENTURY 1700-1740 (1959), and William L. Renwick's ENGLISH LITERATURE 1789-1815 (1963) are selective. The three volumes are part of Oxford University Press's OXFORD HISTORY OF ENGLISH LITERATURE; Volume 8, on the mid-eighteenth century, has not yet appeared.

1.5   ENGLISH THEATRE SCHOLARSHIP. A number of reference works cover the theatre of the British Isles. ENGLISH THEATRICAL LITERATURE 1559-1900: A BIBLIOGRAPHY, comp. James F. Arnott and John W. Robinson

(London: Society for Theatre Research, 1970), is a model of accuracy and thoroughness; it incorporates Robert W. Lowe's A BIBLIOGRAPHICAL ACCOUNT OF ENGLISH THEATRICAL LITERATURE . . . (London: Nimmo, 1888*). James Cameron's A BIBLIOGRAPHY OF SCOTTISH THEATRICAL LITERATURE, Printed Paper no. 4 of the Edinburgh Bibliographical Society (Edinburgh, 1892; supplement 1896) is very brief, as is James J. O'Neill's A BIBLIOGRAPHICAL ACCOUNT OF IRISH THEATRICAL LITERATURE, PART 1: GENERAL THEATRICAL HISTORY, PLAYERS, AND THEATRICAL PERIODICALS (Dublin: Falconer, 1920). Alfred Loewenberg's THE THEATRE OF THE BRITISH ISLES, EXCLUDING LONDON: A BIBLIOGRAPHY (London: Society for Theatre Research, 1950) is of first importance and includes much periodical and pamphlet material. Carl J. Stratman's BRITAIN'S THEATRICAL PERIODICALS 1720-1967: A BIBLIOGRAPHY (New York: New York Public Library, 1972), while still imperfect, is a considerable improvement over the 1962 version. Henry Popkin's "The Drama," in CONTEMPORARY LITERARY SCHOLARSHIP, ed. Louis Leary (New York: Appleton-Century-Crofts, 1958), pp. 289-337, offers a succinct overview of the most important modern scholarship in the field.

1.6   PLAYLISTS. Playlists not restricted to the 1660-1800 period, but covering all or part of it, include Alfred Harbage's ANNALS OF ENGLISH DRAMA 975-1700 . . ., rev. by Samuel Schoenbaum (London: Methuen, 1964), and Allardyce Nicoll's A SHORT-TITLE ALPHABETICAL CATALOGUE OF PLAYS PRODUCED OR PRINTED IN ENGLAND FROM 1660 TO 1900, 2nd ed. (Cambridge: Cambridge Univ. Press, 1959), which constitutes the sixth volume of his A HISTORY OF ENGLISH DRAMA 1660-1900. Harbage includes an index of playwrights and plays; Nicoll lists both titles and subtitles for most plays (a most helpful arrangement given the contemporary tendency to refer to both indiscriminately), records the presence of manuscripts and gives references to mention or discussion of the work in earlier volumes of his history. THREE CENTURIES OF ENGLISH AND AMERICAN PLAYS: A CHECKLIST, ed. G. William Bergquist (New York: Readex Microprint Corp., 1963), is helpful in determining which plays are available in the Readex Microprint series on English drama 1500-1800, but is really more an index to that series than a complete checklist of plays; some extant plays are not included, and not all included plays are first editions. Carl J. Stratman's A BIBLIOGRAPHY OF ENGLISH PRINTED TRAGEDY 1565-1900 (Carbondale: Southern Illinois Univ. Press, 1966) attempts to list all editions, including a number not in Nicoll's list or the CAMBRIDGE BIBLIOGRAPHY OF ENGLISH LITERATURE; it locates copies and gives first performance dates where known. The definition of "tragedy" used is perhaps unduly restrictive, since only those plays so labeled on the title page are included. Stratman's DRAMATIC PLAY LISTS 1591-1963 (New York: New York Public Library, 1966) discusses nearly one hundred earlier lists, about a third of which belong to the 1660-1800 period.

There are a few play lists of a more specialized sort. One of the most important is Charles H. Shattuck's THE SHAKESPEARE PROMPTBOOKS: A DESCRIPTIVE CATALOGUE (Urbana: Univ. of Illinois Press, 1965), a census of those marked copies used in professional productions of Shakespeare from the 1620's to about 1960-61 which are available in public collections. The list is arranged alphabetically by play. "The Shakespeare Promptbooks: First Supplement" appeared in TN 24 (1969), 5-17. Alfred Loewenberg's ANNALS OF

OPERA 1597-1940 . . ., 2nd ed. rev. and corrected by Frank Walker, 2 vols. (Geneva: Societas Bibliographica, 1955), is standard, and defines opera broadly. A companion work is Oscar G.T. Sonneck's CATALOG OF OPERA LIBRETTOS PRINTED BEFORE 1800, 3 vols. (Washington, D.C.: Library of Congress, 1914*). Edward D. Coleman's THE JEW IN ENGLISH DRAMA: AN ANNOTATED BIBLIOGRAPHY was first printed in BNYPL; it has been reprinted by the library and KTAV Publishing House (1970), with addenda by Flola L. Shepard. Coleman's THE BIBLE IN ENGLISH DRAMA: AN ANNOTATED LIST OF PLAYS . . . was also first published in BNYPL; it was separately printed by the library in 1931 and reprinted jointly with KTAV in 1968, when a survey by Isaiah Sheffer of recent biblical plays was added. Davis D. and L.A. McElroy compiled FOUR CENTURIES OF SEA PLAYS 1550-1950 (London: for the British Drama League, 1960); see also Earl F. Walbridge's "Drames à Clef: A List of Plays with Characters Based on Real People," BNYPL 60 (1956), 159-74, 235-47, 289-97. Productions of Corneille in English are listed by Phyllis Hartnoll in "Corneille in English," TR 1 (1958), 14-16; Edith Wray records "English Adaptations of French Drama between 1780 and 1815" in MLN 43 (1928), 87-90.

Dissertations

1.7   Theses and dissertations are not ordinarily listed in this guide. The most complete bibliography is the COMPREHENSIVE DISSERTATION INDEX 1861-1972 (Ann Arbor: Univ. Microfilms, 1973) which has more than 400,000 entries in its 37 volumes. Virtually all American and some foreign dissertations are included, and annual supplements are planned. Volumes 29 and 30 cover language and literature; Volume 31, communications and the arts. Volumes 33-37 constitute an author index. The best annual cumulation is DISSERTATION ABSTRACTS INTERNATIONAL, also published by Xerox Univ. Microfilms in Ann Arbor. This work began as MICROFILM ABSTRACTS (1938) and became DISSERTATION ABSTRACTS (1952-68) before assuming its present form. The INDEX TO THESES ACCEPTED FOR HIGHER DEGRESS IN THE UNIVERSITIES OF GREAT BRITAIN AND IRELAND (London: Association of Special Libraries and Bureaux of Information, 1953--) goes back only to 1950/51; the corresponding works for France and Germany are the CATALOGUE DES THESES ET ECRITS ACADEMIQUES (1884/85--), published by the Ministère de L'Education Nationale, and the JAHRESVERZEICHNIS DER DEUTSCHEN HOCHSCHULSCHRIFTEN (1885/86--), published since 1937 by Deutsche Buecherei of Leipzig. For works in German published since 1967, one may also consult ENGLISH AND AMERICAN STUDIES IN GERMAN: SUMMARIES OF THESES AND MONOGRAPHS (Tuebingen, Germany: Niemeyer, 1969--), issued annually.

Some works more limited in scope are equally useful and often more convenient. Lawrence F. McNamee's DISSERTATIONS IN ENGLISH AND AMERICAN LITERATURE: THESES ACCEPTED BY AMERICAN, BRITISH, AND GERMAN UNIVERSITIES 1865-1964 (New York: Bowker, 1968), is excellent, and SUPPLEMENT ONE, 1964-1968 (New York: Bowker, 1969) adds listings from Canada, Australia, and New Zealand. More specialized still is Fredric M. Litto's AMERICAN DISSERTATIONS ON THE DRAMA AND THE THEATRE: A BIBLIOGRAPHY (Kent, Ohio: Kent State Univ. Press, 1969). German theses from 1885 to 1960 are covered in Gloria Schwanbeck's BIBLIOGRAPHIE DER DEUTSCHSPRACHIGEN HOCHSCHULSCHRIFTEN ZUR THEATERWISSENSCHAFT VON 1885 BIS 1952, and Hans-Juergen Rojek's continuation 1953-60 under the same title (Berlin: Selbstverlag der Gesellschaft fuer Theatergeschichte, 1956 and 1962). Carl J. Stratman's "Theses and Dissertations in Restoration and Eighteenth-Century Theatre," RECTR 2, no. 2 (1963), 20-45, lists some 350 items; it was added to in 3, no. 1 (1964), 57; in 6, no. 1 (1967), 55-56 (by Paul F. Vernon); and in 7, no. 1 (1968), 1-6 (by Michel P. Perrin). Stratman's "Unpublished Dissertations in the History and Theory of Tragedy 1889-1957," BB 22 (1958), 161-64; 22 (1959), 190-92, 214-16, and 237-40; and 23 (1960), 15-20, is helpful; see also his addenda in 23 (1962), 162-65 and 187-92. Dissertations are also listed in the RECTR and MLA annual bibliographies.

B. WORKS ON THE PERIOD

Historical Background

1.8   There are several overlapping bibliographies of English or British history in this period. Godfrey Davies's BIBLIOGRAPHY OF BRITISH HISTORY: STUART PERIOD, 1603-1714, rev. Mary F. Keeler (Oxford: Clarendon Press, 1970), and the BIBLIOGRAPHY OF BRITISH HISTORY: THE EIGHTEENTH CENTURY, ed. Stanley Pargellis and Dudley J. Medley (Oxford: Clarendon Press, 1951), belong to the same series and are standard guides. William L. Sachse's RESTORATION ENGLAND 1660-1689 (Cambridge: Cambridge Univ. Press, 1971), a Bibliographic Handbook of the Conference on British Studies, is also very good.

English Literature and Literary Scholarship

1.9   A number of bibliographies of English literature and literary scholarship focus on all or part of the period. Primary works are listed in the three volumes of Donald G. Wing's SHORT-TITLE CATALOG OF BOOKS PRINTED IN ENGLAND, SCOTLAND, IRELAND, WALES, AND BRITISH AMERICA, AND OF ENGLISH BOOKS PRINTED IN OTHER COUNTRIES, 1641-1700 (New York: Cambridge Univ. Press, 1945-52); a much-needed revised edition of this basic reference tool is in process, and a first volume has appeared (1972). A TRANSCRIPT OF THE REGISTERS OF THE WORSHIPFUL COMPANY OF STATIONERS FROM 1640 TO 1708 A.D., ed. George E.B. Eyre, also in three volumes (London: privately printed, 1913-14*), is still useful. The appropriate volumes of the NEW CAMBRIDGE BIBLIOGRAPHY and the OXFORD HISTORY OF ENGLISH LITERATURE contain lists of both primary and secondary works and are handier to use, since they confine themselves more specifically to literature. The two relevant volumes in the Introductions to English Literature series, Vivian De Sola Pinto's THE ENGLISH RENAISSANCE 1510-1688, rev. ed. (London: Cresset Press, 1966), and H.V. Dyson et al., AUGUSTANS AND ROMANTICS 1689-1830, rev. ed. (London: Cresset Press, 1961), contain fairly extensive bibliographies updated from those in the original edi-

tions (1938–40). The notes to George Sherburn's excellent survey, "The Restoration and Eighteenth Century 1660–1789," in A LITERARY HISTORY OF
ENGLAND, ed. Albert C. Baugh (New York: Appleton-Century-Crofts,
1948), constitute a first-rate selective bibliography for the entire period;
Donald F. Bond's revision for the second edition (1967) updates both text and
notes. John W. Draper's EIGHTEENTH-CENTURY ENGLISH AESTHETICS: A
BIBLIOGRAPHY (Heidelberg, Germany: Winters, 1913*) is still somewhat useful;
part 4, pp. 61–115, deals with literature and drama. Donald A. Stauffer's THE
ART OF BIOGRAPHY IN EIGHTEENTH-CENTURY ENGLAND: BIOGRAPHICAL
SUPPLEMENT (Princeton: Princeton Univ. Press, 1941), includes "An Alphabetical Index of English Biographies and Autobiographies 1700–1800" which runs
to 278 pages and is evaluatively as well as descriptively annotated.

Current scholarship is well covered in "English Literature 1660–1800: A Current Bibliography," which has appeared annually in PHILOLOGICAL QUAR-
TERLY since 1926. Six volumes of this bibliography, which contains generally
excellent reviews and helpful annotations, have been collected under the title
ENGLISH LITERATURE 1660–1800: A BIBLIOGRAPHY OF MODERN STUDIES
(Princeton: Princeton Univ. Press, 1950–72); they cover the years 1925–1969
and are indexed in every second volume. In recent years the PQ bibliography
has covered the period more broadly and therefore more selectively than in the
past. An overview of the previous year's scholarship appears annually in the
summer issue of STUDIES IN ENGLISH LITERATURE. The essay is written by a
different scholar each year, and it varies in thoroughness and emphasis with
the interests of the author.

English Theatre

1.10   ENGLISH THEATRE SCHOLARSHIP. There is as yet no full descriptive bibliography of Restoration and eighteenth-century drama. The lists in Donald G. Wing, Alfred Harbage, the individual volumes of Allardyce Nicoll's
HISTORY, and the NEW CAMBRIDGE BIBLIOGRAPHY are finding and reference
lists. Fredson T. Bowers has been working for many years on a bibliography
which will fill this need for the 1660–1700 period; he describes his methods
(and setbacks) in "Bibliography and Restoration Drama," in BIBLIOGRAPHY:
PAPERS READ AT A CLARK LIBRARY SEMINAR, MAY 7, 1966 (Los Angeles:
W.A. Clark Library, 1966), pp. 1–25.

A general bibliography of current scholarship has appeared in RECTR since 1962
(for 1961). RESTORATION AND EIGHTEENTH-CENTURY THEATRE RESEARCH
BIBLIOGRAPHY 1961–1968, ed. Carl J. Stratman, comp. Edmund A. Napieral-
ski and Jean E. Westbrook (Troy, N.Y.: Whitston, 1969), cumulates these
bibliographies for the years from 1961 through 1967; it includes nearly 1,200
entries in an alphabetical arrangement interfiling authors and subjects. The
RECTR bibliography has improved in both accuracy and completeness over the
years; it is also annotated, though the annotation is sometimes sketchy and
usually descriptive rather than evaluative. The "News and Notes" section in
each issue of this periodical is the best available guide to work in progress in
the field, despite the constant reannouncing of certain projects.

A more ambitious outgrowth of the RECTR bibliography and of the work of Stratman and his colleagues in RESTORATION AND EIGHTEENTH-CENTURY THEATRE RESEARCH: A BIBLIOGRAPHICAL GUIDE 1900-1968, ed. Carl J. Stratman, David G. Spencer, and Mary E. Devine (Carbondale: Southern Illinois Univ. Press, 1971). The general editors assigned the period to fourteen contributing editors, each of whom covered three to five years. The individual contributions were edited and intercalated into a master list of 6,560 entries on all aspects of theatrical activity in the British Isles during the period. Most entries are at least briefly annotated. The list is alphabetical according to some 780 subject and author headings and includes editions and dissertations as well as published secondary materials. In a work produced by so many hands, it is impossible to avoid errors, omissions, and inconsistencies; this volume sets no standard in these respects. Moreover, its overall usefulness is impaired by ubiquitous and unnecessary duplication of entries, by inadequate cross-reference, and by the inclusion of a remarkable number of entries irrelevant or peripheral to the subject. Despite these limitations, the Stratman bibliography is a most useful and comprehensive guide to twentieth-century scholarship on the drama of the period. The form for both author and title is fuller than in the NEW CAMBRIDGE BIBLIOGRAPHY, publishers are cited, and the brief abstracts are generally helpful. Futhermore, since it is in dictionary form, it is often easier to use than the cumulated issues of the PQ bibliography.

Reference materials of a more specialized sort include the following: THE DRAMATIC RECORDS OF SIR HENRY HERBERT, MASTER OF THE REVELS, 1623-1673, ed. Joseph Q. Adams (New Haven: Yale Univ. Press, 1917); Robert W. Babcock, "Eighteenth-Century Comic Opera Manuscripts," PMLA 52 (1937), 907-08; the list of collections of eighteenth-century playbills given by Frederick T. Wood and others throughout N&Q 190 and 191 (1946), and the discussion by Ifan K. Fletcher in "British Playbills before 1718," TN 17 (1963), 48-50; Alfred Harbage, "Elizabethan and Seventeenth-Century Play Manuscripts," PMLA 50 (1935), 687-99, and 52 (1937), 905-07; Philip H. Highfill, Jr., "Folger Library Manuscripts Relating to THE THEATRIC TOURIST," TN 20 (1966), 121-26 (see also TN 1 [1947], 86-90 and 93-95; 7 [1950], 38-40; 19 [1965], 64-66; 21 [1967], 59-62); Allan S. Jackson, "Little-Known Theatrical Prints of the Eighteenth Century," TN 22 (1968), 113-16; Edward A. Langhans, "New Restoration Theatre Accounts 1682-1692," TN 17 (1963), 118-34, and "Theatre References in the Greenwich Hospital Newsletters," N&Q 209 (1965), 338; Robert G. Noyes and Roy Lamson, Jr., "Broadside-Ballad Versions of the Songs in Restoration Drama," HSN 19 (1937), 199-218. Noyes also compiled "Contemporary Musical Settings of the Songs in Restoration Drama," ELH 1 (1934), 325-44; "Contemporary Musical Settings of the Songs in Restoration Dramatic Operas," HSN 20 (1938), 99-121; and "Songs from Restoration Drama in Contemporary and Eighteenth-Century Poetical Miscellanies," ELH 3 (1936), 291-316. See also William B. Squire, "An Index of Tunes in the Ballad Operas," MA 2 (1910-11), 1-17. James M. Wells discusses the Newberry Library's holdings in the field in RECTR 3, no. 1 (1964), 11-14.

Several studies record play notices in the contemporary press. These include Alfred Jackson, "Play Notices from the Burney Newspapers 1700-1703," PMLA 48 (1933), 815-49; two articles by Sybil M. Rosenfeld, "Dramatic Advertisements in the Burney Newspapers 1600–1700," PMLA 51 (1936), 123–52, and "The Restoration Stage in Newspapers and Journals 1660–1700," MLR 30 (1935), 445–59; and John H. Wilson, "Theatre Notes from the Newdigate Newsletters," TN 15 (1961), 79–84, and 16 (1961–62), 59.

Finally, a number of miscellaneous bibliographical studies should be noted. Johan Gerritsen's "The Dramatic Piracies of 1661: A Comparative Analysis," SB 11 (1958), 117–31, discusses the piracies of Francis Kirkman. Walter W. Greg, in "Authorship Attributions in the Early Play Lists 1665–1671," EBST 2, part 4 (1946), 303–29, considers the credibility of the attributions in the lists of Rogers and Ley (1656), Archer (1656), and Kirkman (1661 and 1671). Edward A. Langhans, "Restoration Manuscript Notes in Seventeenth-Century Plays," RECTR 5, no. 1 (1966), 30–39, and no. 2 (1966), 2–17, locates copies of plays 1656–1710 which contain manuscript annotations; in another article, "Restoration Theatre Scholarship 1960–66: A Resumé and Suggestions for Future Work," RECTR 6, no. 1 (1967), 8–11, Langhans cites the need for critical editions of source material. Hazelton Spencer, in "A Caveat on Restoration Play Quartos," RES 6 (1930), 315–16, cites specific instances in which an early quarto is reissued as a "new" edition simply by adding a new title page. Most studies in analytic bibliography involve one or two specific works or a single author, and are listed under the appropriate heading in Part 2 of this guide.

1.11   PLAYLISTS AND COLLECTIONS. Until Fredson T. Bowers's bibliography is published, the most comprehensive bibliography limited to plays of the 1660–1700 period is Gertrude L. Woodward and James G. McManaway's A CHECKLIST OF ENGLISH PLAYS 1641–1700 (Chicago: Newberry Library, 1945), which should be used with Bowers's SUPPLEMENT . . . (Charlottesville: Bibliographical Society of the Univ. of Virginia, 1949). Montague Summers's A BIBLIOGRAPHY OF THE RESTORATION DRAMA (London: Fortune Press, 1934) is also useful, although the list of performance dates given has been superseded by THE LONDON STAGE (Section 1.12). Summers also gives licensing dates as recorded in the Stationers' Register. Dougald MacMillan's CATALOGUE OF THE LARPENT PLAYS IN THE HUNTINGTON LIBRARY (San Marino, Calif.: Huntington Library, 1939) records some 2,500 items, including most new plays from 1737 to 1824. A few minor corrections were made to the list by Ethel Pearce in "The Larpent Plays: Additions and Corrections," HLQ 6 (1943), 491–94; see also Leonard Conolly, "Some New Larpent Titles," TN 23 (1969), 150–57, which adds titles from the MS Larpent catalog now in the Pforzheimer Library. Most of the Larpent manuscripts are the work of professional copyists, but they offer valuable information about the text of a play, especially differences between produced and printed versions.

The last decade of the eighteenth century is treated in a specialized list, Theodore Grieder's "Annotated Checklist of the British Drama 1789–99," RECTR 4, no. 1 (1965), 21–47, which is based on the Readex Microprint Series' THREE CENTURIES OF DRAMA. Grieder discusses the acting history and popularity of each play and uses symbols to indicate whether a given play treats one or more of certain subjects or themes. Terence A. Tobin, in "A List of Anonymous Pieces Presented at the Theatre Royal, Edinburgh 1767–1800," SSL 7 (1969), 29–34, notes fifty-two such pieces; see also his "Plays Presented in

Scotland 1660-1700," RECTR 12, no. 1 (1973), 51-53, 59, and "A Checklist of Plays Presented in Scotland 1700-1750," RECTR 14, no. 1 (1975), 43-50. "A List of Plays and Entertainments by Scottish Dramatists 1660-1800," also compiled by Tobin, appeared in SB 23 (1970), 103-17; this records all known plays by native Scottish authors written in the period. A bibliography based on these articles is included in Tobin's PLAYS BY SCOTS 1660-1800 (Iowa City: Univ. of Iowa Press, 1974).

Other specialized lists include Elisabeth Heisch, "A Selected List of Musical Dramas and Dramas with Music from the Seventeenth and Eighteenth Centuries," RECTR 11, no. 1 (1972), 33-58, and 11, no. 2 (1972), 37-59; "A Checklist of Operas Produced in London 1705-1744," appended to George E. Dorris, PAOLO ROLLI AND THE ITALIAN CIRCLE IN LONDON 1715-1744 (The Hague, Netherlands: Mouton, 1967), pp. 269-77; and Lenemaja Friedman, "Bibliography of Restoration and Eighteenth-Century Plays Containing Children's Roles," RECTR 11, no. 1 (1972), 19-30. Heisch's list is based on the collections in the W.A. Clark and Huntington libraries; The Friedman list was added to by Peter Buckroyd in "More Children in Tragedy 1695-1750," RECTR 12, no. 1 (1973), 49-51.

Several articles are devoted to special collections. Gerald E. Bentley, in "Restoration Plays at Princeton," PULC 34 (1973), 131-39, surveys the Princeton holdings. Cyrus Day, in "The W.N.H. Harding Collection," RECTR 3, no. 1 (1964), 23-24, discusses the major private collection of theatrical pieces with music. Hugh G. Dick, in "The English Drama to 1700," WILLIAM ANDREWS CLARK MEMORIAL LIBRARY: REPORT OF THE FIRST DECADE, 1934-1944 (Berkeley and Los Angeles: Univ. of California Press, 1946), pp. 26-33, surveys one of the finest collections in the United States. Allan S. Jackson lists the holdings of the Ohio State University in "Bibliography of Seventeenth- and Eighteenth-Century Play Editions in the Rare Book Room of the Ohio State University Library," RECTR 8, no. 1 (1969), 30-58. Although the revised Wing catalog and new National Union Catalog of the Library of Congress locate copies of the published theatrical pieces of the period, specialized lists are useful to scholars working of necessity in particular geographical areas.

1.12   THEATRICAL CALENDARS. Research in the theatre of the period has been immeasurably aided by the publication of THE LONDON STAGE 1660-1800: A CALENDAR OF PLAYS, ENTERTAINMENTS, AND AFTERPIECES, TOGETHER WITH CASTS, BOX-RECEIPTS, AND CONTEMPORARY COMMENT, COMPILED FROM THE PLAYBILLS, NEWSPAPERS, AND THEATRICAL DIARIES OF THE PERIOD (Carbondale: Southern Illinois Univ. Press, 1960-68). This work, to which the adjective "monumental" may fairly be applied, was conceived in 1935 by William Van Lennep, who began PART 1: 1660-1700 but died before it was completed; the volume was finished by Emmett L. Avery and Arthur H. Scouten and published in 1965. PART 2: 1700-1729 was compiled and edited by Avery and published in two volumes in 1960. Scouten prepared PART 3: 1729-1747, also in two volumes (1961); George W. Stone, Jr., edited PART 4: 1747-1776 (3 vols., 1962). PART 5: 1776-1800, edited by Charles B. Hogan, completed the set (3 vols., 1968). The introductions, taken together, provide a detailed and informative history of the management, operation, personnel, and repertory of the London theatres for nearly a century and a half; they are available separately as Arcturus paperbacks (Carbondale: Southern Illinois Univ. Press, 1968). For each theatrical season the editors offer a brief discussion of events and follow it with a calendar arranged chronologically by month and day. Casts and contemporary comment are normally given when available, and sources for the information are usually indicated.

The introductions vary in scope and quality. That to Part 1 is unnecessarily repetitious, probably because of the special nature of the collaboration. Stone, in the introduction to Part 4, adds information about the appearance of new actors and the death of well known ones and gives totals for performances, plays produced, new main pieces, and new afterpieces. The most useful addition he makes, however, is the detailed analysis of the repertory of the two major theatres for the twenty-nine year period. Hogan gives similar information in the introduction to Part 5 and identifies plays by type and number of acts in his index. The scope and amount of detail given in the individual parts also varies somewhat.

A work of this magnitude will inevitably have defects. Sources are not given for every entry, for example. The index to Part 2 is much inferior to those for the other volumes. There are misprints in every volume. The calendar will undoubtedly be added to; James G. McManaway, for example, notes "Unrecorded Performances in London about 1700," in TN 19 (Winter 1964-65), 68-70, and Edward A. Langhans gives "New Early Eighteenth-Century Performances and Casts," in TN 26 (1972), 145-46. But on the whole, THE LONDON STAGE is a magnificent work and an invaluable reference tool. The information in the eleven volumes (and also that in Arnott and Robinson's ENGLISH THEATRICAL LITERATURE) has been computerized at Lawrence University at Appleton, Wisconsin, under the direction of Ben R. Schneider, Jr.; retrieval of a wealth of information on plays, playwrights, actors and actresses, roles, and so on, is now possible. See Ben R. Schneider, Jr., and Will Daland, "The London Stage Information Bank," CH 5 (1971), 209-14.

THE LONDON STAGE replaces earlier calendars by Avery, Scouten, and others. Dougald MacMillan's DRURY LANE CALENDAR 1747-1776 (Oxford: Clarendon Press, 1938), is still useful for the Garrick period, however, since it focuses on a single theatre and adds to the calendar an alphabetical list of plays performed. Another calendar, William C. Smith's THE ITALIAN OPERA AND CONTEMPORARY BALLET IN LONDON 1789-1820: A RECORD OF PERFORMANCES AND PLAYERS WITH REPORTS FROM THE JOURNALS OF THE TIME (London: Society for Theatre Research, 1955), is also helpful. Eric W. White lists "Early Theatrical Performances of Purcell's Operas, with a Calendar of Recorded Performances 1690-1710" in TN 13 (1959), 43-65.

Chapter II

COLLECTIONS OF THEATRICAL PIECES

A. PLAYS

Play Collections, 1700-1900

2.1   The only useful guide for locating plays in early collections is that
given by Emmett L. Avery in Volume 2 of the NEW CBEL. Avery lists the
major early collections in which the individual plays of a given dramatist appeared. The text used in most of these collections tends to be whatever was
at hand; most of them date from the late eighteenth or early nineteenth century and are often based on current or recent production copies. They are
therefore useful in indicating changes in the theatrical history of included
plays, but they rarely constitute the best texts available. Some are remainders
bound up together with a new general title page; others were originally parts
of a series--issued monthly, twice a month, or irregularly.

The best-known early collection is BELL'S BRITISH THEATRE . . . (London,
1776-81, 1791-1802, etc.). The first "edition" comprised 100 plays in 21
volumes. By the time of the 1791-1802 issue, there were 36 volumes and 140
plays; this edition has been reprinted in microfiche (Washington, D.C.: NCR-
Microcard Editions). THE NEW ENGLISH THEATRE . . ., 12 vols. (London,
1776-77), was another contemporary collection made up of plays with varying
imprints. THE BRITISH DRAMA . . . (London: Miller, 1804) was one of the
first nineteenth-century collections; better known was THE BRITISH THEATRE
. . ., 25 vols. (London: Longman et al., 1808*); it contains 125 plays selected by Elizabeth Inchbald (also available from NCR-Microcard Editions).
Inchbald also selected the plays in THE MODERN THEATRE . . ., 10 vols.
(London: Longman et al., 1809*), a collection including some 50 plays by
more than twenty dramatists of the later eighteenth century. A similar enterprise
was THE MODERN BRITISH DRAMA, 5 vols. (London: W. Miller, 1811).
Thomas J. Dibdin's THE LONDON THEATRE . . ., 26 vols. in 13 (London:
for Whittingham and Arliss, c.1815-18), and THE BRITISH DRAMA . . ., 14
vols. (London: C. Cooke, 1817) were even more extensive undertakings. A
SELECT BRITISH THEATRE . . ., ed. John P. Kemble, 8 vols. (London:
Miller, c.1816), included many of Kemble's contemporary acting versions of
Shakespeare. William Oxberry's THE NEW ENGLISH DRAMA . . ., 21 vols.

(London: for Simpkin et al., 1818-25) comprised 113 plays issued two a month; [Thomas] DOLBY'S BRITISH THEATRE (London: Dolby, 1823-27) ran 92 issues in 15 volumes; John Duncombe's edition contained some 532 numbers published between 1825 and about 1852. [John] CUMBERLAND'S BRITISH THEATRE . . ., 48 vols. (London: Cumberland, c.1826-61), was one of the last major nineteenth-century collections to include a substantial number of plays belonging to the period.

The SUPPLEMENT to BELL'S BRITISH THEATRE . . ., 4 vols. (1784), was comprised largely of farces and afterpieces, as was Parsons' THE MINOR THEA-TRE . . ., 7 vols. (London, 1794); [John] CAWTHORN'S MINOR BRITISH THEATRE . . ., 6 vols. (London: Cawthorn, 1805-07); Elizabeth Inchbald's A COLLECTION OF FARCES AND OTHER AFTERPIECES . . ., 7 vols. (London: Longman et al., 1809*); and [John] CUMBERLAND'S MINOR THEATRE . . ., 16 vols. (London: Cumberland, 1828-c.1840).

There were few collections after the middle of the nineteenth century. Leigh Hunt's THE DRAMATIC WORKS OF WYCHERLEY, CONGREVE, VANBRUGH, AND FARQUHAR (London: E. Moxon, 1840) should be mentioned as reintroducing the comedy of the Restoration to Victorian readers; the edition also provoked considerable controversy about the supposed indecency of the plays included. The Dramatists of the Restoration series, edited by James Maidment and William H. Logan (Edinburgh, 1872-79), ran to fourteen volumes (separately noticed in Part 2).

Play Collections 1900--

2.2   The best guide for locating a play in a twentieth-century collection is John H. Ottemiller's INDEX TO PLAYS IN COLLECTIONS: AN AUTHOR AND TITLE INDEX TO PLAYS APPEARING IN COLLECTIONS BETWEEN 1900 AND 1962 (New York: Scarecrow Press, 1964). This guide, first published in 1943, locates nearly 7,000 printings of more than 2,500 plays by 1,300 different authors in more than 800 collections.

The first twentieth-century collection of note was REPRESENTATIVE ENGLISH DRAMAS FROM DRYDEN TO SHERIDAN, ed. Frederick and James W. Tupper (New York: Oxford Univ. Press, 1914; rev. and enl. 1934). David H. Stevens edited TYPES OF ENGLISH DRAMA 1660-1780 (Boston: Ginn, 1923). The most important collections, however, are BRITISH PLAYS FROM THE RES-TORATION TO 1820, ed. Montrose J. Moses, 2 vols. (Boston: Little, Brown, 1929); PLAYS OF THE RESTORATION AND EIGHTEENTH CENTURY, ed. Dougald MacMillan and Howard M. Jones (New York: Holt, 1931); TWELVE FAMOUS PLAYS OF THE RESTORATION AND EIGHTEENTH CENTURY, ed. Cecil A. Moore (New York: Modern Library, c.1933); ENGLISH PLAYS 1660-1820, ed. Arthur E. Morgan (New York: Harper, 1935); and BRITISH DRAMA-TISTS FROM DRYDEN TO SHERIDAN, ed. George H. Nettleton and Arthur E. Case (Boston: Houghton Mifflin, 1939; 2nd ed., rev. George W. Stone, Jr., 1969). Of these, the Nettleton, Case, and Stone is probably the best, though the MacMillan and Jones is also good and is still in print. A recent paper-

back, RESTORATION AND EIGHTEENTH-CENTURY COMEDY, compiled by
Scott McMillin (New York: Norton, 1973), may also be recommended, but
includes only a few plays. A specialized collection is TEN ENGLISH FARCES,
ed. Leo A. Hughes and Arthur H. Scouten (Austin: Univ. of Texas Press,
1948*).

The most recent collection of Restoration plays is RESTORATION COMEDY,
ed. Alexander N. Jeffares, 4 vols. (London: Folio Press, 1974), which in-
cludes edited texts of twenty-four plays. Useful collections include Bonamy
Dobrée's two volumes in the World's Classics series, FIVE RESTORATION
TRAGEDIES and FIVE HEROIC PLAYS (Oxford: Oxford Univ. Press, 1928 and
1961). Edmund Gosse's RESTORATION PLAYS FROM DRYDEN TO FARQUHAR
(London: Dent, 1912), a volume in the Everyman Library series, and REPRE-
SENTATIVE ENGLISH COMEDIES, VOLUME 4: DRYDEN AND HIS CONTEM-
PORARIES, COWLEY TO FARQUHAR, ed. Charles M. Gayley and Alwin
Thaler (New York: Macmillan, 1936), are earlier collections; the latter also
contains several useful essays. RESTORATION COMEDIES, ed. Dennis Davison
(Oxford: Oxford Univ. Press, 1970); SIX RESTORATION PLAYS, ed. John H.
Wilson (Boston: Houghton Mifflin, 1959); and Eugene M. Waith's RESTORA-
TION DRAMA (New York: Bantam, 1968) are paperback editions intended for
classroom use. Three specialized collections have been devoted to Shakespeare.
Montague Summers's SHAKESPEARE ADAPTATIONS: 'THE TEMPEST,' 'THE
MOCK TEMPEST,' AND 'KING LEAR' (Boston: Small, Maynard, 1922) has
been long out of print; Christopher Spencer's FIVE RESTORATION ADAPTA-
TIONS OF SHAKESPEARE (Urbana: Univ. of Illinois Press, 1965) has better
texts if fewer notes. Gwynne B. Evans's SHAKESPEARE PROMPT-BOOKS OF
THE SEVENTEENTH CENTURY (Charlottesville: Bibliographical Society of the
Univ. of Virginia, 1960-66) includes three from the Restoration.

There are also several collections which focus on the eighteenth century. The
twenty volumes of BRITISH THEATRE: EIGHTEENTH-CENTURY ENGLISH
DRAMA (Frankfurt: Minerva GMBH, 1969) are reprints of plays from old an-
thologies, selected and arranged by Natascha Wuerzbach; the collection cannot
be recommended, but it includes a few plays otherwise difficult to find in
print. Three volumes in the World's Classics series are useful--Allardyce
Nicoll's LESSER ENGLISH COMEDIES OF THE EIGHTEENTH CENTURY; William
D. Taylor's EIGHTEENTH-CENTURY COMDEY, rev. and re-edited by Simon
Trussler; and Michael R. Booth's EIGHTEENTH-CENTURY TRADEGY (Oxford:
Oxford Univ. Press, 1927, 1929 [rev. 1969], and 1965). The Everyman's Li-
brary volume EIGHTEENTH-CENTURY PLAYS, selected by John Hampden (Lon-
don: Dent, 1928); EIGHTEENTH-CENTURY PLAYS, introd. Ricardo Quintana
(New York: Modern Library, 1952); and John H. Wilson's SIX EIGHTEENTH-
CENTURY PLAYS (Boston: Houghton Mifflin, 1963) may also be mentioned.
Two specialized collections are Simon Trussler's BURLESQUE PLAYS OF THE
EIGHTEENTH CENTURY and Richard W. Bevis's EIGHTEENTH-CENTURY DRAMA:
AFTERPIECES (London: Oxford Univ. Press, 1969 and 1970). New York's
Garland Publishing, Inc., has announced a collection of 171 contemporary
ballad opera texts to be produced in facsimile in 28 volumes. Nineteen vol-
umes of this were published in 1974, ed. Walter H. Rubsamen.

Collections of Theatrical Pieces

B. PROLOGUES, EPILOGUES, SONGS

2.3   Although prologues and epilogues constitute one of the few genres contributed by the period to poetry, and include in their number some of the finest poems of the period, the only modern collection is RARE PROLOGUES AND EPILOGUES 1642-1700, ed. Autrey N. Wiley (London: Allen & Unwin, 1940*).   Emmett L. Avery adds half a dozen new pieces in "Some New Prologues and Epilogues 1704-1708," SEL 5 (1965), 455-67.   A modern edited collection of representative pieces is long overdue.   Collections were far more popular in the eighteenth century, which produced a dozen or so anthologies like THE COURT OF THESPIS . . . (London, 1769), THE SPOUTER'S COMPANION; OR, THEATRICAL REMEMBRANCES . . . (London, 1770?), A COMPLETE COLLECTION OF PROLOGUES AND EPILOGUES (London, 1771), THE THEATRICAL BOUQUET . . . (London, 1780), and THE NEW THESPIAN ORACLE . . . (London, 1791).   A very extensive example is A COLLECTION AND SELECTION OF ENGLISH PROLOGUES AND EPILOGUES, 4 vols. (London, 1779).   A more complete list is given in the NEW CBEL.

A few collections of songs should be noted as including theatrical pieces. The COVENT GARDEN DROLLERY, ed. George Thorn-Drury (London: Dobell, 1928) is one of these.   The most famous of the contemporary song collections is WIT AND MIRTH; OR, PILLS TO PURGE MELANCHOLY, the best known edition of which was compiled by Thomas D'Urfey.   The two modern collections devoted entirely to theatrical songs are Willard Thorp, ed., SONGS FROM THE RESTORATION THEATRE (Princeton: Princeton Univ. Press, 1934*), and SONGS OF THE RESTORATION THEATRE, ed. Philip J. Stead (London: Methuen, 1948).

Collections of Theatrical Pieces

B. PROLOGUES, EPILOGUES, SONGS

2.3   Although prologues and epilogues constitute one of the few genres contributed by the period to poetry, and include in their number some of the finest poems of the period, the only modern collection is RARE PROLOGUES AND EPILOGUES 1642-1700, ed. Autrey N. Wiley (London: Allen & Unwin, 1940*).   Emmett L. Avery adds half a dozen new pieces in "Some New Prologues and Epilogues 1704-1708," SEL 5 (1965), 455-67.   A modern edited collection of representative pieces is long overdue.   Collections were far more popular in the eighteenth century, which produced a dozen or so anthologies like THE COURT OF THESPIS . . . (London, 1769), THE SPOUTER'S COMPANION; OR, THEATRICAL REMEMBRANCES . . . (London, 1770?), A COMPLETE COLLECTION OF PROLOGUES AND EPILOGUES (London, 1771), THE THEATRICAL BOUQUET . . . (London, 1780), and THE NEW THESPIAN ORACLE . . . (London, 1791).   A very extensive example is A COLLECTION AND SELECTION OF ENGLISH PROLOGUES AND EPILOGUES, 4 vols. (London, 1779).   A more complete list is given in the NEW CBEL.

A few collections of songs should be noted as including theatrical pieces. The COVENT GARDEN DROLLERY, ed. George Thorn-Drury (London: Dobell, 1928) is one of these.   The most famous of the contemporary song collections is WIT AND MIRTH; OR, PILLS TO PURGE MELANCHOLY, the best known edition of which was compiled by Thomas D'Urfey.   The two modern collections devoted entirely to theatrical songs are Willard Thorp, ed., SONGS FROM THE RESTORATION THEATRE (Princeton: Princeton Univ. Press, 1934*), and SONGS OF THE RESTORATION THEATRE, ed. Philip J. Stead (London: Methuen, 1948).

Chapter III

PLAYHOUSES AND PLAYGOERS

A. GENERAL AND MISCELLANEOUS WORKS

Introductory Surveys

3.1   A number of books offer helpful introductions to the English playhouse in all or part of the period. Cecil Price's THEATRE IN THE AGE OF
GARRICK (London: Blackwell, 1973) is the most recent of these. Price makes
excellent use of contemporary sources to discuss acting, costume, spectacle,
opera and ballet, repertory, and both London and provincial theatres. Another
fine book devoted to the London stage in the Garrick period is James J.
Lynch's BOX, PIT, AND GALLERY: STAGE AND SOCIETY IN JOHNSON'S
LONDON (Berkeley and Los Angeles: Univ. of California Press, 1953).
Lynch's study is more detailed than Price's and is particularly valuable for its
excellent discussion of repertory and of the professional conditions affecting
manager, actor, and author. The introduction and notes to each season in
THE LONDON STAGE have already been mentioned as an important source of
information, and one should also consult Allardyce Nicoll's HISTORY.

Early studies include Edward Dutton Cook's A BOOK OF THE PLAY: STUDIES
AND ILLUSTRATIONS OF HISTRIONIC STORY, LIFE, AND CHARACTER, 2
vols. (London: Sampson Low et al., 1876), and his later work, ON THE
STAGE: STUDIES OF THEATRICAL HISTORY AND THE ACTOR'S ART, 2 vols.
(London: Sampson Low et al., 1883). R.J. Broadbent's STAGE WHISPERS
(London: Simpkin et al., 1901) is a later and poorer example of these com-
pendiums. George C.D. Odell's introduction to SHAKESPEARE FROM BETTER-
TON TO IRVING (Section 8.2) is still useful despite its 1920 date, as is
Alwin Thaler's SHAKESPEARE TO SHERIDAN: A BOOK ABOUT THE THEATRE
OF YESTERDAY AND TODAY (Cambridge, Mass.: Harvard Univ. Press, 1922*).
William J. Lawrence's OLD THEATRE DAYS AND WAYS (London: Harrap,
1935*), like most of these books, treats such varied topics as the function of
the prompter, admission systems, rehearsals, first nights, and theatrical owner-
ship. A recent example is ALL RIGHT ON THE NIGHT, by Victor C. Clinton-Baddeley (London: Putnam, 1954), which covers roughly 1737-1843 and
deals with everything from pantomime traditions to the origin of the term
"clap-trap." Montague Summers's THE RESTORATION THEATRE (London:

Routledge & Kegan Paul, 1934*) is less anecdotal but equally concerned with miscellaneous information; advertising, the function of prologue and epilogue, the use of the curtain, and so on, are discussed with Summers's customary digressions and expansive style. The best guide to the court stage of the early part of the period is still Eleanore Boswell's THE RESTORATION COURT STAGE (1660-1702) . . . (Cambridge, Mass.: Harvard Univ. Press, 1932).

Architecture and Design

3.2   Architecture and design are covered in the first three chapters of Richard Southern's THE GEORGIAN PLAYHOUSE (London: Pleiades Books, 1948), and in chapters 4-7 of Richard Leacroft's THE DEVELOPMENT OF THE ENGLISH PLAYHOUSE (London: Eyre, Methuen, 1973); both have a wealth of pertinent illustration. William J. Lawrence, Allardyce Nicoll, and other pioneer students argued about the number and location of proscenium doors and the use of the curtain, among other topics, but Southern and other scholars have now established what contemporary practice was. A useful discussion of the earlier controversy is Donald T. Mackintosh's "Restoration Stage," ER 248 (1928), 172-85, a review article. Nicoll's THE DEVELOPMENT OF THE THEATRE: A STUDY OF THEATRICAL ART FROM THE BEGINNINGS TO THE PRESENT DAY, 5th ed. (London: Harrap, 1966), has two sketchy chapters on the period but many useful illustrations. Illustrations may also be found in A PICTURE HISTORY OF THE BRITISH THEATRE, by Raymond Mander and Joe Mitchenson (London: Hulton, 1957), in the BIOGRAPHICAL DICTIONARY OF ACTORS see Section 4.1 below), in THEATRE PICTORIAL: A HISTORY OF WORLD THEATRE AS RECORDED IN DRAWINGS, PAINTINGS, ENGRAVINGS, AND PHOTOGRAPHS, ed. George Altman et al. (Berkeley and Los Angeles: Univ. of California Press, 1953), and in Donald C. Mullin's THE DEVELOPMENT OF THE PLAYHOUSE: A SURVEY OF THEATRE ARCHITECTURE FROM THE RENAISSANCE TO THE PRESENT (Berkeley and Los Angeles: Univ. of California Press, 1970). The text of the Mullin book is disappointing, however. A contemporary work of some interest is George Saunders's A TREATISE ON THEATRES (London, 1790*), a survey of contemporary theatrical architecture accompanied by the author's own designs.

Scenery and Sets

3.3   Scenery and sets have been extensively studied. Lily B. Campbell's book SCENES AND MACHINERY ON THE ENGLISH STAGE DURING THE RENAISSANCE (Cambridge: Cambridge Univ. Press, 1923) has, despite its title, a long chapter on stage decoration after the Restoration. Webb's designs for THE SIEGE OF RHODES were first printed by William G. Keith in "The Design for the First Movable Scenery on the English Public Stage," BM 25 (1914), 29-33 and 85-98. Allardyce Nicoll's "Scenery in Restoration Theatres," ANGLIA 44 (1920), 217-25, along with other early studies, has been superseded by the definitive work on the subject, Richard Southern's CHANGEABLE SCENERY: ITS ORIGIN AND DEVELOPMENT IN THE BRITISH THEATRE (London: Faber, 1952). Southern notes that his work is based on the work and notebooks of William J. Lawrence, but his own meticulous scholarship and passion for detail is everywhere evident. The illustrations are many and excellent. To this book may be added Southern's "Observations on Lansdowne MS no. 1171," TN 2 (1947), 6–19, and his "Concerning a Georgian Proscenium Ceiling," TN 3 (1948), 6–12.

Other useful studies include Mitchell Wells, "Spectacular Scenic Effects of the Eighteenth-Century Pantomime," PQ 17 (1938), 67–81; Russell Thomas, "Contemporary Taste in the Stage Decorations of London Theatres 1770–1800," MP 42 (1944), 65–78; Lee J. Martin, "From Forestage to Proscenium: A Study of Restoration Staging Techniques," TS 4 (1963), 3–28; William S. Clark, "Corpses, Concealments, and Curtains on the Restoration Stage," RES 13 (1937), 438–48; William M. Petersen and Richard Morton, "Mirrors on the Restoration Stage," N&Q 207 (1962), 10–13 and 63–67; and Allan S. Jackson, "Restoration Scenery 1656–1800," RECTR 3, no. 2 (1964), 25–38, a summary of modern scholarship. James G. McManaway's "L'Héritage de la Renaissance dans la mise en scène en Angleterre 1642–1700," JACQUOT COLLECTION, pp. 459–72, is good and has excellent plates. Stage lighting is discussed in most general surveys; see also P.J. Crean, "Footlights," N&Q 164 (1933), 61–62, and Donald C. Mullin, "Lamps for Garrick's Footlights," TN 26 (1972), 92–94.

Perhaps the best work on scene design is Sybil M. Rosenfeld's A SHORT HISTORY OF SCENE DESIGN IN GREAT BRITAIN (Oxford: Blackwell & Mott, 1973), which also has numerous well chosen illustrations. Individual designers or scene painters have occasionally been the subject of an article, particularly Philip De Loutherbourg and William Capon. The latter is discussed by Ralph G. Allen in "Kemble and Capon at Drury Lane 1794–1802," ETJ 23 (1971), 22–35; by Joseph W. Donohue, Jr., in "Kemble's Production of MACBETH (1794): Some Notes on Scene Painters, Scenery, Special Effects, and Costumes," TN 21 (1967), 63–74; and by Robert Eddison, in "Capon and Goodman's Fields," TN 14 (1960), 127–32. William J. Lawrence wrote articles on both Capon and De Loutherbourg as early as 1895; nearly every discussion of scenery in the Garrick era refers to the latter's work. Volume 2 of THEATRE NOTEBOOK (1948) carries a group of articles on Thomas Lediard, of which the most important is Richard Southern's "Lediard and Early Eighteenth-Century Scene Design," pp. 49–54. M.A. Rooker (1731–1801) is the subject of Sybil M. Rosenfeld's "A Georgian Scene-Painter at Work," BMQ 34 (1969), 33–36.

Costume and Properties

3.4   The broadly conceived books on costume, Lucy Barton's HISTORIC COSTUME FOR THE STAGE (Boston: Baker, 1961 [1935]) and James Laver's COSTUME IN THE THEATRE (London: Harrap, 1964) and DRAMA: ITS COSTUME AND DECOR (London: the Studio, 1951) cover the period rather sketchily. Cecil W. and Phyllis Cunnington's HANDBOOK OF ENGLISH COSTUME IN THE SEVENTEENTH CENTURY, 2nd ed. (London: Faber, 1966), and HANDBOOK OF ENGLISH COSTUME IN THE EIGHTEENTH CENTURY, 2nd ed. (London: Faber, 1964), are much more helpful, as is ENGLISH COSTUME OF THE EIGHTEENTH CENTURY, with drawings by Iris Brooke and text by

James Laver (London: Black, 1931). Perhaps the best of these guides is Iris Brooke's DRESS AND UNDRESS: THE RESTORATION AND EIGHTEENTH CENTURY (London: Methuen, 1958), which is not only well written and illustrated but includes delightful and apt contemporary comment on costume and fashion. Lily B. Campbell's "A History of Costuming on the English Stage between 1660 and 1823," UWS, no. 2 (1918), pp. 187-223, reprinted in her COLLECTED PAPERS (New York: Russell, 1968), relates the development of costume in the theatre to the increasing interest in history and the gradual improvement in stage lighting, and thus provides a more theoretical framework for these costume guides. At the other end of the scale, the Cunningtons and Charles Beard collaborated in the excellent A DICTIONARY OF ENGLISH COSTUME 900-1900 (London: Black, 1960), which comes close to being encyclopedic.

More specialized still are the articles dealing with costume or properties for a single production, such as Bernard E. Barrow's "Macklin's Costume and Property Notes for the Character of Lovegold: Some Traditional Elements in Eighteenth-Century Low-Comedy Acting," TN 13 (1958-59), 66-67; and Muriel St. Clare Byrne's "The Stage Costuming of MACBETH in the Eighteenth Century," ENTHOVEN COLLECTION, pp. 52-64. Donald T. Mackintosh's "'New Dress'd, in the Habits of the Times,'" TLS, 25 Aug. 1927, p. 575, argues that it was George Colman in 1762-63, rather than Macklin, who should be called the father of historical costuming. Raymond J. Pentzell, in "Garrick's Costuming," TS 10 (1969), 18-42, argues that Garrick wore stage costume rather than either historical or conventional dress. The same author, in "Kemble's Hamlet Costume," TS 13 (1972), 81-85, uses a contemporary picture to confirm James Boaden's statement that Kemble was using "Old English" dress before 1785. Philip H. Highfill, Jr., in "Rich's 1744 Inventory of Covent Garden Properties," RECTR 5, no. 1 (1966), 7-17, no. 2 (1966), 17-26, and 6, no. 1 (1967), 27-35; and Sybil M. Rosenfeld, in "The Wardrobes of Lincoln's Inn Fields and Covent Garden," TN 5 (1951), 15-19, reproduce contemporary lists. Thornton S. Graves has an amusing and anecdotal essay, "The Stage Sword and Dagger," in SAQ 20 (1921), 201-12.

Miscellaneous Studies

3.5   Miscellaneous articles relating to the stage of the period include Alwin Thaler's "The 'Freelist' and Theatre Tickets in Shakespeare's Time and After," MLR 15 (1920), 124-36, and two articles by William J. Lawrence, "The Origin of the Theatre Program" and "Early Systems of Admission," LAWRENCE COLLECTION 2, pp. 55-91 and 93-118. St. Vincent Trowbridge provides an excellent analysis in THE BENFIT SYSTEM IN THE BRITISH THEATRE (London: Society for Theatre Research, 1967). Rhoda Payne's "Stage Directions during the Restoration," TA 20 (1963), 41-62, has better illustrations than text. Selma J. Cohen's "Theory and Practice of Theatrical Dancing in England in the Restoration and Early Eighteenth Century . . .," BNYPL 63 (1959), 541-54, and 64 (1960), 41-54 and 95-104; William J. Lawrence's "The English Theatre Orchestra: Its Rise and Early Characteristics," MQ 3 (1917), 9-27; and Donald J. Rulfs's "Entr'acte Entertainment at Drury Lane and Covent Garden 1750-1770," TA 12 (1954), 17-27--all concern nonverbal aspects of the theatre. Charles B. Hogan's "An Eighteenth-Century Prompter's Notes," TN 10 (1956),

37-44, is ostensibly devoted to William Powell, but most useful in showing what the prompt notes to a play can reveal about its production. Promptbooks are also the subject of two interesting articles by Edward A. Langhans, "Three Early Eighteenth-Century Promptbooks," TN 20 (1966), 142-50, and "Three Early Eighteenth-Century Manuscript Promptbooks," MP 65 (1967), 114-29.

One or two studies focus on other aspects of production. Brian Cosgrove relates contemporary acting styles to a production problem in "MACBETH in the Eighteenth Century: Should the Ghost of Banquo Appear on the Stage?" TN 27 (1972), 5-9. See also Albert Wertheim's "Production Notes for Three Plays by Thomas Killigrew," TS 10 (1969), 105-13.

Not nearly enough work has been done, however, either on the way in which plays of the period were produced in their own day or on how they should be produced today. William L. Sharp has a perceptive essay, "Restoration Comedy: An Approach to Modern Production," DS 7 (1968-69), 69-86, but for the most part one must go to the reviews of modern productions to get some sense of the problems and the producer's solution to them. Lyn Oxenford's PLAYING PERIOD PLAYS, PART 3: RESTORATION, GEORGIAN, AND REGENCY PERIODS, 1688-1820 (London: G. Miller, 1957) is hardly more than a beginning.

B. LONDON THEATRES

General Studies

3.6   Though there are dozens of books on London which devote some attention to the theatres of the period, most accounts are derivative and sketchy at best; there is at present no modern work which surveys the Restoration and Georgian playhouses in detail, and a modern scholarly version of a book like Edward W. Brayley's HISTORICAL AND DESCRIPTIVE ACCOUNTS OF THE THEATRES OF LONDON (London: J. Taylor, 1826) would be welcome. Drury Lane and the Royal Opera House in Covent Garden, however, are thoroughly covered in Volume 36 of the SURVEY OF LONDON (London: Athlone Press, Univ. of London, for the Greater London Council, 1970); many plates and drawings accompany a text which treats site, buildings, and management in admirable detail. Edward A. Langhans's two studies, "Pictorial Material on the Bridges Street and Drury Lane Theatres," TS 7 (1966), 80-100, and "The Vere Street and Lincoln's Inn Fields Theatres in Pictures," ETJ 20 (1968), 171-85, are useful supplements to the relevant chapters in the general histories of theatre discussed earlier, and they add some new material. See also Oscar Brownstein, "The Duke's Company in 1667," TN 28 (1974), 18-23.

Several books and articles have been devoted to the formation of the various companies and their rights in earlier drama. John Leslie Hotson's THE COMMONWEALTH AND RESTORATION STAGE (Cambridge, Mass.: Harvard Univ. Press, 1928*) is notable among these, particularly in the use of contemporary documents to resolve questions about the transition from interregnum to Restoration.

John Freehafer, in "The Formation of the London Patent Companies in 1660,"
TN 20 (1965), 6–30, adds further material and makes some corrections to the
account given by Hotson. Allardyce Nicoll's argument in "The Rights of Bees-
ton and D'Avenant in Elizabethan Plays," RES 1 (1925), 84–91, that these managers had access to prompt copies independent of the folios and quartos, has
not been widely accepted and was immediately attacked by Hazelton Spencer
in "The Restoration Play Lists," RES 1 (1925), 443–46. A different explana-
tion of this division of rights is offered by Gunnar Sorelius in "The Rights of
the Restoration Theatrical Companies in the Older Drama," SN 37 (1965),
174–89; he thinks the lists had different purposes and were not complete inven-
tories.

The visits of various foreign troupes to London are discussed by William J.
Lawrence in "Early French Players in England," LAWRENCE COLLECTION 1,
pp. 123–56; by Arno L. Bader, "The Modena Troupe in England," MLN 50
(1935), 367–69; by Emmett L. Avery, "Foreign Performers in the London Thea-
tres in the Early Eighteenth Century," PQ 16 (1937), 105–23; and by M. and
P. Fuchs, "Comédiens français à Londres 1738–1755," RLC 13 (1933), 43–72.
Avery's article and Sybil M. Rosenfeld's FOREIGN THEATRICAL COMPANIES
IN GREAT BRITAIN IN THE SEVENTEENTH AND EIGHTEENTH CENTURIES
(London: Society for Theatre Research, 1955) are the best guides to the sub-
ject.

Miscellaneous studies include William J. Lawrence's "Restoration Stage Nurs-
eries," ARCHIV 132 (1914), 301–15, and Peter Thomson's "Thomas Holcroft,
George Colman the Younger, and the Rivalry of the Patent Theatres," TN 22
(1968), 162–68. Harry W. Pedicord's articles, "Rylands English MS. 1111:
An Early Diary of Richard Cross (d. 1760), Prompter to the Theatres," and
"Course of Plays, 1740–42: An Early Diary of Richard Cross, Prompter to the
Theatres," BJRL 37 (1955), 503–27, and 40 (1958), 432–72, add to the Cross-
Hopkins diaries in the Folger Shakespeare Library another record covering Covent
Garden in 1740–41 and Drury Lane in 1741–42. Paul S. Sawyer examines the
vogue of spectacle in "Processions and Coronations on the London Stage 1727–
61," in TN 14 (1959), 7–12. George W. Whiting, in "The Condition of the
London Theatres 1679–83: A Reflection of the Political Situation," MP 25
(1927), 195–206, shows how the politicizing of the theatres led to a decline
in income and ultimately to the United Company. Shirley S. Kenny, in "Theatrical Warfare 1695–1710," TN 27 (1973), 130–45, discusses the complex period after the breakup of the United Company in 1695.

Theatrical activity outside the major playhouses is the subject of Emmett L.
Avery's "Private Theatricals in and near London 1700–1737," TN 13 (1959),
101–05; private theatricals are also discussed in an article by Sybil M. Rosen-
feld in MK 10 (1965). George Speaight explores the puppet stage in his ar-
ticle "Puppet Theatres in London, 2: The Restoration to the End of the Eigh-
teenth Century," TN 2 (1947), 2–5. Una Ellis-Fermor, in "Studies in the
Eighteenth-Century Stage," PQ 2 (1923), 289–301; Henry Morley, in MEMO-
RIES OF BARTHOLOMEW FAIR (London: Chatto & Windus, 1880*); and Sybil
M. Rosenfeld, in THE THEATRE OF THE LONDON FAIRS IN THE EIGHTEENTH
CENTURY (Cambridge: Cambridge Univ. Press, 1960), discuss a fascinating

underworld of contemporary theatrical life. The Rosenfeld account is the most detailed and accurate; Morley's book is beautifully written and well illustrated. See also LeRoy J. Morrissey, "English Street Theatre 1655-1708," COSTERUS 1 (1972), 105-37.

Individual Theatres (Alphabetically)

3.7   THEATRE ROYAL, BRIDGES STREET. Donald C. Mullin, in "The Theatre Royal, Bridges Street: A Conjectual Restoration," ETJ 19 (1967), 17-29, suggests that Webb used a plan he and Inigo Jones had developed twenty years earlier, altered to take grooves and wings. In a further article, "The Theatre Royal, Bridges Street: An Architectural Puzzle," TN 25 (1970), 14-19, Mullin analyzes the architectural implications of the three drawings discovered by Edward A. Langhans and conjectured to be of the exterior of this theatre. Harold J. Oliver, in "The Building of the Theatre Royal in Bridges Street: Some Details of Finance," N&Q 217 (1972), 464-66, shows from contemporary documents unknown to John Leslie Hotson that a Richard Ryder was the builder if not the designer of the building, and that the cost was some £2,500.

COVENT GARDEN. Henry S. Wyndham wrote THE ANNALS OF COVENT GARDEN THEATRE FROM 1734 to 1897, 2 vols. (London: Chatto & Windus, 1906), and Edwin B. Chancellor produced a similar book, THE ANNALS OF COVENT GARDEN AND ITS NEIGHBORHOOD (London: Hutchinson, 1930), two decades later. A more recent study is Harold D. Rosenthal's TWO CENTURIES OF OPERA AT COVENT GARDEN (London: Putnam, 1958), but very little of this book is relevant to the period, and the account that is given is perfunctory. A useful article on the building of the theatre, Howard P. Vincent's "John Rich and the First Covent Garden Theatre," ELH 17 (1950), 296-306, discusses John Rich's troubles with his contractor. For an accurate account of the theatre, one must go to the SURVEY OF LONDON volume mentioned above (Section 3.6), and to the general and seasonal introductions in THE LONDON STAGE. See also Cecil Price, "Thomas Harris and the Covent Garden Theatre," RICHARDS COLLECTION, pp. 105-22.

DORSET GARDEN. Edward A. Langhans has written an excellent survey, "The Dorset Garden Theatre in Pictures," TS 6 (1965), 134-46, with many illustrations, and "A Conjectural Reconstruction of the Dorset Garden Theatre," TS 13 (1972), 74-93, with drawings and photographs of his reconstructed model.

DRURY LANE. Since Hamilton Bell announced his discovery of a Wren plan in "Contributions to the History of the English Playhouse, 2: On Three Plans by Sir Christopher Wren," ARec 33 (1913), 359-68, it has been assumed that this plan was probably for the 1674 Drury Lane. Richard Leacroft discussed a reconstruction of it in "Wren's Drury Lane," ARec 110 (1951), 43-46, and Richard Southern also discusses it in CHANGEABLE SCENERY (see Section 3.3).

Edward A. Langhans, in "Wren's Restoration Playhouse," TN 18 (1964), 91–100, offers a detailed analysis of Wren's drawing, with plates and models. The latest account, by Donald C. Mullin and Bruce Koenig, "Christopher Wren's Theatre Royal," TN 21 (1967), 180–87, gives a critique of the Leacroft and Langhans reconstructions and offers another based on an analysis of contemporary references to the structure in its various forms. See also Graham Barlow, "Sir James Thornhill and the Theatre Royal, Drury Lane," RICHARDS COLLECTION, pp. 179–93.

The Theatre Royal in Bridges Street and the later Drury Lane are discussed in Walter J. Macqueen-Pope, THEATRE ROYAL, DRURY LANE (London: Allen, 1946), but the book is often inaccurate and overly nostalgic; Brian Dobbs's DRURY LANE: THREE CENTURIES OF THE THEATRE ROYAL (London: Cassell, 1972) is a much better guide for the general reader. THE SURVEY OF LONDON and THE LONDON STAGE are again the best sources for details of management and siting. The Cross-Hopkins diaries in the Folger Library provide many details of theatre income and repertory in the Garrick era (Harry W. Pedicord plausibly identifies John Brownsmith as author in "'The Second Chronicler': A Tentative Identification of the Unknown Hand in the MS Diaries of the Drury Lane Theatre," TS 6 [1964], 79–86). There are also account books extant for some seasons; see Edwin B. Chancellor's articles, "A Manuscript Account Book of Drury Lane Theatre for 1746–48" and "More Concerning a Manuscript Account Book . . .," CONNOISSEUR 75 (1926), 217–21, and 76 (1926), 90–94.

GOODMAN'S FIELDS. A general account of this theatre is given by Frederick T. Wood in "Goodman's Fields Theatre," MLR 25 (1930), 443–56. Robert Eddison, in "Capon and Goodman's Fields," TN 14 (1960), 127–32, explores William Capon's hypothetical reconstruction of the seating and stage as it had been in 1741 and prints Capon's manuscript annotations on various copies of the drawing. Charles B. Hogan's "The New Wells, Goodman's Fields, 1739–1752," TN 3 (1949), 67–72, discusses another theatre in the same area.

QUEEN'S (KING'S) THEATRE, HAYMARKET. Donald C. Mullin, "The Queen's Theatre, Haymarket: Vanbrugh's Opera House," TS 8 (1967), 84–105, gives a good general account and reproduces two ground plans of the building among his illustrations. Emmett L. Avery discusses the seating room in "The Capacity of the Queen's Theatre in the Haymarket," PQ 31 (1952), 85–87; Ronald C. Kern gives a good analysis in "Documents Relating to Company Management 1705–1711," TN 14 (1959–60), 60–65, and Sybil M. Rosenfeld another in "An Opera House Account Book for 1716–17," TN 16 (1962), 83–88. An earlier article by William J. Lawrence, "The Early Years of the First English Opera House," MQ 7 (1921), 104–17, is still pertinent. The fullest study, however, is Daniel Nalbach's THE KING'S THEATRE 1704–1867: LONDON'S FIRST ITALIAN OPERA HOUSE (London: Society for Theatre Research, 1972), but see the review by Judith Milhous, PQ 53 (1974), 576–78.

HAYMARKET. Cyril Maude's THE HAYMARKET THEATRE: SOME RECORDS AND REMINISCENCES, ed. Ralph Maude (London: G. Richards, 1903), is anecdotal and derivative on the early years of the theatre. Walter J.

MacQueen-Pope's HAYMARKET: THEATRE OF PERFECTION (London: Allen, 1948) is readable, but also an anecdotal, loosely organized, and romanticized account. Hubert C. Heffner, "The Haymarket Theatre under Colman the Younger, 1789-1805," SM 10 (1943), 23-29, is sketchy; the best account is, as usual, scattered through the volumes of THE LONDON STAGE.

LINCOLN'S INN FIELDS. A modern reconstruction of this theatre is offered by Elizabeth G. Scanlan in "Reconstruction of the Duke's Playhouse in Lincoln's Inn Fields, 1661-1671," TN 10 (1956), 48-50, with illustrations; see also Edward A. Langhans's critique, pp. 112-14. Frederick T. Wood summarizes the contents of two manuscript account books now in the British Museum in "The Account-Books of Lincoln's Inn Fields Theatre, 1724-1727," N&Q 164 (1933), 220-24, 256-60, 272-74, and 294-98. His work was duplicated, with additional interpretation, by Emmett L. Avery in "The Finances of an Eighteenth-Century Theatre," TA 13 (1955), 49-59. Paul Sawyer, in "The Seating Capacity and Maximum Receipts of Lincoln's Inn Fields Theatre," N&Q 199 (1954), 290, uses account books in the Harvard Theatre Collection to show the maximum capacity of the theatre to be less than 1,400 persons, with maximum receipts of about £216.

OTHER THEATRES. Many of the earliest Restoration theatres are discussed in the general works already cited. William J. Lawrence, in "A Forgotten Restoration Playhouse," ESt 35 (1905), 279-89, discusses the Phoenix or Cockpit in Drury Lane. William Van Lennep chronicles the end of an era in "The Death of the Red Bull," TN 16 (1962), 126-34. Elizabeth G. Scanlan's "Tennis Court Theatres in England and Scotland," TN 10 (1955), 10-15, gives detailed references to source material on these buildings; a late example is studied by David C. Jenkins in "The James Street Theatre at the Old Tennis-Court," TN 23 (1969), 143-50. John H. Wilson, in "A Theatre at York House," TN 16 (1962), 75-78, argues that visiting actors performed in this palace in the Strand in 1672-74.

C. PROVINCIAL THEATRES

General Studies

3.8   "Notes on English Provincial Theatres in the Eighteenth Century," by Frederick T. and Jessie Wood, N&Q 160 (1931), 147-50, 165-69, and 183-87, led to further contributions by several different persons, pp. 209-10, 226-27, 247-48, 253, 267, 283-84, 301, 317-18, 338-39, 356-57, 388; 161 (1931), 30-31. In an article in LN&Q 21 (1931), 69-70, 104-07, and 22 (1932) 19-20, Alfred Welby and John B. King give information on more than a dozen theatres. There is also much material in TN 1 (1947) on James Winston's THEATRIC TOURIST (London, 1805) and on the surviving manuscript of this important work. Chapter 9 of Cecil Price's THEATRE IN THE AGE OF GARRICK, already noted, gives a useful overview of the provincial stage, and Roy M. Wiles's "Crowd-Pleasing Spectacles in Eighteenth-Century England," JPC 1 (1967), 90-105, suggests the effect of a variety of spectacular events, including plays, on the life of the provincial towns.

Strollers and Strolling

3.9   Strolling players accounted for much of the theatrical fare of the country towns. The best and most complete account is Sybil M. Rosenfeld's STROLLING PLAYERS AND DRAMA IN THE PROVINCES 1660-1765 (Cambridge: Cambridge Univ. Press, 1939*). Chapter 1 of this book, titled "The Strolling Life," is a fine introduction to the subject. Earlier studies include Elbridge Colby's "Strolling Players in the Eighteenth Century," N&Q 132 (1952), 454–57; Alwin Thaler's "Strolling Players and Provincial Drama after Shakespeare," PMLA 37 (1922), 243–80, which was reprinted with additions in his SHAKESPEARE AND DEMOCRACY (Knoxville: Univ. of Tennessee Press, 1941); Colby's "A Supplement on Strollers," PMLA 39 (1924), 642–54; Frederick T. Wood's "Strolling Actors in the Eighteenth Century," ESt 66 (1931), 16–53, and "Some Aspects of Provincial Drama in the Eighteenth Century," ES 14 (1932), 65–74; Herschel C. Baker's "Strolling Actors in Eighteenth-Century England," SET (1941), 100–20; and Kenneth M. Cameron's "Strolling with Coysh," TN 17 (1962), 12–16. Clifford Leech, in "A Restoration Touring Company," TLS, 31 May 1934, p. 392, suggests that the first license to tour may have been obtained by George Bayley in 1662; Cecil Price, in "An Eighteenth-Century Theatrical Agreement," TN 2 (1948), 31–34, discusses the rules governing a strolling troupe toward the end of the period.

Specific Locations (Alphabetically)

3.10   Only the more important materials concerning the major provincial towns are referred to in the following list. For additional references to published and unpublished material, see Alfred Loewenberg's bibliography, THE THEATRE OF THE BRITISH ISLES, EXCLUDING LONDON, listed in Section 1.5.

BATH. Belville S. Penley's THE BATH STAGE: A HISTORY OF DRAMATIC REPRESENTATIONS IN BATH (London: Lewis, 1892*) is useful but dated. Frederick T. Wood gives a calendar of performances 1706-1800 in "Theatrical Performances at Bath in the Eighteenth Century," N&Q 192 (1947), 477–78, 486–90, 539–41, 552–58; 193 (1949), 38–40, 92–93, 253–55. Cecil Price traces "SOME MOVEMENTS OF THE BATH COMPANY 1729-1734" in TN 1 (1946), 55–56.

BIRMINGHAM.   John E. Cunningham's THEATRE ROYAL: THE HISTORY OF THE THEATRE ROYAL, BIRMINGHAM (Oxford: Ronald, 1950) is the best account. See also Thomas E. Pemberton, THE THEATRE ROYAL, BIRMINGHAM, 1774-1901 (Birmingham, 1901), and Raymond C. Rhodes, THE THEATRE ROYAL, BIRMINGHAM, 1774-1924: A SHORT HISTORY (Birmingham, England: Moody Brothers, 1924).

BRIGHTON. Henry C. Porter's THE HISTORY OF THE THEATRES OF BRIGH-
TON FROM 1774 TO 1885 (Brighton, England: King & Thorne, 1886) may be
supplemented by Sybil M. Rosenfeld's "Duke Street Theatre, Brighton, 1790-
1806," TN 8 (1954), 60-61.

BRISTOL. The theatre at Bristol has been extensively studied. Older ac-
counts, such as Richard Jenkins's anecdotal MEMOIRS OF THE BRISTOL STAGE
. . . (Bristol, England: Cadell, 1826), Guy T. Watts's THEATRICAL BRISTOL
(Bristol, England: Holloway, 1915), George Rennie Powell's THE BRISTOL
STAGE: ITS STORY (Bristol, England: Bristol Printing, 1919), M.E. Board's
THE STORY OF THE BRISTOL STAGE 1490-1925 (London: Fountain Press,
1926), have been largely superseded for the period by Kathleen N. Barker's
THE THEATRE ROYAL, BRISTOL, 1766-1966: TWO CENTURIES OF STAGE
HISTORY (London: Society for Theatre Research, 1974). Bertram L. Joseph
offers a brief survey, "Famous Theatres, 1: The Theatre Royal, Bristol," DS 2
(1962), 139-45; James Ross performs a similar task in "An Eighteenth-Century
Playhouse: The Theatre Royal, Bristol," EDH 22 (1945), 61-85. Kathleen N.
Barker's "The First Night of the Theatre Royal, Bristol," N&Q 212 (1967),
419-21 (THE CONSCIOUS LOVERS and Murphy's THE CITIZEN), and Sybil M.
Rosenfeld's "Actors in Bristol 1741-1748," TLS, 29 Aug. 1936, p. 700, are
also useful.

CAMBRIDGE. Sybil M. Rosenfeld, "The Players in Cambridge 1662-1800,"
ENTHOVEN COLLECTION, pp. 24-37, discusses the theatrical offerings during
the period.

EAST ANGLIA. Theodore Legay Burley's monograph, PLAYHOUSES AND PLAY-
ERS OF EAST ANGLIA (Norwich, England: Jarrold, 1928), may be consulted.

EXETER. The fullest separate account is William Cotton's THE STORY OF THE
DRAMA IN EXETER . . . 1787 TO 1823 . . . (London: Hamilton, Adams, 1887).

HULL. Thomas Sheppard's EVOLUTION OF THE DRAMA IN HULL AND DIS-
TRICT (Hull, England: Brown, 1927) may be consulted.

LEICESTER. See William Kelly, NOTICES ILLUSTRATIVE OF THE DRAMA
AND OTHER POPULAR AMUSEMENTS . . . (London: Smith, 1865).

LIVERPOOL. The best account is R.J. Broadbent's ANNALS OF THE LIVER-
POOL STAGE, FROM THE EARLIEST PERIOD TO THE PRESENT TIME . . .
(Liverpool: n.p.?, 1908*).

MANCHESTER. A good account of the playhouse of Manchester is provided by
J.L. Hodgkinson and Rex Pogson in THE EARLY MANCHESTER THEATRE (London: Society for Theatre Research, 1960).

MARGATE. Malcolm Morley's posthumously published monograph, MARGATE

AND ITS THEATRES 1730-1965 (London: Museum Press, 1966), is the most recent account, but it is sketchy and lacks documentation.

NEWCASTLE. Harold Oswald, THE THEATRES ROYAL IN NEWCASTLE-UPON-TYNE . . . (Newcastle, England: Northumberland Press, 1936), may be consulted; see also K.E. Robinson, "Stephen Kemble's Management of the Theatre Royal, Newcastle-upon-Tyne," RICHARDS COLLECTION, pp. 137-48.

NORTH SHIELDS. See Robert King, NORTH SHIELDS THEATRE, A HISTORY . . . FROM 1765 . . . (Gateshead-on-Tyne, England: Northumberland Press, 1948), the first chapters of which deal with the period.

NORWICH. See Bosworth Harcourt, THEATRE ROYAL, NORWICH . . . (Norwich, England: Norfolk News, 1903). Sybil M. Rosenfeld discusses "The Players in Norwich 1669-1709" and ". . . 1710-1750" in RES 12 (1936), 129-38 and 285-304. Dorothy H. Eshleman has edited THE COMMITTEE BOOKS OF THE THEATRE ROYAL, NORWICH 1768-1825 (London: Society for Theatre Research, 1970). Sandra A. Burner, in "A Provincial Strolling Company of the 1670's," TN 20 (1965-66), 74-78, deals with the Norwich area.

OXFORD. Players at Oxford are the subject of William J. Lawrence's "Irish Players at Oxford in 1677," LAWRENCE COLLECTION 2, pp. 189-200, and of an exchange between Raymond C. Rhodes, Lawrence, and Frederick S. Boas in TLS, 21 and 28 Feb., 14 March, and 21 April 1929, on "The King's Players at Oxford 1661-1712" (pp. 140, 163, 206, and 295). The subject is further treated in Rosenfeld's book, STROLLING PLAYERS, which incorporates her article in RES for 1943.

RICHMOND (Surrey). Frederick Bingham's A CELEBRATED OLD PLAYHOUSE: THE HISTORY OF RICHMOND THEATRE . . . FROM 1765 TO 1884 (London: Vickers, 1886) is the fullest independent account. Emmett L. Avery's "The Summer Theatrical Seasons at Richmond and Twickenham 1746-1753," N&Q 173 (1937), 290-94, 312-15, and 328-32, may also be consulted.

RICHMOND (Yorkshire). Sybil M. Rosenfeld has a pamphlet, THE EIGHTEENTH-CENTURY THEATRE AT RICHMOND, YORKSHIRE (York, England: Georgian Society, 1947), and a brief note, "Report on Two Georgian Theatres," TN 14 (1961), 100-101, which discuss the reconstruction of this theatre.

SHEFFIELD. See Frederick T. Wood's "Sheffield Theatres in the Eighteenth Century," THAS 6 (1947), 98-116.

SOUTHEND. There is some material on the period in chapter 1 of John K. Melling's SOUTHEND PLAYHOUSES FROM 1793 (Letchworth, England: Citizen Press, 1969).

SUSSEX. In "Sources of Information on Eighteenth- and Early Nineteenth-

Century Theatres in Sussex," TN 12 (1958), 58–64, Francis W. Steer gives much information relevant beyond his specific topic.

WESSEX. Arnold Hare's THE GEORGIAN THEATRE IN WESSEX (London: Phoenix, 1958) is a useful account, illustrated.

WORCESTER. One may consult F[rederick?]. Grice's "The Theatre Royal at Worcester," TN 10 (1956), 83–86, and Barry Duncan's "A Worcestershire Company," TN 2 (1948), 76–78.

YORK. Much information is contained in Tate Wilkinson's MEMOIRS (see Section 4.2), and there is a brief sketch by George Benson, THE THEATRE ROYAL AND THE DRAMA IN YORK (York: n.p.?, 1911).

D. IRELAND, SCOTLAND, WALES

3.11   Older accounts of the Irish stage, like Robert Hitchcock's AN HIS-TORICAL VIEW OF THE IRISH STAGE . . ., 2 vols. (Dublin, 1788–1794), and Joseph F. Molloy's THE ROMANCE OF THE IRISH STAGE . . ., 2 vols. (London: Downey, 1897), have been outdated by the work of William S. Clark. His books, THE EARLY IRISH STAGE: THE BEGINNINGS TO 1720 and THE IRISH STAGE IN THE COUNTRY TOWNS 1720 TO 1800 (Oxford: Clarendon Press, 1955 and 1965) are scholarly, well documented, and thorough. Both volumes have useful appendices: the first on plays and players at the Dublin theatres to 1720, the second on plays and players outside Dublin, 1720–1800. LaTourette Stockwell's DUBLIN THEATRES AND THEATRE CUSTOMS 1637–1820 (Kingsport, Tenn.: Kingsport Press, 1938) and Peter Kavanagh's THE IRISH THEATRE, BEING A HISTORY OF THE DRAMA IN IRELAND . . . (Tralee: The Kerryman, 1946), despite their titles, focus on the later eighteenth and nineteenth centuries. THEATRE IN IRELAND, a new study by Micheal O'hAodha (Oxford: B. Blackwell, 1974), traces the formative processes shaping Irish drama from 1637 to 1971. More specialized articles include Robert C. Bald's "Shakespeare on the Stage in Restoration Dublin," PMLA 56 (1941), 369–78; Hazelton Spencer's response, "Shakespearean Cuts in Restoration Dublin," PMLA 57 (1942), 575–76; William Van Lennep's "The Smock Alley Players of Dublin," ELH 13 (1946), 216–22; and John H. Stewart's "The French Revolution on the Dublin Stage 1790–1794," JRSI 90 (1961), 183–92.

John Jackson's THE HISTORY OF THE SCOTTISH STAGE . . . (Edinburgh, 1793) is the earliest full account of the theatre in Scotland; another is Robb Lawson's THE STORY OF THE SCOTS STAGE (Paisley, Scotland: A. Gardner, 1917*). James C. Dibdin's THE ANNALS OF THE EDINBURGH STAGE: WITH AN ACCOUNT OF THE RISE AND PROGRESS OF DRAMATIC WRITING IN SCOTLAND (Edinburgh, 1888) is anecdotal and miscellaneous; about half of it deals with the period. Jack McKenzie has a note, "Shakespeare in Scotland before 1760," in TN 11 (1956), 24–26. J. Keith Angus, A SCOTCH PLAYHOUSE . . . (Aberdeen, Scotland: D. Wyllie, 1878), is devoted to Aberdeen. Kenneth M. Cameron's article, "The Edinburgh Theatre 1668–1682," TN 18 (1963), 18–25, draws on new sources and documents. Terence Tobin's PLAYS BY SCOTS 1660-1800 (Iowa City: Univ. of Iowa Press, 1974) includes an essay on the Edinburgh theatre of the period. George W. Baynham's THE GLASGOW STAGE (Glasgow: R. Forrester, 1892) may be supplemented by Elbridge Colby's "The Inchbalds' Strolling into Glasgow," N&Q 145 (1923), 343-44. For Wales, one may consult T.J.R. Jones's "Welsh Interlude Players of the Eighteenth Century," TN 2 (1948), 62-66. The best account, however, is Cecil Price's THE ENGLISH THEATRE IN WALES IN THE EIGHTEENTH AND EARLY NINETEENTH CENTURIES (Cardiff: Univ. of Wales Press, 1948).

E. THE AUDIENCE

3.12   Some books already discussed, for example James J. Lynch's BOX, PIT, AND GALLERY and Cecil Price's THEATRE IN THE AGE OF GARRICK, have good sections on theatre audiences in the period. There are, in addition, two books and numerous articles on the subject. Harry W. Pedicord's THE THEATRICAL PUBLIC IN THE TIME OF GARRICK (New York: King's Crown Press, 1954*) was in press when Lynch's book appeared, but in many ways complements it. Pedicord's analysis of the seating capacity of London theatres at various dates during the period is a model of clarity and economy, and his discussions of prices and of the inevitable conflict between authors and critics, on the one hand, and managers, on the other, are also very good. Both books deal with the makeup of the audience and analyze repertory as an index to contemporary taste. Leo A. Hughes's THE DRAMA'S PATRONS: A STUDY OF THE EIGHTEENTH-CENTURY LONDON AUDIENCE (Austin: Univ. of Texas Press, 1971) is more miscellaneous in character and neither as well organized or as well written. Its strengths are its abundance of detail quoted from contemporary sources, its forceful presentation in chapter 1 of the role and rights of the audience, and its discussions of the way the audiences of the period varied with the day of the week, the season, and the occasion.

Emmett L. Avery, in "The Restoration Audience," PQ 45 (1966), 54-61, finds a broader range of upper and middle class people in attendance than was earlier supposed. His argument is more strongly stated by Harold Love in "The Myth of the Restoration Audience," KOMOS 1 (1967), 49-56; Love believes (with reason) that the concept of the audience as whore and fop resulted from Victorian narrow-mindedness and too much reliance on the prologues and epilogues of the period as evidence. Pierre Danchin, "Le Public des théâtres londoniens à l'époque de la Restauration d'après les prologues et les épilogues," GEOFFRIN COLLECTION, II, 847-88, bases his conclusions exclusively on an analysis of some five hundred prologues and epilogues, primarily 1660-85, and thus falls to some extent into the trap exposed by Avery and Love.

The popularity with audiences of some of the less verbal entertainment offered by the theatres is explored in Paul Sawyer's "The Popularity of Various Types of Entertainment at Lincoln's Inn Fields and Covent Garden Theatres 1720-1733," TN 24 (1970), 154-63, and in Donald J. Rulfs's popular article "Entr'acte Entertainment at Drury Lane and Covent Garden 1750-1770," TA 12 (1954), 17-27. The interaction between actors, managers, and audiences is explored by William Angus in "Actors and Audiences in Eighteenth-Century London," STUDIES IN SPEECH AND DRAMA IN HONOR OF ALEXANDER M. DRUMMOND, ed. Donald C. Bryant et al. (Ithaca, N.Y.: Cornell Univ. Press, 1944), pp. 123-38. Dane F. Smith's THE CRITICS IN THE AUDIENCE OF THE LONDON THEATRES FROM BUCKINGHAM TO SHERIDAN: A STUDY OF NEOCLASSICISM IN THE PLAYHOUSE 1671-1779 (Alburquerque: Univ. of New Mexico Press, 1953) discusses the prestige of the critic and his influence on the theatre of the period. The attitude of critics toward the audience's taste is the subject of Julian L. Ross's "Dramatist Versus Audience in the Early Eighteenth Century," PQ 12 (1933), 73-81.

Theatre riots are discussed in the books mentioned above, and by Stephen Tait, "English Theatre Riots," TA 24 (1940), 97-104; St. Vincent Trowbridge, "Theatre Riots in London," ENTHOVEN COLLECTION, pp. 84-97; and by John C. Whitty, "The Half-Price Riots of 1763," TN 24 (1969), 25-32. Of these, only the last is of importance; Whitty shows that this riot had a serious economic basis, and that the Garrick-Fitzpatrick issue was only the surface cause.

Command performances are the subject of Ian Bevan's ROYAL PERFORMANCE: THE STORY OF ROYAL THEATREGOING (London: Hutchinson, 1954), but his account is sketchy, gossipy, and anecdotal; Louis D. Mitchell's "Command Performances during the Reign of Queen Anne," TN 24 (1970), 111-17, is much better. Command performances are also listed in THE LONDON STAGE. The attendance of Masons and other such groups is discussed by Harry W. Pedicord in "White Gloves at Five: Fraternal Patronage of London Theatres in the Eighteenth Century," PQ 45 (1966), 270-88. William J. Lawrence, in "The Delights of Chorussing," MQ 1 (1915), 52-56, notes that the audience sing-along was tried and found wanting. Paul Kaufman's "The Reading of Plays in the Eighteenth Century," BNYPL 73 (1969), 562-80, surveys the catalogs of circulating libraries to confirm the popularity of this pastime and its effect on the performance of plays.

Chapter IV

THEATRICAL BIOGRAPHY

A. COLLECTIONS

4.1   Biographies in contemporary and early nineteenth-century collections
are seldom reliable and must be used judiciously. Such satires as Charles
Churchill's ROSCIAD and APOLOGY (1761) are useful reflections of the in-
tense partisanship common in the period. Churchill's poems and Hugh Kelly's
[?] THESPIS (1766) led to brief pamphlet wars; like the GREEN ROOM MIR-
ROR (1786), they are hardly more than attacks on certain performers. Many
collections, like THE THEATRES (Francis Gentleman, 1772) and THE CHILDREN
OF THESPIS (John Williams, 1786) are mere poetical catalogs. The con-
tent of THE SECRET HISTORY OF THE GREEN ROOMS . . ., 2 vols. (1790)
is suggested by its title. Many works, like Benjamin Crosby's POCKET COM-
PANION TO THE PLAYHOUSES . . . (1796) and John Roach's AUTHENTIC
MEMOIRS OF THE GREEN ROOM . . . (1796), are publishers' ventures; they
purport to include lives of "all the principal London performers," but are usually
inaccurate and anecdotal. William Oxberry's DRAMATIC BIOGRAPHY AND
HISTRIONIC ANECDOTES, 6 vols. (London: Virtue, 1825-27), completed and
edited by Catherine Oxberry after her husband's death, is a more substantial
work, but still requires much sifting of fact from fiction. John Galt's THE
LIVES OF THE PLAYERS, 2 vols. (London: Colburn & Bentley, 1831) is a
journalistic "boil-down," to use Robert W. Lowe's phrase; William C. Russell's
REPRESENTATIVE ACTORS . . . (London: Warne, 1872) is a good deal better,
and it went through several editions.

By the time one comes to the later Victorian period, anecdote and nostalgia
have largely taken over. Such collections as Henry B. Baker's OUR OLD
ACTORS, 2 vols. (London: Bentley, 1878), Edward Dutton Cook's HOURS
WITH THE PLAYERS, 2 vols. (London: Chatto & Windus, 1881), and John
Fyvie's COMEDY QUEENS OF THE GEORGIAN ERA (London: Methuen,
1906) and TRAGEDY QUEENS OF THE GEORGIAN ERA (London: Methuen,
1909) are little more than romantic pastiches for theatre buffs. Later works
are sometimes better, but most are derivative and unscholarly. See, for ex-
amples, Lewis S. Benjamin [Lewis Melville], STAGE FAVORITES OF THE
EIGHTEENTH CENTURY and MORE STAGE FAVORITES OF THE EIGHTEENTH
CENTURY (London: Hutchinson, 1928* and 1929*); Henry W. Lanier, THE
FIRST ENGLISH ACTRESSES . . . (New York: The Players, 1930); Rosamond

Gilder, ENTER THE ACTRESS: THE FIRST WOMEN IN THE THEATRE (Boston: Houghton Mifflin, 1931); and Walter J. MacQueen-Pope, PILLARS OF DRURY LANE (London: Hutchinson, 1955).

The standard source at present is still the DICTIONARY OF NATIONAL BIOG-RAPHY, 63 vols. (London: Smith, Elder, 1885-1901), occasionally supple-mented for authors by Stanley J. Kunitz and Howard Haycraft, BRITISH AU-THORS BEFORE 1800: A BIOGRAPHICAL DICTIONARY (New York: Wilson, 1952). DNB entries conclude with a list of sources, but Arnott and Robinson's ENGLISH THEATRICAL LITERATURE (see Section 1.5) lists many more published works on theatrical people. The new standard for the period may be A BIO-GRAPHICAL DICTIONARY OF ACTORS, ACTRESSES, MUSICIANS, DANCERS, MANAGERS, AND OTHER STAGE PERSONNEL IN LONDON, 1660-1800, by Philip H. Highfill, Jr., Kalman A. Burnim, and Edward A. Langhans (Carbon-dale: Southern Illinois Univ. Press, 1973--). Volumes 1 through 4 of the projected twelve have now appeared. The BDA is an ambitious project, since it includes, in addition to the basic facts known about a performer and his family, discussion of his or her roles and specialities, and an iconography. The volumes are well designed and attractively printed; cross-references and illustrations are plentiful. The entries are well organized and packed with useful information; that for John Bannister, for example, runs to twelve columns plus three half-column illustrations. Though the authors defend their failure to list sources or provide a bibliography and do document many points within the text of an entry, the reader must often take information on faith if he is not already familiar with both printed and manuscript sources.

The BDA will supersede all of the earlier collections in its field, at least in most respects. The student will find William Matthews's BRITISH AUTOBIOG-RAPHIES: AN ANNOTATED BIBLIOGRAPHY OF BRITISH AUTOBIOGRAPHIES PUBLISHED OR WRITTEN BEFORE 1951 and BRITISH DIARIES: AN ANNO-TATED BIBLIOGRAPHY OF BRITISH DIARIES WRITTEN BETWEEN 1442 AND 1942 (Berkeley and Los Angeles: Univ. of California Press, 1955 and 1950) useful guides to further reading, and Arnott and Robinson's ENGLISH THEAT-RICAL LITERATURE will continue to be a major source of information on printed material.

Donald A. Stauffer's THE ART OF BIOGRAPHY IN EIGHTEENTH-CENTURY ENGLAND, 2 vols. (Princeton: Princeton Univ. Press, 1941) contains a help-ful chapter on "Biography and the Drama" (I, 9-64) which considers the influ-ence of the stage on contemporary biography and memoirs, and "An Alphabeti-cal Index of English Biographies and Autobiographies, 1700-1800" (II, 1-278) which has both descriptive and evaluative annotation. Highfill and his BDA co-authors make extensive use of such earlier articles as Sybil M. Rosenfeld and Edward Croft-Murray's "A Check-List of Scene Painters Working in Great Britain and Ireland in the Eighteenth Century," TN 19 (1964-65), 6-20, 49-64, 102-13, 133-45, and 20 (1965), 36-44, 69-72; Rosenfeld's "Scene Painters at the London Theatres in the Eighteenth Century," TN 20 (1966), 113-18, 177-82; Charles B. Hogan's "Eighteenth-Century Actors in the DNB: Additions and Corrections," TN 6 (1952), 45-48, 66-71, 87-96, and 11 (1957), 113-21; and John H. Wilson's "Players' Lists in the Lord Chamberlain's Registers," TN 18

(1963), 25-30. These studies will remain useful until the remaining volumes of the BDA are published, as will John H. Wilson's ALL THE KING'S LADIES: ACTRESSES OF THE RESTORATION (Chicago: Univ. of Chicago Press, 1958), which combines lively narrative with meticulous scholarship. Wilson makes a few additions and corrections to his list of actresses, 1660-1689, in "Biographical Notes on Some Restoration Actresses," TN 18 (1964), 43-47.

The reader should note that much biographical information is contained in the works referred to in Sections 1.10-1.12, 3.1, 3.6-3.12, and 6.1-6.6 of this guide.

B. INDIVIDUAL LIVES (Alphabetically by Performer)

4.2   Contemporary biographies and autobiographies are listed in the NEW CBEL, in the works by William Matthews and Donald A. Stauffer cited above, and in Arnott and Robinson's ENGLISH THEATRICAL LITERATURE. Only a selection of materials is mentioned here, primarily modern studies and those earlier works which have been reprinted. Biographical studies of playwrights who were also performers are listed under the appropriate author entry in Part 2 of this guide.

THE LIFE OF MRS. ABINGTON . . . (London: Reader, 1888) is an anonymous and derivative pastiche. ANTHONY ASTON, STROLLER AND ADVENTURER, by Watson Nicholson (South Haven, Mich.: n.p.?, 1920) may be supplemented by Thornton S. Graves, "Some Facts about Anthony Aston," JEGP 20 (1921), 391-96; many of the facts come from Aston's own sketch, attached to THE FOOL'S OPERA (1731). THE MEMOIRS OF MRS. SOPHIA BADDELEY . . ., 6 vols. (1787), is ostensibly by one Elizabeth Steele; it is typically romantic and quite unreliable. THE MEMOIRS OF JOHN BANNISTER, COMEDIAN, 2 vols. (London: Bentley, 1839), by John Adolphus, is a much better work. A first-class biography of Elizabeth Barry has yet to appear; Lucyle Hook, "Portraits of Elizabeth Barry and Anne Bracegirdle," TN 15 (1961), 129-37, is a good essay on the iconography of the two actresses. AN APOLOGY FOR THE LIFE OF GEORGE ANNE BELLAMY . . ., 6 vols. (1785), probably written by or in collaboration with Alexander Bicknell, has been, despite gaps and distortions, the major source for later biographies. The best and most recent of these is Cyril H. Hartmann's ENCHANTING BELLAMY (London: Heinemann, 1956).

John Bernard's RETROSPECTIONS OF THE STAGE, 2 vols. (London: Colburn & Bentley, 1830), edited by his son William B. Bernard, is generally reliable. Although there is another contemporary biography of Barton Booth, titled LIFE OF THAT EXCELLENT TRAGEDIAN, BARTON BOOTH, ESQ. (1733), Benjamin Victor's MEMOIRS OF THE LIFE OF BARTON BOOTH, ESQ. . . . (1733), is superior. Theophilus Cibber's "The Life and Character of That Excellent Actor Barton Booth . . .," which comprises most of the first and only volume of THE LIVES AND CHARACTERS OF THE MOST EMINENT ACTORS AND ACTRESSES . . . (1753), is the other standard source.

The fascinating autobiography of Colley Cibber's daughter is given in A NAR-RATIVE OF THE LIVE OF MRS. CHARLOTTE CHARKE . . . (1755*); Charles D. Peavy's "The Chimerical Career of Charlotte Charke," RECTR 8, no. 1 (1969), 1-12, is a useful modern survey of her life. The DIARY OF WILLIAM DUNLAP (1766-1839), 3 vols., has been edited by Dorothy C. Barck (New York: New York Historical Society, 1930*). Don B. Wilmeth, "An Index to the Life of George Frederick Cooke by William Dunlap," TD 2, nos. 1 and 2 (1969-70), 109-20, is based on Dunlap's MEMOIRS OF GEORGE FREDERICK COOKE, ESQ. . . ., 2 vols. (London: Colburn, 1815). John C. Trewin has a good character sketch of Cooke, titled "The Old Complaint," in THE NIGHT HAS BEEN UNRULY (London: Hale, 1957), pp. 67-87. A more recent study is Arnold Hare's essay "George Frederick Cooke: The Actor and the Man," RICHARDS COLLECTION, pp. 123-36. Mary J. Young's MEMOIRS OF MRS. CROUCH, 2 vols. (London: Asperne, 1806), and THE MEMOIRS OF J. DECASTRO, COMEDIAN . . . (London: Sherwood & Jones, 1824) are typical productions. Edward Croft-Murray's pamphlet, JOHN DEVOTO: A BAROQUE SCENE PAINTER (London: Society for Theatre Research, 1963), may be recommended.

Theodore A. Cook's THOMAS DOGGETT, DECEASED: A FAMOUS COME-DIAN (London: Constable, 1908) is still the standard biography. THE LIFE AND ADVENTURES OF JOHN EDWIN, COMEDIAN . . . (1791) is an autobiography worth noting, as is George Raymond's MEMOIRS OF ROBERT WIL-LIAM ELLISTON, COMEDIAN, 1744 TO 1810, 2 vols. (London: Mortimer, 1844-45*). R.J. Broadbent, ELIZABETH FARREN, COUNTESS OF DERBY (Edinburgh: Ballantyne, Hanson, 1910), is very brief; contemporary pieces like the anonymous LIFE OF LAVINIA BESWICK, ALIAS FENTON, ALIAS POLLY PEACHUM . . . (1728) are not reliable. The best life is Charles E. Pearce's 'POLLY PEACHUM': BEING THE STORY OF LAVINIA FENTON . . . (London: S. Paul, 1913). John H. Wilson, in MR. GOODMAN THE PLAYER (Pittsburgh: Univ. of Pittsburgh Press, 1964) has written an accurate and popular account of Carlell Goodman; the book is also a good introduction to the King's Company during the 1673-82 years.

Nell Gwyn has never lacked for biographers. Peter Cunningham's THE STORY OF NELL GWYN AND THE SAYINGS OF CHARLES THE SECOND (London: Bradbury & Evans, 1852*), though often reprinted, is mostly romance and anecdote. Lewis S. Benjamin's NELL GWYN: THE STORY OF HER LIFE (London: Hutchinson, 1923), Clifford Bax's PRETTY WITTY NELL: AN ACCOUNT OF NELL GWYN AND HER ENVIRONMENT (London: Chapman & Hall, 1932*), and Arthur I. Dasent's NELL GWYN 1650-1687: HER LIFE'S STORY FROM ST. GILES'S TO ST. JAMES'S . . . (London: Macmillan, 1924*) are all of a kind, focusing more on Nell's amours than on her stage career. The best account is John H. Wilson's NELL GWYN: ROYAL MISTRESS (New York: Pelligrini & Cudahy, 1952); Bryan Bevan's NELL GWYN (London: Hale, 1969), is the most recent.

THE LIFE OF THE LATE FAMOUS COMEDIAN, JO HAYNES . . . (1701) is the source of most later accounts; see the comments on it by John H. Wilson, in "Thomas' LIFE OF JO HAYNES," N&Q 206 (1961), 250-51. A good recent

survey is Kenneth M. Cameron's "Jo Haynes, Infamis," TN 24 (1970), 56-67.
William Van Lennep has a good article, "Henry Harris, Actor, Friend of
Pepys," in the ENTHOVEN COLLECTION, pp. 9-23. Thomas Davies's pam-
phlet, A GENUINE NARRATIVE OF THE LIFE AND THEATRICAL TRANSAC-
TIONS OF MR. JOHN HENDERSON . . . (1777), is the basis of later ac-
counts. John Ireland edited LETTERS AND POEMS BY THE LATE MR. JOHN
HENDERSON, WITH ANECDOTES OF HIS LIFE (1786); he asserts Davies's au-
thorship, which is again proved (in more detail) by Chester F. Burgess, "Thomas
Davies and the Authorship of A GENUINE NARRATIVE . . ., the Life of
John Henderson," RECTR 9, no. 1 (1970), 24-34.

James Boaden's THE LIFE OF MRS. JORDAN . . ., 2 vols. (London: E.
Bull, 1831), went through several editions. There are two early twentieth-
century lives of this actress, Philip W. Sergeant's MRS. JORDAN: CHILD
OF NATURE (London: Hutchinson, 1913) and Clare Jerrold's THE STORY OF
DOROTHY JORDAN (London: Nash, 1914*). The best full-length account is
Brian Fothergill's MRS. JORDAN: PORTRAIT OF AN ACTRESS (London:
Faber, 1965), which uses the material in the Royal Archives but not that in
the Huntington Library. Theodore Hook edited the singer and actor Michael
Kelly's REMINISCENCES . . ., 2 vols. (London: Colburn, 1826), on which
Stewart M. Ellis's THE LIFE OF MICHAEL KELLY (London: Gollancz, 1930)
is in part based. See also James Agate's "Scissors and Paste," WHITE HORSE
AND RED LION: ESSAYS IN GUSTO (London: Collins, 1924), pp. 253-73,
a sketch based on the REMINISCENCES. The only good life of Charles Kemble
is Jane Williamson's CHARLES KEMBLE, MAN OF THE THEATRE (Lincoln:
Univ. of Nebraska Press, 1970). THE MEMOIRS OF CHARLES LEE LEWES
. . ., ed. John Lewes, 4 vols. (London: R. Phillips, 1805), tells the story
of a leading Harlequin. There are two full-length biographies of Harriet Mellon: Margaret H. Baron-Wilson's MEMOIRS OF MISS MELLON, DUCHESS
OF ST. ALBANS, 2 vols. (London: Colburn, 1839), and Charles E. Pearce's
THE JOLLY DUCHESS: HARRIET MELLON, AFTERWARDS MRS. COUTTS AND
THE DUCHESS OF ST. ALBANS (London: S. Paul, 1915).

Thomas S. Munden's MEMOIRS OF JOSEPH SHEPHERD MUNDEN, COMEDIAN
(London: Bentley, 1844) includes useful sections on Munden's early career.
FAITHFUL MEMOIRS OF . . . MRS. ANNE OLDFIELD . . . (1731) is no
better than most of Edmund Curll's productions; the anonymous AUTHENTIC
MEMOIRS OF THE LIFE OF MRS. ANN OLDFIELD (1730) was more popular.
Of the two modern full-length accounts, Robert Gore-Browne's GAY WAS THE
PIT: THE LIFE AND TIMES OF ANNE OLDFIELD, ACTRESS (1683-1730)
(London: Reinhardt, 1957), though mostly on the times, is better than Edward
Robins's THE PALMY DAYS OF NANCE OLDFIELD (London: Heinemann, 1898).
"Memoirs of John Palmer, Esq." are reprinted from the THESPIAN MAGAZINE
for 1793 in RECTR 1, no. 1 (1962), 23-34, and 1, no. 2 (1962), 45-53;
Kathleen N. Barker gives a good sketch of William Powell in "William Powell
--A Forgotten Star," RICHARDS COLLECTION, pp. 73-83.

Paul Sawyer provides a good introductory survey in "John Rich: A Biographical
Sketch," TA 15 (1957-58), 55-68. More specialized are Sawyer's "Father and
Lun: Filling Some Gaps in the Lives of Christopher and John Rich," RECTR

12, no. 2 (1973), 51-58, corrected in RECTR 13, no. 1 (1974), 62; and
"John Rich's Contribution to the Eighteenth-Century London Stage," RICHARDS
COLLECTION, pp. 85-104. "Perdita" Robinson is the subject of MEMOIRS
OF THE LATE MRS. ROBINSON . . ., 4 vols. (London: R. Phillips, 1801),
edited by her daughter Mary Robinson. There is no modern edition of Samuel
W. Ryley's THE ITINERANT, OR MEMOIRS OF AN ACTOR, published in nine
volumes (London: Taylor and Hersey [Vol. 1] and Sherwood et al. [Vols. 2-
9], 1808-27). Stanley W.E. Vince surveys the career of a famous dancer in
"Marie Sallé 1707-56," TN 12 (1957), 7-14. Esther K. Sheldon's THOMAS
SHERIDAN OF SMOCK-ALLEY . . . (Princeton: Princeton Univ. Press, 1967)
is the standard biography of the elder Sheridan.

The great actress Sarah Siddons was the subject of James Boaden's MEMOIRS
OF MRS. SIDDONS . . ., 2 vols. (London: Colburn, 1827), which went
through a number of editions. This was followed by Thomas Campbell's LIFE
OF MRS. SIDDONS, 2 vols. (London: E. Wilson, 1834*), by Nina H. Ken-
nard's MRS. SIDDONS (London: Allen, 1887), and by Mrs. Clement Parsons's
THE INCOMPARABLE SIDDONS (London: Methuen, 1909*). Modern scholar-
ship begins with William Van Lennep's edition of THE REMINISCENCES OF
SARAH KEMBLE SIDDONS, 1773-1785 (Cambridge: Widener Library, 1942).
The best modern life is Yvonne ffrench, MRS. SIDDONS: TRAGIC ACTRESS,
rev. ed. (London: Verschoyle, 1954), a popular biography first published in
1936. Kathleen Mackenzie's THE GREAT SARAH: THE LIFE OF MRS. SID-
DONS (London: Evans, 1968) is more popular still. The most recent full-
length life is Roger Manvell's SARAH SIDDONS: PORTRAIT OF AN ACTRESS
(New York: Putnam, 1971), which is well illustrated. Kalman A. Burnim's
edition of "The Letters of Sarah and William Siddons to Hester Lynch Piozzi
in The John Rylands Library," BJRL 52 (1969), 46-95, adds new material.
"Charles Surface in Regency Retirement: Some Letters from Gentleman Smith,"
ed. Philip H. Highfill, Jr., in SP, Extra Series #4 (1967), 135-66, throws
light on Smith's later years. George Akerby wrote THE LIFE OF MR. JAMES
SPILLER, THE LATE FAMOUS COMEDIAN . . . (1729); see also William J.
Lawrence's essay on Spiller, "A Player Friend of Hogarth," LAWRENCE COL-
LECTION 2, pp. 213-26.

Mollie Sands, in "Mrs. Tofts, 1685?-1756," TN 20 (1966), 100-13, gives a
brief account of the singer; George H. Bushnell, "The Original Lady Randolph,"
TN 13 (1959), 119-23, has a good account of Sarah Ward. Tate Wilkinson's
MEMOIRS OF HIS OWN LIFE, 4 vols. (York, 1790), went through several
editions; his THE WANDERING PATENTEE: OR, A HISTORY OF THE YORK-
SHIRE THEATRE, FROM 1770 TO THE PRESENT TIME . . ., 4 vols. (York,
1795*), is even more interesting; an index to this has been compiled by Charles
B. Hogan (London: Society for Theatre Research, 1973). A very good survey
of Wilkinson's career is Charles B. Hogan's "One of God Almighty's Unaccount-
ables: Tate Wilkinson of York," in THE THEATRICAL MANAGER IN ENG-
LAND AND AMERICA: PLAYERS OF A PERILOUS GAME, ed. Joseph W.
Donohue, Jr. (Princeton: Princeton Univ. Press, 1971), pp. 63-86. There is
no full modern biography of Robert Wilks, the Restoration actor. The contem-
porary accounts are the anonymous MEMOIRS OF THE LIFE OF ROBERT WILKS,
ESQ. . . . (1732) and Edmund Curll's THE LIFE OF THAT EMINENT COME-
DIAN ROBERT WILKS, ESQ. (1733).

Margaret Woffington, like Mrs. Siddons, has attracted many biographers. MEMOIRS OF THE CELEBRATED MRS. WOFFINGTON . . . (1760) is the earliest separate account; Joseph F. Molloy's THE LIFE AND ADVENTURES OF PEG WOFFINGTON . . ., 2 vols. (London: Hurst & Blackett, 1884), is the first modern one, but is mostly romantic anecdote. Angustin Daly's WOFFINGTON: A TRIBUTE TO THE ACTRESS AND THE WOMAN (Philadelphia: Globe Printing, 1888*) is an appreciation, as is Henry Austin [Dobson]'s "Mrs. Woffington," SIDEWALK STUDIES (Oxford: Oxford Univ. Press, 1902), pp. 1-32. William R.H. Trowbridge's account in DAUGHTERS OF EVE (London: Chapman & Hall, 1911), pp. 123-75, is derivative. The only two recent books are Janet C. Lucey, LOVELY PEGGY: THE LIFE AND TIMES OF MARGARET WOFFINGTON (London: Hurst & Blackett, 1952), and Janet Dunbar, PEG WOFFINGTON AND HER WORLD (Boston: Houghton Mifflin, 1968), a popular and readable account.

Chapter V

DRAMATIC THEORY

A. COLLECTIONS

5.1   A fuller listing may be found in the NEW CBEL; only the major col-
lections are noted here.   Joel Spingarn, CRITICAL ESSAYS OF THE SEVEN-
TEENTH CENTURY, 3 vols. (Oxford: Oxford Univ. Press, 1908-09), Willard
H. Durham, CRITICAL ESSAYS OF THE EIGHTEENTH CENTURY 1700-25 (New
Haven: Yale Univ. Press, 1915), and Scott Elledge, EIGHTEENTH-CENTURY
CRITICAL ESSAYS, 2 vols. (Ithaca, N.Y.: Cornell Univ. Press, 1961), all in-
clude some essays relevant to the drama. Barrett H. Clark's EUROPEAN THEORIES
OF THE DRAMA: AN ANTHOLOGY, rev. ed. by Henry Popkin (New York:
Crown, 1965), provides useful if elementary background, as does William K.
Wimsatt, Jr.'s collection in THE IDEA OF COMEDY: ESSAYS IN PROSE
AND VERSE, BEN JONSON TO GEORGE MEREDITH (Englewood Cliffs, N.J.:
Prentice Hall, 1969).   Alois Nagler's A SOURCE BOOK IN THEATRICAL
HISTORY, 2nd ed. (London: Constable, 1959), contains selections from con-
temporary sources in chapters 7 and 10, especially relating to plays in perfor-
mance.

DRAMATIC ESSAYS OF THE NEOCLASSIC AGE, ed. Henry H. Adams and
Baxter Hathaway (New York: Columbia Univ. Press, 1950), contains a variety
of selections from English and European critics.   Charles H. Gray's THEATRI-
CAL CRITICISM IN LONDON TO 1795 (New York: Columbia Univ. Press,
1931*) studies the sources of critical opinion, focusing on the eighteenth century. John C. Loftis's ESSAYS ON THE THEATRE FROM EIGHTEENTH-CEN-
TURY PERIODICALS (Los Angeles: Augustan Reprint Society, 1960) is also
helpful. David N. Smith's EIGHTEENTH CENTURY ESSAYS ON SHAKESPEARE,
2nd ed. (Oxford: Clarendon Press, 1963), is a good specialized collection.
The fifty volumes of THE ENGLISH STAGE: ATTACK AND DEFENCE 1577-
1730, now available from New York's Garland Publishing, Inc., are photographic reprints of contemporary texts and include several pieces as much related to dramatic theory as to the Collier controversy.   A similar reprint series,
EIGHTEENTH-CENTURY SHAKESPEARE, published in New York by A.M. Kelley,
also includes works of general critical and theoretical interest.   The collection
ACTORS ON ACTING: THE THEORIES, TECHNIQUES, AND PRACTICES OF
THE GREAT ACTORS OF ALL TIMES AS TOLD IN THEIR OWN WORDS, ed.
Toby Cole and Helen K. Chinoy, rev. ed. (New York: Crown, 1970), includes

numerous theoretical remarks by English performers (chapter 7, pp. 92-145).

B. CONTEMPORARY WORKS

5.2   Many hundreds of contemporary essays, pamphlets, and periodical pieces devoted to dramatic theory--or to criticism of particular plays, genres, acting styles, or performers--include some theoretical discussion. It is usually impossible to separate theory from practical criticism; indeed, contemporary writers felt no more need to do so than do writers today. Since this is a guide to drama rather than criticism, it is extremely selective in listing individual titles. For fuller treatment, the student should refer to the NEW CBEL, and especially to Arnott and Robinson's ENGLISH THEATRICAL LITERATURE. René Wellek's A HISTORY OF MODERN CRITICISM: 1750-1950, 4 vols. (New Haven: Yale Univ. Press, 1955-65), is most helpful in suggesting trends and important works. Robert D. Stock's SAMUEL JOHNSON AND NEOCLAS-SICAL DRAMATIC THEORY: THE INTELLECTUAL CONTEXT OF THE PREFACE TO SHAKESPEARE (Lincoln: Univ. of Nebraska Press, 1973) offers a good introduction to many of the central issues.

Since much contemporary criticism was produced in defense of a fait accompli, one would expect to find the prefaces and appendixes to printed plays an unusually fruitful source of material. Such is the case, for example, with Sir Robert Howard's prefaces to FOUR NEW PLAYS (1665) and THE GREAT FA-VORITE (1668), Thomas Shadwell's prefaces to THE SULLEN LOVERS (1668) and THE HUMOURISTS (1671), Nahum Tate's preface to A DUKE AND NO DUKE (1693), Charles Johnson's to MEDEA (1731), William Mason's to ELFRIDA (1752), and Joanna Baillie's to Volume 1 of A SERIES OF PLAYS . . . (1798). Perhaps the most famous examples are John Dryden's "A Defence of an Essay of Dramatic Poesy," prefixed to the second edition of THE INDIAN EMPEROR (1668), his "Of Heroic Plays, an Essay" and "Defense of the Epilogue; Or, An Essay on the Dramatic Poetry of the Last Age," prefixed and appended, respectively, to THE CONQUEST OF GRANADA (1672), and "The Grounds of Criticism in Tragedy," prefixed to TROILUS AND CRESSIDA (1679).

Other works of major importance include Dryden's OF DRAMATIC POESY, AN ESSAY (1668), Thomas Rymer's THE TRAGEDIES OF THE LAST AGE CONSID-ERED AND EXAMINED . . . (1678 [for 1677]*) and A SHORT VIEW OF TRAGEDY . . . (1693*), St. Evremond's MIXED ESSAYS UPON TRAGEDIES, COMEDIES, ITALIAN COMEDIES, ENGLISH COMEDIES, AND OPERAS (1685), and John Dennis's THE IMPARTIAL CRITIC (1693), an attack on Rymer's SHORT VIEW. Dryden's criticism is available in the modern collections edited by William P. Ker, 2 vols. (Oxford: Clarendon Press, 1926), and by George Watson, 2 vols. (London: Dent, 1962). Curt A. Zimansky produced an excel-lent edition of THE CRITICAL WORKS OF THOMAS RYMER (New Haven: Yale Univ. Press, 1956), and Edward N. Hooker one of THE CRITICAL WORKS OF JOHN DENNIS, 2 vols. (Baltimore: Johns Hopkins Univ. Press, 1939-43).

Works of importance published 1700-50 include Joseph Trapp, "An Essay Upon the Nature and Art of Moving the Passions in Tragedy," in THE WORKS OF VERGIL (1731), and Corbyn Morris, "Concerning Humor in Comedy," appended to his AN ESSAY TOWARD FIXING THE TRUE STANDARDS OF WIT . . . (1744*). Richard Hurd's "Dissertation concerning the Provinces of the Several Species of the Drama," appended to his edition of Horace's ARS POETICA, 2 vols. (1753), is an important mid-century work. So also are the anonymous RE-FLECTIONS UPON THEATRICAL EXPRESSION IN TRAGEDY (1755), William Guthrie's AN ESSAY UPON ENGLISH TRAGEDY . . . (1757*), David Hume's "Of Tragedy," first published in FOUR DISSERTATIONS (1757), and ESSAY ON THE PRESENT STATE OF THE THEATRE IN FRANCE, ENGLAND, AND ITALY (1760). Later works include William Cooke's THE ELEMENTS OF DRAMATIC CRITICISM . . . (1775); B. Walwyn's AN ESSAY ON COMEDY (1782); John Aikin's "On the Impression of Reality Attending Dramatic Repre-sentations," MLPS 4, part 1 (1793), 96–108; and Horace Walpole's "Thoughts on Comedy, Written in 1775 and 1776" and "Thoughts on Tragedy: In Three Letters to Robert Jephson, Esq." in THE WORKS OF HORATIO WALPOLE . . ., 5 vols. (1798), II, 315–22 and 305–14. Samuel Johnson's succinct pronouncements in THE LIVES OF THE POETS and elsewhere are often of theo-retical interest.

Works on acting include Aaron Hill's poem THE ART OF ACTING (1746) and his "An Essay on the Art of Acting, in Prose" (WORKS [1753], IV, 353–414), based on several numbers of THE PROMPTER; Charles Macklin's "Observations on the Drama and on the Science of Acting," in Kirkman's MEMOIRS OF THE LIFE OF CHARLES MACKLIN (1799); Sir John Hill's THE ACTOR: A TREATISE ON THE ART OF PLAYING . . . (1750*); Roger Pickering's REFLECTIONS UPON THEATRICAL EXPRESSION IN TRAGEDY (1755); and James Boswell's ON THE PROFESSION OF A PLAYER: THREE ESSAYS NOW FIRST REPRINTED FROM THE LONDON MAGAZINE FOR AUGUST, SEPTEMBER, AND OCTOBER, 1770 (London: Mathew & Marrot, 1929). There are also many handbooks like THE SENTIMENTAL SPOUTER: OR, YOUNG ACTOR'S COMPANION . . . (1774) and Henry Siddons's PRACTICAL ILLUSTRATIONS OF RHETORICAL GES-TURE AND ACTION . . . (London: R. Phillips, 1807*).

C. THE COLLIER CONTROVERSY

5.3   Arnott and Robinson, in ENGLISH THEATRICAL LITERATURE, list some 150 works published between 1660 and 1800 which deal with the morality of the theatre, and more than 50 specifically related to the controversy gener-ated by the publication of Jeremy Collier's A SHORT VIEW OF THE ENGLISH STAGE . . . (1698*). Their list is more accurate than those given in Joseph W. Krutch's COMEDY AND CONSCIENCE AFTER THE RESTORATION, rev. ed. (New York: Columbia Univ. Press, 1949), and in Sister Rose Anthony's THE JEREMY COLLIER STAGE CONTROVERSY 1698–1726 (Milwaukee, Wis.: Marquette Univ. Press, 1937*). Maximillian E. Novak has a general article on the controversy, "The Artist and the Clergyman: Congreve, Collier and the World of the Play," CE 30 (1969), 555–61; A.J. Turner, in "The Jeremy Collier Stage Controversy Again," N&Q 218 (1973), 409–12, shows the im-mense support Collier received from many of the religious societies in London.

Anthony's study is still the most detailed analysis of the "literature" generated, but one must discount her strong pro-Collier bias and lack of theoretical sophistication and check her facts against the bibliographical information provided by Arnott and Robinson in ENGLISH THEATRICAL LITERATURE. Krutch's book is also affected by his moral distaste for Restoration comedy, the history of which he distorts considerably.

Collier's work is probably more referred to than read. Both sides in the controversy quickly enlisted foreign support, the Collier forces from François Caffaro's "Discourse of the Lawfulness and Unlawfulness of Plays . . .," which Peter Motteux translated and prefixed to his tragedy BEAUTY IN DISTRESS; the defenders of the stage from the writings of Bossuet, translated as MAXIMS AND REFLECTIONS ON PLAYS. Further defenses came almost at once, especially from the playwrights indicted. Elkanah Settle's A DEFENCE OF DRAMATIC POETRY . . .* and A FURTHER DEFENCE OF DRAMATIC POETRY . . .*, William Congreve's AMENDMENTS OF MR. COLLIER'S FALSE AND IMPERFECT CITATIONS . . .*, and Sir John Vanbrugh's A SHORT VINDICATION OF 'THE RELAPSE' AND 'THE PROVOKED WIFE' . . .* are all interesting, but only John Dennis, in THE USEFULNESS OF THE STAGE . . .,* was a worthy opponent. All these works were published in 1698.

George Ridpath renewed the attack in THE STAGE CONDEMNED . . . (1698*), which was closely followed by Collier's A DEFENCE OF THE SHORT VIEW . . . (1699*), which focuses on Congreve's defense. James Drake's THE ANCIENT AND MODERN STAGES SURVEYED (1699*) is not only one of the few able answers to Collier, but also an important critical work; to answer it, Collier published A SECOND DEFENCE OF THE SHORT VIEW . . . (1700*). The great storm of 26 November 1703 gave further ammunition to the Collier forces, and in Arthur Bedford, a Bristol clergyman, they found a new champion. Bedford's THE EVIL AND DANGER OF STAGE-PLAYS . . . (1706*), one of several outbursts, may be read against Edward Filmer's A DEFENCE OF PLAYS . . . (1707*), to which Collier in turn replied with A FURTHER VINDICATION OF THE SHORT VIEW . . . (1708*). When the attack on the stage was renewed, the focus was no longer on Collier, but the basic arguments remained the same for both sides. The most popular attack was William Law's THE ABSOLUTE UNLAWFULNESS OF THE STAGE-ENTERTAINMENT FULLY DEMONSTRATED (1726); the best answer to Law was John Dennis's THE STAGE DEFENDED . . . (1726*). The moral issue in one form or another was central to nearly all serious dramatic theory in the entire period, and it has obvious relationships to other critical issues, such as poetic justice and the nature of dramatic representation.

D. MODERN STUDIES

5.4   There are many modern studies of general theoretical interest. On dramatic theory generally, Allardyce Nicoll's THE THEORY OF DRAMA (London: Harrap, 1931*) and THE THEATRE AND DRAMATIC THEORY (London: Harrap, 1962) are useful, as are Francis Fergusson's THE IDEA OF A THEATRE . . . (Princeton: Princeton Univ. Press, 1949*) and Eric R. Bentley's THE

LIFE OF THE DRAMA (New York: Atheneum, 1964). IDEAS IN THE DRAMA, ed. John Gassner (New York: Columbia Univ. Press, 1964), collects the English Institute Essays for 1963; to this may be added THE CONTEXT AND CRAFT OF DRAMA, ed. Robert W. Corrigan and James L. Rosenberg (San Francisco: Chandler, 1964), and PERSPECTIVES ON DRAMA, ed. James Calderwood and Harold E. Toliver (New York: Oxford Univ. Press, 1968). The critical readings offered in Cleanth Brooks and Robert B. Heilman, UNDER-STANDING DRAMA: TWELVE PLAYS (New York: Holt, Rinehart, Winston, 1948), are stimulating reflections of new-critical theory.

Works on tragedy include Karl Jaspers, TRAGEDY IS NOT ENOUGH, trans. Harald Reiche et al. (Boston: Beacon Press, 1953); Herbert Weisinger's TRAGEDY AND THE PARADOX OF THE FORTUNATE FALL (East Lansing: Michigan State College Press, 1953); Thomas R. Henn's THE HARVEST OF TRAGEDY (London: Methuen, 1956); Elder Olson's TRAGEDY AND THE THEORY OF DRAMA (Detroit: Wayne State Univ. Press, 1961); Herbert J. Muller's THE SPIRIT OF TRAGEDY (New York: Knopf, 1956); and Moody E. Prior's THE LANGUAGE OF TRAGEDY (New York: Columbia Univ. Press, 1947*). More recent works are Geoffrey Brereton's PRINCIPLES OF TRAGEDY . . . (Coral Gables, Fla.: Univ. of Miami Press, 1968) and Robert B. Heilman's TRAGEDY AND MELODRAMA (Seattle: Univ. of Washington Press, 1968). TRAGEDY: VISION AND FORM, ed. Robert W. Corrigan (San Francisco: Chandler, 1965), collects a number of pertinent essays.

The best guides to comedy are Sigmund Freud's JOKES AND THEIR RELATION TO THE UNCONSCIOUS, trans. and ed. James Strachey (New York: Norton, 1960), and Northrop Frye's ANATOMY OF CRITICISM: FOUR ESSAYS (Princeton: Princeton Univ. Press, 1957). Also useful are James K. Feibleman's IN PRAISE OF COMEDY . . . (London: Allen & Unwin, 1939), which has summaries of earlier comic theory, and Albert S. Cook's THE DARK VOYAGE AND THE GOLDEN MEAN: A PHILOSOPHY OF COMEDY (Cambridge, Mass.: Harvard Univ. Press, 1949). The English Institute Essays for 1954, collected in ENGLISH STAGE COMEDY, ed. William K. Wimsatt, Jr. (New York: Columbia Univ. Press, 1955), are a good introduction to the subject; see also W. Moelwyn Merchant, COMEDY (London: Methuen, 1972), an introductory survey in the Critical Idiom series, and COMEDY: MEANING AND FORM, ed. Robert W. Corrigan (San Francisco: Chandler, 1965).

Theoretical works more nearly focused on the Restoration and eighteenth century include Walter J. Bate's FROM CLASSIC TO ROMANTIC: PREMISES OF TASTE IN EIGHTEENTH-CENTURY ENGLAND (Cambridge, Mass.: Harvard Univ. Press, 1946*), a good background study for literary theory, and Walter J. Hipple, Jr., THE BEAUTIFUL, THE SUBLIME, AND THE PICTURESQUE IN EIGHTEENTH-CENTURY AESTHETIC THEORY (Carbondale: Southern Illinois Univ. Press, 1957), which may profitably be read in conjunction with Bate. The standard history is the first volume of René Wellek's HISTORY OF MODERN CRITICISM, already referred to. John W. Draper's "Aristotelian 'Mimesis' in Eighteenth-Century England," PMLA 36 (1921), 372-400, is still of value; compare Paul S. Wood, "The Opposition to Neo-Classicism in England between 1660 and 1700," PMLA 43 (1928), 182-97. Sarup Singh, in THE THEORY OF

DRAMA IN THE RESTORATION PERIOD (Calcutta: Orient Longmans, 1963), uses a conventional theoretical framework, but includes much useful source material.

Donald F. Bond's "'Distrust' of the Imagination in English Neo-Classicism," PQ 14 (1935), 54-69, and "The Neo-Classical Psychology of the Imagination," ELH 4 (1937), 245-64, are standard studies of a topic central to the literary theory of the period. Peter Seary's "Language versus Design in Drama: A Background to the Pope-Theobald Controversy," UTQ 42 (1972), 40-63, takes the argument over the primacy of language or design back to John Dryden and Thomas Rymer in the Restoration. Poetic justice, another concern central to dramatic theory in the period, is discussed broadly in Michael A. Quinlan, POETIC JUSTICE IN THE DRAMA: THE HISTORY OF AN ETHICAL PRINCIPLE IN LITERARY CRITICISM (South Bend, Ind.: Univ of Notre Dame Press, 1912); John D. Ebbs's THE PRINCIPLE OF POETIC JUSTICE ILLUSTRATED IN RESTO-RATION TRAGEDY (Salzburg, Austria: Institut Fuer Englische Sprache und Litera-tur, Univ. Salzburg, 1973) gives a brief summary of contemporary criticism on the topic, but the analyses in application of the principle are dissappointing. Ebbs's Appendix A, "The Addison-Dennis Controversy," pp. 190-204, is sketchy; see also Amrih Singh, "The Argument on Poetic Justice (Addison versus Dennis)." IJES 3 (1962), 61-77; and Richard H. Tyre, "Versions of Poetic Justice in the Early Eighteenth Century," SP 54 (1957), 29-44.

Important theoretical studies of particular genres include Hugh T. Swedenberg, Jr., THE THEORY OF THE EPIC IN ENGLAND 1650-1800 (Berkeley and Los Angeles: Univ. of California Press, 1944); George B. Dutton, "Theory and Practice in English Tragedy, 1650-1700," ESt 49 (1916), 190-219; Clarence C. Green, THE NEO-CLASSIC THEORY OF TRAGEDY IN ENGLAND DUR-ING THE EIGHTEENTH CENTURY (Cambridge, Mass.: Harvard Univ. Press, 1934); and Baxter Hathaway, "The Lucretian 'Return upon Ourselves' in Eighteenth-Century Theories of Tragedy," PMLA 62 (1947), 672-89. Earl R. Wasserman's "The Pleasures of Tragedy," ELH 14 (1947), 283-307, provides a fine analysis of the sources of the contemporary theory of tragic pleasure; Eric Rothstein's "English Tragic Theory in the Late Seventeenth Century," ELH 29 (1962), 306-23 (included in his RESTORATION TRAGEDY, with revisions), is also very good. Comedy is treated in John W. Draper's "The Theory of the Comic in Eighteenth-Century England," JEGP 37 (1938), 207-23; in Stuart M. Tave's THE AMIABLE HUMORIST: A STUDY IN THE COMIC THEORY AND CRITI-CISM OF THE EIGHTEENTH AND EARLY NINETEENTH CENTURIES (Chicago: Univ. of Chicago Press, 1960); and in Harold Love's "Dryden, Durfey, and the Standard of Comedy," SEL 13 (1973), 422-36. Another important study is Robert D. Hume's attempt in "Theory of Comedy in the Restoration," MP 70 (1973), 302-18, to break the tendency of most critics to discuss Restoration comic theory on the basis of the so-called comedy of manners alone. With this article, one clearly enters the realm of dramatic history and literary criti-cism.

Chapter VI

DRAMATIC HISTORY

A. CONTEMPORARY WORKS

Playlists and Dictionaries

6.1   Contemporary playlists and dictionaries tend to become histories of
the drama or of the stage, and vice versa. Such works are therefore consid-
ered here rather than in Section 1 of this guide. Gerard Langbaine's MOMUS
TRIUMPHANS; OR, THE PLAGIARIES OF THE ENGLISH STAGE (1688*) was
designed primarily to show the debt of contemporary playwrights to earlier
English and European writers. Langbaine often confuses sources with analogs,
but his book begins a long tradition of such scholarship. His ACCOUNT OF
THE ENGLISH DRAMATIC POETS (Oxford, 1691*) was revised by Charles
Gildon in 1698 or 1699 as THE LIVES AND CHARACTERS OF THE ENGLISH
DRAMATIC POETS; despite errors and idiosyncrasies, it is a standard source of
information. William Mears's A TRUE AND EXACT CATALOGUE OF ALL THE
PLAYS THAT WERE EVER YET PRINTED IN THE ENGLISH TONGUE . . .
(1713) went through several editions and "continuations." It is more nearly a
playlist in the modern sense than most other works considered here. Giles
Jacob's THE POETICAL REGISTER; OR, THE LIVES AND CHARACTERS OF THE
ENGLISH DRAMATIC POETS, 2 vols. (1719 and 1720), is another important
source book, since many of its accounts were apparently contributed by the
authors themselves. Only the first volume of THE DRAMATIC HISTORIOG-
RAPHER; OR, THE BRITISH THEATRE DELINEATED . . . (1735) was ever pub-
lished, but it went through several editions. Another useful source is Thomas
Whincop's "A List of All the Dramatic Authors, and Some Account of Their
Lives . . .," appended to SCANDERBEG; OR, LOVE AND LIBERTY (1747).

In 1764 David E. Baker published the two volumes of the COMPANION TO
THE PLAYHOUSE; OR, AN HISTORICAL ACCOUNT OF ALL THE DRAMATIC
WRITERS. . . . This, in successive revisions, became the standard authority
until the time of John Genest, and is still valuable for later eighteenth-
century figures. Isaac Reed did the first revision, published as BIOGRAPHIA
DRAMATICA; OR, A COMPANION TO THE PLAYHOUSE . . ., 2 vols.
(1782); Stephen Jones made a further extensive revision in 1812 (3 vols. in 4),
retaining Reed's title. The "companion" idea was popular, and there were

competing works: THE PLAYHOUSE POCKET-COMPANION OR THEATRICAL VADEMECUM . . . (1779), THE THEATRICAL REMEMBRANCER, CONTAINING A COMPLETE LIST OF ALL THE DRAMATIC PERFORMANCES IN THE ENGLISH LANGUAGE . . . (1788), and THE THESPIAN DICTIONARY; OR, DRAMATIC BIOGRAPHY OF THE EIGHTEENTH CENTURY . . . (London: T. Hurst, 1802).

Histories of the Theatre

6.2   Dramatic history as a self-conscious form is a product of this period, and there are a number of notable examples. Most of them are by modern standards inaccurate and incomplete, but they contain much valuable information on which later scholarship depends. "A Short Treatise of the English Stage . . .," appended to Richard Flecknoe's LOVE'S KINGDOM (1664*), is the earliest example. James Wright's HISTORIA HISTRIONICA: AN HISTORICAL ACCOUNT OF THE ENGLISH STAGE (1699*), a thirty-two page pamphlet, has been often reprinted. A more important work is John Downes's ROSCIUS ANGLICANUS; OR, AN HISTORICAL REVIEW OF THE STAGE . . . (1708*), of which Montague Summers prepared a facsimile edition with more than two hundred pages of explanatory notes (London: Fortune Press, 1928*). There is a good index to this work by David S. Rodes, prepared for the facsimile published in the Augustan Reprint Series (Los Angeles: W.A. Clark Library, 1969).

Edmund Curll published THE HISTORY OF THE ENGLISH STAGE, FROM THE RESTORATION TO THE PRESENT TIME . . . in 1741, probably using Thomas Betterton's notes and collaborating with others. Louis Riccoboni, AN HISTORICAL AND CRITICAL ACCOUNT OF THE THEATRES IN EUROPE . . ., translated from the French and published in 1741, includes valuable information on the English stage. William R. Chetwood's A GENERAL HISTORY OF THE STAGE . . . (1749) and THE BRITISH THEATRE, CONTAINING THE LIVES OF THE ENGLISH DRAMATIC POETS, WITH AN ACCOUNT OF ALL THEIR PLAYS . . . (Dublin, 1750; London, 1752) are mid-century works. The GENERAL VIEW OF THE STAGE (London, 1759), attributed to Thomas Wilkes, is also worth mentioning. Benjamin Victor, THE HISTORY OF THE THEATRES OF LONDON AND DUBLIN FROM THE YEAR 1730 TO THE PRESENT TIME . . ., 2 vols. (1761*), is also standard. Walley C. Oulton's THE HISTORY OF THE THEATRES OF LONDON, CONTAINING AN ANNUAL REGISTER . . . 1771 TO 1795 . . ., 2 vols. (1796), is comprehensive and entertaining; a three-volume continuation was published in 1817-18 by Chapple, covering the years from 1795 to 1817. John Roach's book ROACH'S NEW AND COMPLETE HISTORY OF THE STAGE was published in 1796; Charles Dibdin's well known A COMPLETE HISTORY OF THE ENGLISH STAGE . . ., 5 vols. (1797-1800), and Thomas Gilliand's THE DRAMATIC MIRROR, CONTAINING THE HISTORY OF THE STAGE FROM THE EARLIEST PERIOD TO THE PRESENT TIME . . ., 2 vols. (London: Chapple, 1808), bring dramatic historiography into the nineteenth century.

A few contemporary works deal with more specialized topics, or with areas closely related to the stage. John Weaver's THE HISTORY OF THE MIMES AND PANTOMIMES . . . (1728) is still of interest, as is John Lockman's "An Inquiry into the Rise and Progress of Operas and Oratorios . . .," prefixed to ROSALINDA (1740). Much more important are the two great histories of music produced in the period. Charles Burney's A GENERAL HISTORY OF MUSIC FROM THE EARLIEST AGES TO THE PRESENT PERIOD, 4 vols. (1776-89; ed. Frank Mercer, 2 vols. [New York: Dover, 1957]), is particularly important for its long and detailed accounts of dramatic music and opera in the period; Burney's marked preference for Italian and contemporary music is as useful in these areas as it is annoying. Sir John Hawkins's A GENERAL HISTORY OF THE SCIENCE AND PRACTICE OF MUSIC, 5 vols. (1776; ed. J. Alfred Novello, 2 vols., 1853*), is equally important though less well known; Hawkins's preference for English music and for the past rather than for his own period makes his book a useful corrective to Burney's.

B. MODERN WORKS

Histories of Theatre, English Literature, and English Drama

6.3   Histories of the theatre are usually too general to be of much use to specialists in the English drama of the period. Moreover, they tend to be oversimplified both in specific content and in governing philosophy and to reflect out-of-date critical concepts. A HISTORY OF THE THEATRE, by George Freedley and John A. Reeves, 3rd ed. (New York: Crown, 1968), and Oscar G. Brockett's HISTORY OF THE THEATRE (Boston: Allyn & Bacon, 1968) are considerably better than average, especially the latter. Marion Geisinger's PLAYS, PLAYERS, AND PLAYWRIGHTS: AN ILLUSTRATED HISTORY OF THE THEATRE (New York: Hart, 1971) is not as good, but has excellent illustrations. Karl Mantzius's A HISTORY OF THEATRICAL ART IN ANCIENT AND MODERN TIMES, trans. Louise von Cossel, 6 vols. (London: Duckworth, 1903-21*), is more detailed but now quite dated.

Histories of English literature, in treating the drama of the period, generally focus on Etherege, Dryden, Wycherley, Congreve, and Farquhar; mention Gay and Fielding; glance at sentimental comedy and domestic tragedy; and jump to Goldsmith and Sheridan. The received opinion at the time nearly always prevails. Hippolyte Taine's HISTORY OF ENGLISH LITERATURE, trans. Henri van Laun, dominated late nineteenth-century literary history; it ignores eighteenth-century drama completely, and its brilliantly written account of the Restoration is hardly more than caricature. Louis Cazamian's discussion of the period in A HISTORY OF ENGLISH LITERATURE, rev. ed. (New York: Macmillan, 1967), is still brief and very conventional. Five essays in The Cambridge History of English Literature cover the period. Felix E. Schelling, Charles Whibley, and Augustus T. Bartholomew wrote those on Restoration drama (Vol. 8 [1912], pp. 131-65, 166-201, and 202-23). Schelling's essay is factual; he is interested in sources but overstresses the French influence. Whibley considers later comedy, and Bartholomew the tragedians. George H. Nettleton, "The Drama and the Stage" (Vol. 10 [1913], pp. 75-103), considers the decline of tragedy and the rise of sentimental comedy in the eighteenth century; Harold

V. Routh, "The Georgian Drama" (Vol. 11 [1914], pp. 284-314), considers the period of Sheridan. None of the five essays is memorable; all have since been superseded.

Some later accounts are better. George Sherburn's "The Restoration and Eighteenth Century (1660-1789)," in A LITERARY HISTORY OF ENGLAND, ed. Albert C. Baugh (New York: Appleton-Century-Crofts, 1948), pp. 697-1108, is still the best literary history of the period; it is superbly organized, balanced, and well written. Sherburn is conservative, perhaps conventional, in his evaluation of the drama, but his account is detailed and accurate. The second edition (1967) includes a good "Bibliographical Supplement" by Donald F. Bond. Alan D. McKillop's ENGLISH LITERATURE FROM DRYDEN TO BURNS (New York: Appleton-Century-Crofts, 1948) is succinct and factual and provides good bibliographies; McKillop, like Sherburn, presents the traditional account of drama in the period, but with taste and good judgement. Both accounts are better on drama than Louis I. Bredvold's "The Literature of the Restoration and Eighteenth Century 1660-1798," in A HISTORY OF ENGLISH LITERATURE, ed. Hardin Craig (New York: Oxford Univ. Press, 1950). FROM DRYDEN TO JOHNSON, ed. Boris Ford, rev. ed., vol. 4 (London: Cassell, 1965), contains essays on "The Social Setting" and "The Literary Scene" by Arthur R. Humphreys, pp. 7-40 and 43-85, and one on "Restoration Comedy" by Philip A.W. Collins, pp. 148-64; none of the three is remarkable.

Two volumes in the Oxford History of English Literature include sections on drama. James R. Sutherland's account in ENGLISH LITERATURE OF THE LATE SEVENTEENTH CENTURY (1969) is an excellent essay on the background of the age with good bibliographies; the discussion of drama is balanced and sensible. Sutherland does not indulge in categorization and includes major and many minor dramatists in an essay of some 120 pages. Bonamy Dobrée's thirty-odd pages in ENGLISH LITERATURE IN THE EARLIER EIGHTEENTH CENTURY 1700-1740 (1959) are not very good, though facile and entertaining. David Daiches, in A CRITICAL HISTORY OF ENGLISH LITERATURE, 2nd ed., 2 vols. (New York: Ronald Press, 1970), considers only major figures and sees the drama of the period as initiating the current divorce between art and entertainment. He does not intend a survey and does not give one. The most recent general history is the History of Literature in the English Language series being published in London by Barrie and Jenkins. Volume 3, ENGLISH DRAMA TO 1710, ed. Christopher Ricks (1971), contains a perfunctory and inadequate essay, "The Restoration Theatre," by Glynne Wickham (pp. 370-74), and a essay by John Barnard, "Drama from the Restoration till 1710," pp. 375-411. Barnard considers literary values exclusively, provides a good survey of Etherege, Wycherley, and Congreve, and ignores almost everything else. His attempt to relate heroic tragedy to sentimental comedy through their commen concern with idealism is interesting. Volume 4, DRYDEN TO JOHNSON, ed. Roger Lonsdale (1971), includes a brief survey by Ian Donaldson, "Drama from 1710 to 1780" (pp. 190-225).

Most surveys limited to Restoration literature deal with the drama of the period at least briefly. Richard Garnett's THE AGE OF DRYDEN (London: Bell, 1895*) is better than many later studies, though its focus is on major writers

and the "beauties" approach is overdone. Kathleen M.P. Burton's RESTORA-
TION LITERATURE (London: Hutchinson, 1958) depreciates the drama as immoral and ephemeral. General studies of English drama are also brief on the
period; they spend little more time on the eighteenth century than on the first
two-thirds of the nineteenth, though they usually consider Restoration comedy
in more detail. Ashley Thorndike's two volumes, TRAGEDY (Boston: Houghton
Mifflin, 1908*) and ENGLISH COMEDY (New York: Macmillan, 1929*), are
now dated, but were sensible and well organized histories; Thorndike was not
so offended by the moral issue as some later critics have been, and he discusses representative as well as major figures. Walter P. Eaton's THE DRAMA
IN ENGLISH (New York: Scribner's, 1930) is traditional in interpretation
but perceptive in seeing drama in terms of production, an approach few historians have explored adequately. Allardyce Nicoll's BRITISH DRAMA: AN
HISTORICAL SURVEY FROM THE BEGINNINGS TO THE PRESENT TIME, 5th
ed. (London: Harrap, 1962), is a thorough revision of the 1925 edition and
offers a readable, balanced account despite an overly moralistic tone. The
best of these short histories is probably Alan S. Downer's THE BRITISH DRAMA,
A HANDBOOK AND BRIEF CHRONICLE (New York: Appleton-Century-Crofts,
1950). Ernest J. Burton's THE BRITISH THEATRE: ITS REPERTORY AND
PRACTICE 1100-1900 A.D. (London: Jenkins, 1960) is especially useful to
those interested in production and design. George Wilson Knight's THE GOL-
DEN LABYRINTH: A STUDY OF ENGLISH DRAMA (London: Dent, 1962)
moves at breakneck pace yet gives considerable attention to plays, especially
serious plays, that few historians ever discuss. Despite his tendency to ride
his Dionysian versus Appolonian thesis hard, Wilson Knight's book is provocative; he leads one to revalue the tragedy of the period and to consider
eighteenth-century comedy without preconceptions derived from overemphasis
on its Restoration antecedents. By contrast, Alec Clunes's THE BRITISH
THEATRE (London: Cassell, 1964) is tame, though its many illustrations are useful.

Histories of English Drama in the Period

6.4   GENERAL STUDIES. Early accounts of English drama in the period
have been largely superseded by Allardyce Nicoll's monumental A HISTORY
OF ENGLISH DRAMA 1660-1900, 6 vols. (Cambridge: Cambridge Univ. Press,
1952-59), which is comprised of revised editions of five separate volumes originally issued in the 1920's and the ALPHABETICAL CATALOGUE OF PLAYS
noted in Section 1.6 above, and by the general and season-by-season introductions to the eleven volumes of THE LONDON STAGE. The standard account
prior to Nicoll was John Genest, SOME ACCOUNT OF THE ENGLISH STAGE
FROM THE RESTORATION IN 1660 TO 1830, 10 vols. (Bath, England: Carrington,
1832), a modestly titled but impressive work organized (desultorily) by theatres
and theatrical seasons and full of miscellaneous information. Plots, cast lists,
information about authors and actors, lists of plays and roles, citations from
earlier critics and historians, quotations from prefaces, and even excerpts from
plays are offered the reader in a manner entertaining if neither complete nor
systematic. The fortunes of "old plays" (Elizabethan and later) are dealt with
in Volumes 9 and 10; Volume 10 also includes information on plays printed but
not acted, corrections and additions to the earlier volumes, and an indexed
section on the Irish stage which Genest notes comes largely from Robert

Hitchcock's work (see Section 3.11). Later nineteenth-century works sometimes pale by comparison with Genest, but are often better organized and more
readable. John Doran's account in 'THEIR MAJESTIES' SERVANTS': ANNALS
OF THE ENGLISH STAGE FROM THOMAS BETTERTON TO EDMUND KEAN:
ACTORS, AUTHORS, AUDIENCES, 2 vols. (London: Allen, 1864), is moralis-
tic even by Victorian standards; Aphra Behn, for example, is a harlot dancing
through uncleanness. The version of Doran edited and revised by Robert W.
Lowe, 3 vols. (London: Nimmo, 1888), is superior to the original. Percy H.
Fitzgerald's A NEW HISTORY OF THE ENGLISH STAGE, FROM THE RESTORA-
TION TO THE LIBERTY OF THE THEATRES . . ., 2 vols. (London: Tinsley,
1882), is another standard account by a well known historian. Doran, like
Dibdin before him, concentrates on plays and especially on performers and
performances; Fitzgerald, in contrast, prints or uses many of the relevant docu-
ments, and hence tends to be more reliable and pertinent. Henry Barton
Baker's THE LONDON STAGE: ITS HISTORY AND TRADITIONS FROM 1576
TO 1888, 2 vols. (London: Allen, 1889*), is more loosely organized and anecdotal; a second edition carries the title HISTORY OF THE LONDON STAGE
AND ITS FAMOUS PLAYERS 1576-1903 and was published by Routledge (London) in 1904. Between these works and Nicoll's, the only dramatic history
covering the entire period is George H. Nettleton's ENGLISH DRAMA OF
THE RESTORATION AND EIGHTEENTH CENTURY (1642-1780), published by
Macmillan (New York, 1914). William Archer's THE OLD DRAMA AND THE
NEW: AN ESSAY IN REVALUATION (London: Heinemann, 1923) is not so
much a history as an attempt to promote late nineteenth-century drama at the
expense of everything after 1660; it is a classic depreciation of the drama of
the period. A more specialized work, discussing some one hundred plays by
more than fifty authors, is Terence Tobin's PLAYS BY SCOTS 1660-1800 (see
Section 1.11).

Nicoll's first volume, A HISTORY OF RESTORATION DRAMA, was published
in 1923. Volume 2, EARLY EIGHTEENTH-CENTURY DRAMA, came in 1925;
Volume 3, LATER EIGHTEENTH-CENTURY DRAMA 1750-1800, in 1927. The
Restoration volume was partly revised for editions in 1928 and 1940 and more
substantially for issue as Volume 1 of A HISTORY OF ENGLISH DRAMA 1660-
1900 in 1952. The second volume was issued in a partly revised edition in
1929, and both it and the volume on the later eighteenth century were issued
as new editions in 1952. The cost of resetting successive editions necessitated
having much of the final revision in supplements at the end of the volumes,
but the result is inconvenient for the reader. Each of the volumes in the
HISTORY is still a standard reference work on its period. Nicoll begins each
with an essay on the stage, including information about the acting companies
and their personnel. A survey by types follows, and each volume concludes
with a section of relevant documents and a handlist of plays alphabetically by
author. Numerous errors of fact have been corrected in the successive revisions, but it is important to note that the ALPHABETICAL CATALOGUE is more
up-to-date than the handlists in the individual volumes. Some of the discussion has also been revised, but the HISTORY remains a conservative, somewhat
moralistic survey in the nineteenth-century tradition. Nicoll is primarily an
historian rather than a critic; his analyses of particular plays and of the significance of particular playwrights rarely illuminates their literary achievements.
The value of his work lies in the mass of information accumulated through

years of patient research and made accessible in workable form. the HISTORY is thus an essential work, even though its categories are badly in need of revision and the "degeneration and decay" thesis which Nicoll shares with many other historians of eighteenth-century drama is in my opinion mistaken.

6.5   HISTORIES OF RESTORATION DRAMA. Modern studies devoted exclusively to Restoration or later Stuart drama begin with Adolphus W. Ward's A HISTORY OF ENGLISH DRAMATIC LITERATURE TO THE DEATH OF QUEEN ANNE (2 vols., 1875; rev. ed., 3 vols. [London: Macmillan, 1899*]). Ward stresses the narrowness and non-national character of Restoration drama; he sees its comedy as more flexible if more immoral than earlier comedy, and argues conventionally that the period saw the death of tragedy. His book considers minor as well as major dramatists, but much of the "analysis" given is either moral judgment or plot summary.

Bonamy Dobrée's two books on the Restoration drama have been immensely influential. RESTORATION COMEDY 1660-1720 (Oxford: Clarendon Press, 1924) attacks Victorian moralizing and stresses native rather than continental influences. The style is witty and enjoyable, but Dobrée's love of epigram often betrays him into flip judgment; Etherege cannot be dismissed as a mere "brilliant butterfly." RESTORATION TRAGEDY 1660-1720 (Oxford: Clarendon Press, 1929) is less good. Heroic drama cannot be explained as vicariously satisfying the age's need for heroism; throughout, Dobrée has more style than substance. The chapter on ALL FOR LOVE is the best in the book, and those on Otway, Rowe, and THE MOURNING BRIDE and CATO better than average. Both books consider major figures only. Malcolm Elwin's THE PLAYGOER'S HANDBOOK TO THE RESTORATION DRAMA (London: Cape, 1928*) is a survey of the traditional sort, again focusing on major figures. Elwin's praise of some tragedies is excessive, but his analyses of plays like Lee's LUCIUS JUNIUS BRUTUS are helpful.

Montague Summers's THE PLAYHOUSE OF PEPYS (London: Macmillan, 1935*) is a fascinating book. Summers enjoys attacking other scholars, especially Leslie Hotson; his book is also self-centered, capricious, and excessively mannered in style and judgment. Its virtue lies in its detailed information about the early Restoration period, though one can never be sure how reliable a given "fact" is. The critical evaluations are often interesting and as often grossly exaggerated. Alfred Harbage's CAVALIER DRAMA: AN HISTORICAL AND CRITICAL SUPPLEMENT TO THE ELIZABETHAN AND RESTORATION STAGE (New York: Modern Language Association, 1936) is a scholarly and thorough account of the Cavalier mode and its later influence, particularly on heroic drama. John H. Wilson's account in A PREFACE TO RESTORATION DRAMA (Boston: Houghton Mifflin, 1965*) is perhaps the best introduction-- balanced, succinct, lively, and accurate. John E. Cunningham's RESTORATION DRAMA (London: Evans, 1966) is also intended as a beginning guide. Kenneth Muir's book, THE COMEDY OF MANNERS (London: Hutchinson, 1970), despite its title, is more a survey of Restoration comedy than a critical essay on one aspect of it; Muir considers Shadwell, Otway, and Southerne as well as the usual figures. His book is clear, well organized, and unaffected. A more recent survey, focusing on leading writers and plays, is Donald Bruce's

TOPICS OF RESTORATION COMEDY (New York: St. Martin's Press, 1974).

Practically all accounts of the subject confuse or identify Restoration comedy
with what has come to be called the comedy of manners or the comedy of wit
and thus falsify to one degree or another the history of drama in the period.
A useful corrective is Arthur H. Scouten's article, "Notes toward a History of
Restoration Comedy," PQ 45 (1966), 62-70, which should be read by anyone
seriously interested in the subject. Robert D. Hume's THE DEVELOPMENT OF
THE ENGLISH DRAMA IN THE LATE SEVENTEENTH CENTURY (Oxford:
Oxford Univ. Press, 1976) should do much to establish a sounder approach.

6.6   HISTORIES OF EIGHTEENTH-CENTURY DRAMA. Eighteenth-century
drama has received less attention than that of the Restoration, at least so far
as survey histories are concerned. Thomas Seccombe, in THE AGE OF JOHN-
SON 1748-1798 (London: Bell, 1899; 6th ed. rev. 1913), gives a survey superior to those in the Cambridge History of English Literature and in Nettleton;
like most historians, Seccombe considers plays as "letters" rather than as theatrical works, hence his division of comedy into "irresponsible" (opera, pantomime, etc.) and "moral." The two full-length studies are Frederick W. Bateson's ENGLISH COMIC DRAMA 1700-1750 (Oxford: Clarendon Press, 1929*)
and Frederick S. Boas's AN INTRODUCTION TO EIGHTEENTH-CENTURY
DRAMA 1700-1780 (Oxford: Clarendon Press, 1953). The heart of Bateson's
book is a set of essays on Cibber, Steele, Centlivre, Gay, Carey, and Fielding. To these he adds an introduction and conclusion only tangentially related
to the rest of the book. The theoretical discussion in the opening chapter is
not especially good; in concluding, Bateson sees comedy in decline, eventually
to split into Italian opera at one extreme and the medley program at the other.
The Boas book is much inferior. Basically, it is a collection of plot summaries.
A new work, THE REVELS HISTORY OF DRAMA IN ENGLISH, VOLUME VI:
1750-1880, ed. Michael R. Booth et al., has recently appeared (London:
Methuen, 1974).

Chapter VII

LITERARY CRITICISM AND SCHOLARSHIP

A. CONTEMPORARY WORKS

7.1   Separately published contemporary books and pamphlets are listed in
ENGLISH THEATRICAL LITERATURE.   The typically descriptive titles of these
works, together with the brief annotation often provided by Arnott and Robin-
son in ENGLISH THEATRICAL LITERATURE, make detailed discussion here su-
perfluous.   The most important books and collections include A COMPARISON
BETWEEN THE TWO STAGES . . . (1702), ed. Staring B. Wells (Princeton:
Princeton Univ. Press, 1942*); Thomas Wilkes's A GENERAL VIEW OF THE
STAGE (1759); Francis Gentleman's THE DRAMATIC CENSOR (2 vols., 1770*);
and Thomas Davies's DRAMATIC MISCELLANIES . . . (3 vols., 1783-84*).
Criticism devoted to particular dramatic forms may be exemplified by John
Dennis's AN ESSAY ON THE OPERAS AFTER THE ITALIAN MANNER . . .
(1706*); Francesco Algarotti's AN ESSAY ON THE OPERA (1755, trans. 1767);
John Burgoyne's discussion of comic opera in the preface to THE LORD OF
THE MANOR (1781); and Justus Moeser's HARLEQUIN; OR, A DEFENCE OF
GROTESQUE COMIC PERFORMANCES (trans. 1766).   Many other examples
may be found in the works listed in Section 5.2.

Most contemporary criticism was occasional or polemic and therefore appeared
most frequently either in one of the broad-coverage serials like THE GENTLE-
MAN'S MAGAZINE or THE LONDON MAGAZINE or in pamphlet form.   A
good bibliography of theatrical criticism in contemporary periodicals is long
overdue.   The best guide is still Charles H. Gray's THEATRICAL CRITICISM
IN LONDON TO 1795 (mentioned in Section 5.1), but this is far from complete, a summary of trends rather than a comprehensive account.   Perhaps the
most famous example of periodical criticism is Oliver Goldsmith's "A Comparison Between Laughing and Sentimental Comedy," which appeared in THE WEST-
MINSTER MAGAZINE for January 1773.   A few serials, all short run, were
devoted exclusively to theatrical subjects; the most important were Richard
Steele's THE THEATRE (1729), which has been edited by John Loftis (Oxford:
Clarendon Press, 1962, and THE PROMPTER (1734-36), by Aaron Hill and
William Popple, selections from which have been edited by William W. Appleton and Kalman A. Burnim (New York: Blom, 1966).   The pamphlets often
focused on contemporary productions and more particularly on the merits and
faults of favorite actors and actresses.   Typical examples are A REVIEW OF

MRS. CRAWFORD AND MRS. SIDDONS IN THE CHARACTER OF BELVIDERA
. . . (1782), AN ESSAY ON THE PRE-EMINENCE OF COMIC GENIUS,
WITH OBSERVATIONS ON THE SEVERAL CHARACTERS MRS. JORDAN HAS
APPEARED IN (1786), and Frederick Pilon's AN ESSAY ON THE CHARACTER
OF HAMLET AS PERFORMED BY MR. HENDERSON . . . (1777).

B. MODERN WORKS

General and Miscellaneous Studies

7.2   DRAMATIC THEMES AND TYPES. A number of studies treat specific
dramatic themes or forms relevant to the period. Among them are Murray
Roston's BIBLICAL DRAMA IN ENGLAND: FROM THE MIDDLE AGES TO THE
PRESENT DAY (London: Faber, 1968), which deals sketchily with Dryden and
Handel; Thomas F. Mayo's EPICURUS IN ENGLAND 1650-1725 (Dallas: South-
west Press, 1934), which has a chapter on Epicurus in Restoration comedy;
Dane F. Smith's PLAYS ABOUT THE THEATRE IN ENGLAND FROM 'THE RE-
HEARSAL' IN 1671 TO THE LICENSING ACT IN 1737 (London: Oxford Univ.
Press, 1936), still a standard account; and Charles E. Whitmore's THE SUPER-
NATURAL IN TRAGEDY (Cambridge, Mass.: Harvard Univ. Press, 1915), which
has chapters on both the Restoration and eighteenth century. The legend of King
Edgard's love for Elfridin is the subject of George B. Dutton's "Dramatic Fash-
ions Illustrated in Six Old Plays," JEGP 13 (1914), 398-417; Maurice J.
Valency's THE TRAGEDIES OF HEROD AND MARIAMNE (New York: Columbia Univ. Press, 1940) treats several plays of the period on this theme. Dryden and Fielding, among others, are given brief treatment by James D. Merri-
man in THE FLOWER OF KINGS: A STUDY OF THE ARTHURIAN LEGEND
IN ENGLAND BETWEEN 1485 AND 1835 (Lawrence: Univ. Press of Kansas,
1973).

Philip K. Jason discusses "The Afterpiece: Authors and Incentives," RECTR 12,
no. 1 (1973), 1-13, noting their special circumstances and gradual rise in
popularity and profit. Victor C. Clinton-Baddeley's THE BURLESQUE TRADI-
TION IN THE ENGLISH THEATRE AFTER 1660 (London: Methuen, 1952*)
devotes most of its first hundred pages to the period; the book is full of apt
citation and excellent discussion of representative examples. BURLESQUE, a
volume by John D. Jump in Methuen's Critical Idiom series (London, 1972),
may be recommended as a brief introduction. Josephine Laidler's "A History
of Pastoral Drama in England until 1700," ESt 35 (1905), 193-259, is less
thorough than Jeanette Marks's ENGLISH PASTORAL DRAMA FROM THE RES-
TORATION TO THE DATE OF THE PUBLICATION OF THE 'LYRICAL BALLADS'
(1660-1798) (London: Methuen, 1908). The latter includes a useful bibliography of English and continental pastoral plays, but fails to consider such relevant topics as staging, contemporary appeal, and the relation of music to the
success of specific pastoral plays. Marie Pabisch, in PICARESQUE DRAMAS
OF THE SEVENTEENTH AND EIGHTEENTH CENTURIES (Berlin: Mayer, Muel-
ler, 1910) derives Restoration examples from Molière's FOUBERIES DE SCAPIN
and traces the development of the type in the eighteenth century.

Pantomime, introduced in the Restoration period, became staple theatrical fare in the eighteenth century. The patent houses competed for audiences by mounting ever more elaborate pantomimic spectacles, and harlequinade figures were also frequently introduced into other types of plays. R.J. Broadbent's A HISTORY OF PANTOMIME (London: Simpkin et al., 1901) has a few chapters on English pantomime, as does Maurice W. Disher's CLOWNS AND PANTOMIMES (London: Constable, 1925*); the latter is lavishly illustrated. Cyril W. Beaumont's THE HISTORY OF HARLEQUIN (London: Beaumont, 1926*) is also well illustrated. Albert E. Wilson's PANTOMIME PAGEANT . . . (London: S. Paul, 1946) and THE STORY OF PANTOMIME (London: Home, Van Thal, 1949*) include some useful material. Thelma Niklaus's HARLEQUIN PHOENIX; OR, THE RISE AND FALL OF A BERGAMASK ROGUE (London: The Bodley Head, 1956) is derivative and sketchy on English examples. A more recent book, Raymond Mander and Joe Mitchenson's PANTO-MIME: A STORY IN PICTURES (New York: Taplinger, 1973), again offers sketchy text and well chosen illustration.

Farce, like satire, is perhaps more profitably considered a technique than a form. But hundreds of plays throughout the period are so titled, and critics have followed suit. Leo A. Hughes, in "The Early Career of Farce in the Theatrical Vocabulary," SET (1940), pp. 82–95, derives the term from Latin farcire: to stuff or fill. This essay and the substance of his article, "Attitudes of Some Restoration Dramatists toward Farce," PQ 19 (1940), 268–87, are included in his A CENTURY OF ENGLISH FARCE (1956), the standard discussion of the topic for the period 1660–1750. Samuel A. Golden's article "An Early Defence of Farce," STUDIES IN HONOR OF JOHN WILCOX . . ., ed. A. Dayle Wallace and Woodburn O. Ross (Detroit: Wayne State Univ. Press, 1958), pp. 61–70, discusses Sir Samuel Tuke's 1693 preface to A DUKE AND NO DUKE. No study comparable to the Hughes book but focusing on the last half of the eighteenth century has yet appeared.

Early discussions of the puppet theatre in the period include Alwin Thaler, "Elizabethan 'Motions,'" TLS, 26 February 1920, p. 140, and "The Coming of Mr. Punch," TLS, 23 December 1920, p. 874. George Speaight's "'Powell from the Bath': An Eighteenth-Century London Puppet Theatre," ENTHOVEN COLLECTION, pp. 38–51, is an extended study of a famous puppeteer. Most of Speaight's earlier studies are incorporated in THE HISTORY OF THE ENGLISH PUPPET THEATRE (London: Harrap, 1955), the standard work on the subject. A later article, "A Restoration Puppet Show," TN 12 (1958), 69–71, concerns references in John Lacy's THE OLD TROOP (1668). Speaight's HISTORY was extensively revised and republished as PUNCH AND JUDY: A HISTORY (London: Studio Vista, 1970), but this edition lacks the extensive and useful notes of the first edition.

7.3   CHARACTER TYPES. Studies of character types include Benjamin H. Bissell, "The Indian in Drama," THE AMERICAN INDIAN IN ENGLISH LITERATURE OF THE EIGHTEENTH CENTURY (New Haven: Yale Univ. Press, 1925), pp. 118–62; William J. Lawrence, "Irish Types in Old-Time English Drama," ANGLIA 35 (1912), 347–56; George C. Duggan, THE STAGE IRISH-MAN: A HISTORY OF THE IRISH PLAY AND STAGE CHARACTERS FROM

THE EARLIEST TIMES (New York: Longmans, Green, 1937*); and J.O. Bartley's TEAGUE, SHENKIN, AND SAWNEY (Cork, Ireland: Cork Univ. Press,
1954), which considers Irish, Welsh, and Scottish characters in English drama 1581–
1800. Of the studies of Irish types, the Lawrence is perfunctory, the Duggan
most complete, and the Bartley the most scholarly. See also Florence R.
Scott, "Teg--The Stage Irishman," MLR 42 (1947), 314–20, a response to an
earlier article (1942–43) by Bartley. Myer J. Landa includes some relevant
material in chapters 8–10 of THE JEW IN DRAMA (London: King, 1926*),
especially on Richard Cumberland; Harm R.S. Van der Veen, in JEWISH
CHARACTERS IN EIGHTEENTH-CENTURY ENGLISH FICTION AND DRAMA
(Groningen, Netherlands: Wolters, 1935), stresses Tobias Smollett's ISRAELITES as
an earlier portrait sympathetic to Jews. The focus of Ezra K. Maxfield's "The
Quakers in English Stage Plays before 1800," PMLA 45 (1930), 256–73, is on Su-
sanna Centlivre, but his article also distinguishes the different types of reference to
Friends in the drama of the period. Harold F. Watson, in THE SAILOR IN
ENGLISH FICTION AND DRAMA 1550–1800 (New York: Columbia Univ.
Press, 1931) covers his ground somewhat superficially; Frederick S. Boas, in
"The Soldier in Elizabethan and Later English Drama," EDH, n.s. 19 (1942),
121–56, makes only brief reference to the period. Carson S. Duncan argues
a shift from pedantic astrologer-alchemist to virtuoso as object of attack in the
late seventeenth and eighteenth centuries in "The Scientist as a Comic Type,"
MP 14 (1916), 281–91. Montague Summers offers a useful account of witches
in dramatic literature in chapter 7 of his HISTORY OF WITCHCRAFT AND
DEMONOLOGY (London: Kegan Paul et al., 1926*). One of the most
thorough studies of a character type is Jean E. Gagen's THE NEW WOMAN:
HER EMERGENCE IN ENGLISH DRAMA 1600–1730 (New York: Twayne,
1954), which studies the figure of the "learned," "scientific," or "cultivated"
lady in numerous plays in order to document the gradual rise in the status of
women.

7.4   PROLOGUES AND EPILOGUES. Although they constitute one of
the most important literary kinds in the period, prologues and epilogues have
received little critical attention until quite recently. Robert Hannah's "The
Interpretation of the Prologue and Epilogue," QJS 13 (1927), 123–32, is perfunctory. Autrey N. Wiley notes the marked rise in frequency of prologue
and epilogue in "The English Vogue of Prologues and Epilogues," MLN 47
(1932), 255–57; her article "Female Prologues and Epilogues in English Plays,"
PMLA 48 (1933), 1060–79, is also useful. These articles, and Mary E. Knapp's
PROLOGUES AND EPILOGUES OF THE EIGHTEENTH CENTURY (New Haven:
Yale Univ. Press, 1961), are historical rather than critical studies; though the
last-named discusses in some detail the purpose, themes, and development of
the prologue and epilogue, it does not deal adequately with either the rhetori-
cal function or literary merit of the examples cited. James R. Sutherland's
"Prologues, Epilogues, and Audience in the Restoration Theatre," in OF BOOKS
AND HUMANKIND, ed. John Butt et al. (London: Routledge, 1964), pp.
37–54, is hardly more than a pleasant essay. In fact, there are only two
studies which add anything to Knapp's book: Emmett L. Avery's "Rhetorical
Patterns in Restoration Prologues and Epilogues," in ESSAYS IN AMERICAN
AND ENGLISH LITERATURE PRESENTED TO BRUCE ROBERT MCELDERRY, JR.,
ed. Max F. Schultz et al. (Athens: Ohio Univ. Press, 1967), pp. 221–37,
and David M. Vieth's "The Art of the Prologue and Epilogue: A New Approach

Based on Dryden's Practice," GENRE 5 (1972), 271-92. Both articles are
fundamental to any serious study of the subject. Stanley L. Archer's "The
Epistle Dedicatory in Restoration Drama," RECTR 10, no. 1 (1971), 8-13, may
be mentioned here for convenience; though Archer makes no claim for the literary merit of play dedications, he does show that only half of the examples
in his study include an appeal for patronage.

7.5   CENSORSHIP. The standard works on stage censorship are Watson
Nicholson, THE STRUGGLE FOR A FREE STAGE IN LONDON (Boston: Houghton
Mifflin, 1906*); John L. Palmer, THE CENSOR AND THE THEATRES (London:
Unwin, 1912); and Frank Fowell and Frank Palmer, CENSORSHIP IN ENGLAND
(London: Palmer, 1913*). The first seven chapters of Nicholson's book take
the account to 1800, after which John Palmer's book also becomes especially
useful. Chapters 5 through 7 of the Fowell-Palmer book cover 1660-1800.
The Collier controversy and the political history of Walpole's administration are
of major significance in the censorship issue, and the appropriate secondary
works listed in Sections 5.3 should also be consulted. Joseph W. Krutch has
an article on the former topic, "Governmental Attempts to Regulate the Stage
after the Jeremy Collier Controversy," PMLA 38 (1923), 153-74; P.J. Crean,
"The Stage Licensing Act of 1737," MP 35 (1938), 239-55, and Phyllis Hartnoll, "The Theatre and the Licensing Act of 1737," in SILVER RENAISSANCE,
ed. Alex Natan (London: Macmillan, 1961), pp. 165-86, cover the latter.
Richard C. Frushell's "Contemporary Commentary on the Players' Revolt of 1743
and the Licensing Act of 1737," TS 14, no. 2 (1973), 91-95, is also useful.
For the earlier period Arthur P. White's "The Office of Revels and Dramatic
Censorship during the Restoration Period," WRB, 34 (1931), 5-45, may be consulted.

7.6   MISCELLANEOUS WORKS. A few critical studies otherwise difficult
to classify consider topics relevant to the period as a whole. Martin Price, in
TO THE PALACE OF WISDOM: STUDIES IN ORDER AND ENERGY FROM
DRYDEN TO BLAKE (Garden City, N.Y.: Doubleday, 1964), discusses several
plays with acuity and style. Ian Donaldson's THE WORLD UPSIDE-DOWN:
COMEDY FROM JONSON TO FIELDING (Oxford: Clarendon Press, 1970),
like Price's book, is really a collection of individual essays; the Bergsonian
notion of comic inversion is even less adequate as a theoretical framework than
Price's "order and energy" thesis, but the readings of individual plays are pro-
vocative and interesting. John C. Loftis's essay "The Limits of Historical Ve-
racity in Neoclassical Drama," in ENGLAND IN THE RESTORATION AND
EARLY EIGHTEENTH CENTURY: ESSAYS ON CULTURE AND SOCIETY, ed.
Hugh T. Swedenberg, Jr. (Berkeley and Los Angeles: Univ. of California
Press, 1972), pp. 27-50, is a useful caution to those who see the drama of
the period as a perfect mirror of society. An older essay, Raymond M. Alden's
"The Development of the Use of Prose in the English Drama 1660-1800," MP 7
(1909), 1-22, may still be recommended. Gordon Martin's THE PLAYBILL:
THE DEVELOPMENT OF ITS TOPOGRAPHIC STYLE (Chicago: Illinois Institute
of Technology Institute of Design, 1963) is the fullest treatment of a fascinating
topic. W. Heldt's "A Chronological and Critical Review of the Appreciation
and Condemnation of the Comic Dramatists of the Restoration and Orange Periods," Np 8 (1923), 39-59, 109-28, and 197-204, is useful primarily for its
discussion of German dissertations.

Restoration Drama

7.7   GENERAL AND MISCELLANEOUS STUDIES. A number of useful
collections of materials on Restoration drama may be listed here, although many
of the essays they contain are discussed under the appropriate entries elsewhere
in this guide. Montague Summers's ESSAYS IN PETTO (London: Fortune Press,
1928*) includes a number of relevant pieces, as does THEATRE MISCELLANY:
SIX PIECES CONNECTED WITH THE SEVENTEENTH-CENTURY STAGE (Oxford:
Blackwell, 1953). RESTORATION THEATRE, ed. John R. Brown and Bernard
Harris (London: Arnold, 1965), is a good collection of specially commissioned
articles. RESTORATION DRAMA: MODERN ESSAYS IN CRITICISM, ed.
John C. Loftis (New York: Oxford Univ. Press, 1966) is a judicious selection
of previously published criticism, as is RESTORATION DRAMATISTS: A COL-
LECTION OF CRITICAL ESSAYS, ed. Earl R. Miner (Englewood Cliffs, N.J.:
Prentice Hall, 1966). The Loftis collection is about twice the length of the
Miner, and there is some overlap. RESTORATION LITERATURE: CRITICAL
APPROACHES, ed. Harold Love (London: Methuen, 1972), is made up of
commissioned pieces, including three on Restoration drama.

General essays include the first chapter of Alexandre Beljame's MEN OF LET-
TERS AND THE ENGLISH PUBLIC IN THE EIGHTEENTH CENTURY 1660-1744:
DRYDEN, ADDISON, POPE, trans. Emily O. Lormier, ed. Bonamy Dobrée
(London: Kegan Paul, 1948), pp. 1-135. This study was originally published
in 1881, and is now badly dated. Cyrus H. Hoy's "The Effect of the Restora-
tion on Drama," TSL 6 (1961), pp. 85-91, is conventional in its judgments,
as is James R. Sutherland's "The Impact of Charles II on Restoration Litera-
ture," RESTORATION AND EIGHTEENTH-CENTURY LITERATURE: ESSAYS
IN HONOR OF ALAN DUGALD MCKILLOP (Chicago: Univ. of Chicago
Press for Rice Univ., 1963), pp. 251-63. An interchange in KOMOS between
Harold Love and Andrew S. Bear--"The Myth of the Restoration Audience," 1
(1968), 49-56, and "Criticism and Social Change: The Case of Restoration
Drama," 2 (1969), 23-31--throws light on the relation between literary criticism and the ancillary disciplines of history and sociology. David S. Berkeley's
"Some Notes on Probability in Restoration Drama, N&Q 200 (1955) 237-39
and 342-44, points out the historical latitude allowed in plays dealing with
exotic or otherwise distanced material.

Technical or bibliographical articles include Alfred Harbage, "Elizabethan-Res-
toration Palimpsest," MLR 35 (1940), 287-319, which argues that some Restoration playwrights obtained manuscripts of plays written before 1642 and produced
or published modernized versions of them as their own. The argument is highly
speculative and has not been widely accepted. Arthur L. Woehl, in "Some
Plays in the Repertories of the Patent Houses," in STUDIES IN SPEECH AND
DRAMA IN HONOR OF ALEXANDER W. DRUMMOND, ed. Donald C. Bryant
et al. (Ithaca, N.Y.: Cornell Univ. Press, 1944), pp. 105-22, argues from a
study of plays from 1660 to 1670 that there was strong continuity between the late
Elizabethan and early Restoration theatres--a thesis more in need of demonstration in 1944 than now. John H. Wilson's "Six Restoration Play Dates," N&Q
207 (1962), 221-23, is typical of numerous notes, most of which have now
been superseded by THE LONDON STAGE; another example is James Wilson's

"A Note on the Dating of Restoration Plays," RECTR 1 (1962), 18-19, which discusses an inadequacy in the production dates given by Nicoll. Philip J. Gray, Jr., in "Lenten Casts and the Nursery: Evidence for the Dating of Certain Restoration Plays," PMLA 53 (1938), 781-94, suggests that a partial set of actors' names in a <u>dramatis personae</u> may have seasonal significance and usefulness in dating certain plays. Two later articles are more broadly significant. Curt A. Zimansky's essay, "Editing Restoration Comedy: Vanbrugh and Others," in EDITING SEVENTEENTH-CENTURY PROSE, ed. Donal I.B. Smith (Toronto: Hakkert, 1972), pp. 95-122, is an excellent caveat for editors generally, and particularly for those contemplating modernized texts. And Judith Milhous and Robert D. Hume explore a significant source of information in "Dating Play Premières from Publication Data, 1660-1700," HLB 22 (1974), pp. 374-405, suggesting new dates for forty-five plays.

Comparatively few studies trace particular themes through Restoration drama. Roberta F. Brinkley makes some perceptive remarks about the political significance of the story of Arthur in the period in ARTHURIAN LEGEND IN THE SEVENTEENTH CENTURY (Baltimore: Johns Hopkins Univ. Press, 1932). Charles L. Barber's THE IDEA OF HONOR IN THE ENGLISH DRAMA 1591-1700 (Gothenburg, Sweden: Elanders Boktryckeri, 1957) focuses on a concept obviously central to many Restoration plays. Ulrich Broich's "Libertin und heroischer Held: das Drama der englischen Restaurationzeit und seine Leitbilder," ANGLIA 85 (1967), 34-57, does not deal in sufficient detail with specific plays.

Studies of particular character types include Herbert Silvette's THE DOCTOR ON THE STAGE: MEDICINE AND MEDICAL MEN IN SEVENTEENTH-CENTURY ENGLAND, ed. Francelia Butler (Knoxville: Univ. of Tennessee Press, 1967), which focuses on the virtuoso and on dramatic references to "the French disease" and science and scientists; and Henry L. Snuggs's "The Comic Humours: A New Interpretation," PMLA 62 (1947), 114-22, which argues that Restoration humours are merely "the pseudo-humours of affection and eccentricity" rather than the "temperaments" defined in the science of the period. Louis Wann's article, "The Oriental in Restoration Drama," UWS, no. 2 (1918), pp. 163-86, is primarily a catalog with annotations. Thomas B. Stroup, in "Supernatural Beings in Restoration Drama," ANGLIA, 61 (1937), 186-92, gives instances where ghosts are used to help motivate action.

The political drama of the period is the subject of Rose A. Wright's THE POLITICAL PLAY OF THE RESTORATION (Montesano, Wash.: privately printed, 1916); Allardyce Nicoll's "Political Plays of the Restoration," MLR 16 (1921), 224-42; Virgil L. Jones's "Methods of Satire in the Political Dramas of the Restoration," JEGP 21 (1922), 662-69; George W. Whiting's "Political Satire in London Stage Plays 1680-1683," MP 28 (1930), 29-43; and Harold Love's "State Affairs on the Restoration Stage, 1660-1675," RECTR 14, no. 1 (1975), 1-9. A definitive study has not appeared. William E. Stephenson's "Religious Drama in the Restoration," PQ 50 (1971), 599-609, discusses the reasons why the religious plays of the time were ordinarily closet dramas. Richard H. Perkinson, in "Topographical Comedy in the Seventeenth Century," ELH 3 (1936), 270-90, argues that Restoration settings were dictated by theatrical effectiveness rather than sociological interest, focusing on such plays as EPSOM WELLS, THE SQUIRE OF

ALSATIA, and GREENWICH PARK. Frank H. Ristine's ENGLISH TRAGI-
COMEDY: ITS ORIGIN AND HISTORY (New York: Columbia Univ. Press,
1910) has a chapter on "The Decline of Tragicomedy 1642-1700," pp. 150-87;
Marvin T. Herrick's TRAGICOMEDY: ITS ORIGIN AND DEVELOPMENT IN
ITALY, FRANCE, AND ENGLAND (Urbana: Univ. of Illinois Press, 1955) is
a much better book but includes very little material beyond 1650.

7.8   RESTORATION COMEDY: EARLY STUDIES. Restoration comedy
was condemned by the prudishness of a later age, although altered versions
were produced with some regularity in the eighteenth century. William Hazlitt
attempted to rehabilitate these plays as brilliantly realistic descriptions of an
artificial society; Charles Lamb tried to disarm the descendants of Jeremy Collier by arguing that the values apparently appealed to are part of a "utopia
of gallantry . . . which has no reference whatever to the world that is." To
the extent that Lamb's famous essay "On the Artificial Comedy of the Last
Century" (1822) posits a theatrical world which may not be equated with the
world of everyday reality, it is much more profound than is generally recognized, but the temper of most nineteenth-century comment is more in keeping
with Macaulay's thunderous denouncing of the period in his review of Leigh
Hunt's edition of THE DRAMATIC WORKS OF WYCHERLEY, CONGREVE,
VANBRUGH, AND FARQUHAR, published in THE EDINBURGH REVIEW for
1841.

Much, if not most, early twentieth-century criticism is more accurately described as historical scholarship. Deriving from the philological training in
vogue in the German universities before the war, it tended toward the study
of sources and influences, toward fact-gathering, comparative discussion, and
biography. Perhaps the most compelling issue, other than the moral question,
was whether Restoration comedy owed more to Molière and other continental
dramatists or to the native English tradition. Full-length critical interpretation
was slow to appear in this as in other areas. When it did appear, the moral
question was never far from the center of interest, and the ideas of Hazlitt
and Lamb recur with astonishing frequency in ever more sophisticated dress.

The first major study is John L. Palmer's THE COMEDY OF MANNERS (London: Bell, 1913*). Palmer follows Edmund Gosse in adding Etherege to Leigh
Hunt's four dramatists; the resulting canon has remained relatively unchanged
to the present day. He stresses Hazlitt's view of the plays as documents illustrating the manners of an earlier age. Much of his focus is biographical, but
he helps establish the still-current picture of comedy in the period—Etherege
begins the comedy of manners, Congreve perfects it, Vanbrugh and Farquhar
exhibit its decline, Wycherley is anomalous. Palmer's book had been influential because it is unusually well written and because it is the first detailed
and sympathetic analysis of these writers. Henry T.E. Perry's THE COMIC
SPIRIT IN RESTORATION DRAMA: STUDIES IN THE COMEDY OF ETHEREGE,
WYCHERLEY, CONGREVE, VANBRUGH, AND FARQUHAR (New Haven: Yale
Univ. Press, 1925*) is less important. Perry rides his Meredithian thesis far
too hard and attributes practically all the virtues of the plays discussed to
Molière. The comparison with Bonamy Dobrée's RESTORATION COMEDY,
which appeared about the same time, is sharp.

Kathleen M. Lynch's THE SOCIAL MODE OF RESTORATION COMEDY, Univ. of Michigan Publications in Language and Literature, no. 3 (New York: Macmillan, 1926*), was one of the first full-length studies to insist that Restoration comedy owes more to English models than to Molière and other continental sources. She shows the influence of Ben Jonson, Richard Brome, and James Shirley, but stresses that of the Caroline court writers. Her book is remarkable, especially for its date, though it overstresses the precieuse tradition. The related view that Restoration comedy mirrors the life of a narrow, homogeneous, and highly artificial court group--one of the dominant themes in criticism prior to the 1950's--is typified by Bartholow V. Crawford's "High Comedy in Terms of Restoration Practice," PQ 8 (1929), 339-47.

There are few good studies in the decade or so following the appearance of the Dobrée and Lynch books and the first edition of Nicoll's HISTORY. Perhaps the best is Guy Montgomery's essay, "The Challenge of Restoration Comedy," in ESSAYS IN CRITICISM BY MEMBERS OF THE DEPARTMENT OF ENGLISH, UNIVERSITY OF CALIFORNIA (Berkeley and Los Angeles: Univ. of California Press, 1929*), pp. 133-51, which attacks the circular reasoning of those who "explain" the corruption of Restoration comedy by the corruption of the age. Two other studies worth mentioning are George R. Noyes's essay, "The Development of English Comedy of Manners," in REPRESENTATIVE ENGLISH COMEDIES, 4, ed. Charles M. Gayley and Alwin Thaler (New York: Macmillan, 1936), 538-48, and Elmer E. Stoll's "The 'Real Society' in Restoration Comedy: Hymeneal Pretenses," MLN 58 (1943), 175-81, one of a number of articles in which Stoll insists on the kind of distinction between art and life that critics of Restoration comedy have often been unwilling to make.

7.9   RESTORATION COMEDY: DETRACTION AND DEFENSE. Detractors have not been wanting, though their attack is seldom as bald as Macaulay's (see Section 7.8). Lionel C. Knights and John Wain are perhaps best known among the company, but they are not alone. In "Restoration Comedy: The Reality and the Myth," SCRUTINY 6 (1937*), 122-43, Knights argues that the plays are bad because they are "trivial, gross and dull"; his essay contains a number of concealed and questionable assumptions not always recognized by his admirers. A similar attack, Julian Symons's "Restoration Comedy (Reconsiderations II)," appeared in KR 7 (1945), 185-97, with a rebuttal by Eric R. Bentley, pp. 477-80. Symons attacks Bonamy Dobrée for saying that moral attitudes in the plays do not matter; he finds the plays rather dull (except for Farquhar, whom he sees as a predecessor of Shaw), lacking the force of those written from a clear ethical point of view. Clifford Leech, in "Restoration Comedy: The Earlier Phase," EIC 1 (1951), 165-84, argues that comedy before Etherege and Wycherley was merely a collocation of what would entertain, though the quality improved thereafter. John Wain's "Restoration Comedy and Its Modern Critics," EIC 6 (1956), 367-85, is a depreciation nearly as well known as Knights's; Wain calls the comedy of the period "the fever chart of a sick society" and condemns the split between "impossibly high-flown emotionalism about Love and Honour on the one hand" (tragedy) and "the repudiation of all standards on the other" (comedy). The plays become mere sociological documents, unforgivably narrow in their class bias. A fuller version of Wain's essay appears in PRELIMINARIES (London: Macmillan, 1957).

For Vivian Mercier, Restoration comedy is not a drama of ideas because it usually lacks a fair opposition of ideals ("From Myth to Ideas and Back," in IDEAS IN THE DRAMA: SELECTED PAPERS FROM THE ENGLISH INSTITUTE, ed. John Gassner [New York: Columbia University Press, 1964], pp. 42-70). Similarly, Arnold N. Kaul, in THE ACTION OF ENGLISH COMEDY: STUDIES IN THE ENCOUNTER OF ABSTRACTION AND EXPERIENCE FROM SHAKESPEARE TO SHAW (New Haven: Yale Univ. Press, 1970), argues that good comedy actively contrasts abstraction and experience; Restoration comedy merely inverts customary moral values and opposes abstractions and hence lacks dramatic quality. There is no essential difference between Dorimant and Alderman Gripe or between Mirabell and Fainall. David R.M. Wilkinson's THE COMEDY OF HABIT: AN ESSAY IN THE USE OF COURTESY LITERATURE IN A STUDY OF RESTORATION COMIC DRAMA (Leiden, Netherlands: Universitaire Pers, 1964) takes a different tack. Wilkinson notes that he began his study in an attempt to refute Knights but was led to accept his view. Meaning in these comedies, he argues, is "essentially subordinate to immediate comic effects"; an examination of the plays in relation to contemporary courtesy literature shows that Restoration comic wit "is the product of habit rather than an expression of creative art." Wilkinson overgeneralizes his case and objects to stylization, simplification, patterning, sterotyping--indeed, to many of the central features of the comedy he deals with.

While the critics of Restoration comedy are often quite perceptive about its limitations and weaknesses, their work often presupposes definitions of comedy and comic form and conceptions of the relation between art and morality and art and society which they impose arbitrarily on the plays they discuss. It is no wonder they find them wanting.

The defense has not rested its case and, on the whole, has the better of the argument. Some rebuttal has been direct. Marvin Mudrick, in "Restoration Comedy and Later," in ENGLISH STAGE COMEDY, ed. William K. Wimsatt, Jr. (New York: Columbia Univ. Press, 1954), pp. 98-125, praises such plays as THE COUNTRY WIFE and THE WAY OF THE WORLD over most Elizabethan comedy, including Shakespeare. Frederick W. Bateson's "Second Thoughts 2: L.C. Knights and Restoration Comedy," EIC 7 (1957*), 56-67, attempts a defense based on an historical approach. Restoration comedy must be understood in its own terms; sex can be shown to have a serious function in the plays. Norman N. Holland, in "The Critical Forum: Restoration Comedy Again," EIC 7 (1957), 318-22, attacks Knights and Wain for insisting that the plays of the period are about sex. For Holland, they explore the opposition between natural man and social convention.

7.10   RESTORATION COMEDY: GENERAL STUDIES SINCE 1950. Most recent critics, however, deal with the detractors of the comedy of the period only in passing. The main defense has been to demonstrate the merit of this drama by the detailed examination of selected plays by the major dramatists. Some stress wit, some thematic seriousness, some symbolism, some structure. Nearly all are still at least indirectly preoccupied with one aspect or another of the moral issue.

The earliest study to reflect this approach, and the new-critical climate after World War II, was Thomas H. Fujimura's THE RESTORATION COMEDY OF WIT (Princeton: Princeton Univ. Press, 1952*). Fujimura attacks both the "artificial" school deriving from Lamb and the "manners" school of Palmer; the former denies the plays any serious moral concern, while the latter ignores many of their characteristic features, divorces content from treatment, and turns them into superficial social satires primarily of historical importance. Fujimura defines them in terms of witty dialogue, sexual and skeptical wit, and naturalism; he sees them as heavily indebted to Hobbesian conceptions, and their basic structure as an outwitting situation involving the truewits, the witwouds, and the witless. The plays have a moral concern with naturalness, sincerity, and sense; and a pervasive libertine and empirical temper. They are not merely stylistic documents in photographic realism but serious works of art.

Fujimura's book is a landmark and has features common to many later studies. He exaggerates the Hobbesian elements in the plays and ignores the many dramatists whose works do not lend themselves to his rigid scheme. But he offers detailed and valuable readings of a number of major comedies in support of his views, and he treats them as serious works of art. A second landmark is Norman N. Holland's THE FIRST MODERN COMEDIES: THE SIGNIFICANCE OF ETHEREGE, WYCHERLEY, AND CONGREVE (Cambridge, Mass.: Harvard Univ. Press, 1959*). Holland also attacks both the "moral" and "Manners" critics, stating that the purpose of literature is intellectual pleasure. His thesis is that Restoration comedy has as a basic theme the contrast between appearance and nature, between the publicly perceptible and the private nature of things. Holland's readings of particular plays, though marred by a profusion of jargon and over sophisticated analysis, are often brilliant and always stimulating. The final three chapters on the history of criticism of Restoration comedy since Jeremy Collier's time, on Restoration adaptations of earlier drama, and on staging the plays are especially useful. The chapter on the critics may profitably be read with the initial chapter of Fujimura's book; with Irène Simon's "Restoration Comedy and the Critics," RLV 29 (1963), 397-430; with Pierre Legouis's "Le voies de la critique récente: comment elle étudie la comédie de la Restauration," EA 19 (1966), 412-23; and with Andrew S. Bear's fine essay "Restoration Comedy and the Provoked Critic," LOVE COLLECTION, pp. 1-26.

The work of Fujimura, Holland, and Dale S. Underwood (see under Etherege, Part 2) has probably been both cause and effect of the modern interest in Restoration comedy, an interest which appears steady and serious. Recent books clearly reflect this. Virginia O. Birdsall's WILD CIVILITY: THE ENGLISH COMIC SPIRIT ON THE RESTORATION STAGE (Bloomington: Indiana Univ. Press, 1970) offers close readings of eleven well known plays, stressing the play element and the rake-hero as player. Her book evidences a strong interest in comic theory and psychological criticism, though it tends to ignore both stage history and the many plays without an obvious rake at the center of the dramatic structure. Ben R. Schneider, Jr., in THE ETHOS OF RESTORATION COMEDY (Urbana: Univ. of Illinois Press, 1971), argues for the morality of Restoration drama by means of a computer-assisted survey of 1,127 characters in 83 plays and an extended analysis of LOVE FOR LOVE. When the protagonists of plays are measured against a set of character traits which defines generosity, Schneider finds that neither the libertine nor the "manners" view of the plays holds up. Unfortunately, the study lumps plays from 1660 to 1730 together as Restoration drama, and makes its conclusions almost entirely on plot considerations. If a rake reforms in the last scene, the play (protagonist) is moral whether the reformation is properly motivated or not. Despite these problems, the statistical analysis is interesting.

A more recent book on Restoration comedy in Harriett Hawkins's LIKENESSES OF TRUTH IN ELIZABETHAN AND RESTORATION DRAMA (Oxford: Clarendon Press, 1972). THE MAN OF MODE, LOVE FOR LOVE, and THE WAY OF THE WORLD are discussed as imaginative visions of reality which present truths about human experience; they combine an emphasis on facts about the "presentation of self in everyday social life with an emphasis on facts about the dramatic presentation of characters on the stage." Hawkins properly objects to the "righteous solemnity" of many modern critics, stresses the Ovidian game of love in Etherege, makes a neat attack on symbol-hunting in LOVE FOR LOVE, and stresses the morality of THE WAY OF THE WORLD. The book is perceptive, balanced, and remarkably fresh.

A number of articles have dealt with the period as a whole. Frederick W. Bateson's "Contributions to a Dictionary of Critical Terms: I. 'Comedy of Manners,'" EIC 1 (1951), 89-93, notes that the term is modern; contemporaries used the phrase "genteel comedy" to describe the type. David S. Berkeley's "Préciosité and the Restoration Comedy of Manners," HLQ 18 (1955), 109-28, suggests that the major comedies mingle Platonic and anti-Platonic modes and that the précieuse tradition has been neglected as a background for courtship scenes. C.D. Cecil goes further; in "Libertine and Précieux Elements in Restoration Comedy," EIC 9 (1959), 239-53, he insists that every play still of interest to us "attempts to realize an ideal personality based on some comparison between libertinism and self-control"; the plays are "in one sense extended definitions of good behaviour couched largely in terms of bad," and are thus often satiric in form. A similar conclusion is reached by Charles O. McDonald, in "Restoration Comedy as Drama of Satire: An Investigation into Seventeenth-Century Aesthetics," SP 61 (1964), 522-44. McDonald insists that the plays are moral and that Restoration comedy "is a fully adult form of satiric and comic art." Irving Kreutz, in "Who's Holding the Mirror?" CD 4 (1970), 79-88, suggests that the comedy of manners put appearance on the stage and relied on the audience to distinguish it from reality, a dubious proposition hinted at occasionally by other critics.

Two recent articles suggest the often astonishing differences between modern approaches to these plays. Allan E. Rodway's "Restoration Comedy Re-Examined," RMS 16 (1972), 37-60, looks at them as reflections of a central concern of our own culture: they are not libertine enough because they compromise with older ideas of morality they no longer really believe in, but they are serious about exploring "the possibilities of a different life-style" and about testing "traditional assumptions about sexual morality." Robert D. Hume, in "Diversity and Development in Restoration Comedy 1660-1679," ECS 5 (1972), 365-97, takes a much more historical view. He argues convincingly that the

Etherege-Wycherley type of play never dominated the stage, that "London" comedy is a much sounder term than "comedy of manners," and that the outstanding characteristic of the period is diversity. By 1670 there were four major types of comedy, not one or two, and at least four different comic modes. Hume shows that modern criticism has concentrated on a conception of comedy which is partly fictitious and entirely misleading; his article demonstrates that future criticism must be grounded in broader reading in the dramatic history of the period.

7.11   RESTORATION COMEDY: TYPES, THEMES, CONVENTIONS.
Many books and articles published since World War II have focused on specific character types, themes, or conventions. One such study, Elisabeth L. Mignon's CRABBED AGE AND YOUTH: THE OLD MEN AND WOMEN IN THE RESTORATION COMEDY OF MANNERS (Durham, N.C.: Duke Univ. Press, 1947), traces these stereotyped comic butts through the major comedies. John H. Smith's THE GAY COUPLE IN RESTORATION COMEDY (Cambridge, Mass.: Harvard Univ. Press, 1948) is similar in method, but much more provocative and insightful. The rake-hero has been frequently studied. David S. Berkeley, in "The Penitent Rake in Restoration Comedy," MP 49 (1952), 223-33, offers a semistatistical study; both Virginia O. Birdsall and Ben R. Schneider, Jr., deal extensively with the type in the books mentioned above (Section 7.10). The best study is John L. Traugott's "The Rake's Progress from Court to Comedy: A Study in Comic Form," SEL 6 (1966), 381-407. Robert Jordan's "The Extravagant Rake in Restoration Comedy," LOVE COLLECTION, pp. 69-90, is also good; Barbara Rubin's "'Anti-Husbandry' and Self-Creation: A Comparison of Restoration Rake and Baudelaire's Dandy," TSLL 14 (1973), 583-92, is less successful with a similar approach. David S. Berkeley's THE PRECIEUSE, OR DISTRESSED HEROINE OF RESTORATION COMEDY (Stillwater: Oklahoma State Univ. Press, 1959) looks briefly at another stock character. Ben R. Schneider, Jr., studies "The Coquette-Prude as an Actress' Line in Restoration Comedy during the Time of Mrs. Oldfield," TN 22 (1968), 143-56. His article is one of a very few studies which relate the personnel of contemporary companies to characteristic features of plays in the repertory.

Gellert S. Alleman's MATRIMONIAL LAW AND THE MATERIALS OF RESTORATION COMEDY (Wallingford, Pa., 1942), is among the earliest of the intensive studies of a particular convention. Alleman examines the legal motifs common in more than two hundred plays, demonstrating the relation between "stage law" and actual law. Restoration comedy turns out not to be quite the transcript of life the "realistic" school of critics imagines. Paul F. Vernon's "Marriage of Convenience and the Moral Code of Restoration Comedy," EIC 12 (1962), 370-87, discusses the gay couple's achievement of a meaningful relationship within the marriage-of-convenience convention. Yvonne B. Shafer's analysis, "The Proviso Scene in Restoration Comedy," RECTR 9, no. 1 (1970), 1-10, offers a good summary of previous scholarship on this common convention and discusses both its origins and variations. Ram C. Sharma's "Conventions of Speech in the Restoration Comedy of Manners," IJES 2 (1961), 23-38, becomes a chapter in his THEMES AND CONVENTIONS IN THE COMEDY OF MANNERS (New York: Asia Publishing House, 1965), which also discusses (in somewhat pedestrian fashion) character types, themes, and conventions of action. A more interesting article on the language of the plays is Bernard

Harris's "The Dialect of Those Fanatic Times," BROWN COLLECTION, pp. 10-40. C.D. Cecil's three articles--"Delicate and Indelicate Puns in Restoration Comedy," MLR 61 (1966), 572-78, "Raillery in Restoration Comedy," HLQ 29 (1966), 147-59, and "'Une espèce d'éloquence abrégée': The Idealized Speech of Restoration Comedy," EA 19 (1966), 15-25--all concern aspects of dramatic language; the first is the most interesting. Joyce Miller's "A Study of an Epigram: The Mode of Wit in Restoration Comedy," in STUDIES IN THE DRAMA, ed. Arieh Sachs (SH 19 [1967]), 173-80, deals rather pretentiously with the opening line of THE COUNTRY WIFE as illustrative of witty dialogue in the period.

7.12   THE HEROIC PLAY. The serious drama of the Restoration has never received the critical attention lavished on the comedy of the period. Much of the available literature deals with the heroic play, though studies of tragedy are now beginning to appear. Both forms are intimately associated with John Dryden, and the reader will need to supplement the discussion here with the more specific studies listed under Dryden in Part 2.

Modern criticism of the heroic play was from the beginning preoccupied with the question of sources and influences. Such studies as Lewis N. Chase, THE ENGLISH HEROIC PLAY: A CRITICAL DESCRIPTION OF THE RHYMED TRAGEDY OF THE RESTORATION (New York: Columbia Univ. Press, 1903*); Clarence G. Child, "The Rise of the Heroic Play," MLN 19 (1904), 166-73; and James W. Tupper, "The Relation of the Heroic Play to the Romances of Beaumont and Fletcher," PMLA 20 (1905), 584-621, focus almost entirely on this issue, and on the particular characteristics (rhyme, the nature of the hero) which were held to define the form. Nineteenth-century critics held almost uniformly that it derived from the seventeenth-century heroic romance, with a lesser debt to Corneille and Racine. Tupper's article was one of the first to stress native sources, though he weakened his argument by extending the life of the form to 1720, as William E. Bohn noted in "The Decline of the English Heroic Drama," MLN 24 (1909), 49-54. Allardyce Nicoll took Chase to task in "The Origin and Types of the Heroic Tragedy," ANGLIA 44 (1920), 325-36, for making rhyme a defining characteristic of the type; Nicoll placed more emphasis on plot and character and on Elizabethan models. Mervyn L. Poston, in "The Origin of the English Heroic Play," MLR 16 (1921), 18-22, emphasizes the influence of Caroline drama, especially the works of William Davenant and Lodowick Carlell, a position developed much more fully by Kathleen M. Lynch in "Conventions of Platonic Drama in the Heroic Plays of Orrery and Dryden," PMLA 44 (1929), 456-71. William S. Clark's "The Sources of the Restoration Heroic Play," RES 4 (1928), 49-63, insists that the matter and style of these plays derive from French romance and romatic epic, although he admits that the plays transformed their material into something distinctively English. The exchange between Lynch and Clark, "The Platonic Element in the Restoration Heroic Play," PMLA 45 (1930), 623-26, further clarifies the difference of opinion between the two schools.

Cecil V. Deane's DRAMATIC THEORY AND THE RHYMED HEROIC PLAY (London: Oxford Univ. Press, 1931*) sought to determine how closely the form followed the "rules," concluding predictably enough that it did so with latitude.

William S. Clark, "The Definition of the 'Heroic Play' in the Restoration Period," RES 8 (1932), 437-44, returns to the question of definition: Chase argued that verse was essential, Nicoll that content was more important, Dobrée (in RESTORATION TRAGEDY) that both were. Clark attempts to define the form in contemporary terms; it was "a wholly serious play, composed in rimed verse, with a tone befitting heroic poetry, and concerned with the lofty sentiments of persons in high station." Not satisfied with this, A.E. Parsons, in "The English Heroic Play," MLR 33 (1938), 1-14, offered another definition: "The three heroic kinds were produced by the shaping of romantic material to the epic pattern." Earlier students had given some prominence to epic as a source, either directly or through the heroic romance, but Parsons is one of the first to assert the primacy of this influence. Trusten W. Russell, in VOLTAIRE, DRYDEN, AND HEROIC TRAGEDY (New York: Columbia Univ. Press, 1946), comes to a similar conclusion. Parsons stresses the influence of Joseph Scaliger; Russell emphasizes that of René Rapin, René Le Bossu, and André Dacier. Douglas W. Jefferson in 1940 introduced the notion that the heroic play, at least in the hands of Dryden, had a number of satiric and humorous features; his argument has not convinced many critics (see under Dryden, Part 2).

Recent criticism has tended toward an eclectic position, properly acknowledging the influence of French heroic drama and romance, of French and Italian studies of the epic, and especially of earlier English drama. The history of the controversy is succinctly summarized in the introduction to Volume 9 of the Univ. of California edition of the works of Dryden (1966). Sensitive recent studies include Martin Price's in TO THE PALACE OF WISDOM (1964), pp. 32-52, and Eugene M. Waith's in IDEAS OF GREATNESS: HEROIC DRAMA IN ENGLAND (New York: Barnes and Noble, 1971). Eugene N. James's "'Drums and Trumpets,'" RECTR 9, no. 2 (1970), 46-55, and 10, no. 1 (1970), 54-57, is an account of the management of battle scenes in the heroic plays.

7.13   RESTORATION TRAGEDY. Two substantial studies bridge the gap between the heroic play and the tragedy of the period. Moody E. Prior, in "Tragedy and the Heroic Play," THE LANGUAGE OF TRAGEDY (New York: Columbia Univ. Press, 1947), pp. 154-212, provides one of the best single analyses of these plays. He stresses the importance of epic elevation in both characters and style and argues persuasively that action is not primary but merely a framework for rhetoric and dialectic. Anne Righter's "Heroic Tragedy," BROWN COLLECTION, pp. 134-58, is in most respects an essay in sophisticated depreciation. Restoration tragedy, she feels, is merely a gratuitous reversal of restoration comedy, dedicated to spectacle and excess; it is a "literary" and empty form.

The value question is put again by Clifford Leech, in "Restoration Tragedy: A Reconsideration," DUJ 42 (1950), 106-15; he comes to a conclusion similar to Righter's--emotion is more important than dramatic structure, and there is too much straining for effect. The only recent book on the subject, Eric Rothstein's RESTORATION TRAGEDY: FORM AND THE PROCESS OF CHANGE (Madison: Univ. of Wisconsin Press, 1967), includes a good opening chapter on tragic theory, and there are perceptive sections throughout the book. Rothstein argues, in opposition to Waith, that most of the protagonists in the heroic plays are morally static; the last part of his book traces the change toward pathetic tragedy, in which the protagonists become models of pietas. The chapters on structural conventions and language are especially useful. The most recent general essay, Philip Parsons's "Restoration Tragedy as Total Theatre," LOVE COLLECTION, pp. 27–68, follows Moody E. Prior in stressing the rhetorical patterns and intellectual debates in these plays and also the importance of epic ideals.

A few articles of a miscellaneous character may be noted here. Louis B. Teeter's "The Dramatic Use of Hobbes's Political Ideas," ELH 3 (1936), 140–69, attacks the views of such scholars as Louis I. Bredvold and Mark Van Doren, pointing out that Hobbes was anathema to the court and public alike and that Hobbesian sentiments are almost always reserved for villains. Gerald Gillespie, in "The Rebel in Seventeenth-Century Tragedy," CL 18 (1966), 324–36, discusses Otway's VENICE PRESERVED as an example of the baroque rebel's conflict between heart and reason, between personal interest and political realities. Robert G. Noyes's "Conventions of Song in Restoration Tragedy," PMLA 53 (1938), 162–88, studies the types of songs used and their various dramatic functions. Cyrus H. Hoy, in "Renaissance and Restoration Dramatic Plotting," RD 9 (1966), 247–64, analyzes the baroque patterning, especially of love conflicts, in the serious drama of the period. In a related study, "Restoration Melodrama and Its Actors," KOMOS 2 (1970), 81–88, Philip Parsons argues that this drama is not representational but attempts to pattern emotional states rather than create authentic characters.

One does not have to read very far to realize that much work remains to be done on the serious drama of the Restoration. The studies of Martin Price, Moody E. Prior, and Eric Rothstein are a beginning, and there is of course a large body of excellent criticism on Dryden. But the reader will search in vain for studies on many other dramatists of the period which reveal an intimate acquaintance with contemporary dramatic theory and practice, with "total theatre" as an essential condition for meaningful evaluation, and with the variety of forms serious drama exhibits between 1660 and the early years of the eighteenth century. The accounts in such surveys as those by Nicoll, Dobrée, and Nettleton (see Sections 6.4 and 6.5) are critically inadequate and badly out of date. A recent book, Geoffrey Marshall's RESTORATION SERIOUS DRAMA (Norman: Univ. of Oklahoma Press, 1975), is by far the best introduction to the problems this drama presents to the modern reader.

Eighteenth-Century Drama

7.14   GENERAL AND MISCELLANEOUS STUDIES.   Eighteenth-century drama has received much less critical attention than that of the Restoration. "The drama in decline" is not an unusual label in the literary histories, and, until recently, most anthologies jumped from Congreve to Sheridan with only THE BEGGAR'S OPERA and SHE STOOPS TO CONQUER mentioned in between. The enormous vitality of eighteenth-century acting has always been recognized, but critics are only gradually realizing that the same vitality characterizes theatrical fare throughout the century. As the tendency grows to study the plays of the period in their total dramatic context rather than decry their lack of purely "literary" merit, we may expect to see a revival of interest.

While such an essay as Henry B. Irving's "The English Stage in the Eighteenth Century," OCCASIONAL PAPERS, DRAMATIC AND HISTORICAL (London: Bickers, 1906), pp. 1-63, has the traditional nineteenth-century focus on performers, such studies as John C. Loftis's "The Eighteenth-Century Beginnings of Modern Drama," EUQ 7 (1951), 225-36, stress the innovations and achievements of the century. Loftis's book COMEDY AND SOCIETY FROM CONGREVE TO FIELDING (Stanford, Calif.: Stanford Univ. Press, 1959), is a detailed study of the interaction between comedy and society from 1700 to the closing of the theatres in 1737. Loftis relates changes in comedy to the rise of the mercantile class, and traces the gradual breakdown of the Restoration sterotypes of the middle class and the rise of more realistic characterization. He quite properly denies the existence of sentimental drama as a genre, seeing sentiment as an element common to many different kinds of plays. His book, though not especially well organized, is packed with useful information. Dougald Mac-Millan's "The Rise of Social Comedy in the Eighteenth Century," PQ 41 (1962), 330-38, is a useful supplement to Loftis's book, since it focuses on such dramatists as Inchbald, Holcroft, and Reynolds. In THE POLITICS OF DRAMA IN AUGUSTAN ENGLAND (Oxford: Clarendon Press, 1963), Loftis explores both overt and latent political themes in the drama before 1737. This volume complements his earlier study; it is equally thorough, but the reader occasionally wishes for more analysis of the way in which particular plays work out their political themes. Contrasted with this book, such articles as Clement Ramsland's "Britons Never Will Be Slaves: A Study in Political Propaganda in the British Theatre 1700-1742," QJS 28 (1942), 393-99, are superficial and misleading.

The variety of fare offered may be seen from any season's performances as recorded in THE LONDON STAGE. Paul Sawyer's article, "The Popularity of Various Types of Entertainment at Lincoln's Inn Fields and Covent Garden Theatres 1720-1733, TN 24 (1970), 154-63, is also helpful in this respect. Such articles as Richard J. Dircks's "Les fêtes champêtres 1774: Literary and Theatrical Perspectives," PQ 50 (1971), 647-56; Kirsten G. Holmstroem's MONO-DRAMA, ATTITUDES, TABLEAUX VIVANTS: STUDIES ON SOME TRENDS OF THEATRICAL FASHION 1770-1815 (Uppsala, Sweden: Almquist & Wiksell; 1967); and Emmett L. Avery's "Vaudeville on the London Stage 1700-1737," RSW 5 (1937), 65-77, indicate the popularity of some of the peripheral kinds.

There are a few studies of character types and themes. William W. Appleton, in "The Double Gallant in Eighteenth-Century Comedy," in ENGLISH WRITERS OF THE EIGHTEENTH CENTURY, ed. John H. Middendorf (New York: Columbia Univ. Press, 1971), pp. 145-57, studies the contrasting or rival "heroes" evident in such plays as THE RIVALS. Richard Morton and William M. Peterson, in "Peter the Great and Russia in Restoration and Eighteenth-Century Drama," N&Q 199 (1954), 427-32, note increasing realism in the portrayal of Russia after Peter's visit to England in 1698. Wallace C. Brown's "The Near East in English Drama 1775-1825," JEGP 46 (1947), 63-69, makes a few useful references, as does Dougald MacMillan's "Some Notes on Eighteenth-Century

Essex Plays," MLN 55 (1940), 176-83.

Miscellaneous studies include Robert J. Allen's "The Kit-Cat Club and the Theatre," RES 7 (1931), 56-61; John A. Kelly's GERMAN VISITORS TO ENGLISH THEATRES IN THE EIGHTEENTH CENTURY (Princeton: Princeton Univ. Press, 1936*); George W. Stone, Jr.'s "The Authorship of TIT FOR TAT, a Manuscript Source for Eighteenth-Century Theatrical History," TN 10 (1955), 22-28; and Arthur R. Huseboe's "Pope's Critical Views of the London Stage," RECTR 3, no. 1 (1964), 25-37. Kalman A. Burnim's important study, "Eighteenth-Century Theatrical Illustrations in the Light of Contemporary Documents," TN 14 (1959-60), 45-55, shows the significance of such illustrations for understanding contemporary staging. Sybil M. Rosenfeld's article, "Landscape in English Scenery in the Eighteenth Century," RICHARDS COLLECTION, pp. 171-78, is also useful.

7.15   SENTIMENTAL DRAMA.   The pioneer study of sentiment in eighteenth-century drama is Ernest Bernbaum's book, THE DRAMA OF SENSIBILITY (Boston: Ginn, 1915; Cambridge, Mass.: Harvard Univ. Press, 1925), which discusses both sentimental comedy and domestic tragedy 1696-1780. Bernbaum links sentimentalism with benevolism; in comedy the average man is rewarded for virtue, while in tragedy he is overwhelmed by purely external forces. He dates the rise of sentimental comedy after Colley Cibber's play, LOVE'S LAST SHIFT (1696), discusses the attack on the form by Goldsmith and others (1768-72), and posits a triumph of sentiment after 1773. His book is well written and still very useful for its detail and depth, but he exaggerates the influence of sentimental drama, makes too sharp distinctions, and sees clear patterns and categories that will not bear close scrutiny. Arthur Sherbo's ENGLISH SENTIMENTAL DRAMA (East Lansing: Michigan State Univ. Press, 1957) gives a good analysis of the characteristics of the form as presented by Bernbaum and later critics but rejects the idea that it must be domestic and include nature. He sees the repetition and prolongation of sentimental elements as critical rather than incidental. He demonstrates that the proportion of sentimental plays increases throughout the century but not to the extent Bernbaum and others argued.

Other studies of sentimental comedies include Osborn Waterhouse's "The Development of English Sentimental Comedy in the Eighteenth Century," ANGLIA 30 (1907), 137-72 and 269-305; Stanley T. Williams's "The English Sentimental Drama from Steele to Cumberland," SR 33 (1925), 405-26; Frederick T. Wood's two articles, "The Beginnings and Significance of Sentimental Comedy," ANGLIA 55 (1931), 368-92, and "Sentimental Comedy in the Eighteenth Century," Np 18 (1932-33), 37-44 and 281-89; and DeWitt C. Croissant's "Early Sentimental Comedy," in ESSAYS IN DRAMATIC LITERATURE: THE PARROTT PRESENTATION VOLUME, ed. Hardin Craig (Princeton: Princeton Univ. Press, 1935), pp. 47-71. None of these is especially remarkable. More recent are Paul E. Parnell's "The Sentimental Mask," PMLA 78 (1963), 529-35; Arthur Friedman's "Aspects of Sentimentalism in Eighteenth-Century Literature," in THE AUGUSTAN MILIEU: ESSAYS PRESENTED TO LOUIS A. LANDA, ed. Henry K. Miller et al. (Oxford: Clarendon Press, 1970), pp. 247-61; and Elizabeth M. Yearling's "The Good-Natured Heroes of Cumberland, Goldsmith, and Sheridan," MLR 67 (1972), 490-500. The best modern article is Robert D. Hume's "Goldsmith and Sheridan and the Supposed 'Revolution' of 'Laughing' against 'Sentimental' Comedy," in STUDIES IN CHANGE AND REVOLUTION: ASPECTS OF ENGLISH INTELLECTUAL HISTORY 1640-1800, ed. Paul J. Korshin (Mensten, England: Scolar Press, 1972), pp. 237-76, which criticizes the entire tradition of an attack on sentiment in the plays of Goldsmith and Sheridan and argues convincingly that there was no period in which the sort of comedy analyzed by Bernbaum, Sherbo, and others was dominant.

7.16   DOMESTIC DRAMA. Bernbaum (see Section 7.15) saw the tragedy of the period largely in terms of the development of middle class or domestic plays, and his lead has generally been followed. Several German dissertations deal with the development of this buergerliche drama in England and Germany. Arthur E. Morgan, in "English Domestic Drama," EDH, 2nd ser. 31 (1912), 175-207; Fred O. Nolte, in THE EARLY MIDDLE CLASS DRAMA 1696-1774 (Lancaster, Pa.: n.p.?, 1935); and Lewis M. Magill, in "Poetic Justice: The Dilemma of the Early Creators of Sentimental Tragedy," RSW 25 (1957), 24-32, add nothing to Bernbaum's study and the subsequent histories of Allardyce Nicoll and Frederick S. Boas. Arnold Hauser's discussion, "The Origins of Domestic Drama," in THE SOCIAL HISTORY OF ART (London: Routledge and Kegan Paul, 1952), II, 577-92, though focused on continental drama, offers a useful theoretical approach.

7.17   GOTHIC DRAMA AND MELODRAMA. Gothic drama and melodrama have received little attention until recently, even in the standard histories. Willard Thorp, in "The Stage Adventures of Some Gothic Novels," PMLA 43 (1928), 476-86, discussed seven plays based on gothic novels, and Montague Summers's fascination with both drama and the gothic led him to take the last decades of the century more seriously than most. But it was not until Bertrand Evans's excellent book, GOTHIC DRAMA FROM WALPOLE TO SHELLEY (Berkeley and Los Angeles: Univ. of California Press, 1947), appeared that a full-length study was devoted to the type. Maurice W. Disher, in BLOOD AND THUNDER: MID-VICTORIAN MELODRAMA AND ITS ORIGINS (London: Muller, 1949), begins his account with the last years of the eighteenth century, but his book is not as useful as James L. Rosenberg's essay in THE CONTEXT AND CRAFT OF DRAMA, ed. Robert W. Corrigan and James L. Rosenberg (San Francisco: Chandler, 1964), Eric Bentley's chapter on the genre in THE LIFE OF THE DRAMA (London: Methuen, 1965), and the relevant material in Robert B. Heilman's book, TRAGEDY AND MELODRAMA (Seattle: Univ. of Washington Press, 1968). The Rosenberg, Bentley, and Heilman essays are reprinted in TRAGEDY: VISION AND FORM, ed. Robert W. Corrigan (San Francisco: Chandler, 1965). The most thorough study is perhaps Michael R. Booth's ENGLISH MELODRAMA (London: Jenkins, 1965), which, like many other accounts, focuses on the nineteenth century but is very useful for the earlier period as well. The most recent account--one both succinct and perceptive--is James L. Smith's MELODRAMA, a monograph in Methuen's Critical Idiom series (London, 1973). Smith makes the usual distinction between the internal blocking action of tragedy and the external catastrophes of melodrama and properly emphasizes the theatrical values of the form.

7.18   PANTOMIME. This form, unlike domestic tragedy and gothic drama, is not an exclusively eighteenth-century creation, and hence has been treated in Section 7.2. Several articles, however, focus on the later period. The chapter on spectacle in Cecil Price's book, THE AGE OF GARRICK, gives a useful account of the form. Earlier studies still of use include Emmett L. Avery's "Dancing and Pantomime on the English Stage 1700-1737," SP 31 (1934), 417-52; Mitchell P. Wells's two articles, "Some Notes on the Early Eighteenth-Century Pantomime," SP 32 (1935), 598-607, and "Spectacular Scenic Effects of the Eighteenth-Century Pantomime," PQ 17 (1938), 67-81; and Avery's "The Defence and Criticism of Pantomimic Entertainments in the Early Eighteenth Century," ELH 5 (1938), 127-45. Ralph G. Allen's "THE WONDERS OF DERBYSHIRE: A Spectacular Eighteenth-Century Travelogue," TS 2 (1961), 54-66, and his "Topical Scenes for Pantomime," ETJ 17 (1965), 289-300, both discuss DeLoutherberg extravaganzas staged under Garrick at Drury Lane. Elvena M. Green's analysis, in "John Rich's Art of Pantomime as Seen in His THE NECROMANCER; OR, HARLEQUIN DOCTOR FAUSTUS: A Comparison of the Two Faustus Pantomimes at Lincoln's Inn Fields and Drury Lane," RECTR 4, no. 1 (1965), 47-60, shows why Rich was preeminent in the form. Virginia P. Scott, in "The Infancy of English Pantomime: 1716-1723," ETJ 24 (1972), 125-34, presents an interesting argument based on indirect evidence for deriving the English form from the "night scenes" performed at London fairs by actors from early eighteenth-century French fairs.

Musical Forms

7.19   Throughout the 1660-1800 period, music was a part of drama to an extent difficult to realize today. A typical afternoon at the playhouse began with the performance of serious music, and the audience usually heard additional instrumental or vocal pieces between acts. Songs and dances were not only popular entr'acte fare, but often formed an integral part of the plays. Types as different as ballad opera, pantomime, masque, procession, burletta, and melodrama depended heavily on music; most criticism to the contrary, these dramatic forms can neither be understood nor properly evaluated without full consideration of their aural (and visual) components. Much music from the period has been lost; full use has not been made of what remains.

Few works consider this rich heritage with any thoroughness. Wilfred Mellers's book, HARMONIOUS MEETING: A STUDY OF THE RELATIONSHIP BETWEEN ENGLISH MUSIC, POETRY, AND THEATRE c.1600-1900 (London: Dobson, 1965), includes materials on the major figures--Blow, Purcell, Handel, and Gay. The chapters on Handel are especially good, but the discussion of ballad opera is simply mistaken; THE BEGGAR'S OPERA does not represent the victory of Restoration cynicism, nor is it the beginning of British philistinism. John S. Manifold's THE MUSIC IN ENGLISH DRAMA FROM SHAKESPEARE TO PURCELL (London: Rockliff, 1956) has good chapters on music in the Restoration theatre; Robert E. Moore's book, HENRY PURCELL AND THE RESTORATION THEATRE (Cambridge, Mass.: Harvard Univ. Press, 1961), is, however, much more detailed and is highly recommended. The works listed above improve on the pioneer studies of such scholars as William B. Squire ("Purcell's Dramatic Music," SIMG 5 [1904], 489-564). William J. Lawrence's notes in

Foreign Singers and Musicians at the Court of Charles II," MQ 9 (1923), 217-25, and other such articles as well, will presumably be superseded by the work of Highfill, Burnim, and Langhans in the BIOGRAPHICAL DICTIONARY OF ACTORS. The music for the operatic MACBETH, a topic which has exercised many scholars, is the subject of Roger Fiske's "The MACBETH Music," ML 45 (1964), 114-25, and the much earlier piece by William J. Lawrence, "Who Wrote the Famous MACBETH Music?" LAWRENCE COLLECTION 1, pp. 207-24 (originally in ANGLIA for 1908).

Roger Fiske's massive and exhaustive study, ENGLISH THEATRE MUSIC IN THE EIGHTEENTH CENTURY (Oxford: Oxford Univ. Press, 1973), now offers students a mine of information about a badly neglected period. Fiske covers every type of theatre music between the deaths of Purcell in 1695 and Storace in 1796--masque, pantomime, ballad opera, burlesque, English opera, burletta, and others. He discusses both the music and its composers and performers and provides indexes of both; much of his material is new, and the book will undoubtedly become the standard reference work on its subject. Unfortunately, the author's attempt to combine a chronological approach with topical coverage within catchall periods is unsuccessful; the book is repetitious and badly organized.

Aside from studies of ballad opera and the opera seria, there are few other sources. Andrew D. McCredie's article, "John Christopher Smith as a Dramatic Composer," ML 45 (1964), 22-38, deals with the career of Handel's assistant. Charles Cudworth, in "Two Georgian Classics: Arne and Stevens," ML 45 (1964), 146-53, considers Shakespearian song settings. P.T. Dircks's "The Catch on the Eighteenth-Century Stage: A Consideration of Two Burlettas," TN 25 (1971), 93-96, and "The Eighteenth-Century Burletta: Problems of Research," RECTR 10, no. 2 (1971), 44-52, may also be cited. The latter article contains a useful bibliography. Two essays of general significance should be noted. Bertrand M. Bronson's "Some Aspects of Music and Literature in the Eighteenth Century," in STUART AND GEORGIAN MOMENTS, ed. Earl R. Miner (Berkeley and Los Angeles: Univ. of California Press, 1972), was originally published as a Clark Library Seminar paper in 1953; it is a discussion of the fusion of the two arts in the period by a scholar knowledgeable about both. P.T. Dircks's "Musical Drama and the Artistic Whole: The Necessity for Special Criteria," SBT 15 (1974), 277-86, is ostensibly a review of Peter A. Tasch's book on Isaac Bickerstaffe but should be required reading for anyone studying English drama after 1728.

Little work has been done on dance in the 1660-1800 period, perhaps because of the difficulty of recovering the necessary materials. Ifan K. Fletcher, Selma J. Cohen, and Roger Lonsdale produced articles on the subject which were collected by the New York Public Library under the title FAMED FOR DANCE: ESSAYS ON THE THEORY AND PRACTICE OF THEATRICAL DANCING IN ENGLAND 1660-1740 (1960). General histories of dance or ballet are not sufficiently detailed to be of serious use.

Much more has been done with the development of opera in the period. Eric W. White's book, THE RISE OF ENGLISH OPERA (London: Lehmann, 1951), gives a brief historical sketch in chapters 1-3, though with the usual nation-alistic sniping at "the Handelian catastrophe." Clara L. Myers's "Opera in England from 1656 to 1728," WRB, n.s. 9 (1906), 129-56, and Cecil Forsyth's MUSIC AND NATIONALISM: A STUDY OF ENGLISH OPERA (London: Mac-millan, 1911) are earlier sources. Lillian Gottesman's article, "The Arthurian Romance in English Opera and Pantomime 1660-1800," RECTR 8, no. 2 (1969), 47-53, traces the Arthurian legend through five operatic plays of the period. A. Joseph Armstrong's OPERATIC PERFORMANCES IN ENGLAND BEFORE HANDEL (Waco, Tex.: BAYLOR UNIV. BULLETIN 21, no. 4, 1918) has been superseded by later studies, as has Allardyce Nicoll's "The Italian Opera in England: The First Five Years," ANGLIA 46 (1922), 257-81. Edward J. Dent's FOUNDATIONS OF ENGLISH OPERA: A STUDY OF MUSICAL DRAMA IN ENGLAND DURING THE SEVENTEENTH CENTURY (Cambridge: Cambridge Univ. Press, 1928*), despite its early date, is still a standard work, elegant and wide ranging. Donald M. Walmsley's "The Influence of Foreign Opera on English Operatic Plays of the Restoration," ANGLIA 52 (1928), 37-50, may also be consulted. A recent study, Eugene Haun's BUT HARK! MORE HAR-MONY: THE LIBRETTI OF RESTORATION OPERA IN ENGLISH (Ypsilanti: Eastern Michigan Univ. Press, 1971), is useful for its emphasis on texts, but it is repetitive and disorganized.

Opera in the eighteenth century focuses naturally on Handel, but some studies are more general. Daniel Nalbach's article, "Opera Management in Eighteenth-Century London," TR 13, no. 1 (1973), 75-91, is a useful summary; Cecil Price's chapter on opera and ballet in THEATRE IN THE AGE OF GARRICK is a good overview of the subject. William H. Cummings's "The Lord Chamber-lain and Opera in London 1700-40," PMA 40 (1914), 37-71, cites contempo-rary documents from the period.

The operatic genius of Handel dominates the century despite every nationalistic claim. Several biographies contain excellent discussions of the forty-odd op-eras and pasticcios produced from 1705 through 1741 by this prolific composer; the best of these are Otto E. Deutsch's HANDEL: A DOCUMENTARY BIOG-RAPHY (New York: Norton, 1954) and Paul Henry Lang's GEORGE FRIDERIC HANDEL (New York: Norton, 1966). William C. Smith's book, CONCERN-ING HANDEL, HIS LIFE AND WORKS: ESSAYS (London: Cassell, 1948), contains useful material, especially the essay on ACIS AND GALATEA; Smith also contributed a good bibliography to the revised edition of Newman Flower's GEORGE FRIDERIC HANDEL: HIS PERSONALITY AND HIS TIMES (London: Cassell, 1959). The best and most detailed studies of Handel's theatrical music are Winton Dean's HANDEL'S DRAMATIC ORATORIOS AND MASQUES and HANDEL AND THE OPERA SERIA (London: Oxford Univ. Press, 1959 and 1970).

Miscellaneous articles include Franz Montgomery's "Early Criticism of Italian Opera in England," MQ 15 (1929), 415-25; Phillip Lord's "The English-Italian Opera Companies 1732-33," ML 45 (1964), 239-51; and William J. Lawrence's "Marionette Operas," MQ 10 (1924), 236-43. William C. Smith's seasonal calendar, THE ITALIAN OPERA AND CONTEMPORARY BALLET IN LONDON 1789-1820 (London: Society for Theatre Research, 1955), is a standard reference work for the last decade of the century.

Ballad opera has been saved from the general neglect of musical forms by the genius of John Gay. The standard account is Edmond McAdoo Gagey's book, BALLAD OPERA (New York: Columbia Univ. Press, 1937*), which classifies the plays according to type and which contains a useful bibliography. Gagey's categories will not stand close scrutiny, and he does not deal with the inter-relation of texts and music except in connection with THE BEGGAR'S OPERA. The problem of categories is common to nearly all studies, since distinctions between ballad opera, comic opera, burletta, and extravaganza tend to blur considerably. Allardyce Nicoll's ALPHABETICAL CATALOGUE, for example, cautiously omits the often arbitrary classifications evident in the handlists in individual volumes of his HISTORY. Roger Fiske's ENGLISH THEATRE MUSIC distinguishes between all-sung works, works with spoken dialog, pantomimes, and works with incidental music--in the final analysis, perhaps a more useful approach. Gagey's book avoids the most serious consequences of the problem by defining the form to include only those pieces using familiar tunes, but the question "How many tunes?" remains. Much of the scholarship on the ballad opera focuses on John Gay and is cited in Part 2 of this guide. Specific studies not on Gay include LeRoy J. Morrissey's "An Anonymous Ballad Op-era," N&Q 217 (1972), 223-25, and Edgar V. Roberts's "Mr. Seedo's London Career and His Work with Henry Fielding," PQ 45 (1966), 179-90.

Acting

7.20   Much of the scholarship on acting in the period is of necessity closely related to theatrical biography, and Sections 4.1 and 4.2 above, of this guide should therefore be consulted. This subsection focuses on those studies concerned generally with acting, acting styles, or the theory of acting.

Useful theoretical discussions include a fine essay by Alan S. Downer, "Mr. Dangle's Defense: Acting and Stage History," ENGLISH INSTITUTE ESSAYS 1946 (New York: Columbia Univ. Press, 1947), pp. 159-90, and Thornton S. Graves's "Some Aspects of Extemporal Acting," SP 19 (1922), 429-56, which deals anecdotally with the tendency of performers to improvise material not in the script. A. Nicholas Vardac, in STAGE TO SCREEN: THEATRICAL METHOD FROM GARRICK TO GRIFFITH (Cambridge, Mass.: Harvard Univ. Press, 1949), derives realism in acting and production from the Garrick era, but his discussion is perfunctory. William L. Sharp's book, LANGUAGE IN DRAMA: MEANINGS FOR THE DIRECTOR AND THE ACTOR (Scranton, Pa.: Chandler, 1970), includes a good discussion of how to act Restoration and eighteenth-century comedy today.

Hugh Hunt's article, "Restoration Acting," BROWN COLLECTION, pp. 178-92, is a general survey. Nancy W. Henshaw, in "Graphic Sources for a Modern Approach to the Acting of Restoration Comedy," ETJ 20 (1968), 157-70, makes a convincing case for presenting drama of the period realistically rather than formally. Lily B. Campbell's study, "The Rise of a Theory of Stage Presentation in England during the Eighteenth Century," PMLA 32 (1917),

163-200, reprinted in her COLLECTED PAPERS . . . (New York: Russell and Russell, 1968), is concerned with the development of four stages of acting style; she argues that imitative acting was dominant in the Garrick era and the "grand style" in that of Kean. Alan S. Downer's "Nature to Advantage Dressed: Eighteenth-Century Acting," PMLA 58 (1943), 1002-37, and Earl R. Wasserman's "The Sympathetic Imagination in Eighteenth-Century Theories of Acting," JEGP 46 (1947), 264-72, are important theoretical studies. Brewster Rogerson's "The Art of Painting the Passions," JHI 14 (1953), 68-94, is also helpful, as is George Taylor's "'The Just Delineation of the Passions': Theories of Acting in the Age of Garrick," RICHARDS COLLECTION, pp. 51-72. Joseph W. Donohue, Jr.'s, recent book, DRAMATIC CHARACTER IN THE ENGLISH ROMANTIC AGE (Princeton: Princeton Univ. Press, 1970), despite its title, contains much useful information on the eighteenth century. Donohue demonstrates the evolution of an acting style in which the events of a play become merely agencies for drawing from the characters (performers) symbolic illustrations of the inner self; like many recent critics, he stresses the contemporary emphasis on the particular scene or moment at the expense of dramatic structure as usually conceived.

Walter S. Scott's THE GEORGIAN THEATRE (London: Westhouse, 1946) attempts to reveal the Georgian approach to dramatic representation through contemporary pictures and biographical notes, but it is a thin, popular account. William A. Darlington's book, THE ACTOR AND HIS AUDIENCE (London: Phoenix House, 1949), is more successful in defining the ideal tragic actor through a study of great examples, but the most detailed work using this approach is Bertram L. Joseph's THE TRAGIC ACTOR (New York: Theatre Arts Books, 1959). Donald Brook's A PAGEANT OF ENGLISH ACTORS (London: Rockliff, 1950) is primarily biographical, though it discusses performers' conceptions of certain roles.

Stage conventions are discussed by Robert H. Hopkins, "Rigor Mortis and Eighteenth-Century Tragedy," N&Q 204 (1959), 411-12; by Gilbert Bennett, "Conventions of the Stage Villain," AWR 14 (1964), 92-102; and by Lael J. Woodbury, "Death on the Romantic Stage," QJS 49 (1963), 57-61. Arthur C. Sprague, in SHAKESPEARE AND THE ACTORS: THE STAGE BUSINESS IN HIS PLAYS 1660-1905 (Cambridge, Mass.: Harvard Univ. Press, 1944), succeeds in recreating a series of specific performances, including Betterton and Kemble as Hamlet and Garrick as King Lear; the result is much more valuable than articles like William Angus's "Acting Shakespeare," QQ 72 (1965), 313-33.

Other studies of performers in specific roles include William S.E. Coleman's "Post-Restoration Shylocks Prior to Macklin," TS 8 (1967), 17-36; Robert G. Noyes's "Mrs. Bracegirdle's Acting in Crowne's JUSTICE BUSY," MLN 43 (1928), 390-91; Richard J. Dircks's "Garrick and Gentleman: Two Interpretations of Abel Drugger," RECTR 7, no. 2 (1968), 48-55; Cecil Price's discussion of Garrick's acting in JANE SHORE, in THEATRE IN THE AGE OF GARRICK, pp. 7-14; Joseph W. Donohue, Jr.'s "Kemble and Mrs. Siddons in MACBETH: The Romantic Approach to Tragic Character," TN 22 (1968), 65-86; Robert R. Findlay's "Charles Macklin and the Problem of 'Natural' Acting," ETJ 19 (1967), 33-40; Antony Coleman's "Mossop or Wolsey," TN 25 (1970), 11-14;

Robert H. Ross, Jr.'s "Samuel Sandford: Villain from Necessity," PMLA 76 (1961), 367-72; and E. Pearlman's "The Hamlet of Robert Wilks," TN 24 (1970), 125-33. The Noyes piece is a brief note; the other articles are substantial and rewarding.

Chapter VIII

ANTECEDENTS AND INFLUENCES

A. NATIVE

General Studies

8.1   Most source and influence studies focus on a single author (see Part 2) or a single tradition. The exceptions include Martin Ellehauge, ENGLISH RESTORATION DRAMA: ITS RELATION TO PAST ENGLISH AND PAST AND CONTEMPORARY FRENCH DRAMA, FROM JONSON VIA MOLIERE TO CONGREVE (Copenhagen: Levin & Munksgaard, 1933*); Donald J. Rulfs, "Reception of the Elizabethan Playwrights on the London Stage 1776-1833," SP 46 (1949), 54-69; and Gunnar Sorelius, 'THE GIANT RACE BEFORE THE FLOOD': PRE-RESTORATION DRAMA ON THE STAGE AND IN THE CRITICISM OF THE RESTORATION (Uppsala, Sweden: Ulmquist and Wiksell, 1966). The Ellehauge book has a chapter on drama of the commonwealth period, one on earlier and contemporary French drama, and one on Restoration drama. The European point of view is sometimes interesting, but the analysis is not particularly good; Collier, for example, did not destroy the stage for centuries. The Rulfs article discusses the popularity of thirty-five Elizabethan, non-Shakespearean plays in the period, noting that eight of them were stock favorites. The Sorelius book is a detailed study of the pre-Restoration repertory on the Restoration stage. Sorelius suggests that more than 175 old plays were produced; his analyses and repertory summaries are useful, but he undervalues the influence of Beaumont and Fletcher and frequently overstates his case. The account given of the native influence on the development of Restoration dramatic theory is helpful, as is the extensive bibliographical information provided.

Willard Thorp, in "The Stage Adventures of Some Gothic Novels," PMLA 43 (1928), 476-86, touches on the late eighteenth-century dramatic versions of such novels as Matthew G. Lewis's THE MONK; Robert G. Noyes, in THE NEGLECTED MUSE: RESTORATION AND EIGHTEENTH-CENTURY TRAGEDY IN THE NOVEL 1740-1780 (Providence, R.I.: Brown Univ. Press, 1958), shows an important influence in the other direction and also throws light on certain aspects of contemporary drama.

Antecedents and Influences

Shakespeare

8.2   Shakespeare's has quite naturally been the influence most fully investigated. Robert W. Babcock's "A Preliminary Bibliography of Eighteenth-Century Criticism of Shakespeare," SP extra series 1 (1929), 58–98, excludes editions, adaptations, and alterations. Herbert S. Robinson's ENGLISH SHAKESPEARIAN CRITICISM IN THE EIGHTEENTH CENTURY (New York: Wilson, 1932) is a good anthology of contemporary comment; Robert D. Stock's SAMUEL JOHNSON AND NEO-CLASSICAL DRAMATIC THEORY has already been mentioned as a useful guide to contemporary attitudes. Some of the relevant editions are listed in Henrietta C. Bartlett and Alfred W. Pollard, A CENSUS OF SHAKESPEARE'S PLAYS IN QUARTO 1594–1709 (New Haven: Yale Univ. Press, 1935), which was revised and extended by the first author in 1939. Herbert L. Ford, SHAKESPEARE 1700–1740: A COLLATION OF THE EDITIONS AND SEPARATE PLAYS . . . (Oxford: Oxford Univ. Press, 1935), carries the record toward mid-century. Charles H. Shattuck lists prompt-books of the period in THE SHAKESPEARE PROMPTBOOKS: A DESCRIPTIVE CATALOGUE (Urbana: Univ. of Illinois Press, 1965). William Jaggard's SHAKESPEARE BIBLIOGRAPHY: A DICTIONARY OF EVERY KNOWN ISSUE OF THE WRITINGS OF OUR NATIONAL POET AND OF RECORDED OPINION THEREON IN THE ENGLISH LANGUAGE (Statford-on-Avon: Shakespeare Head Press, 1911) is also occasionally useful.

Many contemporary adaptations and alterations are being reprinted in facsimile by London's Cornmarket Press; the first group appeared in 1969, and the series is continuing. Montague Summers's SHAKESPEARE ADAPTATIONS: 'THE TEMPEST,' 'THE MOCK TEMPEST,' AND 'KING LEAR' (London: Cape, 1922*) is a long, rambling account of Shakespearean adaptations in the period; a better collection is FIVE RESTORATION ADAPTATIONS OF SHAKESPEARE, ed. Christopher Spencer (Urbana: Univ. of Illinois Press, 1965). Three Restoration promptbooks are included in the five volumes of SHAKESPEAREAN PROMPT-BOOKS OF THE SEVENTEENTH-CENTURY, ed. Gwynne B. Evans (Charlottesville: Bibliographical Society of the Univ. of Virginia, 1963–70). Eleven volumes of J.P. Kemble's promptbooks are being edited by Charles H. Shattuck for Johnson Reprint's series, THE FOLGER FACSIMILES.

Critical studies of Shakespeare's influence include works like Frank E. Halliday's THE CULT OF SHAKESPEARE (London: Duckworth, 1957) and Louis Marder's HIS EXITS AND HIS ENTRANCES: THE STORY OF SHAKESPEARE'S REPUTATION (Philadelphia: Lippincott, 1963). The story of a landmark in bardolatry is told by Christian Deelman in THE GREAT SHAKESPEARE JUBILEE (New York: Viking, 1964) and by Martha W. England in GARRICK'S JUBILEE (Columbus: Ohio State Univ. Press, 1964). For David Garrick's contribution to the Shakespeare industry, and for studies of his adaptations, see Part 2 of this study.

The stage history of some twenty plays is reviewed by William Winter in the three series of SHAKESPEARE ON THE STAGE (New York: Moffat, Yard, 1911, 1915, 1916), but George C.D. Odell's SHAKESPEARE FROM BETTERTON TO IRVING, 2 vols. (New York: Scribner's, 1920*), is superior.

Odell's focus is as much on stage presentation--scenery, lighting, costume, direction--as on the individual adaptations and alterations. Hazelton Spencer's SHAKESPEARE IMPROVED: THE RESTORATION VERSIONS IN QUARTO AND ON THE STAGE (Cambridge, Mass.: Harvard Univ. Press, 1927*) includes a long section on the stage history of Shakespeare in the period, as well as analysis of the Restoration texts in Part II. Spencer's book is valuable, but he makes no attempt to understand what the adaptors were doing or why they altered what they did; in these respects his book is an exercise in opprobrious epithets. David N. Smith's SHAKESPEARE IN THE EIGHTEENTH CENTURY (Oxford: Oxford Univ. Press, 1928*) is sketchy and general. The standard account is Charles B. Hogan's SHAKESPEARE IN THE THEATRE 1701-1800, 2 vols. (Oxford: Clarendon Press, 1952 and 1957). Volume 1 of this work is a record of London performances 1701-50; Volume 2, of those 1751-1800. Appendixes show the comparative popularity of Shakespeare's plays and their order of popularity. Hogan estimates that one of every six performances in the eighteenth century was Shakespearean--a total of 7,214 out of 40,664. Some of his figures are challenged in an important article by Arthur H. Scouten, "The Increase in Popularity of Shakespeare's Plays in the Eighteenth Century: A Caveat for Interpreters of Stage History," ShQ 7 (1956), 189-202, which argues persuasively that Garrick was not the prime mover in the Shakespeare revival and that there was not one but a series of revivals.

George C. Branam's EIGHTEENTH-CENTURY ADAPTATIONS OF SHAKESPEAREAN TRAGEDY (Berkeley and Los Angeles: Univ. of California Press, 1956) does for the later tragedy what Spencer's book did for Restoration drama, but Branam's critical perspective is better than Spencer's and he does a better job of showing the rationale and effect of the alterations. Lucyle Hook, in "Shakespeare Improved, or A Case for the Affirmative," ShQ 4 (1953), 289-99, also offers a salutary corrective to Spencer, as does W. Moelwyn Merchant, in "Shakespeare 'Made Fit,'" BROWN COLLECTION, pp. 194-219. Paul S. Sawyer, in "The Popularity of Shakespeare's Plays at Lincoln's Inn Fields Theatre 1714-1717," N&Q 216 (1971), 151-52, shows from box office records that, excluding benefit performances, non-Shakespearean performances brought in an average of 15 percent more income than performances of Shakespeare.

Miscellaneous general studies include Robert W. Babcock, "The Attack of the Late Eighteenth Century upon Alterations of Shakespeare's Plays," MLN 45 (1930), 446-51; Winton Dean, "Shakespeare in the Opera House," ShS 18 (1965), 75-93; Arthur H. Scouten, "Shakespeare's Plays in the Theatrical Repertory When Garrick Came to London," SET (1944), 257-68; James W. Nichols, "Shakespeare as a Character in Drama 1679-1899," ETJ 15 (1963), 24-32; Carol J. Carlisle, SHAKESPEARE FROM THE GREENROOM: ACTORS' CRITICISMS OF FOUR MAJOR TRAGEDIES (Chapel Hill: Univ. of North Carolina Press, 1969); and Robert G. Noyes, THE THESPIAN MIRROR: SHAKESPEARE IN THE EIGHTEENTH-CENTURY NOVEL (Providence, R.I.: Brown Univ. Press, 1953).

Several studies focus on adaptations or alterations of individual plays. Joseph G. Price, in "From Farce to Romance: ALL'S WELL THAT ENDS WELL 1756-1811," SJ 99 (1963), 57-71, analyzes the various versions (Garrick, Pilon,

Kemble); the material is more fully developed in Price's book THE UNFORTU-
NATE COMEDY: A STUDY OF ALL'S WELL THAT ENDS WELL AND ITS
CRITICS (Toronto: Univ. of Toronto Press, 1968). HAMLET is the subject of
James G. McManaway's "The Two Earliest Promptbooks of HAMLET," PBSA 43
(1949), 288-320; Muriel St. Clare Byrne's "The Earliest HAMLET Promptbook
in an English Library," TN 15 (1960), 21-31; Claris Glick's "HAMLET in the
English Theatre--Acting Texts from Betterton (1676) to Olivier (1963)," ShQ 20
(1969), 17-35; and Raymond Mander and Joe Mitchenson's 'HAMLET' THROUGH
THE AGES: A PICTORIAL RECORD FROM 1709, 2nd rev. ed. (London: Rockliff, 1955 [1952]).

Gunnar Sorelius has an important study, "The Smock Alley Promptbooks of 1
and 2 HENRY IV," ShQ 22 (1971), 111-27, which analyzes alterations not
included in Evans's editions. John W. Velz provides "A Restoration Cast List
for JULIUS CAESAR" from a MS list in a Folger copy, N&Q 213 (1968), 132-
33. Philip Hobsbaum has an analysis, "KING LEAR in the Eighteenth Century,"
in MLR 68 (1973), 494-505, and one may also consult Max F. Schulz, "KING
LEAR: A Box-Office Maverick among Shakespearian Tragedies on the London
Stage 1700-01 to 1749-50," TSE 7 (1957), 83-90. The best analysis of the
fortunes of MACBETH in the period is Dennis Bartholomeusz's MACBETH AND
THE PLAYERS (London: Cambridge Univ. Press, 1969). Frederick T. Wood,
"THE MERCHANT OF VENICE in the Eighteenth Century," ES 15 (1933), 209-
18, may be supplemented by Toby B. Lelyveld, SHYLOCK ON THE STAGE
(Cleveland, Ohio: Western Reserve Univ. Press, 1961). MUCH ADO is the subject
of Powell Stewart's "An Eighteenth-Century Adaptation of Shakespeare," UTS
12 (1932), 98-117. Marvin Rosenberg analyzes mid-century prudery in "The
Refinement of OTHELLO in the Eighteenth-Century British Theatre," SP 51
(1954), 75-94, but the best overall study is his book, THE MASKS OF OTHELLO:
THE SEARCH FOR THE IDENTITY OF OTHELLO, IAGO, AND DESDEMONA
BY THREE CENTURIES OF ACTORS AND CRITICS (Berkeley and Los Angeles:
Univ. of California Press, 1961). Christopher Spencer has a speculative article
"'Count Paris's Wife': ROMEO AND JULIET on the Early Restoration Stage,"
TSLL 7 (1966), 309-16; see also Stanley T. Williams's "Some Versions of TIMON
OF ATHENS on the Stage," MP 18 (1920), 269-85.

Other Native Influences

8.3   The influence of Beaumont and Fletcher is the subject of Arthur C.
Sprague's BEAUMONT AND FLETCHER ON THE RESTORATION STAGE (Cambridge, Mass.: Harvard Univ. Press, 1926*) and of John H. Wilson's THE INFLU-
ENCE OF BEAUMONT AND FLETCHER ON RESTORATION DRAMA (Columbus:
Ohio State Univ. Press, 1928*). The stage-history section of Sprague's book is now
out of date, but his analysis of some twenty adaptations and alterations remains
useful, as does his bibliography of altered versions. Wilson's book adds a few details but is not impressive. The most recent studies are Donald J. Rulfs, "Beaumont and Fletcher on the London Stage 1776-1833," PMLA 63 (1948), 1245-
64, and the chapters "Beaumont and Fletcher in the Restoration" and "Beaumont
and Fletcher Since 1700" in William W. Appleton, BEAUMONT AND FLETCHER:
A CRITICAL STUDY (London: Allen & Unwin, 1956*). Rulfs notes twelve
revivals 1775-1810, none of which enjoyed great success; Appleton suggests

that there was no important influence after 1688.

Earlier accounts of Ben Jonson's influence were superseded by Robert G. Noyes's BEN JONSON ON THE ENGLISH STAGE 1660-1776 (Cambridge, Mass.: Harvard Univ. Press, 1935), which devoted a chapter to each of seven plays and provided a bibliography of performances and editions. In a later article, "Ben Jonson's Masques in the Eighteenth Century," SP 33 (1936), 427-36, Noyes studied such works as Colman's THE FAIRY PRINCE (1771) and Henry Woodward's THE DRUIDS (1774). Cary B. Graham noted "Jonson Allusions in Restoration Comedy," RES 15 (1939), 200-204.

There have been two later studies. Gerald E. Bentley's SHAKESPEARE AND JONSON: THEIR REPUTATIONS IN THE SEVENTEENTH CENTURY COMPARED, 2 vols. (Chicago: Univ. of Chicago Press, 1945), a by-product of the author's work on THE JACOBEAN AND CAROLINE STAGE, points out that allusion books and other sources give a mistaken impression of the relative importance of the two playwrights and that only in the last decade of the eighteenth century are there more references to Shakespeare than to Jonson. Jonson's plays were far better known, though several Shakespearean characters are referred to more frequently than any of Jonson's. Bentley also adds hundreds of new Jonson allusions to the record. Egon Tiedje's DIE TRADITION BEN JONSONS IN DER RESTAURATIONSKOMOEDIE (Hamburg: Cram, de Gruyter, 1963) studies similarities in technique, characterization, and themes.

A few articles deal with other authors. Richard H. Perkinson's "A Restoration 'Improvement' of DR. FAUSTUS," ELH 1 (1934), 305-24, concerns the version used from 1662 to 1686. J. Frank Kermode, in "A Note on the History of Massinger's THE FATAL DOWRY in the Eighteenth Century," N&Q 192 (1947), 186-87, discusses Aaron Hill's THE INSOLVENT (1758); James G. McManaway, in "Philip Massinger and the Restoration Drama," ELH 1 (1934), 276-304, is concerned with both performances and adaptations. Robert H. Ball, in THE AMAZING CAREER OF SIR GILES OVERREACH . . . (Princeton: Princeton Univ. Press, 1939), traces the later theatrical fortunes of Middleton's character in A NEW WAY TO PAY OLD DEBTS. Dana G. McKinnen's "A Description of a Restoration Promptbook of Shirley's THE BALL," RECTR 10, no. 1 (1971), 25-28, shows that the play was liked in the Restoration.

B. FOREIGN INFLUENCES

French

8.4   The study of foreign influences on English drama 1660-1800, and especially on the drama of the Restoration, was well advanced before most studies of the period in relation to the native dramatic tradition were undertaken. Such topics were favorite subjects for European dissertations around the turn of the century, and many of the standard English sources also grew out of this tradition. These early works, exemplified by Wallace R. Harvey-Jellie's LES SOURCES DU THEATRE ANGLAIS A L'EPOQUE DE LA RESTAURATION

(Paris: Librairie Général de Droit et de Jurisprudence, 1906) and L. Charlanne's L'INFLUENCE FRANCAISE EN ANGLETERRE AU DIX-SEPTIEME SIECLE: LE THEATRE ET LA CRITIQUE (Paris: Société Française d'Imprimerie et de Librairie, 1906), often confuse sources with analogs and tend either to ignore the enormous differences in tone and treatment between a French play and an English one or to limit their discussion to a catalog of resemblances. Thomas C. Macaulay's "French and English Drama in the Seventeenth Century: Some Contrasts and Parallels," E&S 20 (1935, for 1934), 45-74, for example, is perfunctory. There is no doubt about continental influence, particularly on English plots and situations; Willard A. Kinne, in REVIVALS AND IMPORTATIONS OF FRENCH COMEDIES IN ENGLAND 1749-1800 (New York: Columbia Univ. Press, 1939), estimated that 25 percent of all comic performances listed in Genest for the period studied, including revivals and new offerings, were indebted in some way to French sources. Later scholarship, however, has been careful in limiting the extent of continental influence and in recognizing the distinctive uses of the borrowed material made by English dramatists.

Molière's influence is paramount on comedy and has been extensively discussed. W. Moseley Kerby's MOLIERE AND THE RESTORATION COMEDY IN ENGLAND (London: n.p., 1907) and Dudley H. Miles's THE INFLUENCE OF MOLIERE ON RESTORATION COMEDY (New York: Columbia Univ. Press, 1910*) are the earliest full-length accounts in English; Miles tends to exaggerate the French influence, particularly on Etherege and Wycherley, and does not adequately distinguish borrowing from the use of common materials. Joseph E. Gillet's MOLIERE EN ANGLETERRE 1660-1670 (Paris: Champion, 1913) is much more thorough and concentrates on adaptations of Molière in the decade covered. John Wilcox's THE RELATION OF MOLIERE TO RESTORATION COMEDY (New York: Columbia Univ. Press, 1938*) and André de Mandach's MOLIERE ET LA COMEDIE DE MOEURS EN ANGLETERRE 1660-1668: ESSAI DE LITTERATURE COMPAREE (Neuchatel, Switzerland: Seiler, 1945) are the best of these studies. The Wilcox book is especially good because it sets clear criteria for determining what is and is not a source or an influence. Claude E. Jones, in "Molière in England to 1775: A Checklist," N&Q 202 (1957), 383-89, gives a tentative list of plays translated, adapted, or borrowed from Molière, but it is frankly derived from secondary sources. Norman Suckling's essay, "Molière and English Restoration Comedy," BROWN COLLECTION, pp. 92-107, is useful, as are the four essays presented by Pierre Danchin under the title "Quatre adaptations de Molière sur la scène anglaise a l'époque de la Restauration," GEOFFRIN COLLECTION, I, 327-71.

The influence of French tragedy is discussed by Dorothea F. Canfield in CORNEILLE AND RACINE IN ENGLAND: A STUDY OF THE ENGLISH TRANSLATIONS . . . (New York: Columbia Univ. Press, 1904), but she uses the English material only to demonstrate the superiority of the French. Francis Y. Eccles's RACINE IN ENGLAND (Oxford: Clarendon Press, 1922) is slight in comparison with Katherine E. Wheatley's RACINE AND ENGLISH CLASSICISM (Austin: Univ. of Texas Press, 1956*), the most exhaustive study of the subject. Wheatley concludes that English dramatists simply could not read nor comprehend Racine, and lacked dramatic imagination--conclusions most readers will not find helpful.

Voltaire's influence is the subject of Harold L. Bruce's VOLTAIRE ON THE
ENGLISH STAGE (Berkeley and Los Angeles: Univ. of California Press, 1918).
Herbert W. Hill, in "La Calprenède's Romances and the Restoration Drama,"
UNS 2, no. 3 (1910), 1-56, and 3 (1911), 57-158, studies the general influence of these heroic romances in Part 1 and the particular influences of CAS-
SANDRA and CLEOPATRA in Part 2. Marie-Rose Rutherford has a short article, "The Abbé Prévost and the English Theatre 1730-1740," TN 9 (1955),
111-18, and Josephine Grieder a good discussion, "Marmontel's Prose Fiction
on the English Stage," EE 4 (1973), 46-59. Many other sources and attributions are noted under the appropriate headings in Part 2 of this guide.

Spanish, Italian, German

8.5   The evidence suggests that Spanish influence was not nearly so great
or so direct as French. Hilda U. Stubbings, RENAISSANCE SPAIN IN ITS
LITERARY RELATIONS WITH ENGLAND AND FRANCE: A CRITICAL BIBLI-
OGRAPHY (Nashville, Tenn.: Vanderbilt Univ. Press, 1969), lists many useful
studies. Such early surveys as Martin A.S. Hume, SPANISH INFLUENCE ON
ENGLISH LITERATURE (London: E. Nash, 1905*), include little discussion of the
period; such influence as is noted is limited to intrigue plotting. Max Oppen-
heimer, Jr., in "Supplementary Data on the French and English Adaptations of
Calderón's EL ASTROLOGO FINGIDO," RLC 22 (1948), 547-60, focuses on THE
FEIGNED ASTROLOGER and Dryden's MOCK ASTROLOGER (both 1668). The
most important studies are those of John C. Loftis; his earlier articles on the
topic form the basis of his book THE SPANISH PLAYS OF NEO-CLASSICAL
ENGLAND (New Haven: Yale Univ. Press, 1973). A close reading of Loftis's
evidence, and of such ancillary studies as Floriana T. Hogan's "Notes on
Thirty-One English Plays and Their Spanish Sources," RECTR 6, no. 1 (1967),
56-59, convinces one that direct influence was slight. This is essentially the
conclusion of Patricia M. Seward's article, "Was the English Restoration Theatre Significantly Influenced by Spanish Drama?" RLC 46 (1972), 95-125. The
author concludes (and Loftis agrees) that only eight of some 244 plays show
direct Spanish influence and adds that only twenty-nine show clear use of
specifically Spanish forms. Direct borrowing or adaptation is seen in only
twenty-four plays at most--about one in ten.

Italian influence in the period is slight except on pantomime (via France) and
on opera. The operatic influence was so overwhelming as to stifle English
opera; it is discussed in the works cited in Section 7.19. Ifan K. Fletcher,
"Italian Comedians in England in the Seventeenth Century," TN 8 (1954), 86-
91, is one of very few articles on dramatic influence. The works on pantomime cited in Sections 7.2 and 7.18 will be helpful, as will THE LONDON
STAGE.

German drama becomes important only toward the last decade of the period.
Theodore Grieder gives a good account of the influence (in tabular form) in
"The German Drama in England 1790-1800," RECTR 3, no. 2 (1964), 39-50.
Specific influences are discussed in Sydney H. Kenwood, "Lessing in England,"
MLR 9 (1914), 197-212; Thomas Rea, SCHILLER'S DRAMAS AND POEMS IN

ENGLAND (London: Unwin, 1906); Geoffrey Buyers, "The Influence of Schiller's Drama and Fiction upon English Literature in the Period 1780-1830," ESt 48 (1915), 349-93; Margaret W. Cooke, "Schiller's ROBBERS in England," MLR 11 (1916), 156-75; Leonard A. Willoughby, "English Translations and Adaptations of Schiller's ROBBERS," MLR 16 (1921), 297-315; and Frederic Ewen, THE PRESTIGE OF SCHILLER IN ENGLAND 1788-1859 (New York: Columbia Univ. Press, 1932). Most of these studies focus on the romantic period and on other genres than drama. Douglas Milburn, Jr.'s article, "The Popular Reaction to German Drama in England at the End of the Eighteenth Century," in STUDIES IN GERMAN IN MEMORY OF ANDREW LOUIS, ed. Robert L. Kahn (Houston: Rice Univ. Press, 1969), shows that the outcry against Kotzebue's "immorality" has been exaggerated and that eleven of fifteen plays performed during more than one season from 1790 to 1840 were translations or adaptations of his plays.

Part 2

INDIVIDUAL AUTHORS

The alphabetical list which follows includes, with some exceptions, only authors who had three or more plays other than adaptations and translations produced and published in London between 1660 and 1800. (A more complete list of minor figures may be found in the sources listed in Part 1, Section 1, of this guide.) Within a given entry the usual arrangement is as follows: bibliographies, collected editions, editions of individual plays, biography and letters, and criticism (arranged from the general to the most specific). Since such an elaborate arrangement is required only for major authors, most entries are simpler. Biographical information is given only for lesser known writers and has been kept to a minimum. Lists of plays are given only for those writers whose works are not easily available in a modern collected edition or reprint, or for whom there is no adequate bibliography. The nondramatic work of an author is usually ignored. The list of editions and reprints of the more popular plays is selective, as is the treatment of outdated or inconsequential criticism. For full citation of a secondary work referred to in Part 2 by author and short title, consult the first page number listed under the appropriate entry in the author-subject index.

JOSEPH ADDISON (1672-1719)

Addison's three plays were included in his MISCELLANEOUS WORKS IN VERSE
AND PROSE . . . (1726), but the best edition is in the second volume of
THE MISCELLANEOUS WORKS OF JOSEPH ADDISON, ed. Adolph C. Guthkelch, 2 vols. (London: Bell, 1914). CATO (1713) is available in facsimile
from London's Scolar Press. Thomas Tickell's preface to the 1721 WORKS is
biographically important, as is the discussion by Thomas Birch in his translation
of Bayle's GENERAL DICTIONARY . . ., vol. 1 (c.1734). The best biography
is Peter Smithers, THE LIFE OF JOSEPH ADDISON, 2nd ed. (Oxford: Clarendon Press, 1968). Samuel Johnson's biography and estimate in the LIVES OF
THE POETS (1781*), Macaulay's in ER 78 (1843*), 193-260, William J. Courthope's ADDISON in the English Men of Letters series (London: Macmillan,
1884*), and Bonamy Dobrée's essay "The First Victorian," ESSAYS IN BIOG-
RAPHY 1660-1726 (London: Oxford Univ. Press, 1925*) may also be consulted;
they include some discussion of the plays.

Most criticism has focused on CATO, beginning with such contemporary pieces
as John Dennis's REMARKS UPON 'CATO, A TRAGEDY' and George Sewell's
OBSERVATIONS UPON 'CATO, A TRAGEDY' . . . (both 1713). Stuart
Atkins has a textual note, "Addison's CATO I.i.47-53," PQ 21 (1942), 430-
33; Robert Halsband an important article, "Addison's CATO and Lady Mary
Wortley Montagu," PMLA 65 (1950), 1122-29, showing that Addison followed
several of Lady Mary's suggestions about sentiments and diction. More recent
articles include Malcolm M. Kelsall's "The Meaning of Addison's CATO," RES
17 (1966), 149-62, and James S. Malek's "The Fifth Act of Addison's CATO,"
NM 74 (1973), 515-19. Kelsall argues that Cato unites public and private
virtue, but that neither character nor action defines what liberty means in the
play. Malek relates the shift in Cato's character between acts 1-4 (1704) and
act 5 (1713) to the periodical essays of the two periods. Ian Donaldson, in
"Cato in Tears: Stoical Guises of the Man of Feeling," STUDIES IN THE
EIGHTEENTH CENTURY II, ed. R.F. Brissenden (Toronto: Univ. of Toronto
Press, 1973), pp. 377-95, discusses Addison's treatment of Stoicism in the
play. There is some discussion of CATO in John C. Loftis's POLITICS OF
DRAMA and in Eugene M. Waith's IDEAS OF GREATNESS; see also Bonamy
Dobrée's RESTORATION TRAGEDY and Frederick S. Boas's EIGHTEENTH-CEN-
TURY DRAMA.

William E.A. Axon's essay THE LITERARY HISTORY OF THE COMEDY OF
'THE DRUMMER' was published in the PAPERS of the Manchester Literary Club
21 (1895). Lee W. Heilman, in "Addison's THE DRUMMER," TLS, 1 Oct.
1931, p. 754, studies the relationship of the 1716 and 1722 editions of the
play. Donald C. Baker, in "Witchcraft, Addison, and THE DRUMMER," SN
31 (1959), 174-81, argues that Lady Truman represents a commonsense middle
way between Mr. Tinsel's shallow skepticism and the superstition of the servants
in the play. Chapter 4 of Virgil B. Heltzel's FAIR ROSAMOND: A STUDY
OF THE DEVELOPMENT OF A LITERARY THEME (Evanston, Ill.: Northwestern
Univ. Studies in the Humanities, no. 16, 1947) treats Addison's play along
with others on the same theme.

MILES PETER ANDREWS (d. 1814)

Andrews, the son of a London tradesman, rose to become a wealthy business-man and member of Parliament. His plays are all comedies, comic operas, or farces; he was also well known as a writer of prologues and epilogues. The plays include THE CONJUROR (1774), THE ELECTION (1774), BELPHEGOR (1778), SUMMER AMUSEMENT (1779, with William Miles), FIRE AND WATER (1780), DISSIPATION (1781), THE BARON KINKVERVANKOTSDORSPRAKEN-GATCHDERN (1781), THE BEST BIDDER (1782), REPARATION (1784), THE ENCHANTED CASTLE (1786), BETTER LATE THAN NEVER (1790), and MYS-TERIES OF THE CASTLE (1795). THE ELECTION and THE BEST BIDDER are farces; most of the others prior to REPARATION are comic or ballad operas. The last two plays were done in collaboration with Frederick Reynolds. There are no collected or modern editions and only brief references in modern dra-matic histories.

THOMAS AUGUSTINE ARNE (1710-78)

Arne, one of the more famous English composers of the eighteenth century, was fond of writing the libretti for his operas and other musical pieces. He is usually credited with the texts of DON SAVERIO (1750), THE GUARDIAN OUTWITTED (1764), THE COOPER (1772, from LE TONNELIER), THE ROSE (1772), BEAUTY AND VIRTUE (1772, from Metastasio), THE SOT (1775, from Fielding), and PHOEBE AT COURT (1776, from Robert Lloyd's CAPRICIOUS LOVERS). All are pieces whose primary interest is musical. There are no collected editions. For Arne's career as a composer, see the works cited in Part 1, Section 7.19. Burney's life of Arne is included in Rees's CYCLOPE-DIA (1819).

SAMUEL JAMES ARNOLD (1774-1852)

Samuel Arnold, son of the Samuel Arnold who was composer to the Haymarket Theatre, was educated as an artist and eventually became a magistrate and Fellow of the Royal Society. He was a manager of Drury Lane and of the English Opera House (Lyceum) as well as a prolific writer of comedies, comic operas, and melodramas. Only four of his pieces appeared before the nineteenth century--AULD ROBIN GRAY (1974), WHO PAYS THE RECKONING? (1795), THE SHIPWRECK (1796), and THE IRISH LEGACY (1797). All had music by the senior Samuel Arnold. THE SHIPWRECK was particularly successful; THE IRISH LEGACY failed. Among Arnold's many later works are THE VETERAN TAR (1801), FOUL DEEDS WILL RISE and MAN AND WIFE (1804), UP ALL NIGHT (1809), THE MANIAC (1810), THE DEVIL'S BRIDGE (1812), THE WOODMAN'S HUT (1814), THE UNKNOWN GUEST (1815), THE WIZARD (1817), and BROKEN PROMISES (1825). His last play was THE SERGEANT'S WIFE (1835).

THOMAS BAKER (fl. 1701-09)

Little is known of Baker, who wrote four plays produced at Drury Lane between 1701 and 1708. THE FINE LADY'S AIRS (1708) has been issued in facsimile by The Augustan Reprint Society (Los Angeles, 1950), with an introduction by John H. Smith. The other acted plays are THE HUMOUR OF THE AGE (1701), TUNBRIDGE WALKS (1703), and HAMPSTEAD HEATH (1705). TUNBRIDGE WALKS, Baker's most popular play, was revived several times during the century. There are no collected editions and only scattered references to Baker in modern dramatic histories. AN ACT AT OXFORD (pub. 1704) was banned.

JOHN BANCROFT (d. 1696)

Three tragedies produced between 1679 and 1692 are attributed to Bancroft, who was a surgeon by profession. There are no collected or modern editions and only scattered references in the standard histories. The plays are THE TRAGEDY OF SERTORIUS (1679), KING EDWARD THE THIRD (1690), and HENRY THE SECOND (1692); the last two of these are included in SIX PLAYS WRITTEN BY MR. MOUNTFORT (1720).

JOHN BANKS (c.1650-c.1700)

There is no collected edition of Banks's seven tragedies, two of which were prohibited. THE UNHAPPY FAVORITE has been edited by Thomas M.H. Blair (New York: Columbia Univ. Press, 1939); the text, however, is photo-offset from the first edition (1682). Blair provides extensive notes, a study of Banks's life and works, and of the stage history, sources, and analogs of the play. Robert M. Lumiansky clears up a minor point in Blair's discussion of sources in "A Note on Blair's Edition of THE UNHAPPY FAVORITE," MLN 56 (1941), 280-82. Henry W. Knepler, "Maxwell Anderson, a Historical Parallel--Problems for The Poetic Dramatist," QQ 64 (1957), 250-63, makes some interesting parallels between Banks's plays and Anderson's. Edythe N. Backus, "The MS. Play ANNA BULLEN," PMLA 47 (1932), 741-52, discusses a possible source of Banks's VIRTUE BETRAYED. Fredson T. Bowers's "The Variant Sheets in John Banks's CYRUS THE GREAT (1696)," SB 4 (1952), 174-82, is a highly technical analysis of two variant sheets in the first quarto of the play. James J. Devlin, in "The Dramatis Personae and The Dating of John Banks's THE ALBION QUEENS," N&Q 208 (1963), 213-15, corrects Avery's cast list (based on Genest) for the play. Aside from Blair, the only substantial published study is Hans Hochuli's monograph, JOHN BANKS . . . (Bern, Switzerland: Francke, 1952), which presents Banks as a transitional figure. Some attention is also given Banks in Eric Rothstein's RESTORATION TRAGEDY. Plays not mentioned above include THE RIVAL KINGS (1677), THE DESTRUCTION OF TROY (1678), and THE ISLAND QUEENS (not acted; printed 1694).

APHRA BEHN (d. 1689)

Behn's plays were first collected in PLAYS WRITTEN BY THE LATE INGENIOUS
MRS. BEHN, 2 vols. (1702). The 1716 edition (4 vols.) included eight addi-
tional plays; the third edition (4 vols., 1724) added THE YOUNGER BROTHER
(1696). The edition published by Pearson (6 vols., 1871) reprints the 1724
PLAYS. The standard modern edition is THE WORKS OF APHRA BEHN, ed.
Montague Summers, 6 vols. (London: Heinemann, 1915*). Summers's notes
are extensive and helpful, but the text is badly edited and therefore unreliable.
TEN ENGLISH FARCES, ed. Leo A. Hughes and Arthur H. Scouten (Austin:
Univ. of Texas Press, 1948), includes a good text of THE EMPEROR OF THE
MOON (1687); SELECTED WRITINGS OF THE INGENIOUS MRS. APHRA
BEHN (New York: Grove Press, 1950*) includes an uncritical text of THE
DUTCH LOVER (1673). THE ROVER (1677), Behn's most popular play, has
been edited by Frederick M. Link for the Regents Restoration Drama series
(Lincoln: Univ. of Nebraska Press, 1967); both this play and THE LUCKY
CHANCE (1686) are included in Alexander N. Jeffares's collection, RESTORA-
TION COMEDY (1974).

More attention has been paid to Aphra Behn's life than to her plays. The
best general biography is George Woodcock's THE INCOMPARABLE APHRA
(London: Boardman, 1948); see also Evangeline W. Blashfield, PORTRAITS
AND BACKGROUNDS . . . (New York: Scribner's, 1917*), pp. 113-283,
and Walter and Clare Jerrold, FIVE QUEER WOMEN (London: Brentano's,
1929). Neither APHRA BEHN, by Emily Hahn (London: Cape, 1951), nor
APHRA BEHN: THE INCOMPARABLE ASTREA, by Victoria Sackville-West
(New York: Viking, 1928*), can be recommended. The earliest biography is
the "Memoirs . . ." prefixed to THE HISTORIES AND NOVELS . . . (1696),
often ascribed to Charles Gildon. Robert A. Day, in a brilliant article,
"Aphra Behn's First Biography," SB 22 (1969), 227-40, shows that there were
three versions of this in several different styles and tries to assign the different
styles to their respective authors. His article throws light on the controversies
about Behn's birth, parentage, and residence in Surinam, arguments which go
back to Edmund Gosse's article in the DNB, and Ernest Bernbaum's two articles, "Mrs. Behn's Biography a Fiction," PMLA 28 (1913), 432-53, and "Mrs.
Behn's ORONOOKO," in ANNIVERSARY PAPERS BY COLLEAGUES AND PU-
PILS OF GEORGE LYMAN KITTREDGE (Boston: Ginn, 1913), pp. 419-35.
Bernbaum argues that Behn was never in Surinam; the overwhelming evidence
against his view is well summarized in William J. Cameron's NEW LIGHT ON

APHRA BEHN . . . (Auckland, N. Zealand: Univ. of Auckland Press, 1961).
See also Harrison G. Platt, Jr., "Astraea and Celadon: An Untouched Portrait
of Aphra Behn," PMLA 49 (1934), 544-59, and Henry A. Hargreaves, "New
Evidence of the Realism of Mrs. Behn's OROONOKO," BNYPL 74 (1970),
437-44.

Standard sources and library catalogs to the contrary, no one knows when
Aphra Behn was born or what her parentage was; see A. Purvis, AH 1, no. 9
(1953-54), inside front cover, and Percy C.D. Mundy, "Aphra Behn, Novelist
and Dramatist (1640?-1689)," N&Q 199 (1954), 199-201, and 200 (1955), 23
and 456-57. Earlier studies are summarized by Henry A. Hargreaves in "The
Birth of Mrs. Behn," HAB 16 (1965), 19-21; Hargreaves also has an interesting
note, "A Case for Mr. Behn," N&Q 9 (1962), 203-05.

The fullest published discussion of the Behn plays is Frederick M. Link, APHRA
BEHN (New York: Twayne, 1968), which also includes a useful bibliography.
Woodcock includes some comment on the plays in his biography, and there are
brief surveys in Nicoll, in Bernbaum's DRAMA OF SENSIBILITY, in Elisabeth
L. Mignon's CRABBED AGE AND YOUTH, and (of the Spanish influence) in
John A. Lofits's THE SPANISH PLAYS OF NEOCLASSICAL ENGLAND. Richard Southern's CHANGEABLE SCENERY makes occasional reference to her stage-
craft and examines one example in detail. There are a few articles on individual plays. John H. Wilson discusses ABDELAZER (1676) as a representative
example of villain tragedy in his PREFACE TO RESTORATION DRAMA. The
notes to Summers's edition supersede much earlier scholarship on sources and influences, but see Charles L. Batten, Jr., "The Source of Aphra Behn's THE
WIDOW RANTER," RECTR 12, no. 1 (1974), 12-18, for an important addition.
William Van Lennep, in "Two Restoration Comedies," TLS, 28 Jan. 1939, pp.
57-58, notes Luttrell copies which help date the production of THE FALSE
COUNT (1681) and THE REVENGE (1680, from Marston)--the latter a play
often ascribed to Behn. Edward A. Langhans, "Three Early Eighteenth-Century
Promptbooks," TN 20 (1966), 142-50, discusses a promptbook of THE ROVER
probably dating from the 1720's. Paul C. Wermuth, in "Bacon's Rebellion in
the London Theatre," VC 7 (1957), 38-39, gives a brief comparison of THE
WIDOW RANTER (1684) with the historical rebellion on which it is based;
"Aphra Behn's Strange News from Virginia," by Anne Witmer and John Freehafer, LC 34 (1968), 7-23, is superior on the same topic and goes on to conjecture that Bacon's character was modeled on that of William Scot, whom
Aphra Behn presumably met in Surinam.

THOMAS BETTERTON (c.1635-1710)

Most of the plays attributed to Betterton are anonymously published adaptations. The majority of them, like THE SEQUEL OF HENRY THE FOURTH (c.1704), THE ROMAN ACTOR (1722, from Massinger), THE REVENGE (1680, from Marston), and THE COUNTERFEIT BRIDEGROOM (1677, from Middleton), are probably the work of others; the best case for Betterton as adaptor must be made on the basis of THE AMOROUS WIDOW (1670, from Thomas Corneille and Molière) and THE WOMAN MADE A JUSTICE (1670, probably from Mont-fleury but never printed). See the excellent article by Judith Milhous, "Thomas Betterton's Playwriting," BNYPL 77 (1974), 375-92. There are no collected editions of these adaptations. The text and score to THE PROPHETESS (1690, from Massinger and Fletcher), ed. Sir Frederick J. Bridge and John Pointer, was published by Novello in 1900 under its subtitle DIOCLESIAN. This play and THE ROMAN VIRGIN (1669, from Webster) are lightly adapted from their originals; the case for Betterton's hand is reasonable. KING HENRY IV (1700, from Shakespeare), a doubtful attribution, has been issued in facsimile by Cornmarket Press (London, 1969). THE LIFE OF MR. THOMAS BETTERTON . . ., by Charles Gildon, was published in 1710*; the best biography is Robert W. Lowe's THOMAS BETTERTON (London: Kegan Paul et al., 1891*). John Downes's ROSCIUS ANGLICANUS (1708*) should also be consulted.

There is little criticism of Betterton's work but a great deal of discussion of his acting. Montague Summers's "The Comedies of Thomas Betterton," N&Q 170 (1936), 454-56, gives brief notes on the plays and their sources. John H. Smith, in "Thomas Corneille to Betterton to Congreve," JEGP 45 (1946), 209-13, traces the "amorous widow" through LE BARON D'ALBIKRAC, THE AMOROUS WIDOW, and THE WAY OF THE WORLD. Fredson T. Bowers, in "A Bibliographical History of the Fletcher-Betterton play, THE PROPHETESS (1690)," LIBRARY 5th ser. 16 (1961), 169-75, studies the early editions and issues; there are critical discussions of the play in the standard works on Henry Purcell and early English opera. Henry N. Paul's article, "Players' Quartos and Duodecimos of HAMLET," MLN 49 (1934), 369-75, discusses the 1683 text of this dubious attribution to Betterton; see also Dennis Bartholomeusz, "The Davenant-Betterton MACBETH," KOMOS 1 (1967), 41-48. Charles E. Ward attributes the operatic TEMPEST to Betterton in "THE TEMPEST: A Restoration Opera Problem," ELH 13 (1946), 119-30, although it is now generally agreed that this was a cooperative venture. William A. Armstrong's article, "The Acting of Thomas Betterton," ENGLISH 10 (1954), 55-57, is slight and derivative; more interesting is the exchange in TN 1 (1946 and 1947), 54-55, 75, 99-100, and 115-16, between Arthur C. Sprague and others, titled "Did Betterton Chant?"

ISAAC BICKERSTAFFE (c.1733-c.1808)

Bickerstaffe, the best and one of the most popular writers of comic opera in the 1760's, was driven into exile in 1772 when accused of homosexuality; little or nothing is known about the last decades of his life. Such works as THOMAS AND SALLY (1760), LOVE IN A VILLAGE (1762), THE MAID OF THE MILL (1765), LIONEL AND CLARISSA (1768), THE PADLOCK (1768), and THE SULTAN (1775) deserve to be much better known; they were widely reprinted in contemporary and early nineteenth-century collections, but there is no collected edition and no modern editions except for the books of LIONEL AND CLARISSA and LOVE IN A VILLAGE as produced at the Lyric Theatre in Hammersmith (London: Secker, 1925 and 1928).

The only full-length study is Peter A. Tasch's THE DRAMATIC COBBLER: THE LIFE AND WORKS OF ISAAC BICKERSTAFFE (Lewisburg, Pa.: Bucknell Univ. Press, 1972), which gives a detailed account of Bickerstaffe's career, including much information about the production and stage history of the plays. Tasch's book, though it often ignores the important dimension of music, surpasses the briefer accounts in Nicoll's HISTORY and in Frederick S. Boas's EIGHTEENTH-CENTURY DRAMA and earlier articles like Everett H. Emerson's "The Date of Isaac Bickerstaffe's Death," N&Q 197 (1952), 496; Ethel Macmillan's "The Plays of Isaac Bickerstaffe in America," PQ 5 (1926), 58-69; and René Guiet's "An English Imitator of Favart: Bickerstaffe," MLN 38 (1923), 54-56. Recent articles include Tasch's "Bickerstaffe, Colman, and the Bourgeois Audience," RECTR 9, no. 1 (1970), 44-50, and Robert Fahrner's "David Garrick Presents THE PADLOCK: An Eighteenth-Century 'Hit,'" TS 13 (1972), 52-69. Tasch's article contrasts Bickerstaffe's LOVE IN THE CITY (1767) with Colman's ENGLISH MERCHANT; Fahrner emphasizes the enormous popularity of Bickerstaffe in the period.

Plays not mentioned above include DAPHNE AND AMINTOR and an alteration of THE PLAIN DEALER (1765), THE ROYAL GARLAND (1768), THE HYPOCRITE (1768, from Cibber and Molière), THE DOCTOR LAST IN HIS CHARIOT (1769), THE CAPTIVE (1769, from Dryden's DON SEBASTIAN), THE EPHESIAN MATRON (1769), THE SCHOOL FOR FATHERS (1770, an alteration of LIONEL AND CLARISSA), 'TIS WELL IT'S NO WORSE and THE RECRUITING SERGEANT (1770), HE WOULD IF HE COULD (1771, from Pergolesi). THE SPOILED CHILD (1790) has sometimes been attributed to Bickerstaffe, but it is probably by another hand.

SAMUEL BIRCH (1757-1841)

Birch was a dramatist and pastry cook who entered London politics, becoming a member of the Common Council, Sheriff of London in 1811, and Lord Mayor in 1814. His first play, THE MARINERS, was produced in 1793. THE PACKET BOAT, THE ADOPTED CHILD, THE SMUGGLERS, FAST ASLEEP (from J. Powell's unacted 1787 play THE NARCOTIC), and ALBERT AND ADELAIDE (from des Vivetières CAMILLE and Bontet de Monvel's LES VICTIMES CLOI-TREES) followed at yearly intervals. These were all musical farces or melo-dramas; the first five had music by Thomas Attwood. THE ADOPTED CHILD and THE SMUGGLERS were the most popular of Birch's pieces in the 1790's.

JAMES BOADEN (1762-1839)

Boaden was a successful journalist and theatrical biographer as well as a play-wright. His plays, all melodramas, include OZMYN AND DARAXA (1793), FONTAINVILLE FOREST (1794, from Ann Radcliffe), THE SECRET TRIBUNAL (1795, from Count Skjoeldebrand's HERMANN VON UNNA), THE ITALIAN MONK (1797, from Ann Radcliffe's THE ITALIAN), CAMBRO-BRITONS (1798), and AURELIO AND MIRANDA (1799). THE VOICE OF NATURE (1802) and THE MAID OF BRISTOL (1803) were his only dramatic pieces after the turn of the century. FONTAINVILLE FOREST, THE ITALIAN MONK, and CAMBRO-BRITONS were popular for two or three seasons after their initial production; they belong to the Gothicism of the 1790's and to the history of melodrama. THE MAN OF TWO LIVES: A NARRATIVE WRITTEN BY HIMSELF, written under the pseudonym of Edward Sydenham, was published by Colburn in 1828.

FRANCES [MOORE] BROOKE (1724-89)

Frances Moore, daughter of a clergyman, married the Reverend Mr. Brooke about 1756, the same year in which her tragedy VIRGINIA (Dublin, 1754) was rejected by Garrick. She is best known for her novels and translations, but also had three plays produced in the last quarter of the century. THE SIEGE OF SINOPE, a tragedy based on Sarti's opera MITRIDATE A SINOPE (1779), appeared in 1781; MARIAN, a successful operatic farce based on Favart, was produced in 1788. In between came her most popular piece, the comic opera ROSINA (1782), which held the stage for many seasons.

GEORGE VILLIERS, 2ND DUKE OF BUCKINGHAM (1628-87)

The WORKS . . ., 1 vol. (1704) and 2 vols. (1715), remain the only collected editions. THE REHEARSAL has been widely printed and anthologized;
it was included in Edward Arber's English Reprint series (1869) and was edited
by Montague Summers (Stratford-on-Avon: Shakespeare Head Press, 1914).
There are numerous school editions. A key to the play was provided as early
as 1705, and many contemporary editions print text and key together. The
best biography is John H. Wilson's A RAKE AND HIS TIMES: GEORGE VIL-
LIERS, 2ND DUKE OF BUCKINGHAM (New York: Farrar et al., 1954);
Hester W Chapman's GREAT VILLIERS: A STUDY OF GEORGE VILLIERS,
SECOND DUKE OF BUCKINGHAM, 1628-1687 (London: Secker & Warburg,
1949) is also a very readable account.

General studies of THE REHEARSAL include Peter Lewis's "THE REHEARSAL: A
Study of Its Satirical Methods," DUJ 62 (1970), 96-113, and Sheridan Baker's
"Buckingham's Permanent REHEARSAL," MQR 12 (1973), 160-71. The most
detailed analysis, however, is in Dane F. Smith's PLAYS ABOUT THE THEA-
TRE . . . (Part 1, Section 7.2). Emmett L. Avery's article "The Stage Popularity of THE REHEARSAL 1671-1777," RSW 7 (1939), 201-04, lists many performances not mentioned by Smith. Bartholow V. Crawford, in "The Dance
of the Kings," PQ 2 (1923), 151-53, refers this episode to ceremonial dances
at the Inner Temple.

CHRISTOPHER BULLOCK (c.1690-1724)

This well-known actor wrote or adapted some half-dozen plays between 1715 and 1717, mostly farces. There are no collected editions of his works, no modern editions of any of the plays, and only scattered references in modern histories of the drama. The plays written by or attributed to Bullock include THE SLIP and A WOMAN'S REVENGE (1715); THE COBBLER OF PRESTON, THE ADVENTURES OF HALF AN HOUR and WOMAN IS A RIDDLE (1716); and THE PERJUROR (1717). Most of them lasted for several seasons; A WOMAN'S REVENGE was perhaps the most popular.

JOHN BURGOYNE (1722-92)

Studies of Burgoyne focus on his life and military career, not on his plays. They include Francis J. Hudleston, GENTLEMAN JOHNNY BURGOYNE . . . (New York: Bobbs Merrill, 1927), and Paul Lewis, THE MAN WHO LOST AMERICA . . . (New York: Dial Press, 1973). Burgoyne's plays were collected in THE DRAMATIC AND POETICAL WORKS . . ., 2 vols. (London: for Longman et al., 1807); they include THE MAID OF THE OAKS (1774), THE LORD OF THE MANOR (1780), and THE HEIRESS and RICHARD COEUR DE LION (1786).

WILLIAM BURNABY (c.1672-1706)

Burnaby's four plays are collected in THE DRAMATIC WORKS OF WILLIAM
BURNABY, ed. Frederick E. Budd (London: Scholartis Press, 1931); Budd provides a biography and detailed commentary. The plays are THE REFORMED
WIFE (1700), THE LADIES VISITING DAY (1701), THE MODISH HUSBAND
(1702), and LOVE BETRAYED (1703). All were published anonymously.

HENRY CAREY (1687?-1743)

The only collected edition of Carey's plays is THE DRAMATIC WORKS OF
HENRY CAREY (1743), which omits HANGING AND MARRIAGE (1722).
Frederick T. Wood's edition, THE POEMS OF HENRY CAREY (London: Schol-
artis Press, 1930), includes a biography, and William H. Hudson has an essay
on Carey in A QUIET CORNER IN A LIBRARY (Chicago: Rand McNally,
1915), pp. 59-91. There are discussions of Carey in Frederick W. Bateson's
ENGLISH COMIC DRAMA, pp. 104-14, and in Frederick S. Boas's EIGHTEENTH-
CENTURY DRAMA, pp. 191-203. Frederick T. Wood, in "THE DISAPPOINT-
MENT," RES 5 (1929), 66-69, presents evidence that this play is Carey's; in
"Henry Carey's BETTY," RES 9 (1933), 64-66, Wood argues that this lost play
of 1732 was probably a reworking of HANGING AND MARRIAGE. Leo A.
Hughes and Arthur H. Scouten, in "The First Season of THE HONEST YORK-
SHIREMAN," MLR 40 (1945), 8-11, argues that 1734-35 was the first season
and the edition of January 1735-36 the first authentic edition. Samuel L.
Macey, in "Carey's CHRONONHOTONTHOLOGOS: A Plea," LHR (1969),
pp. 17-23, suggests that this piece has been unduly neglected. Works not
mentioned above include THE CONTRIVANCES (1715), AMELIA and TERAMINTA
(1732), THE DRAGON OF WANTLEY (1737), MARGERY (1738), and NANCY
(1739, later titled THE PRESS GANG [1755] and altered as TRUE BLUE [1787]).

SUSANNA CENTLIVRE (c.1670-1723)

THE WORKS OF THE CELEBRATED MRS. CENTLIVRE . . ., 3 vols. (1760-61), is the only collected edition; this was reprinted by Pearson under the title THE DRAMATIC WORKS . . ., 3 vols. (London, 1872*). THE BUSY BODY (1709) has been reprinted in the Augustan Reprint series, with an introduction by Jess Byrd (Los Angeles, 1949); A BOLD STROKE FOR A WIFE (1718) is included in the Regents Restoration Drama series (Lincoln: Univ. of Nebraska Press, 1967), ed. Thalia Stathas. Jane E. Norton provides a bibliography of first editions in "Some Uncollected Authors 14: Susanna Centlivre," BC 6 (1957), 172-78.

The best biography is John W. Bowyer's THE CELEBRATED MRS. CENTLIVRE (Durham, N.C.: Duke Univ. Press, 1952*), which focuses largely on the plays. See also James R. Sutherland, "The Progress of Error: Mrs. Centlivre and the Biographers," RES 18 (1942), 167-82, and John H. Mackenzie, "Susan Centlivre," N&Q 198 (1953), 386. General accounts include Mona Wilson's essay in THESE WERE MUSES (London: Sidgwick & Jackson, 1924); Walter and Clare Jerrold's essay in FIVE QUEER WOMEN (New York: Brentano's, 1929); Frederick T. Wood's "The Celebrated Mrs. Centlivre," Np 16 (1931), 268-78; Frederick W. Bateson's ENGLISH COMIC DRAMA, pp. 61-77; and Frederick S. Boas's EIGHTEENTH-CENTURY DRAMA, pp. 100-116. Specialized materials include an unconscionable number of mechanical German dissertations (listed in Stratman's BIBLIOGRAPHICAL GUIDE); Alan D. McKillop, "Mrs. Centlivre's THE WONDER: A Variant Imprint," BC 7 (1958), 79-80; and Ezra K. Maxfield, "The Quakers in English Stage Plays before 1800," PMLA 45 (1930), 256-73 (with Bowyer's response, "Quakers on the English Stage," pp. 957-58). Robert Strozier's "A Short View of Some of Mrs. Centlivre's Celebrated Plays . . .," DISCOURSE 7 (1964), 62-80, is superficial. There is some material in the standard histories and in such studies as John C. Loftis's COMEDY AND SOCIETY FROM CONGREVE TO FIELDING.

Aside from the two mentioned above, Centlivre's acted plays include THE PERJURED HUSBAND (1700), THE BEAU'S DUEL and THE STOLEN HEIRESS (1702), LOVE'S CONTRIVANCE (1703), THE GAMESTER and THE BASSET TABLE (1705), LOVE AT A VENTURE and THE PLATONIC LADY (1706), THE MAN'S BEWITCHED (1709), A BICKERSTAFFE'S BURYING and MARPLOT (1710), THE PERPLEXED LOVERS (1712), THE WONDER: A WOMAN KEEPS A SECRET

(1714), A WIFE WELL MANAGED (c.1715), THE CRUEL GIFT (1716), and
THE ARTIFICE (1722).

COLLEY CIBBER (1671-1757)

Leonard R.N. Ashley, in "Colley Cibber: A Bibliography," RECTR 6, no. 1 (1967), 14-27, and no. 2, 51-57, provides an annotated checklist; see the addenda in RECTR 7, no. 1 (1968), 17. PLAYS WRITTEN BY MR. CIBBER, 2 vols. (1721), contains ten plays; THE DRAMATIC WORKS . . ., 4 vols. (1760), adds another six. The best collected edition is THE DRAMATIC WORKS . . ., 5 vols. (1777), which includes all but two plays and has a biography by D.E. Baker. COLLEY CIBBER: THREE SENTIMENTAL COMEDIES, ed. Maureen Sullivan (New Haven: Yale Univ. Press, 1973), is the only modern collection. THE CARELESS HUSBAND (1704) has been edited by William W. Appleton for the Regents Restoration Drama series (Lincoln: Univ. of Nebraska Press, 1966). RICHARD III (c.1700) is included in Christopher Spencer's FIVE RESTORATION ADAPTATIONS OF SHAKESPEARE; both the 1700 and 1718 versions have been reprinted by Cornmarket Press (London: 1969), which has also issued (1969) a facsimile of KING JOHN, produced in 1745 as PAPAL TYRANNY IN THE REIGN OF KING JOHN. THE RIVAL QUEANS (1710) has been issued in facsimile with an introduction by William M. Peterson (Painesville, Ohio: Lake Erie College Studies no. 5, 1965). Scolar Press of London offers a facsimile of SHE WOULD AND SHE WOULD NOT (1702).

The best edition of Cibber's autobiography, AN APOLOGY FOR THE LIFE OF . . . (1740), is that of Robert W. Lowe, 2 vols. (London: Nimmo, 1889*); there is also a recent edition by Byrne R.S. Fone (Ann Arbor: Univ. of Michigan Press, 1969). The best biography is Richard H. Barker's MR. CIBBER OF DRURY LANE (New York: Columbia Univ. Press, 1939*); F. Dorothy Senior's THE LIFE AND TIMES OF COLLEY CIBBER (New York: Henkle, 1928) is inadequate. Frederick T. Wood, in "A Letter of Cibber," N&Q 191 (1946), 15, prints the letter from Cibber to his daughter in which he states he will disown her unless she gives up Charke; Fred S. Tupper, in "Colley and Caius Cibber," MLN 55 (1940), 393-96, adds some biographical material not in Barker. Cibber's quarrel with Pope is well covered by Charles D. Peavy, "The Pope-Cibber Controversy: A Bibliography," RECTR 3, no. 2 (1964), 51-55; see also Thomas B. Gilmore, Jr., "Colley Cibber's Good Nature and His Reaction to Pope's Satire," PLL 2 (1966), 361-71.

General studies include DeWitt C. Croissant, "Studies in the Work of Colley

Cibber," BUK 1 (1915), 1-69, originally published in 1912; Diederikus M.E. Habbema, AN APPRECIATION OF COLLEY CIBBER . . . (Amsterdam: Paris, 1928*), a perfunctory work which includes a reprint of THE CARELESS HUS-BAND; and Leonard R.N. Ashley, COLLEY CIBBER (New York: Twayne, 1965), recent but somewhat uneven. Frederick W. Bateson, in ENGLISH COMIC DRAMA (pp. 14-41), and Frederick S. Boas, in EIGHTEENTH-CEN-TURY DRAMA (pp. 86-100), give useful summaries. Cibber is also discussed in John C. Loftis's COMEDY AND SOCIETY FROM CONGREVE TO FIELDING and in all the studies of sentimental drama listed in Part 1, Section 7.15.

Specialized studies focus on individual plays. Harry Glicksman's "The Stage History of Colley Cibber's THE CARELESS HUSBAND," PMLA 36 (1921), 245-50, has been superseded by the material in THE LONDON STAGE. Reginald H. Griffith's "A 'Wildfrau Story' in a Cibber Play," PQ 12 (1933), 298-302, discusses this play as an exemplum of the motif. Frederick W. Bateson's arti-cle, "THE DOUBLE GALLANT of Colley Cibber," RES 1 (1925), 343-46, is devoted to the sources of the play (1707). Emmett L. Avery, in "Cibber, KING JOHN, and the Students of the Law," MLN 53 (1938), 272-75, discus-ses Cibber's attempt to pacify those who were attacking his as yet unacted play. Dougald MacMillan, in "The Text of LOVE'S LAST SHIFT," MLN 46 (1931), 518-19, discusses refinements in the 1721 edition of the play. Byrne R.S. Fone's article, "Colley Cibber's LOVE'S LAST SHIFT and Sentimental Comedy," RECTR 7, no. 1 (1968), 33-43, discusses the history and sources of the play; his later article, "LOVE'S LAST SHIFT and Sentimental Comedy," RECTR 9, no. 1 (1970), 11-23, attacks those who label plays as sentimental without adequately defining their terms. Paul E. Parnell, "An Incorrectly Attributed Speech-Prefix in LOVE'S LAST SHIFT," N&Q 204 (1959), 212-13, corrects the text of III.ii; in a more important article, "Equivocation in Cib-ber's LOVE'S LAST SHIFT," SP 57 (1960), 519-34, Parnell argues that the play resists classification because Cibber deliberately balances wit and senti-ment to appeal to two different segments of his audience. The Fone and Par-nell studies may be supplemented by Alan Roper's perceptive analysis in "Lan-guage and Action in THE WAY OF THE WORLD, LOVE'S LAST SHIFT, and THE RELAPSE," ELH 40 (1973), 44-69.

John Fuller's "Cibber, THE REHEARSAL AT GOATHAM, and the suppression of POLLY," RES 13 (1962), 125-34, relates LOVE IN A RIDDLE (1729) to the suppression of Gay's play. THE NON-JUROR (1717) has attracted considerable comment, beginning with such contemporary pieces as John D. Breval's A COMPLETE KEY . . . (1718). Dudley H. Miles, in "The Original of THE NON-JUROR," PMLA 30 (1915), 195-214, argues convincingly that Cibber's source was Medburne's translation of TARTUFFE (1670) and not the Molière play. Miles's other articles, "The Political Satire of THE NON-JUROR," MP 13 (1915), 281-304, and "A Forgotten Hit: THE NON-JUROR," SP 16 (1919), 66-77, deal with the contemporary impact and stage history of the play. Frederic C. White's "Pre-Malaprop Malapropisms," N&Q 179 (1940), 443-44, concerns the character Mawworm in this play. Cibber's adaptation of RICH-ARD III is analyzed in conventional terms by Richard Dohse in COLLEY CIB-BERS BUEHNENBEARBEITUNG VON SHAKESPEARES RICHARD III, BBA 2 (1899), 1-61; see also Arthur C. Sprague, "A New Scene in Colley Cibber's RICHARD III," MLN 42 (1927), 29-32; Albert E. Kalson, "The Chronicles in Cibber's

RICHARD III," SEL 3 (1963), 253–67; and Kalson's useful "Eighteenth-Century Editions of Colley Cibber's RICHARD III," RECTR 7, no. 1 (1968), 7–17. William Peterson's brief discussion, "Cibber's THE RIVAL QUEANS," N&Q 204 (1959), 164–68, is subsumed in his edition of the play, mentioned above. Peterson's article, "The Text of Cibber's SHE WOULD AND SHE WOULD NOT," MLN 71 (1956), 258–62, follows MacMillan's on LOVE'S LAST SHIFT, comparing the text of the first edition with that in the 1721 PLAYS; his "Cibber's SHE WOULD AND SHE WOULD NOT and Vanbrugh's AESOP," PQ 35 (1956), 429–35, argues that AESOP is one source of the Don Manuel-Octavio plot in Cibber's play. Several German dissertations (listed in Stratman's BIBLIOGRAPHICAL GUIDE) also discuss the sources and analogs of a number of the plays.

Cibber plays not mentioned above include WOMAN'S WIT (1696), XERXES (1699), LOVE MAKES A MAN (1700), THE SCHOOLBOY (1702, from WOMAN'S WIT), PEROLLA AND ISADORA (1705), THE COMICAL LOVERS and THE LADY'S LAST STAKE (1707), THE RIVAL FOOLS (1709), XIMENA (1712), MYRTILLO and VENUS AND ADONIS (1715), THE REFUSAL (1721), CAESAR IN EGYPT (1724), THE PROVOKED HUSBAND (1728, from Vanbrugh), and DAMON AND PHILLIDA (1729).

THEOPHILUS CIBBER (1703-58)

Colley Cibber's son was also an actor and manager, but a man of extravagant taste and rather disreputable habits. He is satirized in AN APOLOGY FOR THE LIFE OF MR. THEOPHILUS CIBBER, COMEDIAN . . . (1740). His acted plays include . . . KING HENRY VI and APOLLO AND DAPHNE (1723), PATIE AND PEGGY (1730, from THE GENTLE SHEPHERD), THE LOVER (1731), THE HARLOT'S PROGRESS (1733), and ROMEO AND JULIET (1744). The first and last are adaptations. Arthur H. Scouten, in "Theophilus Cibber's THE HUMOURISTS," N&Q 200 (1955), 114-15, discusses an adaptation of Shakespeare's 2 HENRY IV not previously attributed to Cibber.

CATHARINE [RAFTOR] CLIVE (1711-85)

Kitty Clive was the daughter of an Irish lawyer who fought for James II but was later pardoned and moved to London. Catharine was brought on the stage at seventeen by Colley Cibber and became a famous actress in comic roles. She married George Clive, a barrister, about 1733 and was active at Drury Lane from 1741 until her retirement in 1769. The best biography is still Percy Fitzgerald's THE LIFE OF MRS. CATHARINE CLIVE . . . (London: Reader, 1888*); see also P.J. Crean, "Kitty Clive," N&Q 174 (1938), 309-10, and THE CASE OF MRS. CLIVE SUBMITTED TO THE PUBLIC (1744). The latter has been reprinted in facsimile by the Augustan Reprint Society (Los Angeles: W.A. Clark Library, 1973).

Catharine Clive wrote a number of brief dramatic sketches, mostly farces. THE REHEARSAL (1750) was the first of them, followed by EVERY WOMAN IN HER HUMOUR (1760) and SKETCH OF A FINE LADY'S RETURN FROM A ROUT (1763). THE ISLAND OF SLAVES (1761, from Marivaux) is sometimes attributed to her. P.J. Crean, in "THE LONDON 'PRENTICE," N&Q 163 (1932), 346-47, argues persuasively for her authorship of this 1754 play. THE FAITHFUL IRISHWOMAN (1765) is probably hers as well; see Richard C. Frushell, "The Textual Relationship and Biographical Significance of Two Petite Pieces by Mrs. Catharine (Kitty) Clive," RECTR 9, no. 1 (1970), 51-58, which agrees with Crean in presenting the piece as a rewritten version of the SKETCH . . . of 1763. The only recent essay on Clive's plays is Frushell's "Kitty Clive as Dramatist," DUJ 32 (1971), 125-32, which focuses on THE REHEARSAL and EVERY WOMAN IN HER HUMOUR. See also his note, "The Cast of Kitty Clive's SKETCH OF A FINE LADY'S RETURN FROM A ROUT," N&Q 214 (1969), 350-51.

JAMES COBB (1756-1818)

Cobb joined the East India Company as a youth and rose to become its secretary in 1814. His first play was THE CONTRACT (1779); he went on to produce some two dozen others, most of them farces or comic operas. His first hit was THE HUMOURIST (1785); others include THE FIRST FLOOR (1787), THE DOCTOR AND THE APOTHECARY (1788), THE HAUNTED TOWER (1789), THE SIEGE OF BELGRADE (1791), THE PIRATES (1792), THE CHEROKEE (1794), and RAMAH DROOG (1798). THE STRANGERS AT HOME (1785), also fairly popular, was revised as THE ALGERINE SLAVE in 1792. Less successful plays include THE WEDDING NIGHT (1780), WHO'D HAVE THOUGHT IT? and KENSINGTON GARDENS (1781), HURLY-BURLY (1785, with Thomas King), ENGLISH READINGS (1787), LOVE IN THE EAST (1788), POOR OLD DRURY (1791), FORTUNE'S WHEEL (1793), THE SHEPHERDESS OF CHEAPSIDE (1796), and PAUL AND VIRGINIA (1800). Cobb's plays are mostly afterpieces--the farces in one or two acts, the comic operas in the customary three-act form.

CHARLES COFFEY (d. 1745)

Coffey wrote several ballad operas produced between 1729 and 1735, of which THE DEVIL TO PAY (1731, adapted from Jevon, in collaboration with John Mottley) was the most popular. He is discussed briefly in the standard works on the form (see under John Gay, below), by William J. Lawrence in "Early Irish Ballad Opera and Comic Opera," MQ 8 (1922), 397-412, and by Frederick S. Boas in EIGHTEENTH-CENTURY DRAMA, pp. 212-19. His other acted plays include THE BEGGAR'S WEDDING (2 versions, 1729), THE DEVIL UPON TWO STICKS and SOUTHWARK FAIR (1729), THE FEMALE PARSON (1730), THE BOARDING SCHOOL (1733), and THE MERRY COBBLER (1735). Except for the first, none was particularly successful and several were failures.

GEORGE COLMAN THE ELDER (1732-94)

THE DRAMATIC WORKS OF GEORGE COLMAN, 4 vols. (1777), omits several of Colman's adaptations and the eight or so plays produced after 1776. There is no later collected edition. THE HISTORY OF KING LEAR (1768) is available in facsimile (London: Cornmarket Press, 1969); THE JEALOUS WIFE (1761), ed. Allardyce Nicoll, was published by Oxford University Press in 1925. Colman's SOME PARTICULARS OF THE LIFE OF THE LATE GEORGE COLMAN, ESQ., WRITTEN BY HIMSELF (1795) mostly concerns the events of 1767. Much correspondence is included in Richard B. Peake's MEMOIRS OF THE COLMAN FAMILY . . ., 2 vols. (London: Bentley, 1841*); see also John D. Gordan's "New in the Berg Collection 1952-56," BNYPL 61 (1957), 303-11 and 353-63, which mentions letters by Garrick and Colman. The standard biography is Eugene R. Page's GEORGE COLMAN THE ELDER: ESSAYIST, DRAMATIST, AND THEATRICAL MANAGER, 1732-1794 (New York: Columbia Univ. Press, 1935), which may be supplemented by Coleman O. Parsons's "Francis and Mary Colman: Biographical Glimpses 1691-1767," N&Q 192 (1947), 288-93 and 310-14, and by Howard P. Vincent's "Christopher George Colman, 'Lunatic,'" RES 18 (1942), 38-48.

There is not nearly as much discussion of Colman's work as is merited by its quality and extent. Joseph M. Beatty, Jr., in "Garrick, Colman, and THE CLANDESTINE MARRIAGE," MLN 36 (1921), 129-41, argues that Colman contributed the basic characterization and most of the important characters, as well as most details of plot in acts 1-4; Garrick provided some of act 4 and all of act 5; see also the Bergmann article listed under David Garrick, below. William Scott suggests that Colman used a contemporary library catalog for the list of novels mentioned in POLLY HONEYCOMBE (1760), in "George Colman's POLLY HONEYCOMBE and Circulating Library Fiction in 1760," N&Q 213 (1968), 465-67. Kathleen M. Lynch, in "PAMELA NUBILE, L'ECOSSAISE, and THE ENGLISH MERCHANT," MLN 47 (1932), 94-96, argues that Colman used Goldoni's play or an English translation of it. Arthur J. Harris's "Garrick, Colman, and KING LEAR: A Reconsideration," ShQ 22 (1971), 57-66, argues convincingly that it was Colman's 1768 adaptation rather than Garrick's (printed 1773) which restored much of Shakespeare's text. For THE FAIRY TALE (1763), see George W. Stone, Jr.'s article on A MIDSUMMER NIGHT'S DREAM, listed under Garrick, below.

Colman produced many plays altered or adapted from both English and continental playwights. These include, in addition to KING LEAR and THE FAIRY TALE, PHILASTER (1763, from Beaumont and Fletcher), THE ENGLISH MERCHANT (1767, from Voltaire), THE PORTRAIT (1770, from Anseaume), THE FAIRY PRINCE (1771, from Jonson), COMUS (1773, from Milton), ACHILLES IN PETTICOATS (1773, from Gay), EPICOENE (1776, from Jonson), POLLY (1777, from Gay), THE SHEEP SHEARING (1777, from A WINTER'S TALE), THE SPANISH BARBER (1777, from Beaumarchais), THE FEMALE CHEVALIER (1778, from Taverner), BONDUCA (1778, from Beaumont and Fletcher), FATAL CURIOSITY (1782, from Lillo), TIT FOR TAT (1786 [1785 in Dublin], from Joseph Atkinson and Marivaux), and THE VILLAGE LAWYER (from de Brueys).

A number of other pieces are one-act preludes or afterpieces: AN OCCASIONAL PRELUDE (1772), THE MANAGER IN DISTRESS and THE GENIUS OF NONSENSE (1780), A PRELUDIO (to THE BEGGAR'S OPERA) and MEDEA AND JASON (both 1781, perhaps not by Colman), HARLEQUIN TEAGUE (1782, with O'Keeffe), and UT PICTURA POESIS (1789). Longer pieces include, in addition to those mentioned above, THE MUSICAL LADY (1762), THE DEUCE IS IN HIM (1763), THE OXONIAN IN TOWN (1767), MAN AND WIFE (1769), MOTHER SHIPTON (1770, with Arnold), THE MAN OF BUSINESS (1774), THE SPLEEN (1776), THE SUICIDE (1778), THE SEPARATE MAINTENANCE (1779), and THE ELECTION OF THE MANAGERS (1784).

GEORGE COLMAN THE YOUNGER (1762-1836)

The only collected edition of the younger Colman's plays is THE DRAMATIC
WORKS OF GEORGE COLMAN THE YOUNGER, with a biography by J.W.
Lake, 4 vols. (Paris: Malepeyre, 1823-24; Baudry, 1827), which includes
only eight plays. While the plays appear frequently in contemporary collec-
tions, the only modern edition is Michael R. Booth's of THE IRON CHEST
(1796) in the World's Classics volume, EIGHTEENTH-CENTURY TRAGEDY.
Colman's RANDOM RECORDS . . ., 2 vols. (London: Bentley, 1830), is an
autobiography to about 1790. The only good biography is Jeremy F. Bagster-
Collins, GEORGE COLMAN THE YOUNGER 1762-1836 (New York: King's
Crown Press, 1946); see also Howard P. Vincent's "George Colman the Younger:
'Adopted Son,'" PQ 15 (1936), 219-20, and Hubert C. Heffner, "The Haymarket Theatre under Colman the Younger 1789-1805," SM 10 (1943), 23-29; and
Peter Thomson, "The Early Career of George Colman the Younger," ESSAYS
ON NINETEENTH-CENTURY BRITISH THEATRE, ed. Kenneth Richards and
Peter Thomson (London: Methuen, 1971), pp. 67-82. Laurence M. Price, in
his INKLE AND YARICO ALBUM (Berkeley and Los Angeles: Univ. of California Press, 1937), devotes several pages to Colman's version of the story
(1787).

The best known of Colman's pre-1800 plays include, in addition to INKLE
AND YARICO and THE IRON CHEST, WAYS AND MEANS (1788), THE BAT-
TLE OF HEXHAM (1789), THE SURRENDER OF CALAIS (1791), THE MOUN-
TAINEERS (1793), NEW HAY AT THE OLD MARKET (1795, but more popular
when excerpted as SYLVESTER DAGGERWOOD [1796]), THE HEIR AT LAW
(1797), and BLUEBEARD (1798, from Sedaine). Other works include THE FE-
MALE DRAMATIST (1782), TWO TO ONE (1784), TURK AND NO TURK
(1785), THE FAMILY PARTY (1789, ascribed to Colman), POOR OLD HAY-
MARKET (1792), MY NIGHTGOWN AND SLIPPERS (1797), BLUE DEVILS
(1798, from Patrat), FEUDAL TIMES (1799), and THE REVIEW (1800). Nineteenth-century pieces include THE POOR GENTLEMAN (1801), JOHN BULL
(1803), LOVE LAUGHS AT LOCKSMITHS (1803, from Bouilly), THE GAY DE-
CEIVERS (1804, from Hell), WHO WANTS A GUINEA? (1805), WE FLY BY
NIGHT (1806), THE AFRICANS (1808), and several other farces and entertainments.

WILLIAM CONGREVE (1670-1729)

There is as yet no complete bibliography of Congreve. THE JOHN C. HODGES COLLECTION OF WILLIAM CONGREVE IN THE UNIVERSITY OF TENNESSEE LIBRARY: A BIBLIOGRAPHICAL CATALOG, ed. Albert M. Lyles and John Dobson (Knoxville: Univ. of Tennessee Libraries, 1970), is useful but not complete. Zoltán Haraszti, in "Early Editions of Congreve's Plays," MB 9 (1934), 81-95, considers only Boston Public Library holdings. Laurence Bartlett, "Bibliography for William Congreve and Restoration Comedy," RECTR 10, no. 2 (1971), 41-43, supplements the listing in Stratman (see Part 1, Section 1.10).

THE WORKS OF MR. WILLIAM CONGREVE was first published in three volumes in 1710; Avery notes that the 1774 edition (2 vols.) contains a revised text of the plays. THE COMPLETE WORKS OF WILLIAM CONGREVE, ed. Montague Summers (London: Nonesuch Press, 1923*), is a typical Summers production--lavish, expansively annotated, and textually unreliable. Frederick W. Bateson's edition, THE WORKS OF CONGREVE (London: Davies, 1930), is better, but an edition that might fairly be called definitive has not yet appeared. There have been many editions of the plays and comedies, beginning with the DRAMATIC WORKS, 2 vols. (1773), and including Leigh Hunt's edition of 1840. The Mermaid edition, ed. Alexander C. Ewald (London: Vizetelly, 1887), includes five plays and is still in print. The comedies were edited by George S. Street, 2 vols. (London: Methuen, 1895); by Bonamy Dobrée (Oxford: Oxford Univ. Press, 1925); and by Joseph W. Krutch (New York: Macmillan, 1927). Dobrée also edited THE MOURNING BRIDE, POEMS, AND MISCELLANIES, BY WILLIAM CONGREVE (Oxford: Oxford Univ. Press, 1928). The two Dobrée volumes, included in the World's Classics series, are still useful, as is the Bateson WORKS. THE COMPLETE PLAYS OF WILLIAM CONGREVE, ed. Herbert Davis (Chicago: Univ. of Chicago Press, 1967), is perhaps the best available edition of the plays. David D. Mann has published A CONCORDANCE TO THE PLAYS OF WILLIAM CONGREVE (Ithaca, N.Y.: Cornell Univ. Press, 1973) based on the Davis edition.

There are many editions of the two popular comedies; all four plays are available in facsimile from Scolar Press of London. The best editions of LOVE FOR LOVE are Emmett L. Avery's for the Regents Restoration series (Lincoln: Univ. of Nebraska Press, 1966), Alexander N. Jeffares's for Macmillan's English

Classics (London: Macmillan, 1967), and Malcolm M. Kelsall's for the New Mermaid series (London: Benn, 1969). THE WAY OF THE WORLD has been edited by Kathleen M. Lynch for the Regents series (Lincoln: Univ. of Nebraska Press, 1965), by Alexander N. Jeffares (with INCOGNITA) for Arnold's English Texts (London: Arnold, 1966), by Brian Gibbon for the New Mermaid series (London: Benn, 1971), and by John Barnard for the Fountainwell series (Edinburgh: Oliver & Boyd, 1972).

Earlier collections of Congreve's letters have been replaced by WILLIAM CONGREVE: LETTERS AND DOCUMENTS, ed. John C. Hodges (New York: Harcourt, Brace, World, 1964). Hodges's THE LIBRARY OF WILLIAM CONGREVE (New York: New York Public Library, 1955) is also standard. Edmund Gosse's A LIFE OF WILLIAM CONGREVE (London: W. Scott, 1888; rev. ed. 1924*), though well written, is not very satisfactory; D. Crane Taylor's WILLIAM CONGREVE (Oxford: Oxford Univ. Press, 1931*) is superior. The standard biography is John C. Hodges's WILLIAM CONGREVE THE MAN: A BIOGRAPHY FROM NEW SOURCES (New York: Modern Language Association, 1941). Kathleen M. Lynch, in A CONGREVE GALLERY (Cambridge, Mass.: Harvard Univ. Press, 1951*), adds a set of studies of Congreve and his friends; see also her article, "References to Congreve in the Evelyn Manuscripts," PQ 32 (1953), 337-40. Robert G. Howarth, in "Congreve and Ann Bracegirdle," ESA 4 (1961), 159-61, challenges Hodges's account of this relationship; J.P. W. Rogers, in "Congreve's First Biographer: The Identity of 'Charles Wilson,'" MLQ 31 (1970), 330-44, challenges the ascription of this work to Oldmixon.

Early estimates of Congreve's work may be found in Samuel Johnson's LIVES OF THE POETS, Thomas Davies's DRAMATIC MISCELLANIES, William Hazlitt's LECTURES ON THE ENGLISH COMIC WRITERS (1819), Leigh Hunt's introduction to his edition of Restoration dramatists (1840), and in Macaulay's famous review of that work ER 72 (1841), 490-528. Congreve's comedies are discussed by every modern student of Restoration comedy, beginning with John L. Palmer in 1913, and including especially Bonamy Dobrée (RESTORATION COMEDY, 1924), Kathleen M. Lynch (SOCIAL MODE, 1926), Thomas H. Fujimura (1952), Norman N. Holland (1959), and Virginia O. Birdsall (1970). (See Part 1, Sections 7.8 and 7.10.) Other assessments include Henry S. Canby's "William Congreve as a Dramatist," SR 21 (1913), 421-27, and "Congreve as a Romanticist," PMLA 31 (1916), 1-23; Dragosh Protopopesco's UNE CLASSIQUE MODERNE: WILLIAM CONGREVE . . . (Paris: Editions "la Vie universitaire," 1924); Lytton Strachey's encomium in "Congreve, Collier, Macaulay, and Mr. Summers," PORTRAITS IN MINIATURE AND OTHER ESSAYS (London: Chatto & Windus, 1931), pp. 41-49; and Virginia Woolf's appreciation, "Congreve's Comedies: Speed, Stillness, and Meaning," TLS, 25 Sept. 1937, pp. 681-82, reprinted in her COLLECTED ESSAYS (New York: Harcourt, Brace, World, 1967), I, 76-84.

More recent studies include Clifford Leech's article, "Congreve and the Century's End," PQ 41 (1962), 275-93, which stresses Congreve's seriousness and feeling, and Kenneth Muir's essay, "The Comedies of William Congreve," BROWN COLLECTION, pp. 220-37. William Van Voris, in THE CULTIVATED STANCE: THE DESIGNS OF CONGREVE'S PLAYS (London: Oxford

William Congreve

Univ. Press, 1965), presents Congreve as a witty and elegant hedonist; Van Voris's analyses are uneven, but those of THE MOURNING BRIDE and THE WAY OF THE WORLD are provocative. Maximillian E. Novak's two articles, "The Clergyman and the Artist: Collier, Congreve, and the World of the Play," CE 30 (1969), 555-61, and "Love, Scandal, and the Moral Milieu of Congreve's Comedies," CONGREVE CONSIDERED . . . (Los Angeles: W.A. Clark Library, 1971), pp. 23-50, are good general studies; his WILLIAM CONGREVE (New York: Twayne, 1971) is one of the best in the English Authors series and has a useful annotated bibliography. An initial chapter offering a succinct overview of Congreve's life and milieu is followed by a discussion of each play and a brief conclusion. The most recent book on the dramatist is WILLIAM CONGREVE (London: Benn, 1972), a collection of critical essays edited by Brian Morris. The nine papers included were presented at the third York Symposium in 1970, and together give a current view of Congreve's work. George Parfitt's contribution, "The Case against Congreve," is less satisfying than Reginald A. Foakes's "Wit and Convention in Congreve's Comedies," pp. 55-71; William Myers's "Plot and Meaning in Congreve's Comedies" is better still (pp. 73-92). Malcolm M. Kelsall's paper, "Those Dying Generations," pp. 113-29, is a perceptive discussion of Congreve's treatment of age. Kenneth Muir's "Congreve on the Modern Stage," pp. 131-54, discusses twentieth-century British performances; Gareth L. Evans's "Congreve's Sense of Theatre," pp. 155-69, analyzes Congreve's ability to combine literary excellence with dramatic realization of his materials.

More specialized studies include Rose Snider's SATIRE IN THE COMEDIES OF CONGREVE, SHERIDAN, WILDE, AND COWARD (Orono: Univ. of Maine Studies, 1937); Emmett L. Avery's excellent book, CONGREVE'S PLAYS ON THE EIGHTEENTH-CENTURY STAGE (New York: Modern Language Association, 1951); Darwin T. Turner's "The Servant in the Comedies of William Congreve," CLAJ 1 (1958), 68-74; and Aubrey Williams's unconvincing argument, in "Poetical Justice, the Contrivances of Providence, and the Works of William Congreve," ELH 25 (1968), 540-65, that Congreve's comedies illustrate providential order operating in human events.

In "The Date of THE OLD BACHELOR," TLS, 13 June 1936, p. 500, Robert G. Howarth argues for early 1689 as the date of composition; his thesis was picked up and added to by Hodges in "The Composition of Congreve's First Play," PMLA 58 (1943), 971-76, an article to which Howarth responded (61 [1946], 596-97). Anthony Kaufman, in "A Possible Allusion to the Death of Mountfort in Congreve's THE OLD BACHELOR," N&Q 217 (1972), 463-64, suggests Wittol and Bluffe might have suggested Richard Hill and Lord Mohun to contemporary audiences; Bert C. Bach, "Congreve's Gulliver: The Character of Vainlove in THE OLD BACHELOR," BSF 9, no. 2 (1968), 70-75, makes a rather strained comparison. Substantial critical essays on the play include Maximillian Novak's "Congreve's THE OLD BACHELOR: From Formula to Art," EC 20 (1970), 182-99, and Brian Gibbons's fine article in the Morris collection, "Congreve's THE OLD BACHELOR and Jonsonian Comedy," pp. 1-20.

THE DOUBLE-DEALER, Congreve's second play, is the subject of John Barnard's contribution to the Morris collection, titled "Passion, 'Poetical Justice,' and

Dramatic Law in THE DOUBLE-DEALER and THE WAY OF THE WORLD," pp. 93-112, and of Anthony Gosse's interesting attempt at rehabilitation, "Plot and Character in Congreve's DOUBLE-DEALER," MLQ 29 (1968), 274-88. Brian Corman, in "'The Mixed Way of Comedy': Congreve's THE DOUBLE-DEALER," MP 71 (1974), 356-65, analyzes the play as a conscious if unsuccessful attempt to fuse the punitive comedy of Jonson with the Fletcherian comedy of wit seen in the work of Dryden and Etherege. In a bibliographical note, "The Cancel Leaf in Congreve's DOUBLE-DEALER (1694)," PBSA 43 (1949), 78-82, Fredson T. Bowers shows that G1 of the first edition was a cancel.

Specialized articles on LOVE FOR LOVE include Anthony Gosse, "The Omitted Scene in Congreve's LOVE FOR LOVE," MP 61 (1963), 40-42 (scene 11); John C. Hodges, "The Ballad in Congreve's LOVE FOR LOVE," PMLA 48 (1933), 953-54; Arthur W. Hoffman, "Congreve's LOVE FOR LOVE, II.i.171-259," Exp 28 (1970), item 72; Edward T. Norris, "A Possible Origin of Congreve's Sailor Ben," MLN 49 (1934), 334-35 (in Ravenscroft); and Barry N. Olshen, "Early Nineteenth-Century Revisions of LOVE FOR LOVE," TN 24 (1970), 160-75. Perhaps the best article on the play is Charles R. Lyons, "Congreve's Miracle of Love," CRITICISM 6 (1964), 331-48. Ben R. Schneider, Jr.'s analysis of the play in THE ETHOS OF RESTORATION COMEDY and Harriett Hawkins's in LIKENESSES OF TRUTH IN ELIZABETHAN AND RESTORATION DRAMA are also very rewarding. See, in addition, F.P. Jarvis, "The Philosophical Assumptions of Congreve's LOVE FOR LOVE," TSLL 14 (1972), 423-34, and Aubrey Williams, "The 'Utmost Trial' of Virtue and Congreve's LOVE FOR LOVE," TSL 17 (1972), 1-18.

Congreve's one tragedy was performed more than two hundred times between 1702 and 1776, as Emmett L. Avery shows in "The Popularity of THE MOURNING BRIDE in the London Theatres in the Eighteenth Century," RSW 9 (1941), 115-16. In another article, "The Première of THE MOURNING BRIDE," MLN 57 (1942), 55-57, Avery shows that the play was first performed on 20 February 1696/97. S.W. Brossman, "Dryden's Cassandra and Congreve's Zara," N&Q 201 (1956), 102-03, suggests the influence of CLEOMENES; James P.W. Crawford, "On the Relation of Congreve's MOURNING BRIDE to Racine's BAJAZET," MLN 19 (1904), 193-94, exaggerates Congreve's use of the French play. More general studies include Francis Gentleman's analysis in THE DRAMATIC CENSOR (1770); Bonamy Dobrée's in RESTORATION TRAGEDY; Elmer B. Potter's depreciation "The Paradox of Congreve's MOURNING BRIDE," PMLA 58 (1943), 977-1001, and the response to this article by Thomas R. Carper, "Congreve's Popular Tragedy," THOTH 12, no. 1 (1971), 3-10; and Eric Rothstein's interesting analysis of the play in RESTORATION TRAGEDY. Aubrey Williams's recent study, "The 'Just Decrees of Heaven' and Congreve's MOURNING BRIDE," CONGREVE CONSIDERED . . . (Los Angeles: W.A. Clark Library, 1971), pp. 1-22, uses the play as an example of Congreve's insistence on a providentially governed universe in his works, a thesis which seems quite forced.

THE WAY OF THE WORLD is generally considered to be the finest Restoration comedy and has naturally been the subject of extensive criticism. The relevant

sections in John L. Palmer, Kathleen M. Lynch, and Bonamy Dobrée's RES-
TORATION COMEDY are worth reading but not in a class with the detailed
analyses of Thomas H. Fujimura and Norman N. Holland, however oversophis-
ticated these may be. (See Part 1, Sections 7.8 and 7.10.) John H. Wilson's brief discussion in his PREFACE TO RESTORATION DRAMA is good; there
are also full analyses in Virginia O. Birdsall's WILD CIVILITY, in Ian Donald-
son's WORLD UPSIDE-DOWN (1970), and in Harriett Hawkins's LIKENESSES OF
TRUTH. Arnold N. Kaul's remarks on the play in THE ACTION OF ENGLISH
COMEDY (1970) may be set against Martin Price's perceptive comments in TO
THE PALACE OF WISDOM (1964) and against Alan Roper's in "Language and
Action in THE WAY OF THE WORLD, LOVE'S LAST SHIFT, and THE RELAPSE,"
ELH 40 (1973), 44-69. The monograph, A NEW VIEW OF CONGREVE'S
'WAY OF THE WORLD,' by Paul and Miriam Mueschke (Ann Arbor: Univ.
of Michigan Press, 1958), offers a balanced and sensitive discussion of the
play; so does the briefer analysis in Cleanth Brooks and Robert B. Heilman's
UNDERSTANDING DRAMA (New York: Holt, 1948). The Mueschkes' study
places Congreve in the moral tradition of Jonsonian comedy, a view attacked
by Paul T. Nolan in "THE WAY OF THE WORLD: Congreve's Moment of
Truth," SPJ 25 (1959), 75-95. Nolan stresses the artifice of the play rather
than its morality; his view is further developed in "Congreve's Lovers: Art and
the Critic," DS 1 (1962), 330-39. Jean E. Gagen's perceptive article, "Congreve's Mirabell and the Ideal of the Gentleman," PMLA 79 (1964), 422-27,
takes the Mueschkes, Fujimura, Holland, and others to task for positing Mirabell's reformation or need for reformation in the play; she argues convincingly
that he already represents the contemporary ideal. Paul J. Hurley, in "Law
and the Dramatic Rhetoric of THE WAY OF THE WORLD," SAQ 70 (1971),
191-202, discusses the legal imagery and legal framework of the play as Congreve's strategy for involving his audience in the action. In "Disguise, Identity, and Personal Value in THE WAY OF THE WORLD," ETJ 23 (1971), 258-
68, Charles R. Lyons analyzes the comic movement of the play from confusion
and concealment of feeling to clarity and the open expression of emotion.
David S. Zeidberg's "Fainall and Marwood: Vicious Characters and the Limits
of Comedy," THOTH 12, no. 1 (1971), 33-38, perhaps overstresses the suffer-
ing of the two, but makes the point that the essential difference between the
protagonists and the blocking characters is that the former act to unify their
world by integrating social and personal values. Both Philip Roberts's "Mirabell
and Restoration Comedy" and John Barnard's "Passion, 'Poetical Justice,' and
Dramatic Law in THE DOUBLE-DEALER and THE WAY OF THE WORLD" (referred to above) are useful essays in the Morris collection; H. Teyssandier's "Congreve's WAY OF THE WORLD: Decorum and Morality," ES 52 (1971), 124-
31, is rather slight.

More specialized articles on the play include E. Millicent Pool's "A Possible
Source of THE WAY OF THE WORLD," MLR 33 (1938), 258-60, which confuses analogs with sources; M.J. O'Regan's "Two Notes on French Reminiscences in Restoration Comedy," HERMATHENA 93 (1959), 63-70, which suggests
parallels between Corneille's LE BARON D'ALBIKRAC and Congreve's play;
Mary Wagoner's "The Gambling Analogy in THE WAY OF THE WORLD," TSL
13 (1968), 75-80 (imagery in the play paralleling sex and gambling); and
Robert D. Hume's "A Revival of THE WAY OF THE WORLD in December 1701
or January 1702," TN 26 (1971), 30-36, which discusses a production not

listed in THE LONDON STAGE.

SEMELE, Congreve's unjustly neglected opera, is discussed in several of the
sources listed in Part 1, Section 7.19, and in two good articles by Stoddard
Lincoln, "The First Setting of Congreve's SEMELE," ML 44 (1963), 103–17,
and "Eccles and Congreve: Music and Drama on the Restoration Stage," TN
18 (1963), 7–18.

SQUIRE TRELOOBY, an adaptation of Molière presented at Lincoln's Inn Fields
in the spring of 1704, was by Congreve, Vanbrugh, and Walsh. A printed
SQUIRE TRELOOBY, published a few weeks later, was by Ozell. Another
translation, SQUIRE LUBBERLY (1732), was followed by THE CORNISH SQUIRE
(1734), which James Ralph asserted to be substantially the same text used in
the original production. John C. Hodges, in "The Authorship of SQUIRE TRE-
LOOBY," RES 4 (1928), 404–13, argued that Ralph put the 1734 piece together
and palmed it off as by Congreve, Vanbrugh, and Walsh. His view was disputed by John B. Shipley in "The Authorship of THE CORNISH SQUIRE," PQ
47 (1968), 145–56, but upheld by Graham D. Harley in "SQUIRE TRELOOBY
and THE CORNISH SQUIRE: A Reconsideration," PQ 49 (1970), 520–29.
Harley shows that these two pieces are closely related, and also that SQUIRE
LUBBERLY and THE CORNISH SQUIRE have material in common that is not in
SQUIRE TRELOOBY; there is no evidence that any extant text represents that
of the original 1704 production. For the possible but conjectural relation of
SQUIRE TRELOOBY to THE GORDIAN KNOT UNTIED, see the exchange between Dennis Arundell and William J. Lawrence in TLS, 4 June 1925, pp.
384, 400, and 416.

THOMAS COOKE (1703-56)

"Hesiod" Cooke, a hack writer and translator of the classics, wrote four miscellaneous pieces for the stage. They are: PENELOPE (1728, in collaboration
with John Mottley), THE TRIUMPHS OF LOVE AND HONOR (1731), THE
EUNUCH (1737, from Terence), and LOVE THE CAUSE AND CURE OF GRIEF
(1743, published in 1739 as THE MOURNFUL NUPTIALS). None of them was
especially successful; there are no modern editions and only infrequent references in the standard histories.

HANNAH [PARKHOUSE] COWLEY (1743-1809)

THE WORKS OF MRS. COWLEY: POEMS AND DRAMAS, 3 vols. (London: Wilkie & Robinson, 1813), includes a biography and all of the plays except THE SCHOOL FOR ELOQUENCE (1780) and THE WORLD AS IT GOES (1781). Cowley's best comedies were often reprinted in contemporary collections, but there are no modern editions. There were acting editions of THE BELLE'S STRATAGEM (1780) throughout the nineteenth century, but no satisfactory text has yet appeared. Scattered references to Hannah Cowley appear in the standard histories; see also an article, "The Belle's Stratagem," RES 5 (1929), 129-42, by Raymond C. Rhodes. J.E. Norton's bibliography in "Some Uncollected Authors 16: Hannah Cowley 1743-1809," BC 7 (1958), 68-76, was corrected by William B. Todd in "Hannah Cowley: Re-impressions, Not Reissues," BC 7 (1958), 301.

Major plays not mentioned above include THE RUNAWAY (1776), WHO'S THE DUPE? and ALBINA, COUNTESS RAIMOND (1779), WHICH IS THE MAN? (1782), A BOLD STROKE FOR A HUSBAND and MORE WAYS THAN ONE (1783), A SCHOOL FOR GREYBEARDS (1786, from Aphra Behn's LUCKY CHANCE), THE FATE OF SPARTA (1788), A DAY IN TURKEY (1791), and THE TOWN BEFORE YOU (1794).

JOHN CARTWRIGHT CROSS (d. c.1810)

Cross was an actor-dramatist who about 1796 became manager of the Royal Circus in Southwark. He was an active playwright in the "spectacle theatre" for a decade and a half after 1793, specializing in the shorter musical forms: farces, ballet-pantomimes, one-act interludes, and melodramas. Plays by Cross produced in London in the period include A DIVERTISEMENT (1790, a framework for Dibdin songs); THE PURSE, BRITISH FORTITUDE AND HIBERNIAN FRIENDSHIP, and THE APPARITION (all 1794); THE WAY TO GET UNMARRIED, THE POINT AT HERQUI, and THE CHARITY BOY (all 1796); THE SURRENDER OF TRINIDAD, AN ESCAPE INTO PRISON (from Elizabeth Inchbald's HUE AND CRY), THE ROUND TOWER, and HARLEQUIN AND QUIXOTE (all 1797); JOAN OF ARC, HARLEQUIN'S RETURN, THE RAFT, THEY'VE BIT THE OLD ONE, and THE GENOESE PIRATE (all 1798). NAPLES BAY and THE NEW DIVERTISEMENT (both 1794) are also attributed to Cross. Numerous other pieces were produced at Sadler's Wells and at the Royal Circus.

PARNASSIAN BAGATELLES . . . (1796) includes THE WAY TO GET UNMARRIED and THE VILLAGE DOCTOR (1796). CIRCUSIANA . . ., 2 vols. (London: Lackington, Allen, 1809), reprinted as THE DRAMATIC WORKS OF J. C. CROSS (London: T. Tegg, 1812), contains THE ROUND TOWER, THE GENOESE PIRATE (Blackbeard), CORA (1799), JULIA OF LOUVAIN (1797), and a number of Cross's many nineteenth-century pieces.

132

JOHN CROWNE (d. 1703)

George P. Winship gives a bibliography of early editions of Crowne's plays in THE FIRST HARVARD PLAYWRIGHT: A BIBLIOGRAPHY OF THE RESTORATION DRAMATIST JOHN CROWNE . . . (Cambridge, Mass: Harvard Univ. Press for E.H. Wells of New York, 1922). THE DRAMATIC WORKS OF JOHN CROWNE, ed. James Maidment and William H. Logan, 4 vols. (Edinburgh, 1873-74*), includes a brief memoir and notes but omits three plays. CITY POLITICS (1683), ed. John H. Wilson, is available in the Regents Restoration Drama series (Lincoln: Univ. of Nebraska Press, 1967). Part 1 of THE DE-STRUCTION OF JERUSALEM BY TITUS VESPASIAN (1677) is included in Bonamy Dobrée's FIVE HEROIC PLAYS. SIR COURTLY NICE (1685), is included in Volume 2 of Alexander N. Jeffares's RESTORATION COMEDY and in Montague Summers's RESTORATION COMEDIES and has been edited by Charlotte B. Hughes in Mouton's Studies in English Literature series (The Hague, 1966). The Hughes edition includes a biography and useful notes on the source and stage history of the play. Both HENRY THE SIXTH (1681) and THE MISERY OF CIVIL WAR (c.1680) have been issued in facsimile by Cornmarket Press (London, 1969).

The only full-scale study of Crowne is Arthur F. White's JOHN CROWNE: HIS LIFE AND DRAMATIC WORKS (Cleveland, Ohio: Western Reserve Univ. Press, 1922). Adolphus W. Ward's essay, "Crowne's Place in Restoration Comedy," REPRESENTATIVE ENGLISH COMEDIES 4, 241-55, may also be consulted. A detailed study of a production of CALISTO (1675) is included in Eleanore Boswell's THE RESTORATION COURT STAGE (1932). The exchange between William M. Peterson and David S. Berkeley, "Sentiment in Crowne's THE MARRIED BEAU, N&Q 198 (1953), 483-85, and 199 (1954), 179, is not productive. Hazelton Spencer, in "A Caveat on Restoration Play Quartos," RES 6 (1930), 315-16, notes that the 1681 quarto of THE MISERY OF CIVIL WAR, labeled "second edition," is merely a reissue of Q1 (1680). Patricia M. Seward, in "An Additional Source for John Crowne's SIR COURTLY NICE," MLR 67 (1972), 486-89, argues persuasively for the influence of Moreto's EL LINDO DON DIEGO on the play.

Plays not mentioned above include JULIANA (1671), THE HISTORY OF CHARLES THE EIGHTH OF FRANCE (c.1671), ANDROMACHE (1674), THE COUNTRY WIT (1676), THE AMBITIOUS STATESMAN (1679), THYESTES (c.1680), DARIUS,

KING OF PERSIA (1688), THE ENGLISH FRIAR (1690), REGULUS (1692), CALIGULA (1698), and JUSTICE BUSY (c.1699).

RICHARD CUMBERLAND (1732-1811)

THE POSTHUMOUS DRAMATIC WORKS OF THE LATE RICHARD CUMBERLAND, 2 vols. (London: G. and W. Nicol, 1813), includes most of the previously published plays but omits several plays produced during Cumberland's long career. The more popular plays were frequently reprinted in contemporary collections; Elizabeth Inchbald's BRITISH THEATRE, for example, includes nine of them. THE WEST INDIAN (1771) is included in the Nettleton, Case and Stone anthology and in several other modern collections; TIMON OF ATHENS (1771) is available in facsimile (London: Cornmarket Press, 1969). A good modern edition of Cumberland's best plays is long overdue.

THE MEMOIRS OF RICHARD CUMBERLAND, WRITTEN BY HIMSELF . . ., 2 vols. (London: Lackington, Allen, 1806-07), was edited by Henry Flanders (Philadelphia: Parry & McMillan, 1856*). William Mudford's THE LIFE OF RICHARD CUMBERLAND, ESQ. . . . (London: Sherwood et al. 1812; rev. ed., 2 vols., 1812) is generally unsympathetic to its subject; Louis I. Newman's RICHARD CUMBERLAND, CRITIC AND FRIEND OF THE JEWS (New York: Bloch Publishing Co., 1919) is perhaps overly sympathetic. The only satisfactory account aside from the brief discussions in the standard histories is Stanley T. Williams's RICHARD CUMBERLAND: HIS LIFE AND DRAMATIC WORKS (New Haven: Yale Univ. Press, 1917), which includes a good bibliography. J. Homer Caskey adds new information in "Richard Cumberland's Mission in Spain," PQ 9 (1930), 82-86, as does Richard J. Dircks in "Richard Cumberland's Political Associations," SBT 11 (1970), 1555-70. Cumberland is discussed in Frederick S. Boas's EIGHTEENTH-CENTURY DRAMA, and in Ernest Bernbaum's and Arthur Sherbo's books on sentimental drama (Part 1, Section 7.15). Williams discussed the major plays in "The Early Sentimental Dramas of Richard Cumberland" and "The Dramas of Richard Cumberland, 1779-1785," MLN 36 (1921), 160-65 and 403-08, but these add nothing to his book.

Specialized studies include William B. Todd, "Press Figures and Book Reviews as Determinants of Priority: A Study of Home's DOUGLAS (1757) and Cumberland's THE BROTHERS (1770)," PSBA 45 (1951), 72-76; the notes by Ifan K. Fletcher, William Van Lennep, and Sybil M. Rosenfeld concerning THE PRINCESS OF PARMA (TLS, 15 March 1934, p. 187; 24 Oct. 1936, p. 863; 26 April 1938, p. 264), which establish 1774 as the date of production of this play; and several studies of THE WEST INDIAN. Of these last, Joseph W.

Donahue, Jr.'s account in DRAMATIC CHARACTER IN THE ENGLISH ROMAN-TIC AGE (1970) is the best (he also discusses THE CARMELITE), but Wylie Sypher's "The West-Indian as a 'Character' in the Eighteenth Century," SP 36 (1939), 503-20, and Robert J. Detisch's "The Synthesis of Laughing and Senti-mental Comedy in THE WEST INDIAN," ETJ 22 (1970), 291-300, may also be consulted. Stanley T. Williams's "Richard Cumberland's WEST INDIAN," MLN 35 (1920), 413-17, attests the play's contemporary popularity.

Cumberland's best known plays include, in addition to those mentioned above, THE FASHIONABLE LOVER (1772), THE CHOLERIC MAN (1774), THE MYS-TERIOUS HUSBAND (1783), THE NATURAL SON (1784), THE JEW (1794), THE WHEEL OF FORTUNE and FIRST LOVE (1795), and FALSE IMPRESSIONS (1797). Among pieces produced in the nineteenth century are the comedies LOVERS' RESOLUTIONS (1802), THE SAILOR'S DAUGHTER (1804), A HINT TO HUSBANDS (1806), and THE WIDOW'S ONLY SON (1810).

JAMES DANCE (1722-74)

Dance, who took the stage name James Love, was the son of the London city surveyor and architect George Dance. He attended Oxford but left without a degree and soon became a comic actor at Dublin and Edinburgh. He came to Drury Lane about 1762. His plays include PAMELA (1741, from Richardson's novel), THE WITCHES (1762), THE RITES OF HECATE (1763), THE HERMIT (1766), THE VILLAGE WEDDING (1767), TIMON OF ATHENS (1768, from Shakespeare and Shadwell), THE LADIES' FROLIC (1770, from Brome), and RULE A WIFE AND HAVE A WIFE (1777, from Beaumont and Fletcher, rev. by John P. Kemble). THE CITY MADAM (1771, from Massinger) was produced at a theatre Dance built with his brother at Richmond. There are no collected or modern editions and only infrequent references in modern secondary materials. For PAMELA, see William M. Sale, Jr., "The First Dramatic Version of PAMELA," YLG 9 (1935), 83-88.

SIR WILLIAM DAVENANT (1606-68)

THE WORKS OF SIR WILLIAM DAVENANT . . . (1673) have been reprinted by Blom (2 vols., New York, 1968). THE DRAMATIC WORKS, ed. James Maidment and William H. Logan, 5 vols. (Edinburgh, 1872-74), includes a prefatory memoir and brief notes; this edition has also been reprinted. THE LAW AGAINST LOVERS (1662, from Shakespeare), MACBETH, A TRAGEDY (1664), and THE RIVALS (1664, from Fletcher) are available in facsimile editions (London: Cornmarket Press, 1969-70). LOVE AND HONOR (revised 1661) and THE SIEGE OF RHODES (both parts revised 1661) were edited by James W. Tupper (Boston: Heath, 1909). The alteration of MACBETH is included in Christopher Spencer's FIVE RESTORATION ADPTATIONS OF SHAKESPEARE and has been ably edited by Christopher Spencer in DAVENANT'S 'MACBETH' FROM THE YALE MANUSCRIPT: AN EDITION, WITH A DISCUSSION OF THE RELATION OF DAVENANT'S TEXT TO SHAKESPEARE'S (New Haven: Yale Univ. Press, 1961). SALMACIDA SPOLIA, ed. Terence J.B. Spencer, is included in A BOOK OF MASQUES IN HONOR OF ALLARDYCE NICOLL (Cambridge: Cambridge Univ. Press, 1967); Anthony M. Gibbs has edited THE SHORTER POEMS AND SONGS FROM THE PLAYS AND MASQUES (Oxford: Clarendon Press, 1972).

Both Alfred Harbage's SIR WILLIAM DAVENANT, POET VENTURER, 1606-1668 (Philadelphia: Univ. of Pennsylvania Press, 1935*) and Arthur H. Nethercot's SIR WILLIAM DAVENANT, POET LAUREATE AND PLAYWRIGHT-MANAGER (Chicago: Univ. of Chicago Press, 1938*) are standard biographies. Harbage devotes more time to Davenant's works, while Nethercot is more detailed on his life. See also J.P. Feil, "Davenant Exonerated," MLR 58 (1963), 335-42. Montague Summers devotes much attention to Davenant in THE PLAYHOUSE OF PEPYS, and there is a rather mechanical full-length study by Howard S. Collins, THE COMEDY OF SIR WILLIAM DAVENANT (The Hague, Netherlands: Mouton, 1967). Lothar Hoennighausen's DER STILWANDEL IM DRAMATISCHEN WERK SIR WILLIAM DAVENANTS (Cologne, Germany: Boehlau, 1965), is perhaps the best general study. Most criticism focuses on the adaptations of Shakespeare. The fullest account is in Hazelton Spencer's SHAKESPEARE IMPROVED, chapter 5, though this is marred by Spencer's insistent bardolatry. The studies by Nicholas Delius and Karl Elze, titled "Davenant and Shakespeare" and "Sir William Davenant," JDSG 4 (1869), 6-40 and 121-59, are perfunctory; Rudolf Stamm's article "Sir William Davenant and Shakespeare's Imagery," ES 24 (1924), 65-79 and 97-116, is much more useful.

Articles on specific plays include Henry N. Paul, "Players' Quartos and Duodecimos of HAMLET," MLN 49 (1934), 369-75, which affirms Davenant's hand
in Betterton's HAMLET; Christopher Spencer, "MACBETH and Davenant's THE
RIVALS," ShQ 20 (1969), 225-29; Dennis Bartholomeusz, "The Davenant-Betterton MACBETH," KOMOS 1 (1967), 41-48; James U. Rundle, "Davenant's
THE MAN'S THE MASTER and the Spanish Source," MLN 65 (1950), 194-96,
which makes a tenuous case for direct borrowing from Zorrilla as well as Scar-
ron; and Charles L. Squier, "Davenant's Comic Assault on Préciosité: THE
PLATONIC LOVERS," UCS 10, ed. J.K. Emery (Boulder: Univ. of Colorado
Press, 1966), pp. 57-72. André de Mandach argues in "The First Translator
of Molière: Sir William Davenant or Colonel Henry Howard," MLN 66 (1951),
513-18, that THE PLAYHOUSE TO BE LET (c.1663) should be ascribed to Howard. Thomas B. Stroup, in "PROMOS AND CASSANDRA and THE LAW
AGAINST LOVERS," RES 8 (1932), 309-10, parallels Whetstone's version of
the story with Davenant's. Alwin Thaler, in "Thomas Heywood, Davenant,
and THE SIEGE OF RHODES," PMLA 39 (1924), 624-41, offers a good study
of the influences on this heroic play; see also Eugene Waith's account of the
play in IDEAS OF GREATNESS and the important article by Ann-Mari Hedbaeck,
"The Printing of THE SIEGE OF RHODES," SN 45 (1973), 68-79. Davenant's
adaptations are discussed by Spencer and others; see the studies cited in Part
1, Section 8.2. THE SIEGE OF RHODES and the other heroic plays are discussed in most studies of the heroic play; see Part 1, Section 7.12. For
Davenant's share in THE TEMPEST (1667), see under Dryden, below.

JOHN DELAP (1725-1812)

Delap, a clergyman and occasional poet, was the author of three tragedies produced in the 1780's. There are no collected or individual editions and very few references in the secondary literature. The acted plays are HECUBA (1761), THE ROYAL SUPPLIANTS (1781), and THE CAPTIVES (1786); a number of unacted pieces were collected in DRAMATIC POEMS . . . (Lewes, England: W. & A. Lee, 1803). THE ROYAL SUPPLIANTS was moderately successful; the other two plays were comparative failures.

JOHN DENNIS (1657-1734)

Five tragedies and three comedies by Dennis were produced between 1697 and 1719. Four of these were included in THE SELECT WORKS . . ., 2 vols. (1718); the two Shakespeare adaptations (THE COMICAL GALLANT [1702] and THE IN-VADER OF HIS COUNTRY [1719]) are available in facsimile (London: Cornmarket Press, 1969). An anonymous LIFE OF MR. JOHN DENNIS appeared in 1734, but the standard biography is Harry G. Paul's JOHN DENNIS: HIS LIFE AND CRITICISM (New York: Columbia Univ. Press, 1911). This should be supplemented by the information in Edward N. Hooker's edition of THE CRITICAL WORKS, 2 vols. (Baltimore: Johns Hopkins Univ. Press, 1939-43*), by Fred S. Tupper's "Notes on the Life of John Dennis," ELH 5 (1938), 211-17 (from Public Record Office documents), and by Pat Rogers's "New Light on John Dennis," N&Q 217 (1972), 217-18. A.N. Wilkins, in "John Dennis' Stolen Thunder," N&Q 201 (1956), 425-28, suggests Pope may have invented the famous anecdote.

There is no thorough study of Dennis's plays, though much information is given about them in Hooker, Volume 2, and there is an overview in Frederick S. Boas's EIGHTEENTH-CENTURY DRAMA. Cary B. Graham's article, "The Jonsonian Tradition in the Comedies of Dennis," MLN 56 (1941), 370-72, notes that Dennis used Jonsonian methods in two of his three comedies. Terence P. Logan, in "John Dennis's SELECT WORKS, 1718, 1721," PBSA 65 (1971), 155-56, suggests that Dennis's popularity had declined considerably by 1721. Articles on specific plays include A.N. Wilkins's "John Dennis and Poetic Justice," N&Q 202 (1957), 421-24, which notes that Dennis violates this "rule" in AP-PIUS AND VIRGINIA (1709); Wilkins's "John Dennis on Love as a 'Tragical Passion,'" N&Q 203 (1958), 396-98 and 417-19, which argues that in RINALDO AND ARMIDA (1698) and IPHIGENIA (1699) Dennis the dramatist presented love the way Dennis the critic thought he ought; and Eugene Haun's "John Dennis's RINALDO AND ARMIDA Confused with Handel's RINALDO," N&Q 199 (1954), 249-50, which notes that Herbert Davis confused the two works in a statement in his essay in THEATRE MISCELLANY . . . (Oxford: Blackwell, 1953). Terence P. Logan, in "The Variant Issues of the 1704 Edition of John Dennis's LIBERTY ASSERTED," LIBRARY 25 (1970), 349-50, shows that there were two issues of this edition, each involving two separate states; Wilkins, in "Tragedy and 'The True Politics,'" N&Q 204 (1959), 390-94, shows that the play demonstrates Dennis's idea that tragedy ought to provide political instruction. In another article, "A Prologue by Dennis," N&Q 200 (1955), 525-26, Wilkins argues that the prologue to Gildon's THE PATRIOT was written by Dennis.

Aside from the works referred to above, Dennis wrote two comedies, A PLOT AND NO PLOT (1697) and GIBRALTAR (1705).

JOHN DENT (fl. 1782-95)

Dent's acted plays include THE CANDIDATE and TOO CIVIL BY HALF (1782), THE RECEIPT TAX (1783), THE LAWYER'S PANIC (1785), and THE TELEGRAPH (1795). THE TWO NANNIES (1788) and THE BASTILLE (1789) were acted at the Royal Grove and the Royal Circus. All are one- or two-act preludes, musical entertainments, or farces; TOO CIVIL BY HALF, a two-act musical farce, was Dent's most successful effort.

CHARLES DIBDIN THE ELDER (1745-1814)

A CHARLES DIBDIN BIBLIOGRAPHY, by Edward R. Dibdin (Liverpool, privately printed, 1937), lists and describes both published and unpublished works, nearly all of which were comic operas and musical farces. See also Wilfred G. Partington, CHARLES DIBDIN . . . (London: Alan Keen, 1944), a pamphlet which describes a collection of Dibdin material. The most popular pieces, for which Dibdin usually supplied both text and music, were included in contemporary collections; there are no modern editions and almost no modern criticism. THE PROFESSIONAL LIFE OF MR. DIBDIN, WRITTEN BY HIMSELF, 4 vols. (London: by the author, 1803), includes the words to hundreds of songs. William Kitchener provides A BRIEF MEMOIR OF CHARLES DIBDIN . . . (London: Walbrook, c.1884); the volume PROFESSIONAL AND LITERARY MEMOIRS OF CHARLES DIBDIN THE YOUNGER . . ., ed. George Speaight (London: Society for Theatre Research, 1956), is also relevant. Edward R. Dibdin's "Charles Dibdin as a Writer," ML 19 (1938), 149-70, is perfunctory; so are two bicentenary articles, H.G. Sear, "Charles Dibdin 1745-1814," ML 26 (1945), 61-65, and "Charles Dibdin," TLS, 3 March 1945, p. 103.

Dibdin's most famous and popular plays were written early in his career. They include THE DESERTER (1773), THE WATERMAN (1774), THE QUAKER (1775), POOR VULCAN! (1778), and ROSE AND COLIN (1778, from Sedaine), and THE WIVES REVENGED (1778, from Favart). Other works produced in the period include THE SHEPHERD'S ARTIFICE (1764), THE WEDDING RING (1773, from Goldoni), THE COBBLER (1774), from Sedaine), THE METAMORPHOSES (1776, from Molière), THE SERAGLIO (1776, with Edward Thompson), THE GYPSIES (1778, from Favart), ANNETTE AND LUBIN (1778, from Favart and Lourdet de Santerre), THE TOUCHSTONE and THE CHELSEA PENSIONER (1779), HARLEQUIN EVERYWHERE (1779, altered from THE MIRROR, also 1779), THE SHEPHERDESS OF THE ALPS (1780, from Marmontel), PASQUIN'S BUDGET (1780, a puppet show based on an earlier puppet play, THE COMIC MIRROR [1775]), THE ISLANDERS (1780, from Saint-Foix, altered as THE MARRIAGE ACT, 1781), HARLEQUIN FREEMASON (1780, with James Messink), JUPITER AND ALCMENA (1781, from Dryden's AMPHITRYON), NONE ARE SO BLIND AS THOSE WHO WON'T SEE (1782, partly from Dorvigny), LIBERTY HALL (1785), HARVEST HOME (1787), A LOYAL EFFUSION (1794), and HANNAH HEWIT (1798, from his own 1795 novel). Numerous other pieces were produced at Sadler's Wells and at the Royal Circus across the Thames.

After about 1780, most of Dibdin's enormous output was in the form of individual songs and "entertainments."

THOMAS JOHN DIBDIN (1771-1841)

Thomas John Dibdin was the illegitimate son of Charles Dibdin the elder. He began his stage career in 1775 at the age of four and acted both in London and in the provinces. Most of his plays were written after 1800; those first produced in London before the 1800 season include THE MOUTH OF THE NILE and THE JEW AND THE DOCTOR (1798); THE MAGIC OAK, FIVE THOUSAND A YEAR, THE BIRTHDAY (from Kotzebue), SUNSHINE AFTER RAIN (originally in Manchester, 1793), THE HORSE AND THE WIDOW (from Kotzebue), TAGG IN TRIBULATION, THE NAVAL PILLAR, and THE VOLCANO (with Charles Farley)--all 1799; OF AGE TOMORROW (from Kotzebue), TRUE FRIENDS, ST. DAVID'S DAY, THE HERMIONE, and LIBERAL OPINIONS (expanded in 1801 as THE SCHOOL FOR PREJUDICE)--all before the summer of 1800.

Most of the above are one- and two-act musical farces. Dibdin wrote more than two hundred dramatic pieces, nearly all of them successful. After 1800 he came to specialize in opera and pantomime, especially Christmas panto-mimes, though he also dramatized several Scott novels. THE CABINET (1802) is regarded as his best opera; MOTHER GOOSE (1807), a pantomime featuring the great clown Grimaldi, was one of more than a dozen smash hits. Dibdin also wrote many hundreds of songs.

THE REMINISCENCES OF THOMAS DIBDIN . . ., 2 vols. (London: Colburn, 1827), offers the best account of his life. There are few good secondary sources; see J. Sandoe, "Some Notes on the Plays of Thomas Dibdin," UCS 8 (1940), and "Master of Melodrama," TLS, 20 Sept. 1941, p. 470.

THOMAS DILKE (fl. 1678-98)

Thomas Dilke, born in Lichfield, wrote three comedies produced at Lincoln's Inn Fields between 1695 and 1698. There are no modern editions or collections and few references in secondary materials. The plays are THE LOVER'S LUCK (1695), THE CITY LADY (1696), and THE PRETENDERS (1698).

ROBERT DODSLEY (1703-64)

Dodsley began his career as a footman, and his first publication was a poem on the proper conduct of servants. With the proceeds from this and from his first play (THE TOY SHOP, 1735), he opened a bookseller's business and became over the years an important figure in the literary life of London. Ralph Straus's ROBERT DODSLEY: POET, PUBLISHER, AND PLAYWRIGHT (London: Lane, 1910) is the only full-length study; it includes an extensive bibliography and two chapters on the plays. Aside from THE TOY SHOP, Dodsley's acted plays are THE KING AND THE MILLER OF MANSFIELD (1737), SIR JOHN COCKLE AT COURT (1738), THE BLIND BEGGAR OF BETHNAL GREEN (1741), THE TRIUMPH OF PEACE (1749), and CLEONE (1758). The first and last of these were very successful.

There is no collected edition of Dodsley, nor are there modern editions of any of the plays. Charles J. Hill, "Applause for Dodsley's CLEONE," PQ 14 (1935), 181-84, concerns Richard Graves's reaction to the tragedy; Olav K. Lundeberg, "The True Sources of Robert Dodsley's THE KING AND THE MIL-LER OF MANSFIELD," MLN 39 (1924), 394-97, corrects Goldoni's memoirs by showing that Sedaine and Collé owe to Dodsley rather than he to them.

ROBERT DRURY (fl. 1732-35)

Robert Drury, an attorney, had four pieces produced in the 1730's, all ballad operas with a strong mix of farce--THE DEVIL OF A DUKE (1732), THE MAD CAPTAIN and THE FANCIED QUEEN (both 1733), and THE RIVAL MILLINERS (1736). There are no collected or modern editions and very few references in modern secondary sources.

JOHN DRYDEN (1631-1700)

The only satisfactory bibliography of Dryden's works is Hugh Macdonald's JOHN
DRYDEN: A BIBLIOGRAPHY OF EARLY EDITIONS AND OF DRYDENIANA
(Oxford: Oxford Univ. Press, 1939*); pages 88-153 cover the plays. James
M. Osborn, "Macdonald's Bibliography of Dryden: An Annotated Check List
of Selected American Libraries," MP 39 (1941), 69-98 and 197-212, is useful
for locating copies. Macdonald's work supersedes the earlier bibliographies
and catalogs by Percy Dobell and Thomas J. Wise, but one should also con-
sult John Barnard's list in the NEW CBEL, the entry for Dryden in Stratman's
BIBLIOGRAPHY OF ENGLISH PRINTED TRAGEDY, and the older CHECK LIST
OF ENGLISH PLAYS 1641-1700, by Gertrude L. Woodward and James G.
McManaway (1945). Zoltán Haraszti, "A List of Dryden's Plays in the Boston
Public Library," MB 8 (1933), 100, and William J. Cameron, JOHN DRYDEN
IN NEW ZEALAND (Wellington, N. Zealand: Wellington Library School,
1960), are specialized lists. See also Fredson T. Bowers, "Variants in Early
Editions of Dryden's Plays," HLB 3 (1949), 278-88.

Early editions of Dryden's works are made-up volumes, as was the four-volume
folio WORKS of 1701. The first modern edition was Walter Scott's THE
WORKS OF JOHN DRYDEN, NOW FIRST COLLECTED . . ., 18 vols. (London: W. Miller, 1808). Scott's edition was revised by George Saintsbury,
18 vols. (Edinburgh: W. Paterson, 1882-93), and remained the standard edition until recently. THE WORKS OF JOHN DRYDEN, ed. Edward N. Hooker
et al. (Berkeley and Los Angeles: Univ. of California Press, 1956--) will
surpass the Scott-Saintsbury edition when finished. Three volumes of plays
have so far appeared. Volume 8 (1962) contains THE WILD GALLANT, THE
RIVAL LADIES, and THE INDIAN QUEEN, ed. John H. Smith et al.; Volume 9 (1966) includes THE INDIAN EMPEROR, SECRET LOVE, and SIR MARTIN
MAR-ALL, ed. John C. Loftis and Vinton A. Dearing; Volume 10 (1970) contains THE TEMPEST, TYRANNIC LOVE, and AN EVENING'S LOVE, ed.
Maxmillian E. Novak and George R. Guffey.

THE COMEDIES, TRAGEDIES, AND OPERAS . . ., 2 vols. (1701), was the
first collection of the plays; THE SECULAR MASQUE was added to the second
issue of Volume 2. THE DRAMATIC WORKS were edited by William Congreve,
6 vols. (London, 1717), and by Montague Summers, 6 vols. (London: Nonesuch Press, 1931-32*); Summers's texts are defective. Eight plays were included

John Dryden

in George Saintsbury's Mermaid edition, 2 vols. (London: Unwin, 1904), Volume 1 of which is still in print. SELECTED DRAMAS . . ., ed. George R. Noyes, came out in 1910 (Chicago: Scott, Foresman). Four tragedies are included in DRYDEN: POETRY, PROSE, AND PLAYS, selected by Douglas Grant (London: Hart-Davis, 1952), but the best editions of selected plays are JOHN DRYDEN: FOUR COMEDIES and JOHN DRYDEN: FOUR TRAGEDIES, ed. Lester A. Beaurline and Fredson T. Bowers (Chicago: Univ. of Chicago Press, 1967). William B. Gardner's THE PROLOGUES AND EPILOGUES OF JOHN DRYDEN: A CRITICAL EDITION (New York: Columbia Univ. Press for the Univ. of Texas, 1951) is good and has excellent notes. Some pieces by Dryden are also included in Autrey N. Wiley's volume, RARE PROLOGUES AND EPILOGUES 1642-1700. Cyrus L. Day, THE SONGS OF JOHN DRYDEN (Cambridge, Mass.: Harvard Univ. Press, 1932*) may also be recommended.

There have been many editions of individual plays. ALL FOR LOVE is available in facsimile (London: Scolar Press, 1969); an earlier facsimile edition was published by William A. Clark, Jr. (San Francisco: J.H. Nash, 1929). Perhaps the best school edition, other than those in anthologies like Nettleton, Case, and Stone, is that edited for the Crofts Classics series by John J. Enck (New York: Appleton-Century-Crofts, 1966). The only independent edition of AURENG-ZEBE is that edited by Frederick M. Link for the Regents Restoration Drama series (Lincoln: Univ. of Nebraska Press, 1971). There is no independent edition of THE CONQUEST OF GRANADA, though Scolar Press of London has published a facsimile reprint. THE INDIAN EMPEROR is included in DRYDEN AND HOWARD 1664-1668 . . ., ed. Dennis D. Arundell (Cambridge: Cambridge Univ. Press, 1929), and is also available in facsimile from Scolar Press. THE KIND KEEPER is included in Alexander N. Jeffares's RESTORATION COMEDY, Volume 2. KING ARTHUR, with alterations as adopted by Purcell, was last published separately in 1928 (Cambridge: Cambridge Univ. Press); MARRIAGE A LA MODE, ed. James R. Sutherland, in 1934 (London: Dent). TROILUS AND CRESSIDA is available in facsimile (London: Cornmarket Press, 1969).

Dryden's criticism is included in THE CRITICAL AND MISCELLANEOUS PROSE WORKS OF JOHN DRYDEN . . ., ed. Edmund Malone, 3 vols. in 4 (London: for T. Cadell and W. Davies, 1800), and in ESSAYS OF JOHN DRYDEN, ed. Walter P. Ker, 2 vols. (Oxford: Clarendon Press, 1900*); the most convenient edition is OF DRAMATIC POESY AND OTHER CRITICAL ESSAYS, ed. George Watson, 2 vols. (London: Dent, 1962). THE LETTERS OF JOHN DRYDEN . . ., ed. Charles E. Ward (Durham, N.C.: Duke Univ. Press, 1942), is standard. So little is known about Dryden the man that biographers cannot hope to be exciting. Scott's life, though inaccurate in some respects, is still very readable; Bernard Kreissman's edition (Lincoln: Univ. of Nebraska Press, 1963), makes corrections in the notes. The correspondence in TLS (1931) initiated by Roswell G. Ham's 20 Aug. article, "The Date of Dryden's Birth," was superseded by James M. Osborn's JOHN DRYDEN: SOME BIOGRAPHICAL FACTS AND PROBLEMS (Gainesville: Univ. of Florida Press, 1940; rev. ed., 1965), and by Charles E. Ward's biography THE LIFE OF JOHN DRYDEN (Chapel Hill: Univ. of North Carolina Press, 1961). The biography by Christopher Hollis (London: Duckworth, 1933) is bad; that by Kenneth Young (London: Sylvan Press, 1954*) is not as good as Ward's. A recent article by Osborn, "A Lost Portrait of John Dryden," HLQ 36 (1973), 341-45 (with plates) should be mentioned.

Samuel J. Monk compiled an excellent bibliography of secondary materials, JOHN DRYDEN: A LIST OF CRITICAL STUDIES PUBLISHED FROM 1895 TO 1948 (Minneapolis: Univ. of Minnesota Press, 1950), to which William R. Keast made some peripheral additions in "Dryden Studies 1895-1948," MP 48 (1951), 205-10. Monk's work may now be supplemented by John A. Zamonski, AN ANNOTATED BIBLIOGRAPHY OF JOHN DRYDEN: TEXTS AND STUDIES 1949-1973 (New York: Garland, 1975). Extensive reviews of the secondary literature are included in the introductions and notes to the new California edition of the WORKS; see also Frederick M. Link, "A Decade of Dryden Scholarship," PLL 8 (1972), 427-43, which discusses books on and editions of Dryden during the decade after 1960. ESSENTIAL ARTICLES FOR THE STUDY OF JOHN DRYDEN, ed. Hugh T. Swedenberg, Jr. (Hamden, Conn.: Archon Books, 1966), is a most useful collection reprinting important material. Both DRYDEN'S MIND AND ART . . ., ed. Bruce A. King (Edinburgh: Oliver & Boyd, 1969), and WRITERS AND THEIR BACKGROUND: JOHN DRYDEN, ed. Earl R. Miner (Athens: Ohio Univ. Press, 1972), are also helpful; the former is a collection of previously published articles, the latter a group written specifically for the volume.

Dryden is discussed in dozens of contemporary works. Johnson's account in THE LIVES OF THE POETS is still without peer and may be set against Macaulay's essay, "Dryden," ER 47 (1828), 1-36. Aside from Scott's biography, the best nineteenth-century study is George Saintsbury's DRYDEN (London: Macmillan, 1881). Mark Van Doren's book, THE POETRY OF JOHN DRYDEN (New York: Harcourt, Brace, 1920*; 3rd rev. ed., 1946), was partly responsible for the rise in Dryden's reputation in the present century, though Van Doren neglected the plays. Arthur W. Verrall's LECTURES ON DRYDEN, ed. Margaret Verrall (Cambridge: Cambridge Univ. Press, 1914); T.S. Eliot's essays collected in JOHN DRYDEN: THE POET, THE DRAMATIST, THE CRITIC: THREE ESSAYS (New York: T. & E. Holliday, 1932); Louis I. Bredvold's THE INTELLECTUAL MILIEU OF JOHN DRYDEN . . . (Ann Arbor: Univ. of Michigan Press, 1935*); and Reuben A. Brower's article "Dryden's Epic Manner and Virgil," PMLA 55 (1940), 119-38, are also important contributions. David N. Smith's JOHN DRYDEN (Cambridge: Cambridge Univ. Press, 1950*) is disappointing. Anna M. Crinò, in JOHN DRYDEN (Florence, Italy: Olschki, 1957), provides a general survey of Dryden's work, including four chapters on the plays. Later articles of importance include Eugene M. Waith's "The Voice of Mr. Bayes," SEL 3 (1963), 335-43, and Jean H. Hagstrum's "Dryden's Grotesque: An Aspect of the Baroque in His Art and Criticism," in the Miner collection noted above. Many recent books on Dryden's criticism and poetry contain material relevant to the plays. These include Arthur W. Hoffman, JOHN DRYDEN'S IMAGERY (Gainesville: Univ. of Florida Press, 1962); Alan Roper, DRYDEN'S POETIC KINGDOMS (London: Routledge and Kegan Paul, 1965); Earl R. Miner, DRYDEN'S POETRY (Bloomington: Indiana Univ. Press, 1967); Philip Harth, CONTEXTS OF DRYDEN'S THOUGHT (Chicago: Univ. of Chicago Press, 1968); Stephen Zwicker, DRYDEN'S POLITICAL POETRY: THE TYPOLOGY OF KING AND NATION (Providence, R.I.: Brown Univ. Press, 1972); and William Myers, DRYDEN, Hutchinson Univ. Library (London: Hutchinson, 1973).

Separately published contemporary criticism of Dryden's plays is listed in
Arnott and Robinson's ENGLISH THEATRICAL LITERATURE; it includes Elkanah
Settle's NOTES AND OBSERVATIONS ON THE 'EMPRESS OF MOROCCO' RE-
VISED . . . (1674) and REFLECTIONS ON SEVERAL OF MR. DRYDEN'S
PLAYS . . . (1687); Gerard Langbaine's ACCOUNT OF THE ENGLISH DRA-
MATIC POETS (1691*); John Dennis's THE IMPARTIAL CRITIC (1693*); A COM-
PARISON BETWEEN THE TWO STAGES (1702*); and John Downes's ROSCIUS
ANGLICANUS (1708*). Historians of drama in the period devote substantial
attention to Dryden, and academic dissertations have been abundant. Most
early studies, like Margaret Sherwood's DRYDEN'S DRAMATIC THEORY AND
PRACTICE (Boston: Lamson, Wolffe, 1898), have been improved on by later
works. There are exceptions; Allison Gaw's essay "Tuke's ADVENTURES OF
FIVE HOURS in Relation to the 'Spanish Plot' and to John Dryden," in STUDIES
IN ENGLISH DRAMA, FIRST SERIES, ed. Allison Gaw (Philadelphia: Univ.
of Pennsylvania, 1917), pp. 1-61, is a good example. Later works are more
rewarding. Bruce A. King, in DRYDEN'S MAJOR PLAYS (Edinburgh: Oliver
& Boyd, 1966), discusses a number of plays other critics have slighted, along
with better known works. The serious plays are discussed by Donamy Dobrée
in RESTORATION TRAGEDY, by Eric Rothstein in RESTORATION TRAGEDY
(1967), and in numerous important articles. Among these are Mildred E. Hartsock, "Dryden's Plays: A Study in Ideas," in SEVENTEENTH-CENTURY
STUDIES, SECOND SERIES, ed. Robert Shafer (Princeton: Princeton Univ.
Press, 1937), pp. 71-176; John Winterbottom, "The Development of the Hero
in Dryden's Tragedies," "The Place of Hobbesian Ideas in Dryden's Tragedies,"
and "Stoicism in Dryden's Tragedies," JEGP 52 (1953), 161-73, 57 (1958),
665-83, and 61 (1962), 868-83; Douglas W. Jefferson, "Aspects of Dryden's
Imagery," EC 4 (1954), 20-41, and "'All, all of a piece throughout':
Thoughts on Dryden's Dramatic Poetry," in the BROWN COLLECTION, pp.
158-76; John R. Moore, "Political Allusions in Dryden's Later Plays," PMLA
73 (1958), 36-42; John M. Wallace, "Dryden and History: A Problem in Al-
legorical Reading," ELH 36 (1969), 265-90; Eugene M. Waith, "Dryden and
the Tradition of Serious Drama," in the Miner collection noted above, pp.
58-89; and the long sections devoted to Dryden in John Loftis's THE SPANISH
PLAYS OF NEOCLASSICAL ENGLAND. See also Michael West, "Dryden and
the Disintegration of Renaissance Heroic Ideals," COSTERUS 7 (1973), 131-51.

More specialized studies include Keitaro Irie, "The Auxiliary 'Do' in John
Dryden's Plays," ANGLICA (Osaka) 5 (1962), 1-19; Eugene N. James, "Drums
and Trumpets," RECTR 9, no. 2 (1970), 46-55, on Dryden's battle scenes; and
Elmar Lehmann, "'If the People Have the Power': Zum Motiv des Volksauf-
standes in Drama John Drydens," POETICA 4 (1971), 437-61. In 'THE LINKS
OF A CURIOUS CHAIN': STUDIES IN THE ACTS AND SCENES OF JOHN
DRYDEN'S TRAGEDIES AND TRAGI-COMEDIES (Gothenburg, Sweden: Univ.
of Gothenburg, 1973), Britta Olinder relates Dryden's theory of act and scene
division to his practice.

The heroic plays have received more attention than Dryden's other dramas, except for ALL FOR LOVE. Most of the studies listed in Part 1, Section 7.12
are relevant here because most of them focus on Dryden; Eugene M. Waith's
THE HERCULEAN HERO (New York: Columbia Univ. Press, 1962) and IDEAS
OF GREATNESS (1971) are recent examples, but the interest is as old as THE

John Dryden

REHEARSAL. Aside from a number of German dissertations, the earliest full-length study is Bevin J. Pendlebury's DRYDEN'S HEROIC PLAYS: A STUDY OF THE ORIGINS (London: Selwyn, 1923*), which argues persuasively for the influence (via Italy and France) of the epic and the heroic romance. Margaret Sherwood (in DRYDEN'S DRAMATIC THEORY), Montague Summers (in the introductions to his edition), and William S. Clark (in his edition of Orrery) take similar positions. Allardyce Nicoll stresses the influence of Beaumont, Fletcher, and Davenant. Kathleen M. Lynch, in "Conventions of Platonic Drama in the Heroic Plays of Orrery and Dryden," PMLA 44 (1929), 456-71, stresses Caroline court drama, as does Alfred Harbage in his history of Caroline drama (1936). The nineteenth century took it for granted that France provided the model; recent criticism has been much more eclectic and justifiably so. A good summary of the evidence is provided in Volume 8 of the California edition, in the commentary on THE INDIAN QUEEN (pp. 284-89).

Additional essays of importance on the heroic plays include Frank W. Payne, "The Question of Precedence between Dryden and the Earl of Orrery with Regard to the English Heroic Play," RES 1 (1925), 173-81; William S. Clark, "Dryden's Relations with Howard and Orrery," MLN 42 (1927), 16-20; Trusten W. Russell, VOLTAIRE, DRYDEN, AND HEROIC TRAGEDY (New York: Columbia Univ. Press, 1946); and Scott C. Osborn, "Heroical Love in Dryden's Heroic Drama," PMLA 73 (1958), 480-90. Douglas W. Jefferson, in "The Significance of Dryden's Heroic Plays," PLS 5 (1940), 125-39, was the first to argue that the heroic plays have a strong vein of humor, a theory not widely accepted but still current--see William Myers's DRYDEN for a recent example. Thomas H. Fujimura, in "The Appeal of Dryden's Heroic Plays," PMLA 75 (1960), 37-45, attacks the dubious notion put forth by Allardyce Nicoll and Bonamy Dobrée that these plays appealed to an unheroic age; he believes that the plays celebrate naturalism and that such heroes as Almanzor are passionately committed to sex, glory, and self-aggrandizement. The Osborn article noted above challenges this view, which tends to ignore plot; Jean E. Gagen, in "Love and Honor in Dryden's Heroic Plays," PMLA 77 (1962), 208-20, agrees with Osborn and defines two different concepts of love and honor operating in the plays. For Gagen, these dramas have ethical content. Martin Price, in a sensitive discussion of Dryden's heroic drama (TO THE PALACE OF WISDOM, pp. 32-52) stresses their dialectic and intensity and the movement of their protagonists toward "the moral rigor of neoclassic self-denial."

Four recent books on the subject are Arthur C. Kirsch's DRYDEN'S HEROIC DRAMA (Princeton: Princeton Univ. Press, 1965*), Selma Zebouni's DRYDEN: A STUDY IN HEROIC CHARACTERIZATION (Baton Rouge: Louisiana State Univ. Press, 1965), Anne T. Barbeau's THE INTELLECTUAL DESIGN OF JOHN DRYDEN'S HEROIC PLAYS (New Haven: Yale Univ. Press, 1970), and Michael W. Alssid's DRYDEN'S RHYMED HEROIC TRAGEDIES: A CRITICAL STUDY OF THE PLAYS AND OF THEIR PLACE IN DRYDEN'S POETRY, 2 vols. (Salzburg, Austria: Institut fuer Englische Sprache und Literatur, Univ. Salzburg, 1974). Kirsch's study stresses the influence of French classical drama and especially of the concept of gloire; his analyses are perceptive, especially in emphasizing the rhetorical nature of the heroic plays. Zebouni argues that the heroic plays demonstrate Dryden's belief in the control of passion by reason--a defensible thesis--but she indulges in numerous oversimplified and dubious assertions about Dryden's central characters and about the heroic plays without providing the detailed analysis necessary to make her theses convincing. Barbeau believes strongly in the intellectual and ethical content of the plays and argues persuasively for a view of them in harmony with Dryden's political and social thought. However, she fails to consider the theatrical significance of the plays she discusses, and she tends to ignore the work of such scholars as Arthur C. Kirsch, Bruce A. King, and Philip Harth. Alssid's book provides excellent critical analyses of the plays and of Dryden's use of symbolism to present his themes. Several articles based on this dissertation are cited under individual plays, below.

The adaptations of Shakespeare are discussed in the sources listed in Part 1, Section 8.2, especially in Hazelton Spencer's SHAKESPEARE IMPROVED. Allardyce Nicoll's pamphlet DRYDEN AS AN ADAPTER OF SHAKESPEARE (London: Oxford Univ. Press for the Shakespeare Association, 1922) is not especially good; it was written just before Montague Summers's SHAKESPEARE ADAPTATIONS and Odell's SHAKESPEARE FROM BETTERTON TO IRVING were published, and therefore it dated rapidly.

Dryden's comedies, though comparatively neglected, are the subject of two books and a number of helpful articles. Ned B. Allen, in THE SOURCES OF JOHN DRYDEN'S COMEDIES (Ann Arbor: Univ. of Michigan Press, 1935*), is exhaustive and generally sound except in occasionally confusing sources with analogs. Frank H. Moore's THE NOBLER PLEASURE: DRYDEN'S COMEDY IN THEORY AND PRACTICE (Chapel Hill: Univ. of North Carolina Press, 1963) is useful despite Moore's tendency to oversimplify his categories. John C. Loftis's essay, "Dryden's Comedies," in the Miner collection noted above, pp. 27-57, gives an excellent overview of the subject--one preferable to the accounts in the standard dramatic histories. See also Harold Love, "Dryden, D'Urfey, and the Standard of Comedy," SEL 13 (1973), 422-36. Kathleen M. Lynch's SOCIAL MODE OF RESTORATION COMEDY should be mentioned as devoting considerable attention to Dryden, and there are brief discussions in Kenneth Muir's COMEDY OF MANNERS (1970) and in William Myers's DRYDEN (1973).

ALL FOR LOVE (1677) has always suffered in comparison with Shakespeare's ANTONY AND CLEOPATRA, particularly at the hands of critics who ignore theatrical values and focus their attention exclusively on verbal art. Much of the best criticism on the play must therefore be isolated from discussions which insist on the comparison with Shakespeare and frequently refuse to consider Dryden's play on its own terms. TWENTIETH-CENTURY INTERPRETATIONS OF 'ALL FOR LOVE': A COLLECTION OF CRITICAL ESSAYS, ed. Bruce A. King (Englewood Cliffs, N.J.: Prentice-Hall, 1968), includes a representative group of previously published essays. John Bailey, "Dryden and Shakespeare," POETS AND POETRY (Oxford: Clarendon Press, 1911), pp. 72-79, is an early modern appreciation, as is Bonamy Dobrée's chapter in RESTORATION TRAGEDY. Frank R. Leavis's "ANTONY AND CLEOPATRA and ALL FOR LOVE: A Critical Exercise," SCRUTINY 5 (1936), 158-69, is a classic depreciation. Leavis is concerned exclusively with poetic values and never considers either play as a drama; Shakespeare is therefore a poet, Dryden a mere craftsman. Kenneth Muir takes a similar approach in "The Imagery of ALL FOR LOVE," PLS 5 (1940), 140-47. Ruth Wallerstein's article, "Dryden and the Analysis of Sheakespeare's Techniques," RES 19 (1943), 165-85, is a perceptive study of contrasting styles. Norman Suckling's "Dryden in Egypt: Reflections on ALL FOR LOVE," DUJ 14 (1952), 2-7, and R.E. Hughes's "Dryden's ALL FOR LOVE: The Sensual Dilemma," DC 3 (1960), 68-74, which argues that the inability of Antony to choose reflects Restoration skepticism, are less interesting contributions. The accounts of the play in Moody E. Prior's LANGUAGE OF TRAGEDY (New York: Columbia Univ. Press, 1947) and in Eugene M. Waith's THE HERCULEAN HERO (1962) are good; Prior (pp. 192-212) notes Antony's "oscillation from one allegiance to another" as the structural principle of the play but stresses Dryden's ability to unify his language with his dramatic form. Waith points to the play's affinities with the earlier heroic tragedies. Jean H. Hagstrum makes some perceptive remarks about ALL FOR LOVE in THE SISTER ARTS . . . (Chicago: Univ. of Chicago Press, 1958*). Bruce A. King, in "Dryden's Intent in ALL FOR LOVE," CE 24 (1963), 267-71, argues that Dryden had no moral purpose in the play, a thesis difficult to sustain. Otto Reinert, in "Passion and Pity in ALL FOR LOVE: A Reconsideration," THE HIDDEN SENSE AND OTHER ESSAYS . . . (Oslo, Norway: Universitetsforlaget, 1963), pp. 159-95, attacks both King and Muir; the play does have moral content and does have a pattern of iterative imagery. L.P. Goggin's "This Bow of Ulysses," in ESSAYS AND STUDIES IN LANGUAGE AND LITERATURE, ed. Herbert H. Petit (Pittsburgh: Duquesne Univ. Press, 1964), pp. 49-86, offers a perceptive reading of the play as an original work founded on Dryden's conception of history and shows how Dryden's sources and theme shape his plot and style. Martin Price's reading, in TO THE PALACE OF WISDOM (1964), is also perceptive. In "ALL FOR LOVE, or Comedy as Tragedy," THE CAVE AND THE SPRING: ESSAYS ON POETRY (Adelaide, Australia: Rigby, 1965), pp. 144-63, Alec D. Hope argues that the play is bourgeois and domestic, really a pathetic comedy; his discussion is more sensitive than its title suggests. Of recent interpretations, Earl R. Miner's in DRYDEN'S POETRY and Derek W. Hughes's in "The Significance of ALL FOR LOVE," ELH 37 (1970), 540-63, are perhaps the best, though Arthur C. Kirsch's reading in DRYDEN'S HEROIC DRAMA and Anne D. Ferry's in MILTON AND THE MILTONIC DRYDEN (Cambridge, Mass.: Harvard Univ. Press, 1968) also deserve close attention.

Less important or more specialized materials include the chapter in Arthur W. Verrall's LECTURES ON DRYDEN; DeWitt T. Starnes's articles, "More about Dryden as an Adapter of Shakespeare," UTS, no. 8 (1928), 100-106, and "Imitation of Shakespeare in Dryden's ALL FOR LOVE," TSLL 6 (1964), 39-46 (both greatly exaggerated); H. Kossman's "A Note on Dryden's ALL FOR LOVE, V.165 ff.," ES 31 (1950), 99-100; Everett H. Emerson et al.'s "Intention and Achievement in ALL FOR LOVE," CE 17 (1955), 84-87; the relevant sections of Stanley E. Hyman's POETRY AND CRITICISM . . . (New York: Atheneum, 1961); Peter Nazareth's "ALL FOR LOVE: Dryden's Hybrid Play," ESA 6 (1963), 154-63; Wallace Jackson's "Dryden's Emperor and Lillo's Merchant: The Relevant Bases of Action," MLQ 26 (1965), 536-44; Howard D. Weinbrot's "Alexas in ALL FOR LOVE: His Genealogy and Function," SP 64 (1967), 625-39, which argues convincingly that Dryden's imitation of

Shakespeare is mostly verbal and has been greatly exaggerated; the chapter on the play in Paul Ramsey's THE ART OF JOHN DRYDEN (Lexington: Univ. of Kentucky Press, 1969); David M. Vieth's "Concept as Metaphor: Dryden's Attempted Stylistic Revolution," LS 3 (1970), 197-204; and Carleton S. Tritt's "The Title of ALL FOR LOVE," ELN 10 (1973), 273-75.

Sources, influences, and analogs are treated in Thomas P. Harrison, Jr., "Othello as a Model for Dryden in ALL FOR LOVE," UTS, no. 7 (1927), 136-43; Morris Freedman, "ALL FOR LOVE and SAMSON AGONISTES," N&Q 201 (1956), 514-17; Charles R. Forker, "ROMEO AND JULIET and the 'Cyndus' Speech in Dryden's ALL FOR LOVE," N&Q 207 (1962), 382-83; S. Klima, "Some Unrecorded Borrowings from Shakespeare in Dryden's ALL FOR LOVE," N&Q 208 (1963), 415-18; H. Neville Davies, "Dryden's ALL FOR LOVE and Thomas May's THE TRAGEDY OF CLEOPATRA QUEEN OF EGYPT," N&Q 210 (1965), 139-44, and "Dryden's ALL FOR LOVE and Sedley's ANTONY AND CLEOPATRA," N&Q 212 (1967), 221-27; Peter Caracciolo, "Dryden and the ANTONY AND CLEOPATRA of Sir Charles Sedley," ES (Anglo-American Supplement), 1969, pp. l-lv; and K.E. Faas, "Some Notes on Dryden's ALL FOR LOVE," ANGLIA 88 (1970), 341-46.

AMBOYNA (c.1672) is a bad play and, consequently, has received little attention. Louis I. Bredvold's "Political Aspects of Dryden's AMBOYNA and THE SPANISH FRIAR," UMP 8 (1932), 119-32, is useful. Charles E. Ward, in "The Dates of Two Dryden Plays," PMLA 51 (1936), 786-92, suggests that the play was performed before June 1672, but the evidence is not conclusive. The play is also discussed in J.A. van der Welle's DRYDEN AND HOLLAND (Groningen, Netherlands: Walters, 1962).

AMPHITRYON (1690) is discussed by Ned B. Allen and Frank H. Moore in their studies of Dryden's comedy mentioned above and is covered in several of the studies of French influence listed in Part 1, Section 8.4. See also Alexander L. Bondurant, "The AMPHITRUO of Plautus, Molière's AMPHITRYON, and the AMPHITRYON of Dryden," SR 28 (1925), 455-68, and Margaret K. Merzbach, "The Third Source of Dryden's AMPHITRYON," ANGLIA 73 (1955), 213-14. In "Dryden's Aims in AMPHITRYON," COSTERUS 9 (1973), 1-8, Thomas E. Barden emphasizes Dryden's addition of vulgar comedy to materials taken from Plautus and Molière.

THE ASSIGNATION (1672) is discussed by Allen and Moore; by James U. Rundle, in "The Source of Dryden's 'Comic Plot' in THE ASSIGNATION," MP 45 (1947), 104-11, who argues for the direct influence of Calderón's CON QUIEN VENGO VENGO; by John C. Loftis, in THE SPANISH PLAYS OF NEOCLASSICAL ENGLAND; and by John A. Zamonski, in "The Spiritual Nature of Carnal Love in Dryden's ASSIGNATION," ETJ 25 (1973), 189-92, who argues that Dryden uses spiritual symbolism to present carnal love.

AURENG-ZEBE (1675) is discussed by Bruce A. King in DRYDEN'S MAJOR PLAYS, by Arthur C. Kirsch in DRYDEN'S HEROIC TRAGEDY (stressing the sentimental and domestic aspects of the play), and by Moody E. Prior in THE LANGUAGE OF TRAGEDY. King sees the theme of the play as "the disquieting effects of the imagination" but focuses on what he considers its stylized humor. Prior's discussion stresses AURENG-ZEBE's dialectic; he notes the pervasive intellectual debates that structure the play and the play's recurrent image patterns. Other important essays include Harley Granville-Barker's "Wycherley and Dryden," ON DRAMATIC METHOD (London: Sidgwick & Jackson, 1931), pp. 113-55; Michael W. Alssid's "The Design of Dryden's AURENG-ZEBE," JEGP 64 (1965), 452-69 (on the imagery); Robert S. Newman's "Irony and the Problem of Tone in Dryden's AURENG-ZEBE," SEL 10 (1970), 439-58, which argues unconvincingly for the role of comic irony in the play; and Leslie H. Martin's "The Consistency of Dryden's AURENG-ZEBE," SP 70 (1973), 306-28, which sees the play as an expression of Dryden's continuing interest in epic. See also William Myers's brief discussion in DRYDEN. Articles concerned with sources include Edward LeComte, "SAMSON AGONISTES and AURENG-ZEBE," EA 11 (1958), 18-22; Richard Morton, "'By No Strong Passion Swayed': A Note on John Dryden's AURENG-ZEBE," ESA 1 (1958), 59-68; Harold F. Brooks, "Dryden's AURENG-ZEBE: Debts to Corneille and Racine," RLC 46 (1972), 5-34; and Leslie H. Martin, "AURENG-ZEBE and the Ritual of the Persian King," MP 71 (1973), 169-71. William Frost's "AURENG-ZEBE in Context: Dryden, Shakespeare, Milton, and Racine, JEGP 74 (1975), 26-49, is a sensitive discussion relating the play to KING LEAR, SAMSON AGONISTES, and, especially to Racine's MITHRIDATES.

CLEOMENES (1692) is the subject of S.W. Brossman's "Dryden's Cassandra and Congreve's Zara," N&Q 201 (1956), 102-03, and "Dryden's CLEOMENES and Fletcher's BONDUCA," N&Q 202 (1957), 66-68, both of which are concerned with parallels. Stanley Archer's "A Performance of Dryden's CLEOMENES," N&Q 216 (1971), 460-61, concerns a prologue by Prior to a performance at Christmas of 1695.

DON SEBASTIAN (1689), one of the longest and most interesting of the serious plays, has not received its due. The best discussion is Bruce A. King's, in DRYDEN'S MAJOR PLAYS; there are also some perceptive remarks in Eric Rothstein's RESTORATION TRAGEDY and in William Myers's DRYDEN. King agrees with Sir Walter Scott that DON SEBASTIAN is Dryden's best play and points to the parting of Sebastian and Almeyda as one of the finest scenes in English drama. His analysis of the structure of the play is particularly good.

THE DUKE OF GUISE (1682) had obvious political implications; it was attacked in such contemporary pamphlets as THE TRUE HISTORY OF THE DUKE OF GUISE . . . and SOME REFLECTIONS UPON THE PRETENDED PARALLEL IN THE PLAY CALLED 'THE DUKE OF GUISE' . . . (both 1683). Bruce A. King's "Anti-Whig Satire in THE DUKE OF GUISE," ELN 2 (1965), 190-93, points out pamphlet sources used by Dryden in the play. Charles H. Hinnant, in "The Background of the Early Version of Dryden's THE DUKE OF GUISE," ELN 6 (1968), 102-06, argues that since much of the play was written in 1660, the play therefore does not refer to the exclusion crisis of 1681-82; his argument is convincingly answered by Lawrence L. Bachorik in "THE DUKE OF GUISE and Dryden's Vindication: A New Consideration," ELN 10 (1973), 208-12.

AN EVENING'S LOVE; OR, THE MOCK ASTROLOGER (1668) is discussed by Frank H. Moore and Ned B. Allen (see above), by Maximillian E. Novak in Volume 10 of the California Dryden (a fine essay), and by Salvatore Fiorino in JOHN DRYDEN: "THE MOCK ASTROLOGER": FONTI E PSEUDO-FONTI (Palermo, Italy: G. Libassi, 1959). Fiorino argues that Dryden borrowed directly from Calderón's EL ASTROLOGO FINGIDO, a thesis John C. Loftis disputes in THE SPANISH PLAYS OF NEOCLASSICAL ENGLAND. Ned B. Allen, in "The Sources of Dryden's THE MOCK ASTROLOGER," PQ 36 (1957), 453–64, argues for the direct and indirect influence of Scudéry's IBRAHIM and posits minor debts to Molière and Quinault.

THE CONQUEST OF GRANADA (part 1, 1670; part 2, 1671) is central to most discussions of Dryden's heroic plays. It helped provoke THE REHEARSAL and led to such contemporary pieces as THE CENSURE OF THE ROTA (1673). Leonard Wallace established the approximate dates of performance in "A New Date for the CONQUEST OF GRANADA," MP 16 (1918), 271–72. George H. Nettleton's "Author's Changes in Dryden's CONQUEST OF GRANADA, Part 1," MLN 50 (1935), 360–64, focuses on revisions in act 5. Jerome W. Schweitzer, in "Dryden's Use of Scudéry's ALMAHIDE," MLN 54 (1939), 190–92, and 62 (1947), 262–63, argues for the direct use of the French romance. Alice D. Ball provides a useful note in "An Emendation of Dryden's CONQUEST OF GRANADA, Part 1," ELH 6 (1939), 217–18. The play is discussed by Arthur C. Kirsch in DRYDEN'S HEROIC DRAMA, by Bruce A. King in DRYDEN'S MAJOR PLAYS, by Eugene M. Waith in both THE HERCULEAN HERO and IDEAS OF GREATNESS, and in most of the other studies of heroic drama cited above and in Part 1, Section 7.12. John H. Wilson's PREFACE TO RESTORATION DRAMA includes a good overview of the play; the best and most extensive discussion is in Anne T. Barbeau's THE INTELLECTUAL DESIGN OF JOHN DRYDEN'S HEROIC PLAYS.

THE INDIAN EMPEROR (1665) is also treated in most studies of the heroic play. John C. Loftis's analysis of its background in Volume 9 of the California Dryden is excellent. Fredson T. Bowers has an important article on the text, "The 1665 Manuscript of Dryden's INDIAN EMPEROR," SP 48 (1951), 738–60; the Trinity MS discussed by Bowers becomes the copy text for the Bowers-Beaurline FOUR TRAGEDIES, while Q1 is used in the California edition. See also James S. Steck, "Dryden's INDIAN EMPEROR: The Early Editions and Their Relation to the Text," SB 2 (1949–50), 139–52. Studies of sources and influences include Albert Maillet, "Dryden et Voltaire," RLC 18 (1938), 272–86, and Merle L. Perkins, "Dryden's THE INDIAN EMPEROR and Voltaire's ALZIRE, CL 9 (1957), 229–37; Dougald MacMillan's impressive article, "The Sources of Dryden's THE INDIAN EMPEROR," HLQ 13 (1950), 355–70, which stresses Davenant's CRUELTY OF THE SPANIARDS IN PERU and PURCHAS HIS PILGRIMAGE; Richard N. Ringler, "Two Sources for Dryden's THE INDIAN EMPEROR," PQ 42 (1963), 423–29 (especially Donne); N.D. Shergold and Peter Ure, "Dryden and Calderón: A New Spanish Source for THE INDIAN EMPEROR," MLR 61 (1966), 369–83 (EL PRINCIPE CONSTANTE); and especially John C. Loftis, in THE SPANISH PLAYS OF NEOCLASSICAL ENGLAND, which incorporates his earlier articles on the subject. The best independent critical assessment of the play is Michael W. Alssid's "The Perfect Conquest: A Study of Theme, Structure, and Character in Dryden's THE

INDIAN EMPEROR," SP 59 (1962), 539-59.

THE INDIAN QUEEN (1664) is considered in most discussions of heroic drama, in Volume 8 of the California Dryden, and in Harold J. Oliver's biography, SIR ROBERT HOWARD (1963; see under Howard, below). Thomas B. Stroup's "Scenery for THE INDIAN QUEEN," MLN 52 (1937), 408-09, should also be consulted.

THE KIND KEEPER; OR, MR. LIMBERHAM (1678) is discussed by Ned B. Allen and Frank H. Moore, above, and by Esmond S. deBeer, "Dryden, THE KIND KEEPER, The 'Poet of Scandalous Memory,'" N&Q 179 (1940), 128-29. Recent articles include Susan Staves's "Why Was Dryden's MR. LIMBERHAM Banned?: A Problem in Restoration Theatre History," RECTR 12, no. 1 (1974), 1-11, and Van R. Baker's "Heroic Posturing Satirized: Dryden's MR. LIMBERHAM," PLL 8 (1972), 370-79, which argues that Dryden in the play uses the military metaphors of heroic drama to attack libertinism.

KING ARTHUR (1691) is referred to in most discussions of Restoration opera and in all substantive accounts of Henry Purcell. See especially Edward Dent's THE FOUNDATIONS OF ENGLISH OPERA and Robert E. Moore's HENRY PURCELL AND THE RESTORATION THEATRE. The opera has been recorded, and has been produced at the Nottingham Festival and elsewhere in comparatively recent years.

LOVE TRIUMPHANT (1694) is rarely discussed; perhaps the best account is Bruce A. King's in DRYDEN'S MAJOR PLAYS, but see also Moore and Allen, above.

MARRIAGE A LA MODE (1671 or 1672), generally considered Dryden's best comedy, is discussed by Ned B. Allen and Frank H. Moore, above, and in many of the studies of Restoration comedy listed in Part 1, Sections 7.8-7.11. Bruce A. King's article, "Dryden's MARRIAGE A LA MODE," DS 4 (1965), 28-37, analyzes the play as a comment on Hobbes's theory that man in his natural state is permanently at war for the property of others. John Reichert, "A Note on Buckingham and Dryden," N&Q 207 (1962), 220-21, shows that jibes at the play were introduced into the 1675 edition of THE REHEARSAL. Charles E. Ward, in "The Dates of Two Dryden Plays," PMLA 51 (1936), 786-92, argues that the play was produced before 1671; see the supporting evidence presented by Robert D. Hume in "The Date of Dryden's MARRIAGE A LA MODE," HLB 21 (1973), 161-66. Hume argues persuasively (in opposition to Allardyce Nicoll) for production by early December of 1671. Leslie M. Howard, in "The Source and Originality of Dryden's Melantha," PQ 52 (1973), 746-53, shows that this character is based on one created by Madeleine de Scudéry in LE GRAND CYRUS.

SIR MARTIN MAR-ALL (1667), OEDIPUS (1678), THE RIVAL LADIES (1663 or 1664), and SECRET LOVE (1667) are plays little discussed. The comedies are treated by Allen and Moore, above, and all are mentioned in the standard histories. Moore has an important article, "The Composition of SIR MARTIN

MAR-ALL," SP, Extra Series 4 (1967), 27-38, concerning the relative contri-
butions of Dryden and Newcastle to the play, but the fullest accounts of this
play and of THE RIVAL LADIES are in the introductions to Volume 8 of the
California Dryden. Roswell G. Ham ascribes a Bodleian MS to Dryden in
"Dryden's Epilogue to THE RIVAL LADIES 1664," RES 13 (1937), 76-80. D.
Biggins, in "Source Notes for Dryden, Wycherley, and Otway," N&Q 201
(1956), 298-301, shows the influence of Fletcher and Rowley's MAID IN THE
MILL on the masque in THE RIVAL LADIES. Articles on SECRET LOVE include
Leslie H. Martin's "Dryden and the Art of Transversion," CD 6 (1972), 3-13,
on Dryden's use of Scudéry's GRAND CYRUS, and two articles suggesting that
SECRET LOVE is indebted to James Howard's ALL MISTAKEN rather than vice
versa, as most scholars have assumed. Montague Summers suggested this idea
in THE PLAYHOUSE OF PEPYS; it was developed by James R. Sutherland's
"The Date of James Howard's ALL MISTAKEN; OR, THE MAD COUPLE,"
N&Q 209 (1964), 339-40, and has been recently supported by Robert D. Hume's
"Dryden, James Howard, and the Date of ALL MISTAKEN," PQ 51 (1972),
422-29. John C. Loftis's discussion of the play in Volume 9 of the California
Dryden is excellent.

THE SPANISH FRIAR (1680) is discussed by Louis I. Bredvold in the article
cited under AMBOYNA, above, and in several of the books already mentioned
(see especially Bruce A. King's chapter in DRYDEN'S MAJOR PLAYS and William Myers's remarks in DRYDEN). Charles E. Ward has a note, "Dryden's
SPANISH FRIAR and a Provincial Touring Company," N&Q 176 (1939), 96-97,
which underlines the long popularity of the play on the stage. Pierre Legouis,
in "Quinault et Dryden: une source de THE SPANISH FRIAR," RLC 11 (1931),
398-415, discusses parallels with Quinault's ASTRATE.

THE STATE OF INNOCENCE (published 1677) has attracted attention largely
because of its relation to PARADISE LOST; it has rarely been considered on
its merits or in terms of its operatic intent. Arthur W. Verrall included an
extensive discussion of the play in his LECTURES ON DRYDEN (1914), arguing
that Dryden actually intended to produce the opera. William J. Lawrence,
in "Dryden's Abortive Opera," TLS, 6 Aug. 1931, p. 606, also argued that
the play was intended for the stage, probably for the marriage of James to
Mary of Modena. P.S. Havens's essay, "Dryden's 'Tagged' Version of PARA-
DISE LOST," in ESSAYS IN DRAMATIC LITERATURE: THE PARROTT PRESEN-
TATION VOLUME, ed. Hardin Craig (Princeton: Princeton Univ. Press,
1935*), pp. 383-97, is a careful, sympathetic study. Havens argues that Dryden would not have published the play had not copies been widely circulated
and that it exemplifies Dryden's notion of what a proper heroic drama should
be. George McFadden's article, "Dryden's 'Most Barren Period'--and Milton,"
HLQ 24 (1961), 283-96, looks at the play as a technical experiment. Bruce
A. King, in "The Significance of Dryden's STATE OF INNOCENCE," SEL 4
(1964), 371-91, suggests that parts of the play are comic but looks carefully
at its imagery; he argues that Dryden sets up a paradise within to counteract
the Hobbesian world of degeneration. This article and Bernard Harris's essay,
"'That Soft Seducer, Love': Dryden's THE STATE OF INNOCENCE AND FALL
OF MAN," in APPROACHES TO PARADISE LOST: THE YORK TERCENTENARY
LECTURES, ed. C.A. Patrides (London: Arnold, 1968), pp. 119-36, are the
best studies of the play. Harris is especially acute in showing that Dryden

wishes to make reasonable what Milton offered to faith, in suggesting why the work was conceived as an opera, and in his analysis of the character of Eve. Morris Freedman's "The 'Tagging' of PARADISE LOST: Rhyme in Dryden's THE STATE OF INNOCENCE," MiQ 5 (1971), 18-22, adds little to previous scholarship.

Specialized studies include George B. Churchill, "The Relation of Dryden's STATE OF INNOCENCE to Milton's PARADISE LOST and Wycherley's PLAIN DEALER: An Inquiry into Dates," MP 4 (1906), 381-88; George W. Whiting, "The Ellesmere MS of THE STATE OF INNOCENCE," TLS, 14 Jan. 1932, p. 28; and Gwynne B. Evans, "Dryden's STATE OF INNOCENCE," TLS, 21 March 1942, p. 144, which discusses notes in Dryden's hand in the Harvard College manuscript. Textual studies include Fredson T. Bowers, "The Pirated Quarto of Dryden's STATE OF INNOCENCE," SB 5 (1952-53), 166-69; Marion H. Hamilton, "The Early Editions of Dryden's STATE OF INNOCENCE," SB 5 (1952-53), 163-66, and "The Manuscripts of Dryden's THE STATE OF IN-NOCENCE and the Relation of the Harvard MS to the First Quarto," SB 6 (1953), 237-46.

Restoration versions of THE TEMPEST have occasioned much controversy. Dryden and William Davenant did the first version, produced in November of 1667. The California editors suggest (plausibly) that the production was planned to compete with the King's Company alteration of Fletcher's SEA VOYAGE, produced in September as THE STORM. They also argue that Davenant's role was limited to suggestions for a character like Hippolito, to writing some of the sailors' scenes, and to general supervision. Theodore Spencer agrees with this view in SHAKESPEARE IMPROVED; Montague Summers takes the opposite view in the introduction and notes to his edition, included in SHAKE-SPEARE ADAPTATIONS (1922). See also the studies of Davenant by Alfred Harbage and Arthur H. Nethercot cited under Davenant, above. For the so-called "operatic TEMPEST" of 1674, see under Thomas Shadwell, below. The Dryden-Davenant version is also included in George R. Guffey's facsimile collection titled AFTER 'THE TEMPEST' . . . (Los Angeles: W.A. Clark Library, 1969). The best edition is that in Volume 10 of the California Dryden.

TROILUS AND CRESSIDA (1679) is discussed in the major books on Shakespearean influence listed in Part 1, Section 8.2. Paul S. Dunkin, in "The Dryden TROILUS AND CRESSIDA Imprint: Another Theory," SB 2 (1949-50), 185-89, offers possibilities not mentioned by Fredson T. Bowers in his study of variant imprints in Dryden's plays, listed above. Kenneth Muir's "Three Shakespeare Adaptations," PLS, section 8, part 4 (1959), pp. 233-40, is perfunctory. W.W. Bernhardt's "Shakespeare's TROILUS AND CRESSIDA and Dryden's TRUTH FOUND TOO LATE," ShQ 20 (1969), 129-41, gives an excellent analysis of the structure and theme of the play, arguing that Dryden adjusts a "problem play" to a non-Elizabethan audience. Denzell S. Smith, in "Dryden's Purpose in Adapting Shakespeare's TROILUS AND CRESSIDA, BSF 10, no. 3 (1969), pp. 49-52, notes that Dryden exhibits order in the world, whereas Shakespeare depicts a disrupted universe; his point is emphasized by Dorothy Cook in "Dryden's Adaptation of Shakespeare's TROILUS AND CRESSIDA," CR 7 (1973), 66-72. G. Douglas Atkins's "The Function and Significance of the Priest in Dryden's TROILUS AND CRESSIDA," TSLL 13 (1971), 29-37, argues that Dryden's reversal of Shakespeare in making Calchas the instrument of Cressida's downfall suggests his hostility to the clergy.

TYRANNIC LOVE (1669) is treated fully in the introduction to Volume 10 of the California edition; see also Bruce A. King's "Dryden, Tillotson, and TYRANNIC LOVE," RES 16 (1965), 364-77, which draws some suggestive parallels. Maximillian E. Novak's "The Demonology of Dryden's TYRANNIC LOVE and 'Anti-Scot,'" ELN 4 (1966), 95-98, is included in the introduction just mentioned. Charles E. Ward, "Massinger and Dryden," ELH 2 (1935), 263-66, and Henry H. Adams, "A Prompt Copy of Dryden's TYRANNIC LOVE," SB 4 (1951-52), 170-74, are more specialized articles.

THE WILD GALLANT (1663) is discussed by Ned B. Allen and Frank H. Moore, above, and in Volume 8 of the Univ. of California edition of Dryden. Independent articles, all quite limited in scope, include Richard H. Perkinson, "'Lady du Lake,'" N&Q 168 (1935), 260-61; Fredson T. Bowers, "The First Edition of Dryden's WILD GALLANT, 1669," LIBRARY, 5th ser. 5 (1950-51), 51-54, which corrects MacDonald's Dryden bibliography; Arthur L. Cooke, "Two Parallels between Dryden's WILD GALLANT and Congreve's LOVE FOR LOVE," N&Q 199 (1954), 27-28; and F.C. Osenburg, "The Prologue to Dryden's WILD GALLANT Re-Examined," ELN 7 (1969), 35-39, which takes issue with the editors of the California edition.

SIR HENRY BATE DUDLEY (1745-1824)

Henry Bate (he assumed the name Dudley in 1784) was a clergyman, journalist, magistrate, and man-about-town. His dramatic works include THE RIVAL CANDIDATES (1775), HENRY AND EMMA (1 act 1775, 3 acts 1779), THE BLACKAMOOR WASHED WHITE (1776), THE FLITCH OF BACON (1778), THE DRAMATIC PUFFERS (1782), THE MAGIC PICTURE (1783, from Massinger), THE WOODMAN (1791), and THE TRAVELLERS IN SWITZERLAND (1794). Most of these are musical pieces. THE FLITCH OF BACON introduced the composer William Shield to London audiences; Shield also wrote the music for THE WOODMAN and THE TRAVELLERS IN SWITZERLAND. These were all successful comic operas, as was THE RIVAL CANDIDATES. FAIR GAME, a farce, was produced in 1813. John Fyvie's account of Dudley in NOBLE DAMES AND NOTABLE MEN OF THE GEORGIAN ERA (London: Constable, 1910) is perfunctory.

THOMAS DUFFETT (fl. 1670's)

Duffett, originally a milliner, wrote a comedy (THE SPANISH ROGUE, 1673) and three burlesques between 1673 and 1675; THE AMOROUS OLD WOMAN (1674) has also been attributed to him. THE EMPRESS OF MOROCCO (1673) is included in THE EMPRESS OF MOROCCO AND ITS CRITICS, introd. Maximillian E. Novak (Los Angeles: W.A. Clark Library, 1968); THE MOCK-TEMPEST (1674), in AFTER THE TEMPEST . . ., ed. George R. Guffey (Los Angeles: W.A. Clark Library, 1969); both are photographic facsimiles. The best edition of Duffett, however, is Ronald E. DiLorenzo's THREE BURLESQUE PLAYS OF THOMAS DUFFETT . . . (Iowa City: Univ. of Iowa Press, 1972), which includes PSYCHE DEBAUCHED (1675). DiLorenzo provides a sound introduction, textual and explanatory notes, and a census of extant copies.

Charles Haywood's article, "THE SONGS AND MASQUE IN THE NEW TEM-PEST: An Incident in the Battle of the Two Theatres, 1674," HLQ 19 (1955), 39-56, suggests that the piece burlesques Thomas Shadwell and thus belongs to the struggle between the two companies. Kenneth M. Cameron, in "Duffett's NEW POEMS and Vacation Plays," TS 5 (1964), 64-70, argues that this 1676 volume gives information about the Duchess of Portsmouth's company and other vacation performances (but see John H. Wilson, "The Duchess of Portsmouth's Players," N&Q 208 [1963], 106-07). Victor C. Clinton-Baddeley gives some attention to Duffett in his history of burlesque (Part 1, Section 7.2), and Peter E. Lewis has a survey article, "The Three Dramatic Burlesques of Thomas Duffett," DUJ 58 (1966), 149-56, which emphasizes visual burlesque techniques in these plays. Samuel L. Macey's "Duffett's MOCK-TEMPEST and the Assimilation of Shakespeare during the Restoration and Eighteenth Century," RECTR 7, no. 1 (1968), 44-52, is less ambitious than its title suggests.

THOMAS D'URFEY (1653-1723)

Although perhaps best known today for the collection WIT AND MIRTH; OR, PILLS TO PURGE MELANCHOLY, 6 vols. (1719-20), D'Urfey had an active dramatic career spanning more than thirty years. Between 1676 and 1709 he had twenty-odd comedies, an opera, a comic opera, a tragicomedy, and three tragedies produced on the London stage. Yet there is no modern collection of his plays, and the only serious study of his work dates from 1916. THE IN-JURED PRINCESS (1682, from CYMBELINE) is available in facsimile (London: Cornmarket Press, 1970). The three parts of THE COMICAL HISTORY OF DON QUIXOTE (1694-95) were reprinted in 1889 (Brooklyn, N.Y., n. p.); A FOOL'S PREFERMENT (1688, from Fletcher) was reprinted in Volume 2 of Robert S. Forsythe's A STUDY OF THE PLAYS OF THOMAS D'URFEY, WITH A REPRINT OF 'A FOOL'S PREFERMENT,' 2 vols. (Cleveland, Ohio: Western Reserve Univ. Press, 1916-17). MADAME FICKLE (1617) is included in Jeffares's RESTORATION COMEDY, vol. 2; it adapts Rowley's A MATCH AT MIDNIGHT. WONDERS IN THE SUN (1706) was reprinted by the Augustan Reprint Society in 1964, with an introduction by William W. Appleton (Los Angeles: W.A. Clark Library). The NEW OPERAS . . . of 1721, which is comprised of several unacted pieces, was reprinted by Blom of New York in 1968. A se-lection, THE SONGS OF THOMAS D'URFEY, was edited by Cyrus L. Day in 1933 (Cambridge, Mass.: Harvard Univ. Press).

Forsythe's study, mentioned above, is confined largely to plot summaries and indication of sources, though some attention is given to the stage history of the better known plays; there is no satisfactory full-length account. Cyrus L. Day's DATES AND PERFORMANCES OF D'URFEY'S PLAYS (Charlottesville: Bibliographical Society of the Univ. of Virginia, 1950) is the standard author-ity on this subject. Contemporary criticism includes such pieces as WIT FOR MONEY; OR, POET STUTTER (1691) and frequent references in the TATLER, SPECTATOR, and GUARDIAN in the early years of the eighteenth century. Nineteenth- and early twentieth-century accounts are perfunctory, as is Jack A. Vaughn's "Persevering, Unexhausted Bard: Tom D'Urfey," QJS 53 (1967), 342-48. The only two significant studies are Kathleen M. Lynch, "Thomas D'Urfey's Contribution to Sentimental Comedy," PQ 9 (1930), 249-59, and Cary B. Graham, "The Jonsonian Tradition in the Comedies of Thomas D'Urfey," MLQ 8 (1947), 47-52. Lynch stresses D'Urfey's contribution to the "fair forlorn" stereotype, and Graham the humor characters, episodic structure, and gulling in many of the comedies.

Articles on specific plays have been concerned almost exclusively with dating or bibliographical matters. Fredson T. Bowers, in "The Two Issues of D'Urfey's CYNTHIA AND ENDYMION (1697)," PULC 13 (1951), 32-34, shows that Woodward and McManaway's nos. 526 and 527 are issues, not separate editions (see Part 1, Section 1.11); in "Thomas D'Urfey's COMICAL HISTORY OF DON QUIXOTE (1694)," PBSA 43 (1949), 191-95, Bowers discusses the printing history of this play. Jack A. Vaughn's "A D'Urfey Play Dated," MP 64 (1967), 322-23, shows that the 1676 quarto mentioned by Forsythe and other scholars is a ghost based on a misprint in the licensing date--the play was acted 31 May 1677 and first printed in the same year. Donald W. Sanville places six 1691 editions in proper order in "D'Urfey's LOVE FOR MONEY: A Bibliographical Study," LC 17 (1950), 71-77. Raymond A. Biswanger, Jr. argues, in "The Date of D'Urfey's RICHMOND HEIRESS," N&Q 198 (1953), 105-06, for a date in late April 1693; provides a printing history and analysis of issues, in "Thomas D'Urfey's RICHMOND HEIRESS (1693): A Bibliographical Study," SB 5 (1953), 169-78; and lists words not in or antedating OED entries, in "Several Words First Employed in D'Urfey's THE RICHMOND HEIRESS," MLN 70 (1955), 577-78. Cyrus L. Day, in "A Lost Play by D'Urfey," MLN 49 (1934), 332-34, conjectures plausibly that A WIFE FOR ANY MAN, produced between December 1695 and September 1697 but not printed, should be ascribed to D'Urfey.

Aside from those mentioned above, D'Urfey's plays include THE SEIGE OF MEMPHIS and THE FOOL TURNED CRITIC (1676), A FOND HUSBAND (1677), TRICK FOR TRICK (from Fletcher) and SQUIRE OLDSAPP (1678), THE VIRTUOUS WIFE (1679), SIR BARNABY WHIGG (1681), THE ROYALIST (1682), A COMMONWEALTH OF WOMEN (1685, from Fletcher's SEA VOYAGE), THE BANDITTI (1686), BUSSY D'AMBOIS (1691, an adaptation of Chapman's play), THE MARRIAGE-HATER MATCHED (1692), THE INTRIGUES AT VERSAILLES (1697), THE CAMPAIGNERS (1698), THE FAMOUS HISTORY OF THE RISE AND FALL OF MASSANIELLO (1699), THE BATH (1701), THE OLD MODE AND THE NEW (1703), and THE MODERN PROPHETS (1709).

SIR GEORGE ETHEREGE (1653?-91)

THE WORKS OF SIR GEORGE ETHEREGE: CONTAINING HIS PLAYS AND POEMS was first published in 1704. The edition of A. Wilson Verity had a few critical notes and an introduction (London: Nimmo, 1888). THE DRAMATIC WORKS OF SIR GEORGE ETHEREGE, ed. Herbert F.B. Brett-Smith, 2 vols. (Oxford: Blackwell, 1927*), is generally sound and has very good notes. THE MAN OF MODE has been often anthologized; W.B. Carnochan's edition in the Regents series (Lincoln: Univ. of Nebraska Press, 1966) may be recommended, and the play is also included in the Fountainwell series, ed. John Conaghan (Edinburgh: Oliver & Boyd, 1973). A facsimile reprint is available from Scolar Press of London. SHE WOULD IF SHE COULD, ed. Charlene M. Taylor, is also included in the Regents series (1971).

THE LETTERBOOK OF SIR GEORGE ETHEREGE, ed. Sybil M. Rosenfeld (London: Oxford Univ. Press, 1928*), and her article, "The Second Letterbook of Sir George Etherege," RES 3 (1952), 19-27, have been superseded by the LETTERS OF SIR GEORGE ETHEREGE, ed. Frederick Bracher (Berkeley and Los Angeles: Univ. of California Press, 1974), which includes the substance of his earlier articles on the subject. Bracher is working on a definitive biography; David D. and C.A. Mann are preparing a concordance to the plays.

Etherege was "discovered" by Edmund Gosse, who, in SEVENTEENTH-CENTURY STUDIES (London: K. Paul, Trench, 1883), provided a mass of new biographical material and impetus to the study of the plays. Both John L. Palmer and Bonamy Dobrée gave Etherege significant attention in their books on Restoration comedy; Dobrée also considered Etherege in ESSAYS IN BIOGRAPHY 1660-1726 (London: Oxford Univ. Press, 1925), but this discussion is inferior to that in RESTORATION COMEDY. Palmer follows Gosse in asserting that Restoration comedy begins with LOVE IN A TUB but is much more sensitive in separating Etherege's comedy from analogs in Molière. His analyses of the plays are less important than his view that "Etherege found a form for the spirit of his age." Dobrée treats Etherege as a charming and brilliant butterfly, characterizing LOVE IN A TUB as "rollicking farce," SHE WOULD IF SHE COULD as "vastly amusing," and THE MAN OF MODE as the perfection of the art of allusion. Dorothy Foster contributed important biographical information in a number of notes 1922-28: TLS, 16 and 23 Feb. 1922, pp. 108 and 124; N&Q 142 (1922), 341-44, 362-65, and 414; 153 (1927), 417-19,

435-40, 454-59, and 472-76; 154 (1928), 28; and TLS, 31 May 1928, p.
412. See also John W. Nichol, "Dame Mary Etherege," MLN 64 (1949),
419-22; John H. Wilson, "Etherege's Julia," MLN 62 (1947), 40-42; and
Thomas H. Fujimura, "Etherege at Constantinople," PMLA 71 (1956), 465-81.

The books of Palmer, Dobrée, and Henry T.E. Perry (see Part 1, Section 7.8)
were followed by Frances S. McCamic's SIR GEORGE ETHEREGE: A STUDY OF
RESTORATION COMEDY 1660-1680 (Cedar Rapids, Iowa: Torch Press, 1931*),
an undistinguished essay. The first modern study is Thomas H. Fujimura's, in
chapter 5 of the RESTORATION COMEDY OF WIT (1952), which stresses the
naturalism of the plays. Etherege, Fujimura believes, is not really interested
in manners but in "witty dialogue, naturalistic content, and realistic technique." Dorimant is the perfect truewit, laughing at fools and expressing a
skeptical and libertine view of human life; THE MAN OF MODE perfects techniques used less skillfully in the first two plays. Dale S. Underwood, ETHE-
REGE AND THE SEVENTEENTH-CENTURY COMEDY OF MANNERS (New
Haven: Yale Univ. Press, 1957*), gives a reading of the plays in accord with
the tenets of modern criticism; he finds complexity and irony everywhere and
ignores theatrical values. His book is therefore the antithesis of Dobrée's essay. Nevertheless, his readings are often perceptive, and his judgments in
many respects more balanced than those of earlier critics. He argues that
LOVE IN A TUB has unity of theme if not of action but is neither a radical
departure from earlier comedy nor a mere exemplar of Caroline comedy. SHE
WOULD is treated quite briefly, THE MAN OF MODE at length. Underwood
regards this play as one of the masterpieces of English comedy and analyzes
it in terms of the hero's "conflict with and ultimate conquest of several contrasting 'worlds' within the total world of the play." He relates main plot to
subplot carefully and discusses the city-versus-country opposition in the play;
in the end, however, Etherege suggests no values against which the "comedy
of power" in the play can be judged.

Fujimura and Underwood offer the first detailed analyses of Etherege's art and,
despite their over-solemn approaches, are often acute and always stimulating.
Norman N. Holland devotes a full chapter of THE FIRST MODERN COMEDIES
to each of Etherege's three plays. He follows John Wilcox (THE RELATION
OF MOLIERE TO RESTORATION COMEDY) in stressing the importance of
Frollick to THE COMICAL REVENGE but develops an elaborate notion of the
"downward conversion" of abstractions and ideals to physical reality in the
play pursuant to his appearance-versus-reality thesis. SHE WOULD IF SHE
COULD presupposes a fundamental split between society and natural desires,
Holland argues, and this opposition is symbolized in the play by country against
town. THE MAN OF MODE is amoral; cleverness is the only virtue in the
play, and the stereotype of the rake reformed is undercut by irony. Holland
is often brilliant, but he also often ignores the comic and theatrical values of
Etherege's plays in the pursuit of complex and rather murky levels of meaning
no audience could ever see.

Virginia O. Birdsall's WILD CIVILITY gives two chapters to Etherege. THE
COMICAL REVENGE, she feels, dramatizes the entrance of "Falstaffian tavern
humor" into "a sophisticated and effete court world"; SHE WOULD IF SHE

COULD exhibits the triumph of the new world of Courtall and Freeman over the old realm represented by Lady Lockwood. Dorimant and Harcourt take a similar role, since Birdsall's rake heroes are individuals challenging social and moral authority. Jocelyn Powell, in "George Etherege and the Form of a Comedy," BROWN COLLECTION, pp. 43-69, argues that Etherege belongs not in the tradition of classical comedy of judgment but in that of the comedy of experience. His characters and situations are seen from the inside, subjectively experienced rather than objectively satirized. LOVE IN A TUB thus has unity of mood; our laughter at the Lockwoods is sympathetic, since they are amoral in their energy and vitality. THE MAN OF MODE is the perfect drama of experience; the theme of the play is the emptiness and isolation of the lives of the characters as experienced through Dorimant's relationships with women.

Aside from Purvis E. Boyette's discussion of the dramatic use of songs in the plays in "The Songs of George Etherege," SEL 6 (1966), 409-19, most recent discussions focus on individual plays, especially THE MAN OF MODE. David R.M. Wilkinson presents the play as a fine example of his thesis in THE COMEDY OF HABIT: Dorimant uses all his charm and wit to dupe women and abuse their affection for him, and this shows the moral weakness and inverted values of the comedy of manners generally. Paul C. Davies, in "The State of Nature and the State of War: A Reconsideration of THE MAN OF MODE," UTQ 39 (1969), 53-62, argues that the play presents characters in a state of war; the play presents life in a tough and realistic way, with Dorimant an agressor who may surrender in the end. David Krause's "The Defaced Angel: A Concept of Satanic Grace in Etherege's THE MAN OF MODE," DS 7 (1968-69), 87-103, goes even farther. In this highly colored reading, the symbolism of sin and death in the play is said to suggest Dorimant as a fallen angel who demonstrates the victory of the imagination over reality. John G. Hayman, in "Dorimant and the Comedy of a Man of Mode," MLQ 30 (1969), 183-97, notes the continuing controversy over the character and argues that Wilkinson is correct except for his conclusion: the plot shows the inadequacy of Dorimant's original mode of behavior to the new emotion provoked by Harriet. A somewhat similar argument is presented by Ronald Berman in "The Comic Passions of THE MAN OF MODE," SEL 10 (1970), 459-68, but neither article is wholly convincing. "A Case of Restoration: Terry Hands and Timothy O'Brien Talk to Robert Waterhouse," P&P, Nov. 1971, pp. 14-16 and 84, presents an interesting discussion of the Royal Shakespeare Company's recent production of the play, arguing against the mannered conception of acting Restoration drama so common in modern productions.

The two best recent discussions of the play are Harriett Hawkins's in LIKENESSES OF TRUTH and Robert D. Hume's in "Reading and Misreading THE MAN OF MODE," CRITICISM 14 (1972), 1-11. Hawkins attacks the "righteous solemnity" of such critics as Powell and Underwood; her own reading stresses the love-game elements in the play, and she argues persuasively that the audience's enjoyment of the game is more important than concern for the moral shortcomings of Dorimant. Hume agrees, seeing the play as an example of the sex comedy popular in the 1660's and as a display of Etherege's wit; Dorimant is a Don Juan being tamed by a woman even tougher and more controlled than he is.

More specialized articles include R.G. Howarth, "Untraced Quotations in Etherege," N&Q 188 (1945), 281; Arthur Sherbo, "A Note on THE MAN OF MODE," MLN 64 (1949), 343-44 (parallels with LES PRECIEUSES RIDICULES), and "Sir Fopling Flutter and Beau Hewitt," N&Q 194 (1949), 297-303 (Hewitt was not Etherege's model); David M. Vieth, "Etherege's MAN OF MODE and Rochester's 'Artemisa to Cloe,'" N&Q 203 (1958), 473-74 (parallels); Jean Auffret, "Etherege à l'école de Molière," JAQUOT COLLECTION, I, 395-407 (the influence of five of Molière's comedies); John Conaghan, "A Prompt Copy of Etherege's THE MAN OF MODE," LR 21 (1968), 387-88 (a marked copy of Q1 possibly used for a production in Edinburgh in 1679); and R.S. Cox, Jr., "Richard Flecknoe and THE MAN OF MODE," MLQ 29 (1968), 183-89 (use of Flecknoe in II.i). In "THE MAN OF MODE and THE PLAIN DEALER: Common Origins and Parallels," EA 19 (1966), 209-22, Auffret concocts an elaborate argument that Dorimant is a composite portrait of Rochester and the Earl of Mulgrave.

GEORGE FARQUHAR (1678-1707)

THE COMEDIES OF MR. GEORGE FARQUHAR was first published early in 1708; see Shirley S. Kenny, "George Farquhar," TLS, 17 Sept. 1971, p. 1119. The so-called WORKS OF THE LATE INGENIOUS MR. GEORGE FAR-QUHAR (c.1711) may have been simply a made-up collection, like other "edi-tions" of both sets. Farquhar was included in Leigh Hunt's DRAMATIC WORKS OF WYCHERLEY, CONGREVE, VANBRUGH, AND FARQUHAR (1840). THE DRAMATIC WORKS OF GEORGE FARQUHAR, ed. Alexander C. Ewald, 2 vols. (London: Nimmo, 1892), and GEORGE FARQUHAR, ed. William Archer, Mermaid series (London: Unwin, 1906*), have been superseded by THE COM-PLETE WORKS OF GEORGE FARQUHAR, ed. Charles A. Stonehill, 2 vols. (London: Nonesuch Press, 1930*). The Stonehill edition will undoubtedly be replaced by that now in preparation by Shirley S. Kenny, especially since Stonehill's work is woefully lacking in annotation.

Louis A. Strauss edited A DISCOURSE UPON COMEDY, THE RECRUITING OFFICER, and THE BEAUX' STRATAGEM together for the Belles Lettres series (Boston: Heath, 1914). The introduction to this edition, and that of William Archer to the Mermaid edition, remain useful, readable essays on Farquhar's art. Both plays have been reprinted in facsimile by Scolar Press, London. THE BEAUX' STRATAGEM has been edited by Eric Rothstein (New York: Ap-pleton-Century-Crofts, 1967) and by Alexander N. Jeffares for the Fountainwell series (Edinburgh: Oliver & Boyd, 1972). THE CONSTANT COUPLE is in-cluded in Jeffares's RESTORATION COMEDY, vol. 4. THE RECRUITING OF-FICER is available in the Regents series, ed. Michael Shugrue (Lincoln: Univ. of Nebraska Press, 1965), and in the Fountainwell series, ed. Alexander N. Jeffares (Edinburgh: Oliver & Boyd, 1973). Kenneth Tynan's "Rehearsal Log-book," pp. 12-16 of his edition (London: Hart-Davis, 1965), is an interesting discussion of his approach to the National Theatre production of this play.

The earliest substantial modern life was David Schmid's GEORGE FARQUHAR: SEIN LEBEN UND SEINE ORIGINAL-DRAMEN (Vienna: Braumueller, 1904) in the Vienna Beitraege zur Englischen Philologie series. Schmid's analysis of the plays is mechanical, and his biography is inferior to that by Willard Connely, YOUNG GEORGE FARQUHAR: THE RESTORATION DRAMA AT TWILIGHT (London: Cassell, 1949). The best brief biography is chapter 1 of Eric Roth-stein's GEORGE FARQUHAR (New York: Twayne, 1967), which does not read

Farquhar into his characters the way Connely and many earlier critics and biographers often do.

John Palmer, in his COMEDY OF MANNERS (1913), popularized the notion
that Farquhar destroyed the comedy of manners while furnishing its last brilliant
examples; Farquhar, he claims, treated sex emotionally and romantically and
therefore more lusciously than did Wycherley and Congreve. Depending on
their conceptions of the development of English drama, subsequent critics have
either agreed with Palmer or seen Farquhar as the dramatist who broadened the
narrow concerns of court comedy by including genuine emotion and by using
settings outside London. William Archer's emphasis (in his Mermaid edition) on
Farquhar's naturalness well exemplifies the latter trend. Few critics have tried
seriously to place Farquhar within the broad context of theatrical activity at
the opening of the new century and to consider his seven dramatic pieces on
this basis. Bonamy Dobrée's remarks in RESTORATION COMEDY are readable,
if superficial, and much superior to Henry T.E. Perry's discussion in THE
COMIC SPIRIT. Elisabeth L. Mignon gives a chapter to Farquhar in CRABBED
AGE AND YOUTH; Frederick S. Boas's account in EIGHTEENTH-CENTURY
DRAMA is fuller than most, and there are some perceptive remarks in Kenneth
Muir's THE COMEDY OF MANNERS.

Two good full-length studies of Farquhar have appeared. Eric Rothstein's book,
mentioned above, not only takes issue with the "Restoration comedy in decline"
thesis but offers a sustained, perceptive analysis of all of Farquhar's work.
Eugene N. James, in the introduction to THE DEVELOPMENT OF GEORGE
FARQUHAR AS A COMIC DRAMATIST (The Hague, Netherlands: Mouton, 1972),
presents a useful discussion of traditions in Farquhar scholarship and analyzes the
plays in the light of the dramatist's own criticism. Both Rothstein and James attempt
to document Farquhar's development; the former is perhaps more perceptive, the
latter more thorough. There is also a study by Kaspar Spinner, GEORGE FAR-
QUHAR ALS DRAMATIKER, in Swiss Studies in English (Bern, Switzerland: Francke,
1956).

Specific studies focus on THE BEAUX' STRATAGEM. William J. Lawrence
conjectures in "Foigard in THE BEAUX' STRATAGEM," N&Q 107 (1903), 46-
47, that the Father Fougourdy described by Pepys on 6 February 1664 was the
original of Foigard, but he presents no evidence. Martin A. Larson shows in
"The Influence of Milton's Divorce Tracts on Farquhar's BEAUX' STRATAGEM,"
PMLA 39 (1924), 174-78, that Farquhar used these tracts in the play. Ronald
Berman's "The Comedy of Reason," TSLL 7 (1965), 161-68, presents the play
as a drama of ideas; it shows why men should submit to reason, nature, and
society. A better essay is Alan Roper's "THE BEAUX' STRATAGEM: Image
and Action," in SEVENTEENTH-CENTURY IMAGERY: ESSAYS ON USES OF
FIGURATIVE LANGUAGE FROM DONNE TO FARQUHAR, ed. Earl R. Miner
(Berkeley and Los Angeles: Univ. of California Press, 1971), pp. 169-86. In
Roper's analysis Boniface represents appetite and Lady Bountiful love, hospitality, and charity; the play integrates imagery and plot in the alternate movement from inn to house. Garland J. Gravitt's "A Primer of Pleasure: Neo-
Epicureanism in Farquhar's THE BEAUX' STRATAGEM," THOTH 12, no. 2 (1972),
38-49, argues unconvincingly that the play supports a neo-Epicurean ethic.

Articles on THE CONSTANT COUPLE include George W. Whiting, "The Date of the Second Edition of THE CONSTANT COUPLE," MLN 47 (1932), 147-48, which demonstrates that the last act was altered for the second edition, not the third, and Richard Morton and William M. Peterson, "The Jubilee of 1700 and Farquhar's THE CONSTANT COUPLE," N&Q 200 (1955), 521-25, which shows that the playwright used news accounts of the jubilee in writing his play. James's thesis in "The Burlesque of Restoration Comedy in LOVE IN A BOTTLE," SEL 5 (1965), 469-90 (an essay included in his book), is ingenious if unconvincing; he argues that the play burlesques earlier comedy and that Farquhar did not repeat this approach because the public took the play straight and liked it. Robert L. Hough's two notes, "An Error in THE RECRUITING OFFICER" and "Farquhar: THE RECRUITING OFFICER," N&Q 198 (1953), 340-41, and 199 (1954), 474, suggest the haste in which Farquhar wrote the play. Albert Wertheim compares a modern adaptation, Brecht's PAUKEN UND TROMPETEN (1955), in "Bertolt Brecht and George Farquhar's THE RECRUIT-ING OFFICER," CD 7 (1973), 179-90. Sybil M. Rosenfeld, in "Notes on THE RECRUITING OFFICER," TN 18 (1963-64), 47-48, shows that Farquhar wrote the play with specific actors in mind. In addition to the chapters in James's and Rothstein's books, one may also consult Tucker Brooke's essay, "George Farquhar: THE RECRUITING OFFICER," in Charles M. Gayley and Alwin Thaler's REPRESENTATIVE ENGLISH COMEDIES, 4 (1936), pp. 667-80. William J. Lawrence, in "The Mystery of THE STAGE COACH," MLR 27 (1932), 392-97, conjectures that the play was first performed in April 1701 as an afterpiece to SIR HARRY WILDAIR; the conjecture is plausible, since WILD-AIR is a very short play, but Leo A. Hughes notes in A CENTURY OF ENG-LISH FARCE that there is no hard evidence to support the assertion. Eric Rothstein's essay, "Farquhar's TWIN-RIVALS and the Reform of Comedy," PMLA 79 (1964), 33-41, is substantially included in his book; Rothstein sees the play as an answer to Jeremy Collier, while James stresses the influence of John Locke's principle of enlightened self-interest.

HENRY FIELDING (1707-54)

The fullest bibliographies of Fielding appear in Volume 3 of Wilbur L. Cross's THE HISTORY OF HENRY FIELDING (New Haven: Yale Univ. Press, 1918), pp. 287-366; in Hiran K. Banerji's HENRY FIELDING: . . . HIS LIFE AND WORKS (Oxford: B. Blackwell, 1929*); and in Frederick H. Dudden's HENRY FIELDING: HIS LIFE, WORKS, AND TIMES (Oxford: Oxford Univ. Press, 1952*), II, 1126-55. Of these, Cross's is the most formal, and Dudden's the most up-to-date. Banerji lists selected criticism, but Francesco Cordasco's HENRY FIELDING: A LIST OF CRITICAL STUDIES PUBLISHED FROM 1895 TO 1946 (Brooklyn, N.Y.: Long Island Univ. Press, 1948) is more detailed despite many shortcomings; note additions in PQ 29 (1950), 273-75.

Fielding's plays have been included in various editions of his complete works; the best and most complete is THE COMPLETE WORKS OF HENRY FIELDING, ESQ., ed. William E. Henley, 16 vols. (London: W. Heinemann, 1903*). The Wesleyan edition of the works, ed. W.B. Coley et al. (Middletown, Conn.: Wesleyan Univ. Press, 1967--) will supersede all earlier editions. Two plays, EURYDICE (1737) and THE WEDDING-DAY (1743), were published in Volume 2 of the MISCELLANIES (1743). The DRAMATIC WORKS (2 vols., 1745) includes twenty additional plays, all except the first version of THE TRAGEDY OF TRAGEDIES (1730) and THE GRUB-STREET OPERA (1731). The original 1730 version of THE AUTHOR'S FARCE, ed. Charles B. Woods, is available in the Regents series (Lincoln: Univ. of Nebraska Press, 1966), as are THE GRUB-STREET OPERA, ed. Edgar V. Roberts (1968), and 'THE HISTORICAL REGISTER FOR THE YEAR 1736' AND 'EURYDICE HISSED,' ed. William W. Appleton (1967). THE GRUB-STREET OPERA, ed. LeRoy J. Morrissey, is included in the Fountainwell series (Edinburgh: Oliver & Boyd, 1973). PASQUIN (1736) has been ably edited by O.M. Brack, Jr. et al. (Iowa City: Univ. of Iowa Press, 1973). THE TRAGEDY OF TRAGEDIES (1731) was edited by James T. Hillhouse (New Haven: Yale Univ. Press, 1918*) and is also available with the original version, TOM THUMB: A TRAGEDY (1730), in the Fountainwell series, ed. LeRoy J. Morrissey (Edinburgh: Oliver & Boyd, 1970). A facsimile of the later version is available from Scolar Press (London, 1973); the play is also included in most standard anthologies.

There are two good biographies--Wilbur L. Cross's (3 vols., 1918) and Frederick

H. Dudden's (2 vols., 1952*), both mentioned above. Austin Dobson's HENRY FIELDING: A MEMOIR (London: Macmillan, 1883) is readable, but its two chapters on the plays are not nearly as useful as the extensive discussions of Cross and Dudden. Gertrude M. Godden's HENRY FIELDING: A MEMOIR (London: Samson Low, 1910) is negligible. Banerji devotes two chapters to Fielding the dramatist; Mary P. Willcocks's popular biography, A TRUE-BORN ENGLISHMAN: BEING THE LIFE OF HENRY FIELDING (London: Allen, Unwin, 1947), also discusses the plays. Biographical scholarship of any significance is included in Dudden's life; see also Kenneth D. Wright, "Henry Fielding and the Theatres Act of 1737," QJS 50 (1964), 252-58; George R. Levine, "Fielding's 'Defense' of the Stage Licensing Act," ELN 2 (1965), 193-96 (in a CHAMPION essay); and Martin C. Battestin, "Fielding and 'Master Punch' in Panton Street," PQ 45 (1966), 191-208.

Many of the earlier items in HENRY FIELDING: THE CRITICAL HERITAGE, ed. Ronald Paulson and Thomas Lockwood (London: Routledge & Kegan Paul, 1969), concern contemporary reaction to the plays. Criticism in the nineteenth and twentieth centuries, however, has focused almost exclusively on the novels; Fielding's dramatic career is usually treated as a prelude to empire, and several book-length studies ignore it completely. Of the modern surveys, George H. Nettleton's ENGLISH DRAMA . . . 1642-1780 (1914), Frederick W. Bateson's ENGLISH COMIC DRAMA (1929*), and Frederick S. Boas's EIGHTEENTH-CENTURY DRAMA (1953) contain the fullest accounts; Dane F. Smith's PLAYS ABOUT THE THEATRE (1936) may also be mentioned. Some attention is given Fielding in John C. Loftis's COMEDY AND SOCIETY (1959), more in THE POLITICS OF DRAMA (1963); see also Sheridan Baker, "Political Allusion in Fielding's AUTHOR'S FARCE, MOCK DOCTOR, and TUMBLE-DOWN DICK," PMLA 77 (1962), 221-31. Charles W. Nichols's "Social Satire in Fielding's PASQUIN and THE HISTORICAL REGISTER," PQ 3 (1924), 309-17, shows how Fielding's plays mirror the times; Leo A. Hughes's "The Influence of Fielding's Milieu upon His Humor," SET (1944), 269-97, how the plays were influenced by audience reaction and dramatic conditions.

Interest in the narrator persona in the novels has prompted a number of recent articles tracing the origin of this technique to the plays. See, for example, Anthony J. Hassall, "The Authorial Dimension in the Plays of Henry Fielding," KOMOS 1 (1967), 4-18; J. Paul Hunter, "Fielding's Reflexive Plays and the Rhetoric of Discovery," STUDIES IN THE LITERARY IMAGINATION (Georgia State Univ.) 5, no. 2 (Oct. 1972), 65-100; Claude J. Rawson, "Some Considerations on Authorial Intrusion and Dialogue in Fielding's Novels and Plays," DUJ 33 (1971), 32-44; and J'nan Sellery, "Language and Moral Intelligence in the Enlightenment: Fielding's Plays and Pope's DUNCAID, Part 1," EE 1 (1970), 17-26. Of these, the Hunter piece is the most interesting, though it is unnecessarily expansive. Other studies of technique in the plays include a solid article by Winfield H. Rogers, "Fielding's Early Aesthetic and Technique," SP 40 (1943*), 529-51; L.P. Goggin, "Development of Techniques in Fielding's Comedies," PMLA 67 (1952), 769-81; and remarks by Glenn W. Hatfield in HENRY FIELDING AND THE LANGUAGE OF IRONY (Chicago: Univ. of Chicago Press, 1968). Chapter 8 of Ian Donaldson's THE WORLD TURNED UPSIDE-DOWN (1970) may also be recommended.

Fielding's ballad operas are discussed in Gagey's book on the genre (Part 1, Section 7.19); by Edgar V. Roberts in "Eighteenth-Century Ballad Opera: The Contribution of Henry Fielding," DS 1 (1961), 77-85; by LeRoy J. Morrissey in "Henry Fielding and the Ballad Opera," ECS 4 (1971), 386-402 (a first-rate study of John Watts and the printing of ballad opera); and by Roberts again in "The Songs and Tunes in Henry Fielding's Ballad Operas," RICHARDS COLLECTION, pp. 29-49. Michael Irwin considers "Didacticism in Fielding's Plays" in chapter 3 of HENRY FIELDING: THE TENTATIVE REALIST (Oxford: Clarendon Press, 1967). Both J. Oates Smith's "Masquerade and Marriage: Fielding's Comedies of Identity," BSF 6, no. 3 (1965), 10-21, and Anthony J. Hassall's "Fielding's Puppet Image," PQ 53 (1974), 71-83, deal with image motifs in the plays. French influence (exaggerated somewhat) is the subject of G.E. Parfitt, L'INFLUENCE FRANCAISE DANS LES OEUVRES DE FIELDING . . . (Paris: Presses Modernes, 1928); that of Ralph the subject of Helen S. Hughes, "Fielding's Indebtedness to James Ralph," MP 20 (1922), 19-34. Several earlier notes on performance dates have been incorporated into THE LONDON STAGE. Other notes include Charles W. Nichols, "Fielding's Satire on Pantomime," PMLA 46 (1931), 1107-12; John E. Wells, "Some New Facts concerning Fielding's TUMBLE-DOWN DICK and PASQUIN," MLN 28 (1913), 137-42; and Charles B. Woods, "Notes on Three of Fielding's Plays," PMLA 52 (1937), 359-73 (on contemporary allusion in THE LETTER-WRITERS, THE MODERN HUSBAND, and EURYDICE HISSED).

There are numerous articles on individual plays. Charles B. Woods, "Cibber in Fielding's AUTHOR'S FARCE: Three Notes," PQ 44 (1965), 145-51, discusses hits at Cibber in the play. Jeanne A. Masengill, "Variant Forms of Fielding's COFFEE-HOUSE POLITICIAN," SB 5 (1952), 178-83, shows that RAPE UPON RAPE and two issues of the COFFEE-HOUSE POLITICIAN (all 1730) are variants of a single edition. Bertrand A. Goldgar, in "The Politics of Fielding's COFFEE-HOUSE POLITICIAN," PQ 49 (1970), 424-29, argues that the play alludes to Walpole and hence shows Fielding's early political involvement. Edgar V. Roberts conjectures details of a lost piece in "Henry Fielding's Lost Play DEBORAH; OR, A WIFE FOR YOU ALL (1733) . . .," BNYPL 66 (1962), 576-88. Jack R. Brown's article "Henry Fielding's GRUB-STREET OPERA," MLQ 16 (1955), 32-41, examines the stage history and various versions of the play. Jacques Michon, "Du BEGGAR'S OPERA au GRUB-STREET OPERA," EA 24 (1971), 166-70, makes some comparisons between Gay and Fielding. Martine Raynaud's "Fielding et l'unité dramatique de THE HISTORICAL REGISTER FOR THE YEAR 1736," CALIBAN 9 (1972), 41-53, finds this unity primarily in the satiric attack on Cibber, Rich, and Walpole. Adriaan E.H. Swaen discusses sources in Plautus and Regnard in "Fielding's THE INTRIGUING CHAMBERMAID," NP 29 (1944), 117-20. Both Edgar V. Roberts in "Fielding's Ballad Opera THE LOTTERY (1732) and the English State Lottery of 1731," HLQ 27 (1963), 39-52, and Harold G. Moss in "A Note on Fielding's Selection of Handel's 'Si cari' for THE LOTTERY," N&Q 217 (1972), 225-26, discuss the dramatist's use of contemporary materials.

Charles B. Woods's article, "The Folio Text of Fielding's THE MISER," HLQ 28 (1964), 59-61, shows that this piracy was probably published as a supplement to no. 5 of COTES'S WEEKLY JOURNAL (1734); for his article "The 'Miss Lucy' Plays of Fielding and Garrick," see under David Garrick, below.

L.P. Goggin considers Fielding's use of French originals and translations in "Fielding and the SELECT COMEDIES OF MR. DE MOLIERE," PQ 31 (1952), 344-50, noting that Fielding used the French directly in THE MOCK DOCTOR and both the French and the English in THE MISER. Dorothy Colmer, in "Fielding's Debt to John Lacy in THE MOCK DOCTOR," ELN 9 (1971), 35-39, argues that the play owes something to Lacy's DUMB LADY (1669), at least in four scenes. Charles B. Woods's "Theobald and Fielding's 'Don Tragedio,'" ELN 2 (1965), 266-71, argues convincingly that this character hits at Theobald. Winfield H. Rogers's "The Significance of Fielding's TEMPLE BEAU," PMLA 55 (1940), 440-44, and Samuel L. Macey's "Fielding's TOM THUMB as the Heir to Buckingham's REHEARSAL," TSLL 10 (1968), 405-14, are general essays. LeRoy J. Morrissey's article on the latter play, "Fielding's First Political Satire," ANGLIA 90 (1972), 325-48, shows that it is full of political barbs, many of which were sharpened in revision. Charles W. Nichols's article, "Fielding's TUMBLE-DOWN DICK," MLN 38 (1923), 410-16, examines the play as integrally related to PASQUIN and sees it as a parody of Pritchard's afterpiece THE FALL OF PHAETON. Emmett L. Avery, in "Fielding's UNIVERSAL GALLANT," RSW 6 (1938), 46, notes that this play was completed more than a year before its first performance.

SAMUEL FOOTE (1720-77)

Foote wrote twenty-odd comedies, farces, and burlesques during his long career as an actor and manager. THE WORKS OF SAMUEL FOOTE (4 vols., 1786) was a made-up collection of variously dated plays, as were the earliest editions of THE DRAMATIC WORKS OF SAMUEL FOOTE, ESQ. THE WORKS OF SAMUEL FOOTE . . . were edited by John Bee (John Badcock) in 3 vols. (London: Sherwood et al, 1830); there is no later edition, and Foote is seldom represented in twentieth-century anthologies. There is an edition of one play, SAMUEL FOOTE'S 'PRIMITIVE PUPPET-SHOW' FEATURING 'PIETY IN PATTENS' [1773], ed. Samuel N. Bogorad and Robert G. Noyes (THEATRE SURVEY MONOGRAPHS, being TS 14a [bonus issue], 1973). This has a good introduction and excellent commentary and notes.

Aside from some contemporary pamphlets, the earliest biography is William Cooke's MEMOIRS OF SAMUEL FOOTE, ESQ. . . . , 3 vols. (London: R. Phillips, 1805), which includes three dramatic pieces not previously published in the collected editions of Foote's works. John Forster contributed a solid appreciation of Foote to the QUARTERLY REVIEW in 1854 (Vol. 95, pp. 483-548); John Fyvie's essay in WITS, BEAUX, AND BEAUTIES OF THE GEORGIAN ERA (London: John Lane, 1909) is trivial by comparison. The earliest modern biography is SAMUEL FOOTE: A BIOGRAPHY, by Percy H. Fitzgerald (London: Chatto & Windus, 1910*), a solid and substantial work. Mary M. Belden's THE DRAMATIC WORK OF SAMUEL FOOTE (New Haven: Yale Univ. Press, 1929*) includes a life which adds little to Fitzgerald's and also gives pedestrian accounts of the plays. Gregory Sinko's SAMUEL FOOTE: THE SATIRIST OF RISING CAPITALISM (Breslau, 1950) is a brief Marxist interpretation. The fullest and most up-to-date study is SAM. FOOTE, COMEDIAN, 1720-1777, by Simon Trefman (New York: New York Univ. Press, 1971). Trefman's book is thoroughly documented and generally sound in its criticism, although it perhaps exaggerates the intrinsic importance of Foote's plays and does not always distinguish between anecdotes and facts about Foote's career.

It is perhaps significant that Frederick S. Boas does not mention Foote in his EIGHTEENTH-CENTURY DRAMA; aside from Allardyce Nicoll and the earlier histories, there are few general accounts. Robert V. Wharton, in "The Divided Sensibility of Samuel Foote," ETJ 17 (1965), 31-37, discusses the sentimental strain he sees in at least ten of Foote's plays. Bogorad, in the introduction to the edition of PIETY IN PATTENS cited above, takes the opposite view and is more convincing. Arthur H. Scouten's "On the Origin of Foote's Matinees," TN 7 (1953), 28-31, suggests that Foote took the notion from auctioneers and prizefight promoters already using matinee hours. Betsy C. Corner, in "Dr. Melchisedeck Broadbrim and the Playwright," JHM 7 (1952), 122-35, notes that Dr. John Fothergill took offense at his portrait in THE DEVIL UPON TWO STICKS (1768); he elucidates the play by reference to the contemporary quarrel about Licentiates in the Royal College of Physicians. Michel Berveiller, in "Anglais et français de comédie chez Louis de Boissy et Samuel Foote," CLS 2 (1965), 259-70, suggests that Foote's ENGLISHMAN IN PARIS (1753) was among the earliest examples of comedy based on dépaysement--on a character displaced from his national environment. Marston Balch deals with Foote's satire on enthusiasm and Methodist preaching in THE MINOR (1760) in "The Theatre Reforms the Pulpit," TAM 12 (1928), 753-62; William K. Wimsatt, Jr., discusses the composite sources of Foote's Sir Matthew (in THE NABOB, 1772) in "Foote and a Friend of Boswell's: A Note on THE NABOB," MLN 57 (1942), 325-35. Edward H. Weatherly's article "Foote's Revenge on Churchhill and Lloyd," HLQ 9 (1945), 49-60, deals with an unpublished version of a scene in TASTE (1752) as performed in 1761; this play is also the subject of an illustrated article by Christopher Wood, "TASTE: An Eighteenth-Century Satire on the Art Market by Samuel Foote," CONNOISSEUR 163 (1966), 240-42. Martha W. England's "The Satiric Blake: Apprenticeship at Haymarket?" BNYPL 73 (1969), 440-64 and 531-50, argues that Blake may have derived his "Island in the Moon" from Foote's show, "Tea in the Haymarket."

Acted plays by Foote not referred to above include THE KNIGHTS (1749, revived 1754), THE ENGLISHMAN RETURNED FROM PARIS (1756), THE AUTHOR (1757), THE DIVERSIONS OF THE MORNING (1758), MODERN TRAGEDY (1761), THE LIAR (1762), THE MAYOR OF GARRATT (1763), THE PATRON (1764), THE COMMISSARY (1765), THE TAILORS (1767, perhaps not by Foote), THE LAME LOVER (1770), THE MAID OF BATH (1771), THE BANKRUPT (1773), THE COZENERS (1774), and THE CAPUCHIN (1776, an alteration of A TRIP TO CALAIS). Foote also put on several pastiche "shows" in evasion of the Licensing Act. These include the "Auction of Pictures" (1748), "A Writ of Inquiry" (1754), "Comic Lectures" (1755), "The Orators" (1762), and "Morning Lectures" (1763).

THOMAS FRANCKLIN (1721-84)

Francklin, the son of a bookseller, went to Trinity College, Cambridge, and eventually became Doctor of Divinity in 1770. For a time a professor at Trinity, he resigned in 1759 and became a popular preacher in London. His plays, like his several translations, were intended to supplement his inadequate income. The first of them, THE ORPHAN OF CHINA (1756) was unacted but went through several editions during the century. Two other tragedies, THE EARL OF WARWICK (1766) and MATILDA (1775), were popular and were included in several contemporary collections. THE CONTRACT (1776), a farce, was less successful. Francklin also adapted ORESTES (1769) and ELECTRA (1774) from Voltaire; these two plays were included in THE WORKS OF MR. DE VOLTAIRE, 25 vols. (1761-65). He is mentioned in Nicoll and in earlier histories, but there are no modern editions or studies.

ANDREW FRANKLIN (d. 1845)

Little is known of Franklin, who was a native of Ireland. His plays include THE MERMAID (1792), THE WANDERING JEW and A TRIP TO THE NORE (1797), THE OUTLAWS (1798), THE EMBARCATION and GANDER HALL (1799), and THE EGYPTIAN FESTIVAL (1800). These are all one- and two-act afterpieces except the last, a comic opera in three acts. There are no collected or modern editions, and there are only scattered references in modern secondary sources. THE COUNTERFEIT, a farce, was produced in 1804.

DAVID GARRICK (1717-79)

Since Garrick was not only the greatest actor of his century but a prolific dramatist and a great theatrical manager as well, both contemporary and modern criticism concerning him is extensive. The literature of the many pamphlet wars which swirled about him during his career is documented in Arnott and Robinson's ENGLISH THEATRICAL LITERATURE and also listed by Emmett L. Avery in the NEW CBEL; material relating to the Shakespeare Jubilee and to his Shakespearean adaptations is listed in Part 1, Section 8.2 of this study. There is unfortunately no adequate bibliography of Garrick on which scholars may rely; aside from the sources mentioned above, the most convenient reference is Gerald M. Berkowitz, "David Garrick--An Annotated Bibliography," RECTR 11, no. 1 (1972), 1-18, which is limited to works dealing with Garrick as a writer.

The earliest collection of Garrick's plays is THE DRAMATIC WORKS OF DAVID GARRICK, ESQ., 3 vols. (1768), which includes sixteen plays. A three-volume edition with the same title, published in 1798*, includes twenty-four plays but still omits three original pieces and nine adaptations previously published. A modern critical edition is long overdue. 'THE LYING VALET,' 'A PEEP BEHIND THE CURTAIN,' 'BON TON; OR, HIGH LIFE ABOVE STAIRS': THREE FARCES BY DAVID GARRICK, ed. Louise B. Osborn (New Haven: Yale Univ. Press, 1925), has a brief introduction and few notes; THREE PLAYS BY DAVID GARRICK, ed. Elizabeth P. Stein (New York: Rudge, 1926*), has a more extensive apparatus and commentary; it includes HARLEQUIN'S INVASION, THE JUBILEE, and THE MEETING OF THE COMPANY. THE POETICAL WORKS . . ., 2 vols. (1785), includes many prologues and epilogues. Many individual plays are included in contemporary collections, but modern printed editions are rare. Many of the Shakespearean adaptations are now available in facsimile from London's Cornmarket Press, including ROMEO AND JULIET (1750), THE FAIRIES (1755), CATHARINE AND PETRUCHIO (1756), FLORIZEL AND PERDITA and ANTONY AND CLEOPATRA (1758), and A MIDSUMMER NIGHT'S DREAM (1763).

THE LETTERS OF DAVID GARRICK, ed. David M. Little and George M. Kahrl, 3 vols. (Cambridge, Mass.: Harvard Univ. Press, 1963), is standard and replaces earlies and partial collections except for THE LETTERS OF DAVID GARRICK AND GEORGIANA COUNTESS SPENCER 1759-1779, ed. Earl Spencer and Christopher Dobson (Cambridge: Roxburghe Club, 1960), for which permission to reprint was refused. James C. Nicholls, in "Some Emendations to THE LETTERS OF DAVID GARRICK, N&Q 213 (1968), 219-20, makes some minor corrections; see also John B. Shipley, "A Note on David Garrick's Correspondence," N&Q 213 (1968), 220-21, and the relevant entries in the Berkowitz bibliography mentioned above. THE DIARY OF DAVID GARRICK: BEING A RECORD OF HIS MEMORABLE TRIP TO PARIS IN 1751 was edited by Ryllis C. Alexander in 1928 (New York: Oxford Univ. Press*); George W. Stone, Jr., edited THE JOURNAL OF DAVID GARRICK, DESCRIBING HIS VISIT TO FRANCE AND ITALY IN 1763 (New York: Modern Language Association, 1939).

The earliest substantial biography is Thomas Davies's MEMOIRS OF THE LIFE OF DAVID GARRICK, ESQ. . . . (2 vols., 1780), revised in 1808 (London: Longman et al.*). Arthur Murphy's THE LIFE OF DAVID GARRICK, ESQ., 2 vols. (London: J. Wright, 1801*), adds nothing to Davies's account; the best nineteenth-century biographies are Percy H. Fitzgerald's THE LIFE OF DAVID GARRICK . . ., 2 vols. (London: Tinsley Bros., 1868*), rev. ed., 2 vols. (London: Simpkin et al., 1889), and Joseph Knight's DAVID GARRICK (London: Kegan Paul et al., 1894*), which corrects Fitzgerald in some respects. The emphasis in Florence M. Parsons's GARRICK AND HIS CIRCLE (London: Methuen, 1906*) is on the theatrical history of the period; her book is illustrated and readable but adds little to earlier accounts. Frank A. Hedgcock's A COSMOPOLITAN ACTOR: DAVID GARRICK AND HIS FRENCH FRIENDS (London: S. Paul, 1912; orig. pub. in French in 1911) is more specialized but adds a number of previously unpublished letters. There are two good modern biographies. Margaret Bolton's GARRICK (London: Faber, 1948) is sound and easier to read than Carola Oman [Lenanton]'s DAVID GARRICK (London: Hodder & Stoughton, 1958); the latter, however, is somewhat more substantial.

Specialized materials of biographical interest include chapter 8 of JOHN ZOFFANY, R.A., HIS LIFE AND WORKS 1735-1810, by Victoria A. Manners and G.C. Williamson (London: John Lane, 1920); Sybil M. Rosenfeld, "Garrick and Private Theatricals," N&Q 181 (1941), 230-31 (reply by Paul deCastro, 182 [1942], 234); T.H. Vail Motter, "Garrick and the Private Theatres, with a list of Amateur Performances in the Eighteenth Century," ELH 11 (1944), 63-75; Lewis M. Knapp, "Smollett and Garrick," in ELIZABETHAN STUDIES AND OTHER ESSAYS IN HONOR OF GEORGE F. REYNOLDS, Univ. of Colorado Studies in the Humanities, Vol. 2, no. 4 (Boulder: Univ. of Colorado Press, 1945), pp. 233-43; Edward H. Weatherley, "The Personal and Literary Relations of Charles Churchill and David Garrick," in STUDIES IN HONOR OF A.H.R. FAIRCHILD, ed. Charles T. Prouty, University of Missouri Studies, Vol. 21, no. 1 (Columbia: Univ. of Missouri Press, 1946), pp. 151-60; Kalman A. Burnim, "Garrick's Quarrel with Lacy in 1745," YLG 33 (1958), 29-34; John B. Shipley, "David Garrick and James Ralph: Remarks on a Correspondence," N&Q 208 (1958), 403-08; Paul Sawyer, "The Garrick--Mrs. Cibber Relationship," N&Q 205 (1960), 303-05; Kalman A. Burnim, "David Garrick's Early Will," TR 7 (1965), 26-44; Ronald Hafter, "Garrick and TRISTRAM SHANDY," SEL 7 (1967), 475-89; and Peter Walch, "David Garrick in Italy," ECS 3 (1970), 523-31.

Contemporary appraisals of Garrick are legion. Among the best are those of Samuel Johnson and Joshua Reynolds. Austin Dobson's essay, "Exit Roscius," in EIGHTEENTH CENTURY VIGNETTES, 3rd ser. (New York: Dodd, Mead, 1896*), pp. 1-28, is typical of turn-of-the-century accounts. James Laver's essay in FROM ANNE TO VICTORIA, ed. Bonamy Dobrée (London: Cassell, 1937), pp. 341-54, is unremarkable, as is William Angus's "An Appraisal of David Garrick, Based Mainly upon Contemporary Sources," QJS 25 (1939), 30-42. Edward C. Wagenknecht's study in MERELY PLAYERS (Norman: Univ. of Oklahoma Press, 1966), on the other hand, is a sensitive and well written appreciation.

Dougald MacMillan, in "David Garrick as Critic," SP 31 (1934), 69-83, concludes a useful survey of Garrick's critical remarks by denying him any stature as a critic on the somewhat unreasonable grounds that he had no fixed principles. MacMillan's "David Garrick, Manager: Notes on the Theatre as a Cultural Institution in England in the Eighteenth Century," SP 45 (1948), 630-46, focuses on Garrick's personal relationships and official duties. The best study of Garrick as manager, however, is Kalman A. Burnim's DAVID GARRICK, DIRECTOR (Pittsburgh: Univ. of Pittsburgh Press, 1961). Burnim first studies Garrick's management and production techniques in considerable detail and then devotes a chapter each to five specific productions: MACBETH, ROMEO AND JULIET, KING LEAR, HAMLET, and THE PROVOKED WIFE. Burnim's study draws on but adds greatly to the accounts of Garrick's treatment of Shakespeare in the sources listed in Part 1, Section 8.2.

The only full-length study of Garrick's dramatic work is DAVID GARRICK, DRAMATIST, by Elizabeth P. Stein (New York: Modern Language Association, 1938*), a solid and useful book. The author classifies the plays into five fairly convenient groups and devotes a chapter to each, concluding with an excellent bibliography of editions and secondary materials. She does not discuss Garrick's Shakespeare but does include his adaptations from the French.

The Stratford jubilee has been given perhaps more attention than it deserves. In addition to the works by Christian Deelman and Martha W. England mentioned in Part 1, Section 8.2 (and earlier studies by the latter subsumed in her book), there is also Johanne M. Stockholm's book, GARRICK'S FOLLY: THE SHAKESPEARE JUBILEE OF 1769 AT STRATFORD AND DRURY LANE (London: Methuen, 1964). Allardyce Nicoll, in "Garrick's Lost JUBILEE, First Stratford Celebration: A Manuscript Copy," THE TIMES (London), 25 June 1927, pp. 13-14, announced his possession of a copy of this 1769 skit, the original of which was lost in the Drury Lane fire of 1809. In addition to sections on Garrick in the works by Montague Summers, George C.D. Odell, Hazelton Spencer, and George C. Braham mentioned in Part 1, Section 8.2, there are a number of important articles on the subject of the Shakespearean adaptations--most of them by George W. Stone, Jr. In "The God of His Idolatry: Garrick's Theory of Acting and Dramatic Composition with Especial Reference to Shakespeare," in JOHN QUINCY ADAMS MEMORIAL STUDIES, ed. James G. McManaway et al. (Washington, D.C.: Folger Shakespeare Library, 1948), pp. 115-28, Stone reproduces Garrick's statements on the subject and argues that Shakespeare dominated his theory of acting and sense of dramatic values.

David Garrick

In "David Garrick's Significance in the History of Shakespeare Criticism: A Study of the Impact of the Actor upon the Change of Critical Focus during the Eighteenth Century," PMLA 65 (1950), 183-97, Stone argues Garrick's central importance in changing the critical attitudes toward Shakespeare in the period and in disseminating knowledge of the plays.

Stone's essays on individual plays include "Garrick's Presentation of ANTONY AND CLEOPATRA," RES 13 (1937), 20-38; "Garrick's Long Lost Alteration of HAMLET," PMLA 49 (1934), 890-921 (including a table of comparison between six versions 1703-73); "Garrick's Production of KING LEAR: A Study in the Temper of the Eighteenth-Century Mind," SP 45 (1948), 89-103 (including an extensive comparison with Tate's version); "Garrick and an Unknown Operatic Version of LOVE'S LABORS LOST," RES 15 (1939), 323-28; "Garrick's Handling of MACBETH," SP 38 (1941), 609-28; "A MIDSUMMER NIGHT'S DREAM in the Hands of Garrick and Colman," PMLA 54 (1939), 467-82 (includes THE FAIRIES and three other versions by Garrick and Colman); "Garrick and OTHELLO," PQ 45 (1966), 304-20; "Bloody, Cold, and Complex Richard: David Garrick's Interpretation," in ON STAGE AND OFF: EIGHT ESSAYS IN ENGLISH LITERATURE, ed. John W. Ehrstine et al. (Pullman: Washington State Univ. Press, 1968), pp. 12-25; "ROMEO AND JULIET: The Source of Its Modern Stage Career," ShQ 15 (1964), 191-206; and "Shakespeare's TEMPEST at Drury Lane during Garrick's Management," ShQ 7 (1956), 1-7. Stone's articles are meticulously detailed, though he tends to minimize the contributions of others to the return to Shakespeare's text (Colman, for example) and perhaps to maximize the speed with which this return took place. Other relevant articles include Gwynne B. Evans's "Garrick's THE FAIRIES (1755): Two Editions," N&Q 204 (1959), 410-11 (Jaggard's bibliography confuses editions with issues), and Charles Haywood's "William Boyce's 'Solemn Dirge' in Garrick's ROMEO AND JULIET Production of 1750," ShQ 11 (1960), 173-87.

Richard J. Dircks's "Garrick and Gentleman: Two Interpretations of Abel Drugger," RECTR 7, no. 2 (1968), 48-55, studies Garrick in THE ALCHEMIST and in Francis Gentleman's THE TOBACCONIST (1770). Joseph M. Beatty, Jr.'s article on THE CLANDESTINE MARRIAGE is listed under Colman the Elder, above; see also Fredrick L. Bergmann, "David Garrick and THE CLANDESTINE MARRIAGE," PMLA 67 (1952), 148-62, which again focuses on Garrick's interest in adapting roles to available actors, and Helmut E. Gerber, "THE CLANDESTINE MARRIAGE and Its Hogarthian Associations," MLN 72 (1957), 267-71, which discusses antecedents of the play and parallels situations in it to some of Hogarth's work. In "Garrick's INSTITUTION OF THE GARTER," RECTR 6, no. 2 (1967), 37-43, Lillian Gottesman reconstructs this "new masque" for 1771. LETHE is a primary topic of Mary E. Knapp's essay, "Garrick's Last Command Performance," in THE AGE OF JOHNSON: ESSAYS PRESENTED TO C.B. TINKER (New Haven: Yale Univ. Press, 1949), pp. 61-71; Charles B. Woods relates this play to Fielding's OLD MAN TAUGHT WISDOM in "The 'Miss Lucy' Plays of Fielding and Garrick," PQ 41 (1962), 294-310. Lillian Gottesman, in "Garrick's LILLIPUT," RECTR 11, no. 2 (1972), 34-37, offers a brief account of this 1756 entertainment.

"David Garrick and THE LONDON CUCKOLDS" [by Paul Sawyer?], N&Q 201

186

(1956), 263-64, argues that this play was revived in 1748 to compete with the Covent Garden Lord Mayor's Day performance and abandoned in 1750 because it lacked box-office appeal. J.D. Hainsworth suggests in "David Garrick and Thomas Fitzpatrick," N&Q 217 (1972), 227-28, that Fribble in MISS IN HER TEENS attacks a type rather than an individual. Peter A. Tasch, in "Garrick's Revisions of Bickerstaffe's THE SULTAN," PQ 50 (1971), 141-49, discusses the manner in which Garrick fitted this afterpiece to Mrs. Abington's abilities as an actress and to the public taste. Edgar Wind relates a scene in THE THEATRICAL CANDIDATES to a Joshua Reynolds painting in "Harlequin between Tragedy and Comedy," JWI 6 (1943), 224-25. And in "Garrick's ZARA," PMLA 74 (1959), 225-32, Fredrick L. Bergmann discusses the nature and extent of Garrick's alteration of Aaron Hill's play.

JOHN GAY (1685-1732)

The most complete edition of Gay is the POETICAL, DRAMATIC, AND MIS-
CELLANEOUS WORKS OF JOHN GAY, 6 vols. (1795), which includes John-
son's biography. THE WORKS OF MR. JOHN GAY, 4 vols. (Dublin 1770,
London 1772), contains five plays in Volume 4, reprinted from PLAYS WRITTEN
BY MR. JOHN GAY . . . (1760). THE PLAYS OF JOHN GAY, 2 vols.
(London: Chapman & Dodd, 1923), adds THE MOHOCKS and THE WHAT D'YE
CALL IT. THE POETICAL WORKS OF JOHN GAY, ed. Geoffrey C. Faber
(London: Oxford Univ. Press, 1926*), includes a good bibliography as well as
good texts of THE BEGGAR'S OPERA and POLLY. For secondary works, one
may consult Julie T. Klein, JOHN GAY: AN ANNOTATED CHECKLIST OF
CRITICISM (Troy, N.Y.: Whitston, 1973).

A facsimile edition of THE BEGGAR'S OPERA (1729 ed.), including the music,
was published in 1961 (Larchmont, N.Y.: Argonaut Books) with commentary
by Louis Kronenberger and Max Goberman; Goberman's study of the sources
of the songs is helpful. Another facsimile (3rd ed., 1729), also with music,
is available from Scolar Press in London. There are many modern editions; the
better ones are those of Frederick W. Bateson (London: Dent, 1934), Edward
J. Dent (London: Oxford Univ. Press, 1954), Nettleton, Case, and Stone
(in the rev. ed. of their anthology), Benjamin W. Griffith, Jr. (Great Neck,
N.Y.: Barron's, 1962), and Edgar V. Roberts and Edward Smith, Regents
series (Lincoln: Univ. of Nebraska Press, 1969). The last three are the best
of these; they also include at least the tunes of the airs, without which no
adequate understanding of the work can be gained. A more recent edition is
that of Peter Lewis (New York: Barnes & Noble, 1973). Faber's edition of
POLLY in THE POETICAL WORKS remains the best. THREE HOURS AFTER
MARRIAGE was edited by Richard Morton and William Peterson from the first
edition of 1717 (Painesville, Ohio: Lake Erie College Studies, Vol. 1, 1961)
and by John H. Smith from the Dublin SUPPLEMENT TO THE WORKS OF
ALEXANDER POPE, 1758 (Los Angeles: Augustan Reprint Society, 1961).
Smith argues that the 1717 edition is the three-act version intended by the
authors, while the 1758 edition is the five-act version as acted. A text of
ACIS AND GALATEA is in the standard edition of Handel's works.

THE LETTERS OF JOHN GAY, ed. Chester F. Burgess (Oxford: Clarendon
Press, 1966), is standard. Edmund Curll's LIFE OF MR. JOHN GAY (1733)

is unreliable; Samuel Johnson's (in LIVES OF THE POETS) is more useful for
its comments on Gay's works than as a biography. Lewis Benjamin [Lewis
Melville], LIFE AND LETTERS OF JOHN GAY 1685-1732, AUTHOR OF 'THE
BEGGAR'S OPERA' (London: O'Connor, 1921*), is superior to Oscar Sherwin,
MR. GAY: BEING A PICTURE OF THE LIFE AND TIMES OF THE AUTHOR
OF 'THE BEGGAR'S OPERA' (New York: John Day, 1929), and to Phoebe
F. Gaye, JOHN GAY: HIS PLACE IN THE EIGHTEENTH CENTURY (London:
Collins, 1938*), both of which are journalistic and overwritten. The best bi-
ography, however, is William H. Irving, JOHN GAY: FAVORITE OF THE
WITS (Durham, N.C.: Duke Univ. Press, 1940*), which includes much mate-
rial on Gay's circle and the literary history of the period.

General accounts of Gay's career include William Hazlitt's remarks in LEC-
TURES ON THE ENGLISH POETS (1818) and William Thackeray's in ENGLISH
HUMORISTS (1853). George H. Nettleton devotes some attention to Gay in
his ENGLISH DRAMA (1914); there is a silly essay by Augustine Birrell in
THE COLLECTED ESSAYS . . ., 3 vols. (London: Dent, 1922), I, 100-106,
and better ones by Iolo A. Williams ("The Author of THE BEGGAR'S OPERA,"
LM 3 [1920], 166-79) and James R. Sutherland ("John Gay," in POPE AND
HIS CONTEMPORARIES: ESSAYS PRESENTED TO GEORGE SHERBURN [Ox-
ford: Clarendon Press, 1949], pp. 201-14). Both Frederick W. Bateson in
ENGLISH COMIC DRAMA (1929) and Frederick S. Boas in EIGHTEENTH-CEN-
TURY DRAMA (1953) have substantial chapters on Gay's dramatic work, focus-
ing on THE BEGGAR'S OPERA. The most recent study in English is Patricia
M. Spacks's JOHN GAY (New York: Twayne, 1965) in Twayne's English
Authors series; chapters 5 and 6 deal with the plays, and the volume includes
a useful bibliography. Articles primarily biographical in nature include John
Fuller, "Cibber, the REHEARSAL AT GOATHAM, and the Suppression of
POLLY," RES 13 (1962), 125-34; Chester F. Burgess, "John Gay and POLLY
and a Letter to the King," PQ 47 (1968), 596-98; Leonard W. Conolly, "Anna
Margaretta Larpent, Duchess of Queensbury, and Gay's POLLY in 1777," PQ
51 (1972), 955-57; and chapter 13 of Norman Ault's NEW LIGHT ON POPE
(London: Methuen, 1949).

Most of the criticism of individual plays concerns THE BEGGAR'S OPERA, but
there are a few exceptions. Alexander Burnet's 'ACHILLES' DISSECTED: BE-
ING A COMPLETE KEY OF THE POLITICAL CHARACTERS IN THAT NEW
BALLAD OPERA . . . (1733) is a useful contemporary pamphlet; the play is
also the subject of Peter E. Lewis's "John Gay's ACHILLES: The Burlesque
Element," ARIEL 3 (1972), 17-28, which concludes that the burlesque is neither precise nor specific enough. The only good study of a minor masterpiece
is "The True Proportions of Gay's ACIS AND GALATEA," PMLA 80 (1965*),
325-31, by Bertrand H. Bronson; Bronson is one of the very few critics of mu-
sical plays in the entire period who understands that texts and music must be
considered together. Thomas B. Stroup suggests burlesque parallels in "Gay's
MOHOCKS and Milton," JEGP 46 (1947), 164-67; there is a similar essay,
"Another Look at John Gay's THE MOHOCKS," MLR 63 (1968), 790-93, by
Peter E. Lewis. Adriaan E.H. Swaen's study, "The Airs and Tunes of John
Gay's POLLY," ANGLIA 60 (1936), 403-22, is standard; James R. Sutherland's
"POLLY among the Pirates," MLR 37 (1942), 291-303, tells the story of the
pirates and Gay's legal suit against them. Edward Parker's A COMPLETE KEY

TO THE NEW FARCE CALLED 'THREE HOURS AFTER MARRIAGE' . . . (1717) is a typical contemporary pamphlet. The best articles on this play are George Sherburn's "The Fortunes and Misfortunes of THREE HOURS AFTER MARRIAGE," MP 24 (1926), 91–109, and Peter E. Lewis's "Dramatic Burlesque in THREE HOURS AFTER MARRIAGE," DUJ 33 (1972), 232–39. A COMPLETE KEY TO THE LAST NEW FARCE 'THE WHAT D'YE CALL IT' . . . [Benjamin Griffin and Lewis Theobald], published in 1715, is really an attack on the play; recent articles include Peter Lewis's "Gay's Burlesque Method in THE WHAT D'YE CALL IT," DUJ 29 (1967), 13–25, and Edward Heuston's "Gay's TRIVIA and THE WHAT D'YE CALL IT," SCRIBBLERIAN 5 (1972), 39–42; the latter is peripheral.

Edward McAdoo Gagey devotes substantial time to Gay's ballad operas in his book on the form (1937; Part 1, Section 7.19), focusing on THE BEGGAR'S OPERA. There are also three full-length studies of this play. Charles E. Pearce's 'POLLY PEACHUM': BEING THE STORY OF LAVINIA FENTON (DUCHESS OF BOLTON) AND 'THE BEGGAR'S OPERA' (London: S. Paul, 1913*) is a readable study including material on the play, its background and stage history, as well as on the actress who created the role of Polly. Frank Kidson's book, 'THE BEGGAR'S OPERA': ITS PREDECESSORS AND SUCCESSORS (Cambridge: Cambridge Univ. Press, 1922*), considers earlier and later ballad operas much as Gagey does but concentrates on THE BEGGAR'S OPERA and POLLY. The best and most thorough study is William E. Schultz, GAY'S 'BEGGAR'S OPERA': ITS CONTENT, HISTORY, AND INFLUENCE (New Haven: Yale Univ. Press, 1923*). The first half of this book discusses the original and succeeding productions of the play through the Hammersmith Lyric Theatre revival in the 1920's; the last half has chapters on the genius of the play and its relation to Italian opera and contemporary political and social affairs. It includes discussions of the music and of the morality of the play, and there is also some discussion of POLLY. Appendix 1 is an annotated list of ballad operas; appendix 2 lists the original versions of the songs, with extensive notes. None of the four authors gives an adequate critical account of the play, which would require an integrated analysis of text and music.

The best study of the play is Bertrand H. Bronson's "THE BEGGAR'S OPERA," originally published in STUDIES IN THE COMIC, University of California Publications in English, Vol. 8, no. 2 (Berkeley and Los Angeles: Univ. of California Press, 1941), pp. 197–231, and several times reprinted, most recently in FACETS OF THE ENLIGHTENMENT (Berkeley and Los Angeles: Univ. of California Press, 1968), pp. 60–90. Other useful essays include Adriaan E.H. Swaen, "The Airs and Tunes of John Gay's BEGGAR'S OPERA," ANGLIA 43 (1919), 152–90; David H. Stevens, "Some Immediate Effects of THE BEGGAR'S OPERA," in THE MANLY ANNIVERSARY STUDIES . . . (Chicago: Univ. of Chicago Press, 1923*), pp. 180–89; and St. Vincent Trowbridge, "Making Gay Rich, and Rich Gay," TN 6 (1951), 14–20 (on the financial success of the play). The chapter on the play in Sven M. Armens's JOHN GAY: SOCIAL CRITIC (New York: King's Crown Press, 1954*) is superficial and ignores dramatic values; that in William Empson's SOME VERSIONS OF PASTORAL (London: Chatto & Windus, 1935), may be often oblique or pretentious in examining the ironies in the play but is also often extremely perceptive. Chester F. Burgess, in "The Genesis of THE BEGGAR'S OPERA," CITHARA 2 (1962), 6–12, argues that Gay was interested in the subject before Swift made his famous suggestion; in "Political Satire in John Gay's THE BEGGAR'S OPERA," MwQ 6 (1965), 265-76, Burgess gives a standard account of the play in relation to contemporary political affairs. Martin Price's brief section in TO THE PALACE OF WISDOM (1964) and Ian Donaldson's chapter in THE WORLD UPSIDE-DOWN (1970), both noted in Part 1, Section 7.6, are among the most stimulating and perceptive accounts of the play. Horst Hoehne's "Gay's BEGGAR'S OPERA und POLLY," ZAA 13 (1965), 232-60 and 341-59, is based on his inaugural dissertation. John Preston, in "The Ironic Mode: A Comparison of JONATHAN WILD and THE BEGGAR'S OPERA," EC 16 (1966), 268-80, shows that Gay's use of irony is far more complex than Fielding's.

Other articles and notes on the play include Arthur V. Berger, "THE BEGGAR'S OPERA, the Burlesque, and Italian Opera," ML 17 (1936), 93-105; Jean B. Kern, "A Note on THE BEGGAR'S OPERA," PQ 17 (1938), 411-13 (the quarrel between Peachum and Lockit is not a burlesque of an actual one between Walpole and Townsend but refers instead to the general friction between them); Walter E. Knotts, "Press Numbers as a Bibliographical Tool: THE BEGGAR'S OPERA (1728)," HLB 3 (1949), 198-212 (an argument William B. Todd demolished in PQ 29 [1950], 239-40); and John O. Rees, Jr., "A Great Man in Distress: Macheath as Hercules," UCS 12 (1966), 73-77, which relates Macheath between Polly and Lucy to the Choice of Hercules. Two articles compare Gay's play with Brecht's THREEPENNY OPERA. Ulrich Weisstein, in "Brecht's Victorian Version of Gay: Imitation and Originality in the DREIGROSCHENOPER," CL 7 (1970), 314-35, merely uses Gay as a whipping boy for praise of Brecht's play. Judith J. Sherwin's "'The World is Mean and Man Uncouth,'" VQR 35 (1959), 258-70, is more balanced if also more obvious in comparing the two works.

FRANCIS GENTLEMAN (1728-84)

Gentleman was born in Dublin and, after a short career in the army, became an actor, dramatist, and occasional poet-critic. He was active after about 1748 in Dublin, London, and the provinces. Several tragedies by him were acted or published at Bath, including THE SULTAN, SEJANUS (from Jonson), and ZAPHNA. Plays produced in London include THE ROYAL SLAVE (1769, from Southerne's OROONOKO), THE TOBACCONIST (1771, from Jonson's ALCHEMIST), THE COXCOMBS (1771, also from Jonson), CUPID'S REVENGE (1772), THE PANTHEONITES (1773), and THE MODISH WIFE (1773; Chester 1770). Of these, only THE TOBACCONIST had real success. THE DRAMATIC CENSOR, 2 vols. (1770), is Gentleman's best known work.

CHARLES GILDON (1665-1724)

Three tragedies and two adaptations are attributed to this well known hack writer and critic. The tragedies are THE ROMAN BRIDE'S REVENGE (1696), PHAETON (1698), LOVE'S VICTIM (1701); the adaptations are MEASURE FOR MEASURE (1700) and THE PATRIOT (1702, from Lee's LUCIUS JUNIUS BRUTUS). There are no collected or modern editions of Gildon's plays and only scattered comments on the tragedies in secondary sources. The Shakespearean adaptation is, however, discussed in several of the sources listed in Part 1, Section 8.2.

OLIVER GOLDSMITH (1730?-74)

The fullest bibliography of Goldsmith is Temple Scott's OLIVER GOLDSMITH BIBLIOGRAPHICALLY AND BIOGRAPHICALLY CONSIDERED (New York: Bowling Green Press, 1928); it is based on the Elkins collection now in the Free Library of Philadelphia. Ernest R. Dix, "The Works of Oliver Goldsmith: A Hand-List of Dublin Editions before 1801," TBSI 3 (1928), 93-101, and Iolo A. Williams's chapter on Goldsmith in SEVEN EIGHTEENTH-CENTURY BIBLI-OGRAPHIES (London: Dulau, 1924), may also be consulted; the latter is limited to first editions. The best list of Goldsmith's works is that by Author Friedman in the NEW CBEL. Katharine C. Balderston's A CENSUS OF THE MANUSCRIPTS OF OLIVER GOLDSMITH (New York: Brick Row Bookshop, 1926) is exhaustive.

The standard edition of Goldsmith's major writings is THE COLLECTED WORKS OF OLIVER GOLDSMITH, ed. Arthur Friedman, 5 vols. (Oxford: Oxford Univ. Press, 1966); the plays are in Volume 5. THE WORKS OF OLIVER GOLDSMITH, ed. J.W.M. Gibbs, 4 vols. (London: G. Bell & Sons, 1884-86), is the best of the earlier editions. Nineteenth-century editions of the MISCELLANEOUS WORKS, including plays, begin with an Edinburgh edition in 1791 (2 vols. in 1). The best known are THE MISCELLANEOUS WORKS OF OLIVER GOLDSMITH, M.B.: A NEW EDITION, 4 vols. (London: J. Johnson et al., 1801); THE MISCELLANEOUS WORKS OF OLIVER GOLD-SMITH, INCLUDING A VARIETY OF PIECES NOW FIRST COLLECTED, ed. James Prior, 4 vols. (New York: Putnam, 1850); and THE MISCELLANEOUS WORKS . . . WITH BIOGRAPHICAL INTRODUCTION BY PROFESSOR MAS-SON (London: Macmillan, 1868), better known as the Globe edition. The POEMS AND PLAYS BY OLIVER GOLDSMITH, M.B. was first published in Dublin in 1777; the Austin Dobson edition, 2 vols. (London: Dent, 1889), was later used for the Everyman Library edition (London: Dent, 1910); the plays were issued separately by Dent in 1901 and were also edited by Charles E. Doble and George Ostler (London: Oxford Univ. Press, 1909; 1928 [Oxford Standard Authors]). Dobson did the introduction and George P. Baker the text to the Belles Lettres edition of the two major plays (Boston: Heath, 1903).

THE GOOD-NATURED MAN is not available in a sound separate edition. THE GRUMBLER, acted only once (1773), was printed from the Larpent MS, ed. Alice I.P. Wood (Cambridge, Mass.: Harvard Univ. Press, 1931). There are many editions of SHE STOOPS TO CONQUER, including those edited by Katharine C. Balderston for the Crofts Classics Series (New York: Appleton-Century-Crofts, 1951), by Alexander N. Jeffares for Macmillan's English Classics (London: Macmillan, 1965), and by Arthur Friedman (Oxford: Oxford Univ. Press, 1968). The play is also available in facsimile from Scolar Press of London (1970).

THE COLLECTED LETTERS OF OLIVER GOLDSMITH, ed. Katharine C. Balderston (Cambridge: Cambridge Univ. Press, 1928*), is standard, though seven additional items have since been published. Goldsmith seems always to have attracted biographers. Aside from the contemporary accounts of him given by Sir Joshua Reynolds, Thomas Davies, Samuel Johnson, Sir John Hawkins, James Boswell, and others, the first real biography is Thomas Percy's MEMOIRS OF DR. GOLDSMITH . . . (1773; revised by Percy and others for THE MISCELLANEOUS WORKS . . ., 4 vols. [London: J. Johnson et al., 1801]). THE HISTORY AND SOURCES OF PERCY'S 'MEMOIR OF GOLDSMITH,' by Katharine C. Balderston (Cambridge: Cambridge Univ. Press, 1926), is an excellent study of this work, and both this and her edition of Goldsmith's letters reprint contemporary biographical materials. Richard Glover's "Authentic Anecdotes of the Late Dr. Goldsmith" appeared in THE UNIVERSAL MAGAZINE 54 (1774), 252-55, shortly after Goldsmith's death. James Prior's THE LIFE OF OLIVER GOLDSMITH . . ., 2 vols. (London: Murray, 1837), and John Forster's THE LIFE AND ADVENTURES OF OLIVER GOLDSMITH . . . (London: Bradbury & Evans, 1848; rev. ed., 2 vols., 1854*, as THE LIFE AND TIMES OF OLIVER GOLDSMITH), along with Austin Dobson's briefer LIFE OF OLIVER GOLDSMITH (London: W. Scott, 1888*), were the best of the nineteenth-century biographies. There have been a dozen or so more in the present century, beginning with Richard King's OLIVER GOLDSMITH (London: Methuen, 1910). The best is Ralph Wardle's OLIVER GOLDSMITH (Lawrence: Univ. of Kansas Press, 1957); Ricardo Quintana's OLIVER GOLDSMITH: A GEORGIAN STUDY (New York: Macmillan, 1967) is as much a critical appraisal as a biography.

GOLDSMITH: THE CRITICAL HERITAGE, ed. George S. Rousseau (London: Routledge & Kegan Paul, 1974), includes some material on the plays. There are brief accounts in the histories of George H. Nettleton and Frederick S. Boas, and Ricardo Quintana has a good discussion of irony in the plays in the book mentioned above. Clara M. Kirk's OLIVER GOLDSMITH (New York: Twayne, 1967) is unremarkable but does include a substantial section on the plays. Arthur L. Sells, in LES SOURCES FRANCAISES DE GOLDSMITH (Paris: Champion, 1924), argues debts to Marivaux and others. William B. Todd, "The First Editions of THE GOOD-NATURED MAN and SHE STOOPS TO CONQUER," SB 11 (1958), 133-42, shows that all the "editions" W. Griffin published of the two plays (1768 and 1773) are in each case merely impressions of a single edition.

John H. Smith's "Tony Lumpkin and the Country Booby Type in Antecedent English Comedy," PMLA 58 (1943), 1038-49, and Robert B. Heilman's "The Sentimentalism of Goldsmith's GOOD-NATURED MAN," in STUDIES FOR WILLIAM A. READ . . ., ed. Nathaniel M. Caffee and Thomas A. Kirby (Baton

Rouge: Louisiana State Univ. Press, 1940), pp. 237-53, may both be recommended; the latter essay denies that the play is sentimental and argues that young Honeywood is an object of laughter. Allan E. Rodway, in "Goldsmith and Sheridan: Satirists of Sentiment," in RENAISSANCE AND MODERN ESSAYS . . ., ed. George R. Hibbard (London: Routledge & Kegan Paul, 1966), pp. 65-72, takes a more conventional view of the play. Other articles include Robert G. Howarth, "Proverbs in THE GOOD-NATURED MAN," N&Q 174 (1938), 245, and Byron Gassman, "French Sources of Goldsmith's THE GOOD-NATURED MAN," PQ 39 (1960), 56-65 (only two of six suggested by earlier critics seem demonstrable).

Alexander N. Jeffares's A CRITICAL COMMENTARY ON "SHE STOOPS TO CONQUER" (London: Macmillan, 1966) is a sound discussion of the play. B. Eugene McCarthy, in "The Theme of Liberty in SHE STOOPS TO CONQUER," UWR 7 (1971), 1-8, argues that the play exhibits contrast and deception on several levels and agrees with Quintana that it has a much stronger structure than most critics have allowed it. See also Jack D. Durant, "Laughter and Hubris in SHE STOOPS TO CONQUER: The Role of Young Marlowe," SSJ 37 (1972), 269-80. Katharine C. Balderston discusses the Larpent copy in "A Manuscript Version of SHE STOOPS TO CONQUER," MLN 45 (1930), 84-85; Coleman O. Parsons examines the same topic in much more detail in "Textual Variations in a Manuscript of SHE STOOPS TO CONQUER," MP 40 (1942), 57-69. Studies of sources and analogs include Robert S. Forsythe, "Shadwell's Contribution to SHE STOOPS TO CONQUER and to THE TENDER HUSBAND," JEGP 11 (1912), 104-11 (THE LANCASHIRE WITCHES); Gertrude Ingalls, "Some Sources of Goldsmith's SHE STOOPS TO CONQUER," PMLA 44 (1929), 565-68 (SPECTATOR 289 and 427); Maurice Baudin, "Une source de SHE STOOPS TO CONQUER," PMLA 45 (1930), 614 (unconvincing; M.A. LeGrand's GALANT COUREUR, 1722); Mark Schorer, "SHE STOOPS TO CONQUER: A Parallel," MLN 48 (1933), 91-94 (THE MAN'S BEWITCHED); and John Hennig, "The Auerbachs Keller Scene and SHE STOOPS TO CONQUER," CL 7 (1955), 193-97 (an unconvincing parallel).

GEORGE GRANVILLE, LORD LANSDOWNE (c.1666-1735)

Granville is primarily known as a minor poet; his plays include THE SHE GAL-
LANTS (1695 or 1696), HEROIC LOVE (1697 or 1698), THE JEW OF VENICE
(1701, from Shakespeare), and THE BRITISH ENCHANTERS (1706). The last
of these was the most popular. The first three were collected in 1713 as
THREE PLAYS . . .; all four were included in FOUR PLAYS OF THE RIGHT
HONORABLE LORD LANSDOWNE . . . (1732); in THE GENUINE WORKS,
IN VERSE AND PROSE . . ., 2 vols. (1732); and in THE DRAMATIC WORKS
OF THE RIGHT HONORABLE GEORGE GRANVILLE, LORD LANSDOWNE
(Glasgow, 1752). THE JEW OF VENICE is included in Christopher Spencer's
FIVE RESTORATION ADAPTATIONS OF SHAKESPEARE (1965); there are no
other modern editions. The standard biography is Elizabeth Handasyde's GRAN-
VILLE THE POLITE: THE LIFE OF GEORGE GRANVILLE, LORD LANSDOWNE,
1666-1735 (London: Oxford Univ. Press, 1933), which includes a bibliography.
See also Herbert M. Cashmore, "Lord Lansdowne's Comedies," N&Q 155
(1928), 464-65. John H. Wilson discusses THE JEW OF VENICE in "Granville's 'Stock-Jobbing' Jew," PQ 13 (1934), 1-15; see also the works listed
in Part 1, Section 8.2. There is a brief discussion of THE BRITISH ENCHANTERS
in Stoddard Lincoln's article, "The Anglicization of AMADIS DE GAUL," in
ON STAGE AND OFF: EIGHT ESSAYS IN ENGLISH LITERATURE, ed. John
W. Ehrstine et al. (Pullman: Washington State Univ. Press, 1968), pp. 46-
52. The Handasyde biography offers also the fullest account of Granville's
plays.

BENJAMIN GRIFFIN (1680-1740)

Griffin, the son of a clergyman, began his career as a strolling player in the provinces. His plays include a tragedy, INJURED VIRTUE (1714, from Massinger); a comedy, WHIG AND TORY (1720); and three farces--LOVE IN A SACK (1715), THE HUMOURS OF PURGATORY (1716), and THE MASQUERADE (1717). Of these, the comedy was the most successful; see William M. Peterson, "Performances of Benjamin Griffin's WHIG AND TORY," N&Q 202 (1957), 17-19. There are no modern editions of Griffin's plays, and there are only scattered references in the standard modern histories.

ELIZABETH GRIFFITH (1720?-93)

Elizabeth Griffith is best known today for her fiction and for THE MORALITY
OF SHAKESPEARE'S COMEDY ILLUSTRATED (1775), but she also wrote fiction
and half a dozen rather sentimental comedies, five of which were acted, be-
tween 1765 and 1779. These are THE PLATONIC WIFE (1765), THE DOUBLE
MISTAKE (1766, attributed to her), THE SCHOOL FOR RAKES (1769), A WIFE
IN THE RIGHT (1772), and THE TIMES (1779, from Goldoni). THE SCHOOL
FOR RAKES was her most popular play. Jane E. Norton gives a bibliography
of early editions in "Some Uncollected Authors, 22: Elizabeth Griffith," BC
8 (1959), 418-24; there is a biographical sketch in Joyce M.S. Tompkins's
THE POLITE MARRIAGE . . . (Cambridge: Cambridge Univ. Press, 1938),
pp. 1-40.

JOSEPH HARRIS (c.1650-c.1715)

Harris, who was also an actor, wrote THE MISTAKES (1690), THE CITY BRIDE (1696, from John Webster), and LOVE'S A LOTTERY (1699, including the masque LOVE AND RICHES RECONCILED). THE CITY BRIDE, Harris's most popular play, has been edited by Vinton A. Dearing for the Augustan Reprint series (Los Angeles: W.A. Clark Library, 1952). There are no modern editions and only scattered references to Harris in standard modern histories of the drama.

WILLIAM HAVARD (1710?-78)

Havard, son of a Dublin vintner, became a prominent actor, specializing in secondary roles. His plays are SCANDERBEG (1733, a failure), KING CHARLES THE FIRST (1737), REGULUS (1744), and THE ELOPEMENT (1763); the first three are tragedies, the last a farce. KING CHARLES THE FIRST, written in imitation of Shakespeare, is Havard's best play, though David Garrick's acting carried REGULUS through several performances. There are no modern editions and only scattered references in the secondary literature.

WILLIAM HAYLEY (1745-1820)

Hayley, considered by his contemporaries a major poet, was born in Chichester and was educated at Eton and Cambridge, leaving the university in 1767 without a degree. His first dramatic efforts were rejected by Garrick and Colman, but eventually five of his plays were produced in London--MARCELLA (1789, from THE CHANGELING), THE TWO CONNOISSEURS and LORD RUSSELL (1784), EUDORA (1790), and ZELMA (1792, with Jeremiah Meyer). PLAYS OF THREE ACTS WRITTEN FOR A PRIVATE THEATRE (1784) included the first three of these and THE HAPPY PRESCRIPTION and THE MAUSOLEUM. The plays included in POEMS AND PLAYS . . ., 6 vols. (1785, 1788), are from this edition. THREE PLAYS . . . (London: for T. Cadell and W. Davies, 1811) included EUDORA, THE VICEROY, and THE HEROINE OF CAMBRIA. Early editions are discussed in N.J. Barker's "Some Notes on the Bibliography of William Hayley," TCBS 3 (1959-62), 103-12, 167-76, and 339-60. The best biography is still THE MEMOIRS OF THE LIFE AND WRITINGS . . . WRITTEN BY HIMSELF . . ., ed. J. Johnson, 2 vols. (London: Colburn, 1823); see also William T. LeViness, THE LIFE AND WORKS OF WILLIAM HAYLEY 1745-1820: A BICENTENNIAL TRIBUTE (Santa Fe, N.M.: Rydal Press, 1945), a twenty-page pamphlet.

ELIZA HAYWOOD (c.1693-1756)

Eliza Haywood wrote or collaborated on two tragedies, a comedy, and a burlesque produced between 1721 and 1733; the best was her comedy A WIFE TO
BE LET (1723). She is known today for her fiction. THE WORKS OF MRS.
ELIZA HAYWOOD, 4 vols. (1724), is the only collected edition; there are
no modern editions of any of the plays. The best secondary accounts are
George F. Whicher's THE LIFE AND ROMANCES OF MRS. ELIZA HAYWOOD
(New York: Columbia Univ. Press, 1915) and Walter and Clare Jerrold's study
in FIVE QUEER WOMEN (New York: Brentano's, 1929); Whicher's book in-
cludes a bibliography, pp. 176-204. John R. Elwood's article, "The Stage
Career of Eliza Haywood," TS 5 (1964), 107-16, may be supplemented by THE
LONDON STAGE, and by Marcia Heinemann, "Eliza Haywood's Career in the
Theatre," N&Q 218 (1973), 9-13. Donald M. Walmsley, in "Eliza Haywood:
A Bicentenary," TLS, 24 Feb. 1956, p. 117, establishes the date of death by
means of a contemporary obituary.

Haywood's plays include THE FAIR CAPTIVE (1721), A WIFE TO BE LET (1723),
FREDERICK, DUKE OF BRUNSWICK-LUNENBURGH (1729), and THE OPERA
OF OPERAS (1733, attributed to her and William Hatchett). ARDEN OF
FEVERSHAM (1736) is also possibly hers.

PAUL HIFFERNAN (1719-77)

Hiffernan was born in Ireland. His parents intended him for the Roman Catholic priesthood; he studied abroad, took a degree from the university in Montpellier, and lived in Paris for some years. He came to London about 1753. His first play was THE MAIDEN WHIM (1756; as THE LADY'S CHOICE, 1759). There followed THE NEW HIPPOCRATES (1761), an unsuccessful farce, THE NATIONAL PREJUDICE (1768, from Favart), and THE HEROINE OF THE CAVE (1794, an expanded version of Henry Jones's unfinished play, THE CAVE OF IDRA). Thereafter, Hiffernan turned to miscellaneous writing. There are no collected or modern editions of his work and only infrequent references to him in standard modern sources.

AARON HILL (1685-1750)

Hill was vitally interested in opera and drama all his life and wrote periodical and other criticism on many topics related to the stage. His plays were mostly tragedies, although he also translated Rossi's opera, RINALDO, for Haymarket production in 1711 and wrote a farce to go with his first play (ELFRID, 1710). His best known tragedies are THE FATAL EXTRAVAGANCE (1721, possibly in collaboration with Joseph Mitchell) and three adaptations from Voltaire, ZARA (1736), ALZIRA (1736), and MEROPE (1749). THE DRAMATIC WORKS OF AARON HILL, ESQ., 2 vols. (1760), includes all his produced plays as well as a number of unacted works. KING HENRY THE FIFTH (1723) is available in facsimile (London: Cornmarket Press, 1969).

The best biography is Dorothy Brewster's AARON HILL: POET, DRAMATIST, PROJECTOR (New York: Columbia Univ. Press, 1913), which includes a good bibliography. Alan D. McKillop's "Letters from Aaron Hill to Richard Savage," N&Q 199 (1954), 388-91, adds material not used by Brewster. Austin Dobson's essay, "Aaron Hill," collected in ROSALBA'S JOURNAL AND OTHER PAPERS (London: Chatto & Windus, 1915), pp. 229-62, was originally a review of the Brewster biography. Kalman A. Burnim demonstrates Hill's interest in realism in "Some Notes on Aaron Hill and Stage Scenery," TN 12 (1957), 29-33. Paul S. Dunkin, in "The Authorship of THE FATAL EXTRAVAGANCE," MLN 60 (1945), 328-30, and Paul P. Kies, in a similarly titled note in RSW 13 (1945), 155-58, agree that the play was written in collaboration with Joseph Mitchell, but Kies gives a much greater role to Mitchell than do Brewster and Dunkin. See the further note by Kies, RSW 14 (1946), 88. Hill's adaptation of HENRY V is discussed in the relevant sources listed in Part 1, Section 8.2, and by Landon C. Burns, Jr., "Three Views of King Henry V," DS 1 (1962), 278-300, an article which also discusses Orrery's version. Hill's four adaptations of Voltaire are discussed in Harold Bruce's VOLTAIRE ON THE ENGLISH STAGE (1914); see also Phyllis Horsley, "Aaron Hill: An English Translator of MEROPE," CLS 12 (1944), 17-23, and Robert Eddison, "Topless in Jerusalem," TN 22 (1967), 24-27 (a somewhat vague article on ZARA).

BENJAMIN HOADLY (1706-57)

Hoadly, son of a famous Bishop of Winchester, was a prominent doctor and was physician to the Prince of Wales. He wrote only two plays, the SUSPICIOUS HUSBAND (1747) and THE TATLERS (produced posthumously in 1797). The former comedy was popular throughout the century; a generation of playgoers enjoyed David Garrick in the role of Ranger. Contemporary and nineteenth-century dramatic histories are more informative than modern sources; see also AN EXAMEN OF THE NEW COMEDY CALLED 'THE SUSPICIOUS HUSBAND' . . . and Samuel Foote's THE ROMAN AND ENGLISH COMEDY CONSIDERED AND COMPARED . . . (both 1747). There are no separate modern editions.

PRINCE HOARE (1775-1834)

Hoare was the son of an artist, and exhibited at the Royal Academy before turning to the drama. Although he began with a tragedy (Bath, 1788), he is known for his musical pieces--farces, opera, comic operas, and "entertainments"--most of them produced in London in the two decades after 1790. Stephen Storace wrote the music for most of these pieces, though William Shield and Michael Kelly were also collaborators; many of them were alterations or adaptations. Early nineteenth-century theatre histories give most information about Hoare's career; there are no collected modern editions and only scattered references in modern secondary materials. Allardyce Nicoll, who believes Hoare "may be completely neglected," limits his comments in THE HISTORY OF ENGLISH DRAMA to a discussion of sources.

Plays produced in London through the 1799-1800 season include NO SONG NO SUPPER (1790), THE CAVE OF TROPHONIUS (1791, partly from Casti), DIDO, QUEEN OF CARTHAGE (1792, from Metastasio), THE PRIZE (1793), MY GRANDMOTHER (1793, partly from Anseaume), THE THREE AND THE DEUCE (1795), LOCK AND KEY and MAHMOUD (1796), JULIA (1796, originally at Bath, 1788), A FRIEND IN NEED and ITALIAN VILLAGERS (1797), THE CAPTIVE OF SPILBURG (1798, from Marsollier des Vivetières), SIGHS (1799, from Kotzebue), and THE CHILDREN and INDISCRETION (1800). The first, fourth, fifth, and seventh of these were extremely popular.

THOMAS HOLCROFT (1745-1809)

Some seventeen of Holcroft's twenty-odd dramatic pieces (excluding THE GER-
MAN HOTEL [1790], probably not his), were produced between 1781 and 1800.
DUPLICITY (1781, altered as THE MASKED FRIEND, 1796), SEDUCTION
(1787), THE SCHOOL FOR ARROGANCE (1791, from Destouches), THE DE-
SERTED DAUGHTER (1795, partly from Richard Cumberland), and especially
THE ROAD TO RUIN (1792), were popular comedies frequently included in
contemporary collections. Elbridge Colby, A BIBLIOGRAPHY OF THOMAS
HOLCROFT (New York: New York Public Library, 1922), collects earlier
N&Q and BNYPL notes and is the fullest bibliography. See Virgil R. Stall-
baumer, "Translations by Holcroft," N&Q 173 (1937), 402-05, for questions
about four of Colby's attributions. There are no collected editions of Holcroft's plays and only one modern edition, THE ROAD TO RUIN, ed. Ruth I.
Aldrich (Lincoln: Univ. of Nebraska Press, 1968).

THE MEMOIRS OF THE LATE THOMAS HOLCROFT, WRITTEN BY HIMSELF
. . ., completed and edited by William Hazlitt, was first published in 1816
(3 vols., Longman et al.); it is included in the edition of Hazlitt's works
edited by Percival P. Howe, 21 vols. (London: Dent, 1930-34), and has been
separately edited by Elbridge Colby, 2 vols. (London: Constable, 1925*).
For supplementary material, see the contemporary dramatic histories, Charles
Kegan Paul's WILLIAM GODWIN: HIS FRIENDS AND CONTEMPORARIES, 2
vols. (London: H. King, 1876); T. Vincent Benn, "Holcroft en France," RLC
6 (1926), 331-37; and Frederick Rosen, "Godwin and Holcroft," ELN 5 (1968),
183-86. Elbridge Colby's "Thomas Holcroft: Man of Letters," SAQ 22 (1923),
53-70, is a good general article, the last half of which deals with Holcroft's
plays. Virgil R. Stallbaumer's "Thomas Holcroft: A Satirist in the Stream of
Sentimentalism," ELH 3 (1936), 31-62, is also a general essay. Colby's
"Thomas Holcroft: Translator of Plays," PQ 3 (1924), 228-36, documents Holcroft's debts to his French and German contemporaries; in "Financial Accounts
of Holcroft Plays," N&Q 146 (1924), 42-45 and 60-63, Colby analyzes records
now in the British Museum. Articles relevant to specific plays include Stewart
S. Morgan, "The Damning of Holcroft's KNAVE OR NOT? and O'Keefe's SHE'S
ELOPED," HLQ 22 (1958), 51-62 (political censorship in 1798), and Peter
Thomson, "Thomas Holcroft, George Colman the Younger, and The Rivalry of
the Patent Theatres," TN 22 (1968), 162-68 (THE RIVAL QUEENS).

Plays produced before 1800 not mentioned above include THE CRISIS (1778), THE NOBLE PEASANT (1784), THE CHOLERIC FATHERS (1785), and THE OLD CLOTHES MAN (1799), all comic operas; LOVE'S FRAILTIES (1794, from von Gemmingen), THE MAN OF TEN THOUSAND and THE FORCE OF RIDICULE (1796), HE'S MUCH TO BLAME (1798, from Pont-de-Veyle and Goethe), and THE INQUISITOR (1798, from Unzer). DEAF AND DUMB (1801), A TALE OF MYSTERY (1802), and HEAR BOTH SIDES (1803) were popular plays early in the new century.

JOSEPH GEORGE HOLMAN (1764-1817)

Holman, from Oxfordshire, was an actor as well as a dramatist. Four of his plays belong to the period. ABROAD AND AT HOME (1796) and THE VOTARY OF WEALTH (1799) were successful; THE RED-CROSS KNIGHTS (1799, based on Schiller's ROBBERS) and WHAT A BLUNDER! (1800) were less so. There are no collected or modern editions and only scattered remarks--mostly on Holman as an actor--in the standard histories. The last years of Holman's life were spent in America, where he died.

JOHN HOME (1722-1808)

Home, a Scottish clergyman, wrote five tragedies after DOUGLAS (Edinburgh 1756, London 1757), all of which were produced. But it is for DOUGLAS that he is remembered; the play was part of the standard repertory throughout the period. Jean M. Lefevre's "John Home: A Check List of Editions," BIBLIOTHECK 3 (1961), 121-38, may be supplemented by Carl J. Stratman, "John Home: A Check List Continued," BIBLIOTHECK 3 (1962), 222-26. THE WORKS OF JOHN HOME, ESQ. . . ., 3 vols. (Edinburgh: Constable, 1822), includes a biography by Henry Mackenzie. THE DRAMATIC WORKS OF JOHN HOME (1760) includes only three of the plays; THE DRAMATIC WORKS . . ., 2 vols. (Edinburgh, 1798), is complete. DOUGLAS was included in nearly every contemporary collection and has been edited by Hubert J. Tunney, BUK 3, no. 3 (1924); the text is based on Mackenzie's edition. The play is included in several modern collections and has recently been well edited by Gerald D. Parker in the Fountainwell series (London: Oliver & Boyd, 1972).

The contemporary controversy surrounding the initial productions of the play is referred to in Arnott and Robinson's ENGLISH THEATRICAL LITERATURE and in the NEW CBEL. It is focused almost exclusively on the moral issue raised by a clergyman's writing a play--one conservative Presbyterians considered offensive--and has little critical significance for modern readers. See also Edward Forse et al., "Norval," N&Q 181 (1941), 106-07, 148, 149, 163, and 181. The only full twentieth-century study is Alice E. Gipson's JOHN HOME: A STUDY OF HIS LIFE AND WORKS, WITH SPECIAL REFERENCE TO HIS TRAGEDY OF 'DOUGLAS' AND THE CONTROVERSIES WHICH FOLLOWED ITS FIRST REPRESENTATIONS (Caldwell, Idaho: Caxton Printers, 1917). This work includes a biography, chapters on DOUGLAS, the DOUGLAS controversy, and chapters on each of the other plays. Frederick S. Boas devotes a full chapter in EIGHTEENTH-CENTURY DRAMA to Home and his work. The most interesting analysis of DOUGLAS is Joseph W. Donohue, Jr.'s, in DRAMATIC CHARACTER IN THE ENGLISH ROMANTIC AGE (1970), pp. 57-65. More specialized articles on the play include Dougald MacMillan, "The First Editions of Home's DOUGLAS," SP 26 (1929), 401-09 (the first Edinburgh edition is more authoritative than its London contemporary); William B. Todd, "Press Figures and Book Reviews as Determinants of Priority: A Study of Home's DOUGLAS (1757) and Cumberland's THE BROTHERS (1770)," PBSA 45 (1951), 72-76 (the original English "edition" consists of two separate editions); MacDonald

Emslie, "Home's DOUGLAS and Wully Shakespeare," SSL 2 (1964), 128-29; and Ernest C. Mossner, "Hume and the Scottish Shakespeare," HLQ 3 (1940), 419-41 (on the impact of Hume's dedication).

James S. Malek, in "The Ossianic Source of John Home's THE FATAL DISCOVERY," ELN 9 (1971), 39-42, argues for fragment 9 of FRAGMENTS OF ANCIENT POETRY (1759); in another article, "John Home's THE SIEGE OF AQUILEIA: A Re-evaluation," SSL 10 (1973), 232-40, Malek compares THE SIEGE with Edward Jerningham's play THE SIEGE OF BERWICK (1794) and argues that this 1760 play is better than DOUGLAS in several important respects.

Home's other plays are AGIS (1758), ALONZO (1773), and ALFRED (1778).

JOHN HOOLE (1727-1803)

Hoole, an auditor for the East India company, was primarily a translator from the Italian; his versions of Tasso's JERUSALEM DELIVERED and RINALDO and of Ariosto's ORLANDO FURIOSO were known well into the nineteenth century. His three tragedies, produced between 1768 and 1775, are indebted to Metastasio, whose works Hoole also translated. The three are included in the 1797 edition of Bell's collection of plays; there are no collected or modern editions. Samuel Hoole published ANECDOTES RESPECTING THE LIFE OF THE LATE JOHN HOOLE . . . (London: Evans, 1803), but this is a brief pamphlet. There are scattered references in secondary materials--and one published dissertation, Authur Saegesser's JOHN HOOLE: HIS LIFE AND HIS TRAGEDIES (Bern, Switzerland: Fischer-Lehmann, 1922).

The plays are CYRUS (1768), TIMANTHES (1770), and CLEONICE, PRINCESS OF BYTHNIA (1775); CYRUS and TIMANTHES were successful, CLEONICE much less so.

213

CHARLES HOPKINS (d. 1700)

Hopkins, son of a bishop of Londonderry, grew up in Ireland; he became a poet and dramatist after a brief military career. Four tragedies by him were produced between 1695 and 1699--PYRRHUS, KING OF EPIRUS (1695), NE-GLECTED VIRTUE (1696), BOADICEA, QUEEN OF BRITAIN (1697), and FRIEND-SHIP IMPROVED (1699). BOADICEA was the most successful of the four and is also the best known, probably because it is a late example of rhymed trag-edy. There are no collected or modern editions of Hopkins's plays and only scattered references in modern dramatic histories. Biographical information is given in Alice E. Jones, "A Note on Charles Hopkins (c.1671-1700)," MLN 55 (1940), 191-94. Baldwin Maxwell discusses Shakespearean and Fletcherian influence in "Notes on Charles Hopkins's BOADICEA," RES 4 (1928), 79-83.

EDWARD HOWARD (1624-c.1700)

Howard's plays include a tragedy, THE USURPER (1664); two tragicomedies, THE CHANGE OF CROWNS (1667) and THE WOMEN'S CONQUEST (1670); and two comedies, THE SIX DAYS' ADVENTURE (1671) and THE MAN OF NEWMARKET (1678). The plays have never been collected; the only modern edition is Frederick S. Boas's of THE CHANGE OF CROWNS (London: Oxford Univ. Press for the Royal Society of Literature, 1949)--a play not printed in the period. Boas announced the discovery of the prompt copy of this play in "A Lost Restoration Play Restored," TLS, 28 Sept. 1946, p. 468. Richard Southern worked out the staging in "The Scene Plot of THE CHANGE OF CROWNS," TN 4 (1950), 65-68.

SIR ROBERT HOWARD (1626-98)

Howard, a royalist imprisoned during the Commonwealth, was rewarded by
Charles II with a knighthood and (in 1677) a lucrative position as auditor of
the exchequer. His FOUR NEW PLAYS (1665) included THE SURPRISAL and
THE COMMITTEE (both comedies produced in 1662) and THE INDIAN QUEEN
and VESTAL VIRGIN (tragedies produced in 1664). THE INDIAN QUEEN was
written in collaboration with Dryden. THE GREAT FAVORITE; OR, THE DUKE
OF LERMA, produced in 1668, was added in FIVE NEW PLAYS (1692); this
edition was reprinted later under the title THE DRAMATIC WORKS OF SIR
ROBERT HOWARD (1722). A sixth play, THE COUNTRY GENTLEMAN, written in collaboration with Buckingham, has recently been discovered. See
Arthur H. Scouten and Robert D. Hume, "A Lost Restoration Comedy Found:
THE COUNTRY GENTLEMAN, by Sir Robert Howard and the Duke of Buckingham," TLS, 28 Sept. 1973, pp. 1105-06.

For editions and discussion of THE INDIAN QUEEN, see under Dryden. Howard's best play has been edited by Carryl N. Thurber, SIR ROBERT HOWARD'S
COMEDY 'THE COMMITTEE,' UIS 7, no. 1 (1921). Thurber provides extensive notes but unfortunately uses a text dating from 1776. THE GREAT FA-
VORITE is included in Arundell's DRYDEN AND HOWARD, also mentioned
under Dryden. There are no modern collections.

The standard biography is Harold J. Oliver, SIR ROBERT HOWARD 1626-1698:
A CRITICAL BIOGRAPHY (Durham, N.C.: Duke Univ. Press, 1963), which
has a good bibliography. Several earlier articles and notes by Florence Scott,
Esmond S. deBeer, and others are superseded by Oliver's study; see also the
Scott pamphlet, THE LIFE AND WORKS OF SIR ROBERT HOWARD (New York:
New York Univ. Press, 1946).

JOHN HUGHES (1677-1720)

Hughes, scion of a middle-class dissenting family, is best known as a minor poet and essayist, but his tragedy THE SIEGE OF DAMASCUS (1720) was widely known in print and frequently staged. CALYPSO AND TELEMACHUS (1712) and APOLLO AND DAPHNE (1716) are musical works--opera and masque, respectively. Both pieces are included in POEMS ON SEVERAL OCCASIONS, Vol. 2 (1735). There are no collections or modern editions of the plays. Johnson included a biography of Hughes in THE LIVES OF THE POETS; see also the DNB account. John R. Moore, in "Hughes's Source for THE SIEGE OF DAMASCUS," HLQ 21 (1958), 362-66, shows the relation of the play to Simon Ockley's THE HISTORY OF THE SARACENS, 2 vols. (1708, 1718), a work to which Hughes subscribed. J. Merrill Knapp, in "A Forgotten Chapter in English Eighteenth-Century Opera," ML 42 (1961), 1-16, discusses CALYPSO AND TELEMACHUS, the music for which was written by J.E. Galliard.

THOMAS HULL (1728-1808)

Hull was an actor, novelist, and theatrical manager as well as a playwright; most of his plays are alterations of older works. Neither THE ABSENT MAN (1764) nor PHARNACES (1765), an opera adapted from Lucchini, were very successful. THE SPANISH LADY (1765), a musical interlude, had a good run after it was altered in 1770. THE TWINS (1762, 1779) was adapted from THE COMEDY OF ERRORS; ALL IN THE RIGHT (1776), from Destouches; THE PER-PLEXITIES (1767), from Tuke; THE ROYAL MERCHANT (also 1767), from Beaumont and Fletcher's BEGGAR'S BUSH; EDWARD AND ELEANORA (1775), from James Thomson; LOVE FINDS THE WAY (1777), from Arthur Murphy's SCHOOL FOR GUARDIANS; IPHIGENIA (1778), from Boyer's alteration of Racine; THE COMEDY OF ERRORS (1779), from Shakespeare; TIMON OF ATHENS (1786), from Shadwell and Shakespeare; and DISINTERESTED LOVE (1798), from Massinger's BASHFUL LOVER. THE FAIRY FAVOR (1767) and THE FATAL INTER-VIEW (1782), masque and tragedy, respectively, were not successful; Hull's best known plays are HENRY THE SECOND (1773, based on the 1749 version by Hawkins) and TRUE BLUE (1776), his alteration of Henry Carey's NANCY. There are no collections or modern editions of any of Hull's plays and only scattered references in modern dramatic histories.

THOMAS HURLSTONE (fl. 1792-95)

Hurlstone was an actor and journalist who also wrote three pieces produced in the period. These are JUST IN TIME (1792), a comic opera; TO ARMS! (1793), a one-act interlude revived in 1795 as THE BRITISH RECRUIT; and CROTCHET LODGE (1795), a farce. There are no modern editions and only infrequent references in modern secondary sources.

ELIZABETH [SIMPSON] INCHBALD (1753-1821)

Elizabeth Inchbald--actress, dramatist, and novelist--had her first play produced in 1784. George L. Joughin's "An Inchbald Bibliography," SET 14 (1934), 59-74, does not include letters or distinguish between issues and editions; it is based on the Harvard collection and gives some locations. Inchbald's plays have never been collected, nor are there any modern separate editions; many, however, are included in contemporary collections, and EVERYONE HAS HIS FAULT is included in Allardyce Nicoll's LESSER ENGLISH COMEDIES OF THE EIGHTEENTH CENTURY (1931). She is best known for farces like THE MID-NIGHT HOUR (1787) and ANIMAL MAGNETISM (1788); for comedies like SUCH THINGS ARE (1787), EVERYONE HAS HIS FAULT (1793), THE WED-DING DAY (1794), and WIVES AS THEY WERE AND MAIDS AS THEY ARE (1797); and for her adaptations of Kotzebue, especially LOVERS' VOWS (1798).

The only good biography is James Boaden's MEMOIRS OF MRS. INCHBALD, INCLUDING HER FAMILIAR CORRESPONDENCE . . ., 2 vols. (London: Bentley, 1833); Boaden appends two unacted pieces, THE MASSACRE and A CASE OF CONSCIENCE. Samuel R. Littlewood's ELIZABETH INCHBALD AND HER CIRCLE: THE LIFE STORY OF A CHARMING WOMAN 1753-1821 (London: O'Connor, 1921) is based on Boaden and is undocumented; two chapters and part of a third concern the plays. Lucy Stebbins's chapter, "My Lady Restless," in LONDON LADIES: TRUE TALES OF THE EIGHTEENTH CENTURY (New York: Columbia Univ. Press, 1952), pp. 29-58, is also undocumented. There is a good brief account in Allardyce Nicoll's HISTORY OF ENGLISH DRAMA, and somewhat longer ones in the standard nineteenth-century sources listed in Part 1, Sections 6.3, 6.4, and 6.6, of this study. Esmond S. deBeer has an article, "LOVERS' VOWS: 'The Dangerous Insignificance of the But-ler,'" N&Q 207 (1962), 421-22.

ISAAC JACKMAN (fl. 1777-88)

Isaac Jackman was born in Dublin around the middle of the eighteenth century but was writing for the London stage as early as 1777, when both THE MILE-SIAN and ALL THE WORLD'S A STAGE were produced. The latter, a two-act farce, was very successful and was performed beyond the end of the century. THE DIVORCE (1781), with music by Shield, was also a success. THE MAN OF PARTS, produced in Dublin in 1785, was altered by the actor Thomas Ryder as SUCH THINGS HAVE BEEN (1789). Jackman's later career was apparently in journalism; according to the DNB, he may have been one of the editors of the MORNING POST 1786-95. Two burlesques, HERO AND LEANDER (1787) and ALMIRINA (1788), were played at the Royalty Theatre. There are no collected or modern editions of Jackman's plays, and there are few references in modern dramatic histories.

ROBERT JEPHSON (1736-1803)

Allardyce Nicoll, in his HISTORY OF ENGLISH DRAMA, places Jephson next to Home among "pseudo-romantic" tragedians of the later eighteenth century, primarily on the basis of BRAGANZA (1775), THE COUNT OF NARBONNE (1781), and CONSPIRACY (1796). THE LAW OF LOMBARDY (1779) derives from Ariosto's version of MUCH ADO, THE COUNT OF NARBONNE from Horace Walpole's CASTLE OF OTRANTO, and CONSPIRACY from Metastasio. Jephson also wrote for the Smock Alley theatre in Dublin; THE HOTEL (1784), retitled TWO STRINGS TO YOUR BOW (Covent Garden, 1791), became popular and is included in several contemporary collections. There are no modern editions or collections of Jephson's work. Martin S. Peterson's ROBERT JEPHSON 1736-1803: A STUDY OF HIS LIFE AND WORKS (Lincoln: Univ. of Nebraska Studies, 1930) includes a brief biography and critical comments on the plays but is thin. Horace Walpole discusses BRAGANZA in his "Thoughts on Tragedy" (Part 1, Section 5.2); there is comment on THE LAW OF LOMBARDY in Thomas M. Parrott, "Two Late Dramatic Versions of the Slandered Bride Theme," in JOHN QUINCY ADAMS MEMORIAL STUDIES, ed. James G. McManaway et al. (Washington, D.C.: Folger Shakespeare Library, 1948), pp. 537-51. Jephson's other plays are the comic opera THE CAMPAIGN (1785; altered by O'Keeffe as LOVE AND WAR in 1787) and JULIA (1787), a tragedy.

EDWARD JERNINGHAM (1727-1812)

Jerningham dabbled in both poetry and drama but had no great success in either genre. MARGARET OF ANJOU (1777), a one-act interlude, was his first effort; there followed THE SIEGE OF BERWICK (1793) and THE WELSH HEIRESS (1795). His POEMS AND PLAYS . . ., "9th ed.," 4 vols. in 2 (London: for Nornaville & Fell, 1806), includes these pieces in Vols. 3-4, as well as THE PECKHAM FROLIC (pub. 1799). THE SIEGE OF BERWICK was edited by H.E.H. Jerningham (London: Ridgway, 1882). See also the Malek article on THE SIEGE OF AQUILEIA cited under Home. EDWARD JERNINGHAM AND HIS FRIENDS . . . (London: Chatto & Windus, 1919) is a collection of letters edited by William A.L. Bettany.

CHARLES JOHNSON (1679-1748)

Johnson wrote nearly twenty plays, seventeen of which were produced in London during the period. His first four plays--THE GENTLEMAN CULLY (1701), THE FORCE OF FRIENDSHIP and LOVE IN A CHEST (1710), and THE GENEROUS HUSBAND (1711)--were not very successful. THE WIFE'S RELIEF (1711) and THE COUNTRY LASSES (1715), however, eventually became standard repertory fare and held the boards until the last decades of the century. Three serious plays--THE SUCCESSFUL PIRATE (1712), THE VICTIM (1714, from Racine), and THE SULTANESS (1717)--lasted four to six performances each; MEDEA (1730) and CAELIA (1732) did not get that far. THE COBBLER OF PRESTON (1716), a farce competing with Christopher Bullock's play of the same name, had a successful season; THE MASQUERADE (1719) and THE FEMALE FORTUNE TELLER (1726) were also fairly successful. Other plays include LOVE IN A FOREST (1723), THE VILLAGE OPERA (1729), and THE EPHESIAN MATRON (1732); FORTUNE IN HER LISTS and LOVE AND LIBERTY were unacted. There are no collections of Johnson's plays and only one modern printing, a facsimile of his Shakespearean adaptation LOVE IN A FOREST (London: Cornmarket Press, 1969).

The best general account is Maurice Shudofsky's article, "Charles Johnson and Eighteenth-Century Drama," ELH 10 (1943), 131-58. See also Richard C. Boys, "Rural Setting in the Drama: An Early Example," N&Q 170 (1936), 207, which discusses the realistic setting of THE COUNTRY LASSES; Edward N. Hooker, "Charles Johnson's THE FORCE OF FRIENDSHIP and LOVE IN A CHEST: A Note on Tragi-Comedy and Licensing in 1710," SP 34 (1937), 407-11, which shows from a Folger Library prompt copy that these two pieces were originally designed as a single tragi-comedy titled THE FORCE OF LOVE; and Mary Dias, "A Satire on John Dennis, 1711," RES 19 (1943), 213-14 (on the character Dypthong in THE GENEROUS HUSBAND).

SAMUEL JOHNSON OF CHESHIRE (1691-1773)

Johnson was a dancing-master and occasional dramatist who came to London in the 1720's and had several burlesques produced before retiring to Macclesfield about 1743. His first effort, HURLOTHRUMBO (1729), is also his best known piece; it was followed by THE CHESHIRE COMICS (1730), THE BLAZING COMET (1732), ALL ALIVE AND MERRY (1737), and THE FOOL MADE WISE, played with SIR JOHN FALSTAFF IN MASQUERADE (1741). HURLOTHRUMBO achieved a certain notoriety when produced, but it is difficult to follow; see Valerie C. Rudolph, "HURLOTHRUMBO: Sense and Nonsense," RECTR 12, no. 1 (1973), 28-35, which suggests that it satirizes the heroic play. Biographical notes on Johnson include Austin Dobson and J. Knight, "Samuel Johnson of Cheshire," N&Q 61 (1880), 338-39, and William Harrison, "Maggoty Johnson, Fiddler Johnson, and Lord Flame," N&Q 65 (1882), 157-58. There are no collected or modern editions of Johnson's plays.

HUGH KELLY (1739-77)

THE WORKS OF HUGH KELLY, TO WHICH IS PREFIXED HIS LIFE (1778) includes FALSE DELICACY (1768), A WORD TO THE WISE (1770), CLEMENTINA (his only tragedy, 1771), THE SCHOOL FOR WIVES (1773), and THE RO-MANCE OF AN HOUR (1774). THE SCHOOL FOR WIVES was his most popular play, remaining in the repertory to the end of the century; FALSE DELI-CACY, also popular in the period, is perhaps better known today. The other two comedies were also successful; THE ROMANCE OF AN HOUR, for example, was revived several times. THE MAN OF REASON (1776), however, was a failure. Kelly soon gave up the stage, failed at the law, and then turned to drink.

There is no adequate biography of Kelly, no collected edition since 1778, and no modern edition of any of the plays except FALSE DELICACY, which is oc-casionally anthologized. THE SCHOOL FOR WIVES, however, is in several contemporary collections. FALSE DELICACY is discussed briefly in Joseph W. Donohue, Jr.'s DRAMATIC CHARACTER IN THE ROMANTIC AGE, pp. 113-18. See also Claude J. Rawson, "Some Remarks on Eighteenth-Century 'Deli-cacy,' with a Note on Hugh Kelly's FALSE DELICACY (1768)," JEGP 61 (1962), 1-13, which defines delicacy in relation to sensibility and argues per-suasively that the play is a good-humored attack on delicacy rather than a sentimental espousal of it. Mark Schorer, in "Hugh Kelly: His Place in the Sentimental School," PQ 12 (1933), 389-401, agrees that Kelly's movement is away from the sentimental but depreciates his work as shallowly optimistic, full of platitudes, and overly didactic. There is a brief discussion in Frederick S. Boas's EIGHTEENTH-CENTURY DRAMA, pp. 292-300.

JOHN KELLY (c.1680-1751)

Three plays by John Kelly were produced in London between 1732 and 1735. TIMON IN LOVE (1733, from Sieur de Lisle) and THE PLOT (1735) were ballad operas lasting only long enough for a benefit performance; THE MARRIED PHILOSOPHER, mentioned in dramatic histories as the first introduction of the French Comédie Larmoyante to England, did better but was given only one recorded performance its second season. THE LEVEE, a topical ballad opera, was banned in 1741. There are no collected or modern editions of Kelly's plays and only scattered references in the standard histories.

JOHN PHILIP KEMBLE (1757-1823)

More than twenty alterations and adaptations by this important actor and manager were produced at Drury Lane between 1785 and 1800, including his versions of Shakespearean plays. Several of the latter, including CORIOLANUS and HENRY V (both 1789), are available in facsimile from London's Cornmarket Press. Alterations like THE PANEL (1788, from Bickerstaffe) and LODOISKA (1794, from Dejaure) were very popular; these and many other Kemble pieces appear in contemporary collections, but there are no modern collections or editions other than the facsimiles mentioned.

The standard biography of Kemble is Herschel C. Baker's JOHN PHILIP KEMBLE: THE ACTOR IN HIS THEATRE (Cambridge, Mass.: Harvard Univ. Press, 1942), which also includes critical comments on the plays. James Boaden's MEMOIRS OF THE LIFE OF JOHN PHILIP KEMBLE, ESQ. . . ., 2 vols. (London: Longman et al., 1825*), and Percy H. Fitzgerald's THE KEMBLES . . ., 2 vols. (London: Tinsley Bros., 1871*), may also be consulted. Sir Walter Scott's well known review of Boaden's book is included in his MISCELLANEOUS WORKS (Edinburgh: Black, 1881), XX, 152-233. There is a readable biographical sketch in James Agate's WHITE HORSE AND RED LION: ESSAYS IN GUSTO (London: W. Collins, 1924). Critical comment has focused almost exclusively on Kemble's Shakespearean productions. Harold H. Child's THE SHAKESPEARIAN PRODUCTIONS OF JOHN PHILIP KEMBLE (London: Oxford Univ. Press for the Shakespeare Association, 1935), a sketchy survey, argues that Kemble kept much Shakespeare before the public and staged the plays with more splendor and dignity than did Garrick. Joseph W. Donohue, Jr., in "Kemble's Production of MACBETH (1794): Some Notes on Scene Painters, Scenery, Special Effects, and Costumes," TN 21 (1967), 63-74, recovers many details of Kemble's version; in "Kemble and Mrs. Siddons in MACBETH: The Romantic Approach to Tragic Character," TN 22 (1967-68), 65-86, Donohue shows how Kemble's acting style differed from that of Garrick and other earlier tragic actors. David Rostron, in "John Philip Kemble's CORIOLANUS and JULIUS CAESAR: An Examination of the Prompt Copies," TN 23 (1968), 26-34, shows how these copies reveal Kemble's interest in spectacular effects; in "Contemporary Political Comment in Four of J.P. Kemble's Shakespearean Productions," TR 12 (1972), 113-19, Rostron examines CORIOLANUS, HENRY V, HENRY VIII, and KING JOHN as illustrating Kemble's conservatism and patriotism. The Shakespearean adaptations are also discussed in several sources listed in Part 1, Section 8.2.

WILLIAM KENRICK (c.1729-79)

Kenrick was a clever but quarrelsome journalist; his first play was FALSTAFF'S WEDDING (1766), a "sequel" to 2 HENRY IV revived in several later seasons. THE WIDOWED WIFE (1767) was also successful, THE DUELLIST (1773) and THE SPENDTHRIFT (1778) less so. Kenrick's most popular play was the comic opera, THE LADY OF THE MANOR (1778), based on Charles Johnson's THE COUNTRY LASSES; it was performed for a decade or more.

There is no thorough biography of Kenrick, nor are there any collected or modern editions of his plays. Honor McKusker gives a brief account in "Doctor Kenrick of Grub Street," MB 14 (1939), 3-10; see also G.E. Brewer and Paul Fussell, Jr., "The Birth Date of Kenrick," N&Q 195 (1950), 51-52, and Fussell's "William Kenrick, Eighteenth-Century Scourge and Critic," JRL 20 (1957), 42-59.

THOMAS KING (1730-1805)

King, the son of a tradesman, was educated at Westminster but soon became a strolling actor. His London career lasted more than forty years; he created many famous roles, notably Lord Ogleby in THE CLANDESTINE MARRIAGE and Sir Peter Teazle in THE SCHOOL FOR SCANDAL. His first play, LOVE AT FIRST SIGHT (1763), was only moderately successful. WIT'S LAST STAKE (1768), however, was a popular farce, revived occasionally throughout the century. THE TRIUMPH OF MIRTH; OR, HARLEQUIN'S WEDDING (1782) was a successful pantomime; HURLY-BURLY (1785), a later pantomime, was written in collaboration with James Cobb. King's most successful play was LOVERS' QUARRELS (1790), an adaptation of Vanbrugh's THE MISTAKE. There are no collections or modern editions of King's plays; the scattered references in the standard dramatic histories are usually to King as an actor or manager.

JOHN LACY (c.1615-81)

Lacy was primarily known as an actor in comic roles, but he also wrote four plays: THE OLD TROOP (c.1665), SAUNY THE SCOT (1667), THE DUMB LADY (1669), and SIR HERCULES BUFFOON (1684). The first and last of these were occasionally revived; THE LONDON STAGE lists a revival as late as the 1735-36 season. THE DRAMATIC WORKS OF JOHN LACY, COMEDIAN, edited by James Maidment and William H. Logan, was included in the Dramatists of the Restoration series (London: Sotheran, 1875*). The 1698 Quarto of SAUNY THE SCOT (from Shakespeare's TAMING OF THE SHREW) is available from Cornmarket Press (London, 1969). There is no full biography of Lacy and only passing references to his plays in the secondary literature. Emmett L. Avery and Authur H. Scouten, in "The Opposition to Sir Robert Walpole 1737-1739," EHR 83 (1968), 331-36, discusses Lacy's role in evading government restrictions on the theatre; Charles W. Cooper's "The Triple Portrait of John Lacy: A Restoration Theatrical Portrait, History and Dispute," PMLA 47 (1932), 759-65, is a useful iconographical study.

NATHANIEL LEE (c.1650-92)

Alan L. McLeod, "A Nathaniel Lee Bibliography 1670-1960," RECTR 1, no. 2 (1962), 27-39, includes collected works, editions of individual plays and poems, and secondary materials. THE WORKS OF MR. NATHANIEL LEE, 2 vols. (1713), 3 vols. (1722), and THE DRAMATIC WORKS OF NATHANIEL LEE, 3 vols. (1733-36?), have been superseded by THE WORKS OF NATHANIEL LEE, ed. Thomas B. Stroup and Arthur L. Cooke, 2 vols. (New Brunswick, N.J.: Scarecrow Press, 1954-55*). Numerous German dissertations on Lee are listed in McLeod's bibliography; several of these are editions of individual plays. LUCIUS JUNIUS BRUTUS (1680) is included in the Regents Restoration series, ed. John C. Loftis (Lincoln: Univ. of Nebraska Press, 1967). THE RIVAL QUEENS (1677), available in facsimile (London: Scolar Press, 1971), was edited by William M. Peterson for the Lake Erie College series (Painesville, Ohio, 1965) and is also available in the Regents series, ed. Paul F. Vernon (Lincoln: Univ. of Nebraska Press, 1970). SOPHONISBA (1675) is included in the World's Classics volume FIVE HEROIC PLAYS (1960), ed. Bonamy Dobrée.

The standard biography of Lee is still Roswell G. Ham's OTWAY AND LEE: BIOGRAPHY FROM A BAROQUE AGE (New Haven: Yale Univ. Press, 1931*), which is as much about Lee's plays as about his life. See also Alan L. McLeod, "Lee's Birth Date," MLN 69 (1954), 167-70 (he suggests 1651), and "Nathaniel Lee's Portrait," N&Q 198 (1953), 103-05, in which McLeod calls attention to a picture of Lee in the Garrick Club. General articles on Lee's plays include H.M. Sanders, "The Plays of Nathaniel Lee, Gentleman," TEMPLE BAR 124 (1901), 497-508; Bonamy Dobrée, "Nat Lee (1653-1692) and the Tragedy of Humours," in RESTORATION TRAGEDY (1929); Frances M. Barbour, "The Unconventional Heroic Plays of Nathaniel Lee," SET 20 (1940), 109-16; George Wilson Knight, "The Plays of Nathaniel Lee," VENTURE 1 (1960), 186-96; Eric Rothstein, "Lee, Banks, Otway," in RESTORATION TRAGEDY (1967); Peter Skrine, "Blood, Bombast, and Deaf Gods: The Tragedies of Lee and Lohenstein," GLL 24 (1970), 14-30; and Eugene M. Waith, "Lee and Otway," in IDEAS OF GREATNESS (1971). For Dobrée, Lee is the most typically "heroic" of the writers of heroic drama, the master of rant, an early Expressionist; his plays are "Gothic building run mad" but "held up by terrific stresses, and towering up above the mundane street." The Barbour article notes that the five plays written before 1679-80 picture kings as tyrants accountable for their acts; in the early as well as the later tragedies, Lee is atypical in his Whiggish leanings. Rothstein stresses Lee's sensationalism and pathos, but his discussion is too brief to be more than suggestive. Waith focuses on SOPHONISBA and THE RIVAL QUEENS; he agrees with Colley Cibber and Bonamy Dobrée that the plays are operatic and stresses Lee's lyricism and capacity for presenting tenderness.

More specialized studies include Fredson T. Bowers, "Nathaniel Lee: Three Probable Seventeenth-Century Piracies," PBSA 44 (1950), 62-66, which concerns the 1694 RIVAL QUEENS, the 1696 NERO, and the 1697 SOPHONISBA, and Gustav Cross, "Ovid Metamorphosed: Marston, Webster, and Nathaniel Lee," N&Q 201 (1956), 244-45 and 508-09, which suggests echoes of Golding's translation of Ovid in all three dramatists. A number of articles deal with individual plays. Arthur L. Cooke and Thomas B. Stroup, in "The Political Implications in Lee's CONSTANTINE THE GREAT," JEGP 49 (1950), 506-15, show how the play reflects the Popish and Rye House plots. John C. Loftis includes a similar study of LUCIUS JUNIUS BRUTUS (1680) in THE POLITICS OF DRAMA (1963). Alan L. McLeod shows in "The Douai MS. of Lee's MITHRIDATES," N&Q 205 (1960), 69-70, that Wing's SHORT-TITLE CATALOG is in error in calling this manuscript a holograph. Fredson T. Bowers, "The Prologue to Nathaniel Lee's MITHRIDATES (1678)," PBSA 44 (1950), 173-75, shows that Lee's name appeared in a rare variant of the prologue, but was later deleted.

Allardyce Nicoll, in "THE TRAGEDY OF NERO and PISO'S CONSPIRACY," N&Q 137 (1919), 254-57, suggests that Gerard Langbaine and later historians erred in equating these two plays; George Newall, pp. 299-300, correctly asserts that Langbaine referred to NERO'S TRAGEDY (1671) and THE TRAGEDY OF NERO (1624) and not to Lee's play. See also Edward Bensley, p. 323. Stroup, in "THE PRINCESS OF CLEVE and Sentimental Comedy," RES 11 (1935), 200-203, shows that elements of sentimentalism can be seen much earlier than Cibber's LOVE'S LAST SHIFT. Graham Greene's TLS note, "Rochester and Lee," 2 Nov. 1935, p. 697, concerns Montague Summers's argument for a manuscript of Rochester's VALENTINIAN prior to Lee's play; Greene's argument is countered by William J. Lawrence, p. 722. Fredson T. Bowers's "A Crux in the Text of Lee's PRINCESS OF CLEVE (1689), II.i," HLB 4 (1950), 409-11, explains the omission of a speech as an error. Robert Birley, in "Nathaniel Lee: THE RIVAL QUEENS," SUNK WITHOUT TRACE: SOME FORGOTTEN MASTERPIECES RECONSIDERED (London: Hart-Davis, 1962), pp. 40-75, writes one of the most perceptive essays available on Lee, comparing his drama with baroque art, discussing the sources and rhetorical structure of THE RIVAL QUEENS, and emphasizing its theatrical values. Gwynne B. Evans's "Milton and Lee's THE RIVAL QUEENS (1677)," MLN 64 (1949), 527-28, points out a minor indebtedness; see also the Peterson edition of Cibber's RIVAL QUEANS cited under Colley Cibber. A. José Axelrad, LE THEME DE SOPHONISBE DANS LES PRINCIPALES TRAGEDIES DE LA LITTERATURE OCCIDENTALE . . . (Lille, France: Bibliothèque Universitaire, 1956), considers Lee's play and its place in the tradition.

MATTHEW GREGORY LEWIS (1775-1818)

Lewis, whose gothic novel THE MONK made him famous at twenty, had three
of his plays produced before the end of the period. THE CASTLE SPECTRE
(1797), a melodrama with music by Michael Kelly, was a tremendous success;
THE TWINS (1799, probably based on F.L. Schroeder's DIE ZWILLINGSBRUEDER)
and THE EAST INDIAN (1799) are less significant works. THE MINISTER,
from Schiller, and ROLLA, from Kotzebue, were not produced in the period,
though the former was altered as THE HARPER'S DAUGHTER and produced in
1803. Several other plays belong to the new century, among them ADELMORN
THE OUTLAW (1801), ALFONSO, KING OF CASTILE (1801), ADELGITHA
(1807), VENONI (1808), and TIMOUR THE TARTAR and ONE O'CLOCK
(1811). Upon inheriting his father's estate in 1812, Lewis gave up the drama;
he died at sea of yellow fever in 1818.

There is a bibliography of Lewis's work in Montague Summers, A GOTHIC BIB-
LIOGRAPHY (London: Fortune Press, 1941). Margaret Baron-Wilson's THE
LIFE AND CORRESPONDENCE OF MATTHEW GREGORY LEWIS . . ., 2 vols.
(London: Colburn, 1839), has been superseded by Louis F. Peck's A LIFE OF
MATTHEW G. LEWIS (Cambridge, Mass.: Harvard Univ. Press, 1961), which also
contains a long chapter on Lewis's plays. Karl S. Guthke's ENGLISCHE VOR-
ROMANTIK UND DEUTSCHER STURM UND DRANG: M.G. LEWIS' STELLUNG
IN DER GESCHICHTE DER DEUTSCH-ENGLISCHEN LITERATURBEZIEHUNGEN,
in PALAESTRA, Vol. 223 (Goettingen, Germany: Vandenhoeck & Ruprecht,
1958), studies Lewis in relation to contemporary German literature. Guthke's
article, "F.L. Schroeder, J.F. Regnard, and Lewis," HLQ 27 (1963), 79-82,
compares Lewis's THE TWINS with its source. Another Guthke article, "M.G.
Lewis's THE TWINS," HLQ 25 (1962), 189-223, includes a complete text of the
play; still another, "Some Bibliographical Errors concerning the Romantic Age,"
PBSA 51 (1957), 159-62, points out that THE EAST INDIAN, composed before
Lewis knew German, is not indebted to Kotzebue. Walter C. Adelsperger
studies the promptbook for an 1818 production in "Aspects of Staging in ADEL-
GITHA," OSTB no. 7 (1960), 14-34.

GEORGE LILLO (c.1691-1739)

THE WORKS OF THE LATE MR. GEORGE LILLO (1740) was the first collected edition of Lillo's plays. THE WORKS OF MR. GEORGE LILLO, WITH SOME ACCOUNT OF HIS LIFE, 2 vols. (1775), adds ARDEN OF FEVERSHAM to the plays printed in the 1740 edition and includes a biography by Thomas Davies; this edition was reprinted by W. Lowndes in 1810. Adolphus W. Ward edited THE LONDON MERCHANT (1731) and FATAL CURIOSITY (1736) for the Belles Lettres series (Boston: Heath, 1906); the introduction to this volume is still one of the best accounts of Lillo and his plays. These two plays have also appeared in the Regents Restoration series, ed. William H. McBurney (Lincoln: Univ. of Nebraska Press, 1966 and 1965). THE LONDON MERCHANT is included in many modern collections; MARINA (1738), an alteration of PERICLES, is available in facsimile (London: Cornmarket Press, 1969).

Little is known about Lillo's life, so it is not surprising that there is no full-scale biography. See Drew B. Pallette, "Notes for a Biography of George Lillo," PQ 19 (1940), 261-67; Chester F. Burgess, "Further Notes for a Biography of George Lillo, PQ 46 (1967), 424-28; and William H. McBurney, "What George Lillo Read: A Speculation," HLQ 29 (1966), 275-86. Surveys of Lillo's work include sections in several works on sentimental and domestic drama mentioned in Part 1, Sections 7.16 and 7.17, especially Bernbaum and Sherbo; the relevant sections of William P. Harbeson, THE ELIZABETHAN INFLUENCE ON THE TRAGEDY OF THE LATE EIGHTEENTH AND THE EARLY NINETEENTH CENTURIES (Lancaster, Pa.: Wickersham Printing Co., 1935) and Boas's EIGHTEENTH-CENTURY DRAMA; and two more recent articles, Chester F. Burgess's "Lillo sans Barnwell; or, the Playwright Revisited," MP 66 (1968), 5-29, and George E. Wellwarth, "George Lillo and the Finger-Wagging Drama," PLS 14, no. 3 (1970), 75-97. The best of these studies is that of Burgess, which emphasizes Lillo as a thorough professional, writing for theatrical success.

Michael M. Cohen, in "Providence and Constraint in Two Lillo Tragedies," ES 52 (1971), 231-36, argues that FATAL CURIOSITY is Lillo's best play; its departure from the Calvinist doctrines evident in THE LONDON MERCHANT increases the tragic inevitability of the action. William E.A. Axon, in "The Story of Lillo's FATAL CURIOSITY," N&Q 65 (1882), 21-23, discusses the early seventeenth-century story on which the play is founded; Chester F.

Burgess, "FATAL CURIOSITY in Berkshire," N&Q 215 (1970), 92-93, cites an analog to the story from an unpublished diary of 1762. Joseph W. Donohue, Jr.'s brief discussion of this play in DRAMATIC CHARACTER IN THE ROMANTIC AGE is illuminating. Gerard A. Barker examines THE SHIPWRECK (1784) in "Henry Mackenzie's Adaptation of Lillo's FATAL CURIOSITY," BNYPL 74 (1970), 532-48.

William H. Hudson's article, "George Lillo and THE LONDON MERCHANT," A QUIET CORNER IN A LIBRARY (Chicago: Rand McNally, 1915*), pp. 93-162, offers the conventional account of the play as the forerunner of melodrama and the social problem play. George B. Rodman's "Sentimentalism in Lillo's THE LONDON MERCHANT," ELH 12 (1945), 45-61, notes that the play does not fit the traditional notion of sentimentalism as belief in the natural goodness of average human nature; Rodman argues that Lillo is in fact trying to show the consequences of being ruled by feeling instead of reason. The play is sentimental only because we are expected to be moved by a character who does not deserve our pity. In a later issue ("The Sentimentalism of THE LONDON MERCHANT," pp. 183-87), Raymond D. Havens retorts that the play is sentimental because Barnwell is presented sympathetically and ought not to have been. The weaknesses of the play are succinctly stated in "Notes on THE LONDON MERCHANT" in Cleanth Brooks and Robert B. Heilman's UNDERSTANDING DRAMA (1948), pp. 180-89. Perhaps the most illuminating study is Frank J. Kearful's article "Dramatic Rhetoric in Lillo's LONDON MERCHANT," NM 73 (1972), 849-54, which argues persuasively that Lillo is interested in moral persuasion rather than psychological realism or dramatic naturalism.

Specialized articles on this play include Reginald H. Griffith, "Early Editions of Lillo's LONDON MERCHANT, SET 15 (1935), 23-27, and Lawrence M. Price, "George Barnwell Abroad," CL 2 (1950), 126-56; the latter improves on one or two earlier accounts of the remarkable European influence of the play. Herbert L. Carson's "The Play That Would Not Die: George Lillo's THE LONDON MERCHANT," QJS 49 (1963), 287-94, is superficial.

Lillo plays not referred to above include SYLVIA (an opera, 1730), THE CHRISTIAN HERO and ELMERICK (tragedies, 1735 and 1740), and ARDEN OF FEVERSHAM (1759, completed by John Hoadly). None was long-lived on the stage.

CHARLES MACKLIN (c.1699-1797)

THE PLAYS OF CHARLES MACKLIN (Dublin, 1793) includes THE MAN OF
THE WORLD (Dublin 1764, London 1781), THE TRUE-BORN IRISHMAN (Dublin,
1762; retitled THE IRISH FINE LADY for production in London in 1767), and
LOVE A LA MODE (1759). The best edition of Macklin's work, however, is
FOUR COMEDIES BY CHARLES MACKLIN, ed. J.O. Bartley (Hamden, Conn.:
Archon Books, 1968), which adds to the three just mentioned THE SCHOOL
FOR HUSBANDS (from the Larpent manuscript), produced in 1761 as THE MAR-
RIED LIBERTINE. Facsimiles of THE COVENT GARDEN THEATRE (1752) and
of A WILL AND NO WILL (1746), together with THE NEW PLAY CRITICIZED
(1747), were edited for the Augustan Reprint Society by Jean B. Kern (Los
Angeles: W.A. Clark Library, 1965 and 1967). THE MAN OF THE WORLD
was printed (from the 1792 edition) in the same series, ed. Dougald MacMillan
(1951). Macklin wrote a number of plays which were never produced; those
which were produced and failed include a tragedy, KING HENRY VII (1746),
and THE CLUB OF FORTUNE HUNTERS (1748). Only THE MAN OF THE
WORLD and LOVE A LA MODE were very successful; both became stock plays.

Macklin was primarily known as an actor. The earliest biography was a com-
petent pamphlet by Francis A. Congreve, AUTHENTIC MEMOIRS OF THE LATE
MR. CHARLES MACKLIN, COMEDIAN . . . (1798). This was followed by
James T. Kirkman's MEMOIRS OF THE LIFE OF CHARLES MACKLIN, ESQ.
. . ., 2 vols. (1799), and William Cooke's MEMOIRS OF CHARLES MACKLIN,
COMEDIAN (London: Asperne, 1804). Edward A. Parry's CHARLES MACKLIN
(London: K. Paul et al., 1891) uses all three of the previous works, adding
little new material. The best biography is William W. Appleton, CHARLES
MACKLIN: AN ACTOR'S LIFE (Cambridge, Mass.: Harvard Univ. Press, 1960).
See also J.O. Bartley's "Charles Macklin: Appearances outside London," TN 22
(1967), 4-5; Alfrida Lee's "Macklin in Birmingham," TN 22 (1968), 133; the
material on Macklin in Bartley's book TEAGUE, SHENKIN, AND SAWNEY
(1954); and Robert R. Findlay's "Charles Macklin and the Problem of 'Natural'
Acting," ETJ 19 (1967), 33-40.

The best recent discussion of Macklin's plays is Findlay's article, "The Comic
Plays of Charles Macklin: Dark Satire at Mid-Eighteenth Century," ETJ 20
(1968), 398-407, which emphasizes their unsentimental and satiric character.
Studies of specific plays include two additional articles by Findlay, "Macklin's

Legitimate Acting Version of LOVE A LA MODE," PQ 45 (1966), 749-60 [see W. Matthews, "The Piracies of Macklin's LOVE A LA MODE," RES 10 (1934), 311-18], and "Macklin's 1748 Adaptation of Ford's THE LOVER'S MELANCHOLY," RECTR 8, no. 1, (1969), 13-22; Dougald MacMillan, "The Censorship in the Case of Macklin's THE MAN OF THE WORLD, HLB, no. 10 (1936), 79-101; and Esther M. Raushenbush, "Charles Macklin's Lost Play about Henry Fielding," MLN 51 (1936), 505-14, which notes THE COVENT-GARDEN THEATRE among the Larpent manuscripts.

LEONARD MacNALLY (1752-1820)

MacNally, son of a Dublin merchant, was primarily a successful double agent, working after 1794 for the British against the Irish revolutionaries. His London plays, all produced at Covent Garden, belong to an earlier period in his life; they include RETALIATION (1782), TRISTRAM SHANDY and COALITION (1783), ROBIN HOOD (1784), FASHIONABLE LEVITIES (1785, 5-act version 1792), THE APRIL FOOL (1786, from Middleton), RICHARD COEUR DE LION (1786, from Sedaine), THE CANTABS (1787), and an adaptation of the Fletcher-Massinger play THE KNIGHT OF MALTA (1783). Most of these pieces are musical farces or comic operas in two or three acts; though several of them had modest runs involving more than one season, only ROBIN HOOD was really popular. There are no collected or modern editions of MacNally's plays and only scattered references in the standard dramatic histories.

DAVID MALLET (c.1705-65)

Mallet was born in Perth of a Roman Catholic family named Malloch and came to England as a young man. His plays include three tragedies and two masques, all produced at Drury Lane. The tragedies are EURYDICE (1731), MUSTAPHA (1739), and ELVIRA (1763); the masques are ALFRED (1740; with music by T. A. Arne, 1745; with music by Arne and others, 1751) and BRITANNIA (1755). Samuel Johnson's brief life is unremarkable; Herbert W. Starr's "Notes on David Mallet," N&Q 178 (1940), 277-78, concerns the change of name from Malloch to Mallet. Starr has also an article, "Sources of David Mallet's MUSTAPHA, A TRAGEDY," N&Q 181 (1941), 285-87, which persuasively argues that Knolles's GENERAL HISTORY OF THE TURKS was Mallet's main source. For ELVIRA, one may consult James Boswell et al., CRITICAL STRICTURES ON THE NEW TRAGEDY OF 'ELVIRA' . . . (1763), ed. Frederick A. Pottle (Los Angeles: W.A. Clark Library, 1952), a facsimile in the Augustan Reprint series. For ALFRED, see Alan D. McKillop, "The Early History of ALFRED," PQ 41 (1962), 311-24, an article which discusses the original Thomson-Mallet entertainment at Cliveden (1740), its transformation into an oratorio by Arne, and Mallet's 1751 version. There are no collections or modern editions of Mallet's plays.

MARY DELARIVIÈRE MANLEY (1663-1724)

Mary Manley is now remembered for her scandal chronicles, but she wrote a comedy and three tragedies during her miscellaneous career. The comedy is THE LOST LOVER (1696); the tragedies include THE ROYAL MISCHIEF (1696), ALMYNA (1706), and LUCIUS (1717). None of the four was particularly successful, and the comedy was a failure. There are no collected or modern editions of any of the plays.

The best study of Manley is the chapter in Walter and Clare Jerrold's FIVE QUEER WOMEN (New York: Brentano's, 1929). See also Herbert Carter, "Three Women Dramatists of the Restoration," BJ 13 (1925), 91-97; Paul B. Anderson, "Mistress Delarivière Manley's Biography," MP 33 (1936), 261-78; and two articles by Gwendolyn B. Needham, "Mary de la Rivière Manley, Tory Defender," HLQ 12 (1949), 253-88, and "Mrs. Manley: An Eighteenth-Century Wife of Bath," HLQ 14 (1951), 259-84. See also Henry L. Snyder, "New Light on Mrs. Manley," PQ 52 (1973), 767-70. THE FEMALE WITS (Drury Lane, 1697) satirizes Mrs. Manley and her plays.

MOSES MENDEZ (d. 1758)

Mendez, a grandson of the Portuguese physician-in-ordinary to Catherine of Braganza, became a wealthy London stockbroker for whom the stage and poetry were hobbies. His dramatic pieces include THE DOUBLE DISAPPOINTMENT (1746), a popular farce; THE CHAPLET (1749), a musical entertainment made popular by Kitty Clive as Pastora; ROBIN HOOD (1750); and THE SHEPHERD'S LOTTERY (1751). The latter two pieces were musical entertainments. There are no collected or modern editions and few references in modern secondary sources.

JAMES MILLER (1706-44)

The most popular plays of this clergyman-dramatist were THE MOTHER-IN-LAW (1734) and THE MAN OF TASTE (1735), both comedies; THE UNIVERSAL PASSION (1737), an adaptation of MUCH ADO; and MAHOMET THE IMPOSTER (1744), a tragedy written in collaboration with John Hoadly. Miller's first play, THE HUMOURS OF OXFORD (1730), was also fairly successful. London templars took offense at THE COFFEE HOUSE (1738) and damned it along with Miller's subsequent plays--ART AND NATURE (1738), AN HOSPITAL FOR FOOLS (1739), and THE PICTURE (1745). (Miller's part in MAHOMET was kept secret for a time to avoid their censure.) MISCELLANEOUS WORKS IN VERSE AND PROSE (1741) is said by Emmett L. Avery (NEW CBEL) to include Miller's first four plays; Volume 1 only was issued. There are no modern editions. Charles W. Nichols, "A Reverend Alterer of Shakespeare," MLN 44 (1929), 30-32, and Walter P. Stewart, "An Eighteenth-Century Adaptation of Shakespeare," UTS 12 (1932), 98-117, both deal with THE UNIVERSAL PASSION. There is no biography more recent than the account in the DNB.

EDWARD MOORE (1712-57)

Moore, the son of a dissenting minister, is known as a fabulist as well as a dramatist. He wrote three plays--THE FOUNDLING (1748), GIL BLAS (1751), and THE GAMESTER (1753). GIL BLAS was not particularly successful, even when revived in 1764 as THE COUNTERFEITS; the other two plays, especially THE GAMESTER, eventually became stock pieces in the repertory and were played through the end of the period. POEMS, FABLES, AND PLAYS BY EDWARD MOORE (1756*) contains all three plays, as does THE DRAMATIC WORKS OF EDWARD MOORE, a made-up edition reissued in 1788. THE GAMESTER has been reprinted in facsimile by the Augustan Reprint Society, ed. Charles H. Peake and P.R. Wikelund (Ann Arbor, 1948), and is occasionally anthologized.

THE LIFE AND WORKS OF EDWARD MOORE, by John H. Caskey (New Haven: Yale Univ. Press, 1927), is the standard biography and includes a full discussion of the plays. Ralph L. Collins, in "Moore's THE FOUNDLING--an Intermediary," PQ 17 (1938), 139-43, discusses the play in relation to TOM JONES. E.C. Van Bellen, in "Trois jouers," Np 9 (1924), 161-72, discusses THE GAMESTER in relation to Saurin's BEVERLEY (1768), an adaptation of Moore's play.

THOMAS MORTON (c.1764-1838)

Morton, born in county Durham, was raised by his uncle, a broker, and became a member of Lincoln's Inn. Only seven of his plays belong to the period. These are COLUMBUS (1792), THE CHILDREN IN THE WOOD (1793),
ZORINSKI (1795), THE WAY TO GET MARRIED (1796), A CURE FOR THE
HEARTACHE (1797), SECRETS WORTH KNOWING (1798), and SPEED THE
PLOUGH (1800). All except the first were included in at least one contem-
porary collection, and all were successful on the stage; THE CHILDREN IN
THE WOOD, a dramatic opera with music by Arnold, and SPEED THE PLOUGH
are perhaps the most famous. Plays produced after the 1799-1800 season in-
clude THE BLIND GIRL (1801), BEGGAR MY NEIGHBOR (1802), THE SCHOOL
OF REFORM (1805), TOWN AND COUNTRY (1807), THE KNIGHT OF
SNOWDON (1811), EDUCATION (1813), THE SLAVE (1816), WHO'S MY
FATHER? (1818), A ROLAND FOR AN OLIVER (1819), HENRI QUATRE (1820),
A SCHOOL FOR GROWN CHILDREN (1827), and THE INVINCIBLES (1828).
Despite Morton's long career and stage popularity, there are no independent
modern editions of his plays, only one in a collection, no adequate biography,
and very little discussion of his work in the standard modern sources. See MR.
MORTON'S 'ZORINSKI' AND BROOKE'S 'GUSTAVUS VASA' COMPARED
(1795). SPEED THE PLOUGH is included in Allardyce Nicoll's LESSER ENG-
LISH COMEDIES OF THE EIGHTEENTH CENTURY (1931).

PETER ANTHONY MOTTEUX (1663-1718)

Motteux, born in Normandy, came to London upon the revocation of the Edict of Nantes in 1695; he became a businessman and translator (of Rabelais and Cervantes) as well as a playwright. Robert N. Cunningham's "A Bibliography of the Works of Peter Anthony Motteux, POBS 3, part 3 (1933), 317-37, is standard. Motteux's plays are mostly musical pieces--interludes, farces, or operas. The music of John Eccles and Daniel Purcell was a significant factor in the success of such early pieces as LOVE'S A JEST (1696), THE LOVES OF MARS AND VENUS (1696), and EUROPE'S REVELS FOR THE PEACE (1697). Motteux's most popular plays were THE ISLAND PRINCESS (c.1699, from Fletcher) and ACIS AND GALATEA (c.1702); the former was operatic, the latter a masque. Other plays include three acts of THE NOVELTY (1697), BEAUTY IN DISTRESS (1698), BRITAIN'S HAPPINESS (1704), and FAREWELL FOLLY (1705). Libretti include those for ARSINOE (1705, in collaboration), THE TEMPLE OF LOVE (1706), TOMYRIS, QUEEN OF SCYTHIA (1707), and LOVE'S TRIUMPH (1708, from Ottoboni).

The only substantial study of Motteux is Robert N. Cunningham's PETER ANTHONY MOTTEUX 1663-1718: A BIOGRAPHICAL AND CRITICAL STUDY (Oxford: Blackwell, 1933). Louis Charlanne has a general essay, "Un français, écrivain anglais au dix-septième siècle: Pierre-Antoine Motteux," REVUE BLEUE, 26 Aug. and 2 Sept. 1911, pp. 181-86 and 300-306. Allardyce Nicoll, in "FAREWELL FOLLY and THE AMOROUS MISER," N&Q 137 (1919), 310-12, argues that only the former play, printed in 1707, is Motteux's; Frederick W. Bateson, "Motteux and THE AMOROUS MISER," RES 3 (1927), 340-42, argues convincingly that this play was an unacted version of FAREWELL FOLLY. Fredson T. Bowers has a bibliographical note, "Motteux's LOVE'S A JEST (1696): A Running-Title and Presswork Problem," PBSA 48 (1954), 268-73. Motteux is sometimes thought to have had a hand in Farquhar's THE STAGECOACH; see William J. Lawrence, "The Mystery of THE STAGECOACH," MLR 27 (1932), 392-97, and the Stonehill edition of Farquhar. Lawrence argues for a production date c.1701, but his conjecture has not been accepted by most authorities.

JOHN MOTTLEY (1692-1750)

Mottley was a literary hack who turned out biographies of Peter I of Russia and others in addition to writing plays. His plays include THE IMPERIAL CAPTIVES (1720) and ANTIOCHUS (1721), both tragedies; PENELOPE (1728, with Thomas Cooke) and THE DEVIL TO PAY (1731, mostly by Coffey), both ballad operas; THE CRAFTSMAN (1728), a farce; and THE WIDOW BEWITCHED (1730), a comedy. The latter two reached six performances. There are no collected or modern editions of Mottley's plays and infrequent references in modern secondary sources.

WILLIAM MOUNTFORT (1664-92)

Mountfort, a well known actor, was murdered by Captain Richard Hill in a quarrel over the actress Anne Bracegirdle. SIX PLAYS WRITTEN BY MR. MOUNTFORT, 2 vols. (1720), includes THE LIFE AND DEATH OF DOCTOR FAUSTUS, WITH THE HUMOURS OF HARLEQUIN AND SCARAMOUCH (c. 1686), THE INJURED LOVERS (1688), THE SUCCESSFUL STRANGERS (c.1689), and GREENWICH PARK (1691). ZELMANE (1705) was completed by an unknown hand. KING EDWARD THE THIRD (1690) and HENRY THE SECOND, KING OF ENGLAND (1692), though included in SIX PLAYS, are usually attributed to John Bancroft; a collaboration may have been involved. THE LIFE AND DEATH OF WILLIAM MOUNTFORT, by Albert S. Borgman (Cambridge, Mass.: Harvard Univ. Press, 1935) is an excellent biography. In "The Significance of William Mountfort's GREENWICH PARK," RECTR 12, no. 2 (1973), 35-40, Martin W. Walsh shows that the East End setting of the play is fully consistent with its favorable presentation of the merchant class, since fashionable London was rapidly moving west.

ARTHUR MURPHY (1727-1805)

Murphy, son of a Dublin merchant, was a journalist and lawyer as well as a
dramatist. THE WORKS OF ARTHUR MURPHY, ESQ., 7 vols. (1786), includes
in Volumes 1-4 all of Murphy's acted plays; it has not been reprinted. 'THE
WAY TO KEEP HIM' AND FIVE OTHER PLAYS BY ARTHUR MURPHY, ed.
John P. Emery (New York: New York Univ. Press, 1956), includes THE
APPRENTICE (1756), THE UPHOLSTERER (1758), THE WAY TO KEEP HIM
(1760), THE OLD MAID (1761), THREE WEEKS AFTER MARRIAGE (1776, originally WHAT WE MUST ALL COME TO, 1764; produced in 1767 as MAR-
RIAGE A LA MODE), and KNOW YOUR OWN MIND (1777). These were
all popular plays in the period, some of them lasting well into the nineteenth
century; all are included in contemporary anthologies, and at least two are
available in other modern collections. ALL IN THE WRONG (1761) was also
popular; THE CITIZEN (1761) even more so. THE ENGLISHMAN FROM
PARIS, one of Murphy's few unsuccessful plays, has been published in facsimile
by the Augustan Reprint Society (Los Angeles: W.A. Clark Library, 1969),
with an introduction by Simon Trefman.

Murphy's tragedies include THE ORPHAN OF CHINA (1759), ZENOBIA (1768),
THE GRECIAN DAUGHTER (1772), ALZUMA (1773), and THE RIVAL SISTERS
(1793). The first three of these were the most successful, especially THE
GRECIAN DAUGHTER. Less successful works include THE DESERT ISLAND
(1760), NO ONE'S ENEMY BUT HIS OWN (1764), THE CHOICE (1765), and
THE SCHOOL FOR GUARDIANS (1767). ARMINIUS and HAMLET (a parody)
were unacted. Many of Murphy's plays are partially indebted to Molière and
other French dramatists.

NEW ESSAYS BY ARTHUR MURPHY, ed. Arthur Sherbo (East Lansing: Michi-
gan State Univ. Press, 1963), includes a number of Murphy's dramatic reviews.
The earliest biography is Jesse Foot's THE LIFE OF ARTHUR MURPHY, ESQ.
(London: J. Faulder, 1811), but this is inadequate. Two full-length modern
studies appeared in the same year: John P. Emery's ARTHUR MURPHY: AN
EMINENT ENGLISH DRAMATIST OF THE EIGHTEENTH CENTURY (Philadelphia:
Univ. of Pennsylvania Press for Temple Univ. Publications, 1946) and Howard
H. Dunbar's THE DRAMATIC CAREER OF ARTHUR MURPHY (New York: Mod-
ern Language Association, 1946). The Emery book is a thorough biography
which pays considerable attention to Murphy's legal as well as his dramatic

career; Dunbar's study focuses on the 1754-77 period in which Murphy was an active dramatist and is primarily critical rather than biographical. A good general essay on Murphy as a comic writer is John H. Caskey's "Arthur Murphy and the War on Sentimental Comedy," JEGP 30 (1931), 563-77, which argues that Murphy is much less sentimental than is often assumed. Frederick S. Boas's EIGHTEENTH-CENTURY DRAMA also treats Murphy, though briefly. Simon Trefman's article "Arthur Murphy's Long Lost ENGLISHMAN FROM PARIS: A Manuscript Discovered," TN 20 (1966), 137-41, calls attention to a Newberry Library manuscript; Martin Lehnert, in "Arthur Murphy's HAMLET-Parodie (1772) auf David Garrick," SJ 102 (1966), 97-167, includes the full text of this un-acted play.

WILLIAM CAVENDISH, 1ST DUKE OF NEWCASTLE (1592-1676)

Most of Newcastle's efforts after the Restoration were devoted to rebuilding his estate, which was badly dispersed during the Commonwealth period. Two of his earlier plays, THE COUNTRY CAPTAIN and THE VARIETY, were performed after 1660; new plays included THE HUMOUROUS LOVERS (1667, attributed by Pepys to Newcastle's wife), SIR MARTIN MAR-ALL (1667, with Dryden), THE HEIRESS (1669), and THE TRIUMPHANT WIDOW (1674, with Shadwell). THE FRENCH DANCING-MASTER (1661) was an alteration of THE VARIETY. THE LIFE OF THE . . . DUKE . . . OF NEWCASTLE (1667) was written by Newcastle's wife; it has been edited by Charles H. Firth (London: Nimmo, 1886). THE COUNTRY CAPTAIN, ed. Arthur H. Bullen, was included in Volume 2 of A COLLECTION OF OLD ENGLISH PLAYS (London: privately published, 1883) but attributed to James Shirley. Some of Newcastle's scenes for THE TRIUMPHANT WIDOW are printed by John D. Jump in "The Merry Humour of a Rogue," JGLS 17 (1938), 24–30; see also A PLEASANT AND MERRY HUMOUR OF A ROGUE, ed. Francis Needham in the WELLBECK MISCELLANY NO. 1 (Bungay, England: R. Clay & Sons, 1933).

THOMAS ODELL (1691-1749)

Odell, son of a country squire, was a political hack for a time. He built the theatre in Goodman's Fields in 1729, and eventually became Deputy Licenser (1738-49). His plays are THE CHIMERA (1721), THE PATRON and THE SMUGGLERS (1729), and THE PRODIGAL (1744, from Shadwell); none was long-lived on the stage. There are no collected or modern editions and only infrequent references to the plays in secondary materials.

GABRIEL ODINGSELLS (1690-1734)

Two comedies and a ballad opera by Odingsells were produced in London. THE BATH UNMASKED (1725) has a successful run; THE CAPRICIOUS LOVERS lasted for three performances later the same year, as did BAYES'S OPERA in 1730. Odingsells gradually lost his faculties and in 1734 hanged himself. There are no collected or modern editions and few references in modern dramatic histories.

KANE O'HARA (c.1714-82)

O'Hara was born in Ireland into a musical family and educated at Trinity College, Dublin; he was an artist as well as playwright. His most popular plays were MIDAS (1762) and TOM THUMB (1780, from Fielding); both were played throughout the century. THE GOLDEN PIPPIN (1773) was only slightly less popular. These three pieces are burlettas, MIDAS in three acts and the others in two. O'Hara also wrote THE TWO MISERS (1775), a popular musical farce, and APRIL DAY (1777), a burlesque. The first of these was revived occasionally to the end of the century; APRIL DAY was less successful, and it is the only O'Hara play not represented in contemporary collections.

There are no collected or independent modern editions of O'Hara's plays, nor is there a modern biography. P.T. Dircks, in "The Dublin Manuscripts of Kane O'Hara," N&Q 215 (1970), 99-100, notes that five unpublished plays in manuscript are held by the National Library of Ireland and that the MSS of MIDAS and THE GOLDEN PIPPIN show significant differences from published texts. In another article, "The Catch on the Eighteenth-Century Stage: A Consideration of Two Burlettas," TN 25 (1971), 93-96, Dircks discusses this aspect of the same two plays. The only general survey of O'Hara's work, Margaret F. Maxwell, "Olympus at Billingsgate: The Burlettas of Kane O'Hara," ETJ 15 (1963), 130-35, is brief and disappointing.

JOHN O'KEEFFE (1747-1833)

O'Keeffe, like his younger countryman O'Hara, was an artist as well as a dramatist and was a victim of early blindness. He was an actor in Dublin for a dozen years, moving to London in 1780. During his long career, he wrote more than fifty pieces for the stage; few of them were fairlures, and several were among the most popular productions of the last quarter of the century.

The plays are THE SHE GALLANT (Dublin 1767; as THE POSITIVE MAN*, 1782); TONY LUMPKIN IN TOWN* (1778); THE SON-IN-LAW (1779); THE DEAD ALIVE and THE AGREEABLE SURPRISE (1781); THE BANDITTI (1781; as THE CASTLE OF ANDALUSIA*, 1782); HARLEQUIN TEAGUE (1782, with George Colman, Sr.); LORD MAYOR'S DAY (1782); THE MAID'S THE MIS-TRESS (1783, from Federico's libretto for LA SERVA PADRONA); THE SHAM-ROCK (Dublin 1777; as THE POOR SOLDIER*, 1783); THE YOUNG QUAKER (1783); THE BIRTHDAY* (1783, from Saint-Foix); GRETNA GREEN (1783; by Charles Stuart, with alterations and songs by O'Keeffe); FRIAR BACON (1783; as HARLEQUIN RAMBLER, 1784; written with Charles Bonner); PEEPING TOM and FONTAINBLEAU* (1784); THE BLACKSMITH OF ANTWERP*, A [The?] BEGGAR ON HORSEBACK*, and OMAI (1785); LOVE IN A CAMP* (1786, occasionally acted under the subtitle PATRICK IN PRUSSIA); THE SIEGE OF CURZOLA (1786); THE MAN MILLINER* (1787); LOVE AND WAR (1787, abridged from Jephson's THE CAMPAIGN); THE FARMER* (1787); TANTARA RARA, ROGUES ALL!*, THE PRISONER AT LARGE*, THE HIGHLAND REEL*, and ALADDIN (1788); THE TOY* (1789; as THE LIE OF THE DAY, 1796); THE FARO TABLE (1789, an alteration of Centlivre's GAMESTER); THE LITTLE HUNCHBACK* (1789); LE GRENADIER* (prohibited: published 1789); THE CZAR* (1790; as THE FUGITIVE, also 1790); THE BASKET MAKER* (1790); MODERN ANTIQUES* and WILD OATS* (1791); SPRIGS OF LAUREL* (1793; as THE RIVAL SOLDIERS, 1797); THE LONDON HERMIT* and THE WORLD IN A VILLAGE* (1793); LIFE'S VAGARIES* (1795); THE IRISH MIMIC* (1795, oc-casionally acted as BLUNDERS AT BRIGHTON); MERRY SHERWOOD (1795); LAD OF THE HILLS (1796; as THE WICKLOW MOUNTAINS*, 1796); THE DOLDRUM* and THE MAGIC BANNER* (1796); OLYMPUS IN AN UPROAR (1796, from O'Hara); BRITAIN'S BRAVE TARS (1797); SHE'S ELOPED!, THE ELEVENTH OF JUNE, and NOSEGAY OF WEEDS (1798).

O'Keeffe's outstanding successes were THE SON-IN-LAW, THE AGREEABLE

SURPRISE, THE POOR SOLDIER, PEEPING TOM, and THE FARMER. THE LONDON STAGE lists these as fourth, third, fifth, sixth, and eleventh, respectively, in frequency of performance among afterpieces produced 1776-1800, and THE CASTLE OF ANDALUSIA as fifteenth in popularity among mainpieces during the same period. THE DEAD ALIVE, THE YOUNG QUAKER, FONTAINBLEAU, LOVE IN A CAMP, LOVE AND WAR, THE PRISONER AT LARGE, THE HIGHLAND REEL, WILD OATS, THE LONDON HERMIT, and THE IRISH MIMIC were all popular enough to have made the career of a less prolific writer. O'Keeffe's last four pieces were not particularly successful, nor were THE BLACKSMITH OF ANTWERP, THE MAN MILLINER (a complete failure), TANTARA RARA, THE CZAR, and THE BASKET MAKER.

THE DRAMATIC WORKS OF JOHN O'KEEFFE . . ., 4 vols. (1798) includes the plays with asterisks above; many pieces are also included in contemporary collections. Despite O'Keeffe's theatrical importance, there are no modern collections or independent editions, nor is there an adequate critical or biographical study. RECOLLECTIONS OF THE LIFE OF JOHN O'KEEFFE, WRITTEN BY HIMSELF, 2 vols. (London: Colburn, 1826*) is rambling and anecdotal, but of first importance. Leonard W. Connolly, in "A Case of Political Censorship at the Little Theatre in the Haymarket in 1794: John O'Keeffe's JENNY'S WHIM; OR, THE ROASTED EMPEROR," RECTR 10, no. 2 (1971), 34-40, notes that the piece was banned because it poked fun at Morocco, a neutral government. William A. Huse, in "A Noble Savage on the Stage," MP 33 (1936), 303-16, discusses OMAI; see also Thomas B. Clark, OMAI: FIRST POLYNESIAN AMBASSADOR TO ENGLAND (San Francisco: Colt Press, 1941), chapter 6. Both S.S. Morgan, in "The Damning of Holcroft's KNAVE OR NOT? and O'Keeffe's SHE'S ELOPED," HLQ 22 (1958), 51-62, and Connolly, in "More on John O'Keeffe and the Lord Chamberlain," N&Q 214 (1969), 190-92, deal with SHE'S ELOPED! and the changes O'Keeffe had to make in the play to obtain a license for performance.

ROGER BOYLE, 1ST EARL OF ORRERY (1621-79)

THE DRAMATIC WORKS OF ROGER BOYLE . . ., 2 vols. (1739), has been superseded by the identically titled edition of William S. Clark, 2 vols. (Cambridge, Mass.: Harvard Univ. Press, 1937). Clark is elaborate and thorough; his edition includes historical and critical prefaces, explanatory and textual notes, and a bibliography. THE TRAGEDY OF MUSTAPHA is included in Bonamy Dobrée's FIVE HEROIC PLAYS along with THE HISTORY OF HENRY THE FIFTH, and both plays are available in facsimile (London: Cornmarket Press, 1969). The best biography is Kathleen M. Lynch's ROGER BOYLE, FIRST EARL OF ORRERY (Knoxville: Univ. of Tennessee Press, 1965), which also devotes two chapters to the plays.

Clark's many articles on Orrery are incorporated in his edition and need not be separately listed. Montague Summers's early article, "Orrery's THE TRAGEDY OF ZOROASTRES," MLR 12 (1917*), 24-32, is mostly plot summary but does call attention to the unpublished MS of the play. "Roger Boyle, Earl of Orrery," TLS, 28 April 1921, p. 274, is a general essay focusing on the heroic plays. Frank W. Payne's "The Question of Precedence between Dryden and the Earl of Orrery with Regard to the English Heroic Play," RES 1 (1925), 173-81, is typical of a number of studies; see the works cited on heroic drama in Part 1, Section 7.12, (especially Deane and Waith) and under Dryden, above. Kathleen M. Lynch, in "Conventions of Platonic Drama in the Heroic Plays of Orrery and Dryden," PMLA 44 (1929), 456-71, argues for the influence on both writers of the Caroline court dramatists. Laurens J. Mills's article, "The Friendship Theme in Orrery's Plays," PMLA 53 (1938), 795-806, is one of the few literary-critical essays on Boyle. C. William Miller's "A Source Note on Boyle's THE GENERAL," MLQ 8 (1947), 146-50, and Samuel N. Bogorad's "A Note on Orrery's HENRY THE FIFTH," N&Q 195 (1950), 117-18, add minor points to the information in Clark's edition.

THOMAS OTWAY (1652-85)

THE WORKS OF MR. THOMAS OTWAY (1692); THE WORKS OF MR. THOMAS OTWAY . . ., 2 vols. (1712); THE WORKS OF THOMAS OTWAY, 2 vols. (London: Rivington, 1812); THE WORKS OF THOMAS OTWAY . . ., 3 vols. (London: for T. Turner, 1813); and THE COMPLETE WORKS OF THOMAS OTWAY, ed. Montague Summers, 3 vols. (London: Nonesuch Press, 1926*), have all been superseded by THE WORKS OF THOMAS OTWAY: PLAYS, POEMS, AND LOVE-LETTERS, ed. Jyotish C. Ghosh, 2 vols. (Oxford: Clarendon Press, 1932*). The Summers edition, which Stratman's BIBLIO-GRAPHICAL GUIDE calls definitive, is grossly inaccurate; see Robert W. Babcock's "The Reverend Montague Summers as Editor of Otway," PMLA 48 (1933), 948-50, and Ghosh's introduction. DON CARLOS (1676), THE ORPHAN and THE SOLDIER'S FORTUNE (1680), and VENICE PRESERVED (1682) are included in the Mermaid THOMAS OTWAY, ed. Roden Noel (London: Vizetelly, 1884*). THE ORPHAN (1680) and VENICE PRESERVED were edited by Charles F. McClumpha in the Belles Lettres series (Boston: Heath, 1908). THE HISTORY AND FALL OF CAIUS MARIUS (1679) is available in facsimile from London's Cornmarket Press (1969); facsimile editions of both THE ORPHAN and VENICE PRESERVED are also available (London: Scolar Press, c.1972). VENICE PRESERVED, ed. Malcolm M. Kelsall, is included in the Regents Restoration Drama series (Lincoln: Univ. of Nebraska Press, 1969).

Samuel Johnson included Otway in THE LIVES OF THE POETS, and he is also discussed by Thomas Davies in his DRAMATIC MISCELLANIES (1784-85). The best biography is Roswell G. Ham, OTWAY AND LEE: BIOGRAPHY FROM A BAROQUE AGE (New Haven: Yale Univ. Press, 1931*), though one may also consult the more succinct account in the introduction to Ghosh's edition. Differences between these two accounts are aired in several earlier articles. Ghosh contributed "New Light on Some Episodes in the Life of Thomas Otway," N&Q 147 (1924), 421-24, 439-42, 459-63, and "Thomas Otway and Mrs. Barry," N&Q 144 (1923), 103-05; Ham responded with "Additional Materials for a Life of Thomas Otway," N&Q 150 (1926), 75-77, and "Thomas Otway, Rochester, and Mrs. Barry," N&Q 149 (1925), 165-67. Ham also contributed "The Portraits of Thomas Otway," N&Q 149 (1925), 111-13; "New Facts about Otway," TLS, 14 Jan. 1926, p. 28; and "Otway's Duels with Churchill and Settle," MLN 41 (1926), 73-80. More recent biographical notes include W. H. Challen, "Thomas Otway," N&Q 199 (1954), 316-17, and Noel Blakiston, "Otway's Friend," TLS, 15 Aug. 1958, p. 459.

General surveys of Otway's career include Edmund Gosse's essay, "Thomas Otway," SEVENTEENTH-CENTURY STUDIES (New York: Scribner's, 1914 [originally 1883]), pp. 299-342; Edgar Schumacher's monograph THOMAS OTWAY (Bern, Switzerland: Duerrenmatt-Egger, 1924*); Bonamy Dobrée's essay in RESTORATION TRAGEDY (1929), based on the TLS lead article for 3 March 1927); and the perceptive accounts in Eric Rothstein's RESTORATION TRAGEDY (1967) and Eugene M. Waith's IDEAS OF GREATNESS (1971). The most recent book on the plays is Helmut Klinger's DIE KUENSTLERISCHE ENTWICKLUNG IN DER TRAGOEDIEN THOMAS OTWAYS (Vienna: Braumueller, 1971), which studies Otway's development as a serious dramatist. More specialized works include Gisela Fried's GESTALT UND FUNKTION DER BILDER IM DRAMA THOMAS OTWAYS (Goettingen, Germany: Vandenhoeck & Ruprecht, 1965); Thomas B. Stroup, "Ottway's Bitter Pessimism," in ESSAYS IN ENGLISH LITERATURE . . . PRESENTED TO DOUGALD MACMILLAN, ed. Daniel W. Patterson and Albrecht B. Strauss, SP Extra Series 4 (Chapel Hill: Univ. of North Carolina Press, 1967), pp. 54-75; Eugene M. Waith, "Tears of Magnanimity in Otway and Racine," in FRENCH AND ENGLISH DRAMA OF THE SEVENTEENTH CENTURY: PAPERS READ AT A CLARK LIBRARY SEMINAR MARCH 13, 1971 (Los Angeles: W.A. Clark Library, (1972), pp. 1-22; and Aline M. Taylor, NEXT TO SHAKESPEARE: OTWAY'S 'VENICE PRESERVED' AND 'THE ORPHAN' AND THEIR HISTORY ON THE LONDON STAGE (Durham, N.C.: Duke Univ. Press, 1950). The Fried monograph is a thorough study of the form and content of Otway's imagery in both comedies and tragedies. Stroup derives Otway's cynicism and pessimism from the popularity of Hobbes's ideas. Waith notes that Otway stresses pity without Racine's corresponding magnanimity. The Taylor study traces the stage career of Otway's most famous works, noting that they were the only Restoration tragedies to hold the boards throughout the entire period; the author also gives a good critical analysis of both plays and a calendar of performances.

Most scholarship has focused on VENICE PRESERVED, but there are a number of studies of the other plays. D. Biggins, in "Source Notes for Dryden, Wycherley, and Otway," N&Q 201 (1956), 298-301, derives the rape of Timandra in ALCIBIADES (1675) from Zulema's similar attempt on Almahide in THE CONQUEST OF GRANADA. J.C. Ross argues in "An Attack on Thomas Shadwell in Otway's THE ATHEIST," PQ 52 (1973), 753-60, that the character Daredevil attacks Thomas Shadwell and that the plot involving Daredevil is based on events which occurred in early 1682. CAIUS MARIUS is discussed in several works listed in Part 1, Section 8.2 and also by Louis M. Eich, "A Previous Adaptation of ROMEO AND JULIET," QJS 23 (1937), 589-94 (negligible), and by Hazel M. Batzer, "Shakespeare's Influence on Thomas Otway's CAIUS MARIUS," RUO 39 (1969), 533-61 (stressing Otway's attempt to turn Shakespearean and Plutarchian materials to contemporary political uses). Homer Goldberg, "The Two 1692 editions of CAIUS MARIUS," SB 3 (1951), 252-55, notes that no. 882 in Woodward and McManaway's CHECKLIST OF ENGLISH PLAYS is the third edition, not an issue; the proper order is 880-881-882, while 883 is a ghost, 884 probably a fake, and 885 a reprint of 882. Edward A. Langhans, in "Three Early Eighteenth-Century Promptbooks," TN 20 (1966), 142-50, discusses an acting copy of THE CHEATS OF SCAPIN (Dec. 1676 or Jan. 1677) dating from the 1730's; Jean-Paul Michel, in "Thomas Otway: THE CHEATS OF SCAPIN (1676)," GEOFFRIN COLLECTION, I, 361-71,

Thomas Otway

compares this first English version of Molière's FOURBERIES DE SCAPIN with
its source. DON CARLOS is discussed in Gustave Dulong's L'ABBE DE SAINT-
REAL . . ., 2 vols. (Paris: Champion, 1921), Vol. 2. Aline M. Taylor's
book gives the best account of THE ORPHAN; Geoffrey Marshall, in "The
Coherence of THE ORPHAN," TSLL 11 (1969), 931-43, argues (too ingeniously,
perhaps) that Acasto precipitates the tragedy by speaking ironically rather than
plainly about marriage. André Lefèvre, "Racine en Angleterre au dix-septième
siècle: TITUS AND BERENICE de Thomas Otway," RLC 34 (1960), 251-57,
compares this 1676 play with its source.

VENICE PRESERVED has been extensively studied. Aside from Aline M. Taylor's
account, the best discussions are those of Moody E. Prior, THE LANGUAGE
OF TRAGEDY (1947), stressing Otway's interest in painting the passions; David
R. Hauser, "Otway Preserved: Theme and Form in VENICE PRESERVED," SP
55 (1958), 481-93, which focuses on Otway's presentation of man's ambivalent
nature and of a world where good and evil are inextricably mingled; John H.
Wilson, in his PREFACE TO RESTORATION DRAMA (1965), pp. 95-108; Ronald
Berman, "Nature in VENICE PRESERVED," ELH 36 (1969), 529-43, which views
the play in terms of the disparity Pierre and Jaffeir see between social forms
and the truths underlying them; and Derek W. Hughes, "A New Look at VEN-
ICE PRESERVED," SEL 11 (1971), 437-57, which sees the tragedy as the triumph of impulse over reason and relates the scenes with Antonio to this theme.

The controversial "Nicky-Nacky" scenes are the subject of R.E. Hughes's
"'Comic Relief' in Otway's VENICE PRESERVED," N&Q 203 (1958), 65-66;
of William H. McBurney's "Otway's Tragic Muse Debauched: Sensuality in
VENICE PRESERVED," JEGP 58 (1959), 380-99; and of Robert Pasquarelli,
"On the Nicky-Nacky Scenes in VENICE PRESERVED," RECTR 8, no. 2 (1969),
38-41. Hughes argues that masochism and perversion do not obscure the comic
element in these scenes; McBurney relates their eroticism to Restoration comedy,
especially to Otway's own comedies, and notes that eighteenth-century acting
versions of the play regularly emasculated these scenes. Pasquarelli argues for
the structural significance of the scenes as comic relief and contrast; they are
thematic in that Antonio symbolizes the Venetian senate. The political dimension of the Nicky-Nacky scenes is discussed by John R. Moore in "Contemporary Satire in Otway's VENICE PRESERVED," PMLA 43 (1928), 166-81.

Other studies of the play include Samuel Derrick's REMARKS UPON THE
TRAGEDY OF 'VENICE PRESERVED,' no. 1 of THE DRAMATIC CENSOR . . .
(1752); William Van Voris's "Tragedy Through Restoration Eyes: VENICE
PRESERVED in Its Own Theatre," HERMATHENA 99 (1964), 55-65; Gordon
Williams's "The Sex-Death Motif in Otway's VENICE PRESERVED," TRIVIUM
(Wales) 2 (1967), 59-70; Françoise Rives's "Un dramaturge à la croisée des
chemins: Otway dans VENICE PRESERVED," CALIBAN 6 (1969), 17-25; and
Bessie Proffitt's "Religious Symbolism in Otway's VENICE PRESERVED," PLL 7
(1971), 26-37 (unconvincing). The play's relationship to Hofmannsthal is the
subject of several studies. The most accessible of these are Fritz Wenther,
DAS GERETTETE VENEDIG: EINE VERGLEICHENDE STUDIE (Berkeley and Los
Angeles: Univ. of California Press, 1914); Michel Vanhelleputte, "Hofmannsthal und Thomas Otway: zur Struktur des GERETTETEN VENEDIG," RB 42

(1964), 926-39; H.R. Klieneberger, "Otway's VENICE PRESERVED and Hofmannsthal's DAS GERETTETE VENEDIG," MLR 62 (1967), 292-97. See also
G.W. Crowhurst, "The Dramatic Opening--A Comparative Study of Otway and
Hofmannsthal," THEORIA (Natal) 35 (1970), 51-58. Otway's sources are discussed by Alfred Johnson in . . . LAFOSSE, OTWAY, SAINT-REAL: ORI-
GINES ET TRANSFORMATIONS D'UN THEME TRAGIQUE (Paris: Hachette,
1901); by Gordon H. Gerould, "The Sources of VENICE PRESERVED," JEGP 5
(1903), 58-61, which argues that Belvidera and some other features of the play
are indebted to Lee's CAESAR BORGIA; and by S. Riva, "Otway, Saint-Réal,
e la VENEZIA SALVATA," DANTE, June 1936, pp. 278-82. Minor notes
include Aline Mackenzie [Taylor], "A Note on Pierre's White Hat," N&Q 192
(1947), 90-93 (a Jacobite allusion); Edward H.W. Meyerstein, "The Dagger in
VENICE PRESERVED," TLS, 7 Sept. 1951, p. 565; and a brief but stimulating
discussion at the end of Gerald Gillespie, "The Rebel in Seventeenth-Century
Tragedy," CL 18 (1966), 324-36.

WALLEY CHAMBERLAIN OULTON (c.1770-c.1820)

Oulton was born and educated in Dublin, and many of his early dramatic pieces were first performed there. He came to London around 1786, becoming an occasional poet, journalist, and critic. Besides his plays, he compiled a number of "histories" of contemporary drama. THE HAUNTED CASTLE (1783); THE HAPPY DISGUISE, THE NEW WONDER, and THE MADHOUSE (1784); POOR MARIA and THE RECRUITING MANAGER (1785); and CURIOSITY (1786) were all produced in Dublin. A NEW WAY TO KEEP A WIFE AT HOME (from Fielding) was Oulton's first London production (1783); it was followed by HOBSON'S CHOICE (1787), PERSEVERANCE (1798), AS IT SHOULD BE (1789), ALL IN GOOD HUMOR (1792), THE IRISH TAR (1797), and BOTHERATION (1798). Some half-dozen more of Oulton's plays were produced in the early nineteenth century, including THE SIXTY-THIRD LETTER (1802, sometimes attributed to Prince Hoare), THE MIDDLE DISH (1804), THE SLEEPWALKER (1812), MY LANDLADY'S GOWN (1816), and FRIGHTENED TO DEATH (1817). Most of Oulton's pieces are short farces, entertainments, and interludes. There are no collected or modern editions and only scattered references in modern secondary materials.

HENRY NEVIL PAYNE (fl. 1672-1710)

Payne, a Jacobite agent tried for treason in 1693, wrote three plays--THE
FATAL JEALOUSY (1672), THE MORNING RAMBLE (1672), and THE SIEGE
OF CONSTANTINOPLE (1674). The first of these was edited by Willard
Thorp for the Augustan Reprint series (Los Angeles: W.A. Clark Library, 1948).
There are no collected or other modern editions. The only substantial modern
study of Payne is Thorp's "Henry Nevil Payne: Dramatist and Jacobite Con-
spirator," in THE PARROTT PRESENTATION VOLUME (Princeton: Princeton
Univ. Press, 1935), pp. 347-81. Harold Love, in "State Affairs on the Restoration Stage, 1660-1675," RECTR 14, no. 1 (1975), 1-9, devotes some attention to THE SIEGE OF CONSTANTINOPLE.

WILLIAM PEARCE (fl. 1792-95)

Pearce produced several musical pieces in the 1790's--comic operas, melo-dramas, and farces, often with music by William Shield. The most popular of these was HARTFORD BRIDGE (1792); others are THE NUNNERY (1785), THE MIDNIGHT WANDERERS (1793), NETLEY ABBEY and ARRIVED AT PORTS-MOUTH! (both 1794), WINDSOR CASTLE (1795), and MERRY SHERWOOD (1795, with Mark Lonsdale). There are no collected or modern editions of Pearce's plays and very few references in modern secondary materials.

AMBROSE PHILIPS (1674-1749)

Philips's THREE TRAGEDIES . . . (1725) is a made-up volume; there is no true collected edition of the plays. THE DISTRESSED MOTHER (1712, from Racine's ANDROMACHE) became a stock play, produced well into the 1780's; THE BRITON (1722) and HUMPHRY, DUKE OF GLOUCESTER (1723, from Crowne and Shakespeare) lasted for only a few performances. The last of these is available in facsimile (London: Cornmarket Press, 1969).

Samuel Johnson included a life of Philips in THE LIVES OF THE POETS, but the best biography is in Mary G. Segar's introduction to her edition of THE POEMS OF AMBROSE PHILIPS (Oxford: Blackwell, 1937) in the Percy Reprints series. This includes earlier material published in TLS. See also Aleyn L. Reade, "The Date of Ambrose Philips's Death," TLS, 12 Feb. 1938, p. 108 (confirming Segar's date); S.F. Fogle, "Notes on Ambrose Philips," MLN 54 (1939), 354-59 (two minor corrections and one addition to Segar); and Calhoun Winton, "Some Manuscripts by and concerning Philips," ELN 5 (1967), 99-101.

Philips is rarely discussed except as a poet, though Frederick S. Boas devotes a chapter of EIGHTEENTH-CENTURY DRAMA to his three tragedies. Katherine E. Wheatley, "Andromache as the 'Distressed Mother,'" RR 39 (1948), 3-21, notes the enormous popularity of Philips's play but then turns her attention to its infinite inferiority to Racine's; Englishmen, she concludes, could not possibly understand or approach Racine's genius. Paul E. Parnell's "THE DISTRESSED MOTHER, Ambrose Philips's Morality Play," CL 11 (1959), 111-23, is more concerned with what Philips and his contemporary audiences thought and is, consequently, a more useful article. Adolphus J. Bryan, "Ambrose Philips's HUMPHRY, DUKE OF GLOUCESTER: A Study in Eighteenth-Century Adaptation," in STUDIES FOR WILLIAM A. READ . . ., ed. Nathaniel M. Caffee and Thomas A. Kirby (Baton Rouge: Louisiana State Univ. Press, 1940), pp. 221-36, relates the play to its sources.

WILLIAM PHILIPS (d. 1734)

Little is known of Captain William Philips. THE REVENGEFUL QUEEN (1698, from Machiavelli), ST. STEPHEN'S GREEN (Dublin, 1700), and HIBERNIA FREED (1722) are now considered his work, although published anonymously; BELISARIUS (1724) was published under his name. The latter two plays were relatively successful on the stage. There are no collected or modern editions of Philips and only scattered references in modern dramatic histories.

EDWARD PHILLIPS (fl. 1730-40)

Little is known of Phillips except his plays, which are all afterpieces and mostly ballad operas or musical farces. THE CHAMBERMAID (1730), THE STAGE MUTINEERS (1733), and BRITONS, STRIKE HOME! (1739) were not particularly successful, but Phillips's pantomime THE ROYAL CHASE (1736; also acted as MERLIN'S CAVE and HARLEQUIN SKELETON) became a stock piece until well into the 1780's. THE LIVERY RAKE (1733) was successful but not nearly as popular as another production in the same season, THE MOCK LAW-YER. Phillips also wrote the words for John Galliard's THE NUPTIAL MASQUE (1734). There are no collected or modern editions and only scattered references in the standard modern histories. Charles W. Nichols, in "A Note on THE STAGE MUTINEERS," MLN 35 (1920), 225-27, attributes this play to Phillips on strength of an anonymous contemporary pamphlet; his argument is persuasive.

FREDERICK PILON (1750-88)

Pilon, born in Cork, was a stroller and London journalist before turning to the drama. Most of his plays are farcical afterpieces. They include THE INVASION (1778, revived 1793), THE LIVERPOOL PRIZE and ILLUMINATION (1779), THE DEVICE (1779; altered as THE DEAF LOVER, 1780), THE SIEGE OF GIBRALTER and THE HUMOURS OF AN ELECTION (1780), THELYPHTHORA (1781), THE FAIR AMERICAN (1782), AEROSTATION (1784), THE MAGIC CAVERN (1784, with Ralph Wewitzer), BARATARIA (1785, from D'Urfey), an alteration of ALL'S WELL (1785), and HE WOULD BE A SOLDIER (1786, Pilon's only five-act comedy). THE DEAF LOVER and BARATARIA were hits popular to the end of the century. THE LIVERPOOL PRIZE and HE WOULD BE A SOLDIER were also popular. In fact, nearly all Pilon's pieces had successful runs.

THE DEAF LOVER and HE WOULD BE A SOLDIER were included in several contemporary collections, but there are no independent modern editions of any of Pilon's plays and only scattered references in the secondary literature.

MARY [GRIFFITH] PIX (1666-c.1720)

Mary Pix, daughter of a clergyman, married a merchant tailor in 1684. IBRAHIM (1696), her first and best known play, was followed by THE SPANISH WIVES (1696), THE INNOCENT MISTRESS (1697), THE DECEIVER DECEIVED (1697, reissued as THE FRENCH BEAU), QUEEN CATHARINE (1698), THE FALSE FRIEND (1699), THE BEAU DEFEATED (1700), THE DOUBLE DISTRESS and THE CZAR OF MUSCOVY (1701), THE DIFFERENT WIDOWS (1703), THE CONQUEST OF SPAIN (1705), and ADVENTURES IN MADRID (1706). There are no collected or modern editions of Pix's plays nor any adequate account of her life. Fredson T. Bowers has a bibliographical note, "Underprinting in Mary Pix, THE SPANISH WIVES (1696)," LIBRARY, 5th ser. 9 (1954), 248-54. Herbert Carter's "Three Women Dramatists of the Restoration," BJ 13 (1925), 91-97, is a brief general account. James M. Edmunds, "An Example of Early Sentimentalism," MLN 48 (1933), 94-97, concerns one of the plots in THE SPANISH WIVES. George Thorn-Drury's note, "An Unrecorded Play-Title," RES 6 (1930), 316-18, refers to THE FRENCH BEAU.

THOMAS PORTER (1636-80)

Thomas Porter was a son of Endymion Porter, the royalist. He began his career by kidnapping a wife and went on to be involved in two duels fatal to his opponents. It is perhaps not surprising that his first play, THE VILLAIN (1662), was successful. Later plays include A WITTY COMBAT (c.1663), THE CAR-NIVAL (1663/64 season), and THE FRENCH CONJUROR (1667). There are no collected or modern editions of Porter and only minor references in the secondary literature.

GEORGE POWELL (c.1658-1714)

Powell, son of an actor of the same name, is also best known as an actor. Despite his addiction to alcohol, he was long famous in both tragic and comic roles. His plays include THE TREACHEROUS BROTHERS (1689), ALPHONSO, KING OF NAPLES (1690), A VERY GOOD WIFE (1693), BONDUCA (1695, from Beaumont and Fletcher), . . . BRUTUS OF ALBA (1696, an opera written with John Verbruggen), and THE IMPOSTURE DEFEATED (1697). THE COR-NISH COMEDY (1696), published by Powell, is attributed to him by the editors of THE LONDON STAGE; he may well be the author, though he states the play was written by another. There are no collected or modern editions of any of Powell's plays and minimal references in the standard modern histories.

JAMES RALPH (c.1705-62)

Ralph probably was born in Pennsylvania but went to London with his friend
Benjamin Franklin in 1724.   He was primarily a journalist and periodical essayist, but he wrote poems and a well known contemporary history of England
as well as several dramatic pieces.   The latter include THE FASHIONABLE
LADY (1730), a popular burlesque; THE FALL OF THE EARL OF ESSEX (1731),
a tragedy based on Banks's play; THE CORNISH SQUIRE (1731), a fairly successful alteration of an earlier play by Congreve, Vanbrugh, and Walsh; THE
LAWYER'S FEAST (1743), a successful farce; and THE ASTROLOGER (1744),
an unsuccessful farce.   There are no collected or modern editions of Ralph's
plays.   There is a survey of his career in Robert W. Kenny's article, "James
Ralph: An Eighteenth-Century Philadelphian in Grub Street," PM 64 (1940),
218-42.   Dougald MacMillan, in "Some Notes on Eighteenth-Century Essex
Plays," MLN 55 (1940), 176-83, comments on THE FALL OF THE EARL OF
ESSEX; J.M. Bastian, in "James Ralph's Second Adaptation from John Banks,"
HLQ 25 (1962), 181-88, discusses a manuscript adaptation of ANNA BULLEN.
For discussion of THE CORNISH SQUIRE, see under Congreve.

EDWARD RAVENSCROFT (c.1650-c.1700)

Ravenscroft, who left the study of law for that of the stage, wrote a dozen plays produced between 1672 and 1692. Both THE ANATOMIST (1696), a short farce, and THE LONDON CUCKOLDS (1681), a racy and effective comedy, were stock pieces for more than eighty years. Ravenscroft's other plays are THE CITIZEN TURNED GENTLEMAN (1672; as MAMAMOUCHI, 1675), THE CARELESS LOVERS (1673), THE WRANGLING LOVERS (1676), SCARAMOUCH A PHILOSOPHER, HARLEQUIN A SCHOOLBOY . . . and KING EDGAR AND ALFREDA (1677), THE ENGLISH LAWYER (1677, from IGNORAMUS), TITUS ANDRONICUS (c.1678, from Shakespeare), DAME DOBSON (1683), THE CANTERBURY GUESTS (1694), and THE ITALIAN HUS- BAND (1697).

There is no collected edition of Ravenscroft's plays, and the only modern edi- tions are Montague Summers's of THE LONDON CUCKOLDS in his RESTORA- TION COMEDIES (1921), Alexander N. Jeffares's edition of the same play in RESTORATION COMEDY, vol. 2, and a facsimile of TITUS ANDRONICUS (London: Cornmarket Press, 1969). Nor is there a satisfactory biography. Edward T. Norris, in "The Original of Ravenscroft's ANATOMIST . . .," MLN 46 (1931), 522-26, shows that the play derives from Hauteroche's CRIS- PIN MEDECIN; Raymond E. Parshall makes the same point five years later in "The Source of Ravenscroft's THE ANATOMIST," RES 12 (1936), 328-33. James G. McManaway suggests in "The Copy for THE CARELESS LOVERS," MLN 46 (1931), 406-09, that the play was set from a prompt copy. Curt A. Zimansky, in "Edward Ravenscroft's First Play," PQ 28 (1949), 516-17, con- jectures that KING EDGAR AND ALFREDA was completed a decade before 1677 and that Thomas Rymer borrowed from it for his own EDGAR. Nadia Bugnet, in "Edward Ravenscroft: THE CITIZEN TURNED GENTLEMAN (1672)," GEOFFRIN COLLECTION I, 352-61, compares the play with its sources. Edward T. Norris, in "The Italian Source for Ravenscroft's ITALIAN HUSBAND," RES 10 (1934), 202-05, proves that the source was G.A. Cicognini's IL TRADIMENTO PER L'HONORE (1664) and not Thomas Wright. In another ar- ticle, "TITUS ANDRONICUS," TLS, 11 May 1933, p. 331, Norris suggests that this play must have been produced around 1678-79, though it was not printed until 1687. Henry C. Lancaster's "Calderón, Boursault, and Ravens- croft," MLN 51, (1936), 523-28, argues that THE WRANGLING LOVERS is based directly on Boursault's novel, NE PAS CROIRE CE QU'ON VOID, rather than on a translation of the novel. James U. Rundle, in "More about

Calderón, Boursault, and Ravenscroft," MLN 62 (1947), 383-84, attacked this view, suggesting that both Boursault and Ravenscroft used a Spanish novel translated by Boursault. Lancaster responded, "Still More about . . .," pp. 385-89; Rundle answered in "Footnote on . . .," MLN 63 (1948), 217-19.

JOSEPH REED (1723-87)

Reed, a successful ropemaker by profession, was interested enough in the theatre to move his business to London about 1757. His two-act farce, THE REGISTER OFFICE (1761), was popular for twenty years and is included in several contemporary collections. MADRIGAL AND TRULETTA (1758) is a burlesque, TOM JONES (1769) a comic opera, and THE IMPOSTERS (1776, from GIL BLAS) a farce. DIDO (1767), Reed's tragedy, was refused by the managers before finally seeing the stage at a benefit; it then had a successful run. See Paul Sawyer, "Garrick, Joseph Reed, and DIDO," RECTR 6, no. 2 (1967), 44-50, and 7, no. 1 (1968), 17-32. THE SUPERANNUATED GALLANT, a farce, was printed in Newcastle in 1745. There are no collected or modern editions of Reed's plays and little comment on them in the secondary literature.

FREDERICK REYNOLDS (1764-1841)

Reynolds, son of a prominent Whig attorney, was educated at Westminster; he entered the Middle Temple but soon gave up the law for the stage. Reynolds was a prolific dramatist, and many of his productions were hits. His most popular play in the period was THE DRAMATIST (1789, ed. Allardyce Nicoll in The World's Classics volume LESSER ENGLISH COMEDIES OF THE EIGHTEENTH CENTURY, 1931); this and many other pieces were included in contemporary collections, but there are no collected or other modern editions and no adequate biography. THE LIFE AND TIMES OF FREDERICK REYNOLDS, WRITTEN BY HIMSELF, 2 vols. (London: Colburn, 1826*), is the best account.

Plays produced in the period include WERTER (1785), a very successful tragedy, and ELOISA (1786), a less successful one. THE CRUSADE (1790) was a popular melodrama, as was THE MYSTERIES OF THE CASTLE (1795, with Miles Peter Andrews). Subsequent plays were usually five-act comedies: BETTER LATE THAN NEVER (1790, with Andrews), NOTORIETY (1791, partly from Fletcher), HOW TO GROW RICH (1793), THE RAGE (1794), SPECULATION (1795), FORTUNE'S FOOL (1796), THE WILL and CHEAP LIVING (1797), LAUGH WHEN YOU CAN (1798), and MANAGEMENT (1799). All had successful runs.

Among Reynolds's many nineteenth-century productions are LIFE (1800), FOLLY AS IT FLIES (1801), THE CARAVAN (1803), THE BLIND BARGAIN (1804), THE DELINQUENT (1805), THE EXILE (1808), THE VIRGIN OF THE SUN and THE RENEGADE (1812, the latter an adaptation of DON SEBASTIAN), and adaptations of A MIDSUMMER NIGHT'S DREAM and THE COMEDY OF ERRORS (1816 and 1819). These and a dozen other pieces were published, but most of Reynold's plays after 1820 or so have never been printed.

JOHN ROSE (b. 1754?)

John Rose, rector of St. Martin Outwich, London, wrote several afterpieces produced in the period. They include A QUARTER OF AN HOUR BEFORE DINNER (1788) and THE FAMILY COMPACT (1792), both farces; THE FAIRY FESTIVAL (1797), an interlude; and THE PRISONER (1792, from Boutet de Monvel) and CAERNARVON CASTLE (1793), both melodramas with music by Attwood. A QUARTER OF AN HOUR BEFORE DINNER was Rose's most successful play, though THE PRISONER was also popular. There are no collected or modern editions and only infrequent references in modern dramatic histories.

NICHOLAS ROWE (1674-1718)

Rowe, the son of a well-to-do lawyer, was educated at Westminster; he gave up the study of law after the death of his father and the success of his first play. He was undersecretary of state to the Duke of Queensbury, was made poet laureate upon the accession of George I, and was granted valuable preferment which he did not live to enjoy fully. His one comedy, THE BITER (1704) was a failure; THE AMBITIOUS STEPMOTHER (1700), his first tragedy, was followed by TAMERLANE (1701), THE FAIR PENITENT (1703), ULYSSES (1705), THE ROYAL CONVERT (1707, later revived as ETHELINDA), THE TRAGEDY OF JANE SHORE (1714), and THE TRAGEDY OF THE LADY JANE GREY (1715). TAMERLANE, THE FAIR PENITENT, and JANE SHORE were popular stock plays until the end of the century and beyond; THE ROYAL CONVERT and JANE GREY were played into the seventies.

Emmett L. Avery, in the NEW CBEL, lists THE TRAGEDIES OF NICHOLAS ROWE, 2 vols. (1714). I have not seen a copy of this item; it may be a made-up set. THE DRAMATIC WORKS . . ., 2 vols. (1720*), is made-up, as are THE WORKS OF NICHOLAS ROWE . . ., 3 vols. (1728), and the PLAYS . . ., 2 vols. (1736). The WORKS . . ., 2 vols. (1747), ed. Anne Devenish, appears to be a genuine collected edition and includes a biography. THREE PLAYS BY NICHOLAS ROWE, ed. James R. Sutherland (London: Scholartis Press, 1929), includes TAMERLANE, THE FAIR PENITENT, and JANE SHORE; it also contains a good biography and a bibliography of early editions. THE FAIR PENITENT and JANE SHORE were edited together by Sophie C. Hart for the Belles Lettres series (Boston: Heath 1907); these plays are also included in several modern anthologies. THE FAIR PENITENT, ed. Malcolm Goldstein, is included in the Regents Restoration Drama series (Lincoln: Univ. of Nebraska Press, 1969), as is JANE SHORE, ed. Harry W. Pedicord (1974). A facsimile of JANE SHORE is available from Scolar Press (London, 1973); TAMERLANE has been edited by Landon C. Burns, Jr. (London: Oxford Univ. Press, 1966).

The best modern life of Rowe is Sutherland's, noted above. The best early account is James Welwood's, prefaced to Rowe's translation of Lucan's PHARSALIA (1718). See also Howard N. Doughty, Jr., "Nicholas Rowe and the Widow Spann," MLQ 4 (1943), 465-72, which adds new documents. Critical studies begin with A COMPARISON BETWEEN THE TWO STAGES (1702) and Charles

Gildon's A NEW REHEARSAL (1714), both of which attack Rowe's departures from the rules. Samuel Johnson's life focuses on Rowe's plays but is very brief. Bonamy Dobrée gives a survey in RESTORATION TRAGEDY (1929), as does Frederick S. Boas in EIGHTEENTH-CENTURY DRAMA (1953). Alfred E. Jackson, "Rowe's Historical Tragedies," ANGLIA 54 (1930), 307-30, and George W. Whiting, "Rowe's Debt to PARADISE LOST," MP 32 (1935), 271-79, are more specialized articles. Recent discussions include Eugene M. Waith's in IDEAS OF GREATNESS (1971), and Malcolm Goldstein's "Pathos and Personality in the Tragedies of Nicholas Rowe," in ENGLISH WRITERS OF THE EIGHTEENTH CENTURY, ed. John H. Middendorf (New York: Columbia Univ. Press, 1971), pp. 172-85 (rather thin).

Sir Walter Scott's OBSERVER essays (nos. 88-90, 1790), comparing THE FAIR PENITENT with Massinger's FATAL DOWRY, still make interesting reading. See also Donald B. Clark's "An Eighteenth-Century Adaptation of Massinger," MLQ 13 (1942), 239-52. Lindley A. Wyman, in "The Tradition of the Formal Meditation in Rowe's THE FAIR PENITENT," PQ 42 (1963), 412-16, relates the last scene to earlier literature in the tradition, arguing that Calista does in fact repent. Frank J. Kearful's "The Nature of Tragedy in Rowe's THE FAIR PENITENT," PLL 2 (1966), 351-60, presents the play as a conscious attempt to fuse domestic tragedy and sentimental pathos with a didactic theme. John A. Dussinger, in "Richardson and Johnson: Critical Agreement on Rowe's FAIR PENITENT," ES 49 (1968), 45-47, notes that Johnson, in comparing Rowe and Richardson, follows a letter in CLARISSA on the defects of Calista.

Charles Gildon's REMARKS ON . . . 'LADY JANE GREY' . . . (1715) and A REVIEW OF 'THE TRAGEDY OF JANE SHORE' . . . (1714), by an unknown author, are attack and defense respectively of these two plays; the latter responds to Gildon's attack in THE NEW REHEARSAL (1714). See also Alfred Schwarz, "An Example of Eighteenth-Century Pathetic Tragedy: Rowe's JANE SHORE," MLQ 22 (1961), 236-47, and the somewhat tangential "Shore's Wife," SEL 6 (1966), 447-64, a study by Donald F. Rowan of the literary treatment of this theme. The political allegory of TAMERLANE, mentioned in Johnson's life of Rowe, is amplified by Willard Thorp in "A Key to Rowe's TAMERLANE," JEGP 39 (1940), 124-27. Donald B. Clark finds the play's main source in Knolles's GENERAL HISTORY OF THE TURKS; see "The Source and Characterization of Nicholas Rowe's TAMERLANE," MLN 65 (1950), 145-52. CRITICAL REMARKS ON . . . ULYSSES (1706) offers a rare discussion of one of Rowe's lesser known pieces. William H. Ingram's "Theobald, Rowe, Jackson: Whose AJAX?" LC 21 (1965), 91-96, conjectures that the translation of Sophocles's play published by Lintot in 1714 is Rowe's.

SIR CHARLES SEDLEY (1639?-1701)

Sedley is best known as a courtier and minor poet. His plays are THE MUL-BERRY GARDEN (1668), ANTONY AND CLEOPATRA (1677, from Shakespeare), and BELLAMIRA (1687, adapted from William Hemmings's THE FATAL CON-TRACT). Translations of Corneille (POMPEY THE GREAT, with others) and of de Brueys-de Palaprat (THE GRUMBLER, ascribed to Sedley) were not produced during Sedley's lifetime. Sedley's first play is included in Volume 1 of Alex-ander N. Jeffares's RESTORATION COMEDY.

Vivian de Sola Pinto includes an excellent bibliography in his edition of THE POETICAL AND DRAMATIC WORKS OF SIR CHARLES SEDLEY, 2 vols. (Lon-don: Constable, 1928), which is standard. Contemporary editions are THE MISCELLANEOUS WORKS OF . . . SIR CHARLES SEDLEY . . . (1702, in-cluding one play) and THE WORKS OF . . . SIR CHARLES SEDLEY . . ., 2 vols. (1722), neither of which is reliable. The standard biography, also by Pinto, is SIR CHARLES SEDLEY 1639-1701: A STUDY IN THE LIFE AND LIT-ERATURE OF THE RESTORATION (London: Constable, 1927); it includes criti-cism of the plays as well. Pinto provides a briefer biography in RESTORATION CARNIVAL: FIVE COURTIER POETS (London: Folio Society, 1954). Pinto's work surpasses Max Lissner's biography in "Sir Charles Sedleys Leben und Werke," ANGLIA 28 (1905), 145-254. See also Willard Thorpe's note, "Sed-ley and Beau Fielding," N&Q 192 (1947) 251-52, and the response by Pinto, p. 393. There is a good account of Sedley in John H. Wilson's COURT WITS OF THE RESTORATION (Princeton: Princeton Univ. Press, 1948).

ELKANAH SETTLE (1648-1724)

Settle, born in Dunstable, attended Oxford but took no degree. CAMBYSES, KING OF PERSIA, his first play, was a success when produced in 1671; it was followed by THE EMPRESS OF MOROCCO (1673; at court c.1671), LOVE AND REVENGE (1674, from William Hemmings's FATAL CONTRACT), THE CONQUEST OF CHINA BY THE TARTARS (c.1675), IBRAHIM THE ILLUSTRIOUS BASSA and PASTOR FIDO (1676), THE FEMALE PRELATE and FATAL LOVE (1680), and THE HEIR OF MOROCCO (1682). Settle was involved in political as well as literary pamphleteering in the 1670's and 1680's; he was able to change principles with changing regimes and was eventually appointed city poet (1691). He produced an annual pageant, usually titled "The Triumphs of London," for many years before poverty and ridicule drove him to the annual fairs and eventually to the Charterhouse as a poor Brother.

His later plays are DISTRESSED INNOCENCE (1690), THE FAIRY QUEEN (1692, with music by Henry Purcell), THE AMBITIOUS SLAVE (1694), PHILASTER (1695, from Beaumont and Fletcher), THE WORLD IN THE MOON (1697, with music by Daniel Purcell), THE VIRGIN PROPHETESS (1701), and THE CITY RAMBLE (1711). He is usually credited with THE LADY'S TRIUMPH (1718); Lewis Theobald wrote the masque in act 5 of this piece. THE NEW ATHENIAN COMEDY was printed in 1693; no production is known.

There are no collected editions of Settle. THE EMPRESS OF MOROCCO is included in The World's Classics volume FIVE HEROIC PLAYS (1960), ed. Bonamy Dobrée, and also in the Augustan Reprint Society's volume of facsimiles, THE EMPRESS OF MOROCCO AND ITS CRITICS . . . (Los Angeles: W.A. Clark Library, 1968). THE FAIRY QUEEN is also available in facsimile (London: Cornmarket Press, 1969). The standard biography is Frank C. Brown's ELKANAH SETTLE: HIS LIFE AND WORKS (Chicago: Univ. of Chicago Press, 1910), which contains some discussion of each play and a good bibliography. See also Roswell G. Ham, "Dryden Versus Settle," MP 25 (1928), 409-16, and Ham's comments on Settle in OTWAY AND LEE. William J. Lawrence, in "The Plates in Settle's EMPRESS OF MOROCCO," TLS, 11 July 1935, p. 448, suggests that these illustrations are not wholly dependable guides to contemporary practice. Paul S. Dunkin's "Issues of THE FAIRY QUEEN (1692)," LIBRARY, 4th ser. 26 (1946), 297-304, suggests there may have been nine such issues. The best discussion of this play is Robert E. Moore's in HENRY PURCELL

(1961). Thomas P. Haviland, in "Elkanah Settle and the Least Heroic Romance," MLQ 15 (1954), 118-24, considers IBRAHIM and its French source. PASTOR FIDO is discussed briefly in Edward A. Langhans's note, "Three Early Eighteenth-Century Promptbooks," TN 20 (1966), 142-50; its epilogue is printed by Richard Morton in "An Epilogue to PASTOR FIDO," N&Q 201 (1956), 337-38, with comments. For Settle's connection with the "operatic" TEMPEST, see under Shadwell.

CHARLES SHADWELL (d. 1726)

Charles Shadwell, younger son of Thomas Shadwell, served in the army for a time and was a tax supervisor in Kent in the early eighteenth century. Only three of his plays were acted in London: THE FAIR QUAKER OF DEAL (1710), THE HUMOURS OF THE ARMY (1713), and THE MERRY WIVES OF BROAD STREET (1713, an afterpiece not printed). THE FAIR QUAKER OF DEAL was a stock piece for decades and survived until the later 1780's in THE FAIR QUAKER, an adaptation by Edward Thompson. THE HUMOURS OF THE ARMY was also successful and was revived in 1746. Several other plays were produced at the Smock Alley theatre in Dublin; FIVE NEW PLAYS (1720) included THE HASTY WEDDING, THE SHAM PRINCE, ROTHERICK O'CONNOR, THE PLOTTING LOVERS, and IRISH HOSPITALITY. THE WORKS OF CHARLES SHADWELL, 2 vols. (Dublin, 1720) also contains a brief biography. There are no modern editions of Shadwell's plays and infrequent references in standard modern sources.

THOMAS SHADWELL (c.1642-92)

THE WORKS OF THOMAS SHADWELL, ESQ. (1693) is a made-up collection; the first collected edition is THE DRAMATIC WORKS OF THOMAS SHADWELL, ESQ., 4 vols. (1720), which also includes a brief biography. The Mermaid edition volume, THOMAS SHADWELL, ed. George Saintsbury (London: Unwin, 1903), contains only four plays--THE SULLEN LOVERS (1668), A TRUE WIDOW (c.1678), THE SQUIRE OF ALSATIA (1688), and BURY FAIR (1689). THE WORKS OF THOMAS SHADWELL, ed. Montague Summers, 5 vols. (London: Fortune Press, 1927*), is complete but textually unreliable; Summers's extensive (if digressive) notes are more valuable, and his biographical and critical intro- duction runs to more than 230 pages. EPSOM WELLS (1672) and THE VOL- UNTEERS (1692) were edited together by Donald M. Walmsley for the Belles Lettres series (Boston: Heath, 1930); the biographical introduction corrects errors in Summers and Borgman (see below). THE LIBERTINE (1675) is included in THE THEATRE OF DON JUAN . . ., ed. Oscar Mandel (Lincoln: Univ. of Nebraska Press, 1963). THE SQUIRE OF ALSATIA (1688) is included in Volume 3 of Alexander N. Jeffares's RESTORATION COMEDY. THE TEMPEST (1674) is in Christopher Spencer's FIVE RESTORATION ADAPTATIONS OF SHAKESPEARE (1965) and Montague Summers's SHAKESPEARE ADAPTATIONS (1922); it is available in facsimile from London's Cornmarket Press (1969) and is also included in the Augustan Reprint Society series (1969). THE HISTORY OF TIMON OF ATHENS (1678) is also available in facsimile (London: Corn- market Press, 1969); THE VIRTUOSO (1676) is included in the Regents Restora- tion Drama series, ed. Marjorie H. Nicolson and David S. Rodes (Lincoln: Univ. of Nebraska Press, 1966).

Good biographical accounts are included in Albert S. Borgman, THOMAS SHADWELL: HIS LIFE AND COMEDIES (New York: New York Univ. Press, 1928*), in Summers's edition, and in Michael W. Alssid's THOMAS SHADWELL (New York: Twayne, 1967). The basic source of information is the biography prefaced to the 1720 WORKS, with which Shadwell's son was probably involved. Shadwell's relations with the Duke of Newcastle are explored in Henry T.E. Perry's THE FIRST DUCHESS OF NEWCASTLE . . . (Boston: Ginn, 1918). See also William B. Ober, "Thomas Shadwell: His Exitus Revised," AIM 74 (1971), 126-30, which suggests that the dramatist died of a coronary occlusion.

The books of Borgman and Alssid are both primarily critical studies. The latter is especially good on the plays as literature and has judicious notes dealing with earlier criticism. For an early modern appreciation, see William H. Browne, "Thomas Shadwell," SR 21 (1913), 257-76. The relevant sections of Bonamy Dobrée's RESTORATION COMEDY (1924) and Allardyce Nicoll's HISTORY (I, 201-10) give brief overviews of Shadwell's career. Major articles include John H. Smith, "Shadwell, the Ladies, and the Change in Comedy," MP 46 (1948), 22-33, stressing Shadwell's moralizing in plays after A TRUE WIDOW (1678); Don R. Kunz, "Shadwell and His Critics: The Misuse of Dryden's MACFLECKNOE," RECTR 12, no. 1 (1973), 14-27, an excellent discussion of the bias created in later criticism by Dryden's famous poem; Alan H. Fisher, "The Significance of Thomas Shadwell," SP 71 (1974), 225-46, a good general discussion of Shadwell's development as a dramatist; Thomas B. Stroup, "Shadwell's Use of Hobbes," SP 35 (1938), 405-32; and R. Jack Smith, "Shadwell's Impact upon John Dryden," RES 20 (1944), 29-44. Don R. Kunz, THE DRAMA OF THOMAS SHADWELL (Salzburg, Austria: Institut fuer Englische Sprache und Literatur, Univ. Salzburg, 1972), reproduces a critically useful dissertation.

Numerous articles focus on individual plays. Gerald M. Berkowitz, in "A Source for Shadwell's AMOROUS BIGOT," AN&Q 10 (1971), 35-36, suggests that Corneille's LE MENTEUR is the basic source of the play. Antony Coleman, in "Shadwell's 'Country Hero,'" N&Q 216 (1971), 459-60, discusses Hugh Clodpate in EPSOM WELLS. In "Thomas Shadwell and the Lancashire Dialect," in ESSAYS AND STUDIES . . . BY MEMBERS OF THE ENGLISH DEPARTMENT OF THE UNIVERSITY OF MICHIGAN (Ann Arbor: Univ. of Michigan Press, 1933) pp. 261-78, Harold Whitehall argues that Shadwell in THE LANCASHIRE WITCHES (1681) and elsewhere imitated a definite spoken dialect of the time. Michele Audubert's "Thomas Shadwell: THE MISER (1672)," GEOFFRIN COLLECTION, I, 343-52, discusses the play in relation to its sources; Françoise Mathieu-Arth performs a similar task in "La PSYCHE de Thomas Shadwell d'après Molière," I, 373-93. Robert D. Hume compares Shadwell and Terence in "Formal Intention in THE BROTHERS and THE SQUIRE OF ALSATIA," ELN 6 (1969), 176-84; Ronald Berman considers both Terence and Locke in "The Values of Shadwell's SQUIRE OF ALSATIA," ELH 39 (1972), 375-86, a fine discussion of the play. Carl R. Kropf, in "Educational Theory in THE SQUIRE OF ALSATIA," SAB 37, no. 2 (1972), 16-22, concludes that Ned and Tim in the play represent good and bad notions of education. Richard Perkin, "Shadwell's Poet Ninny: Additional Material in a Manuscript of THE SULLEN LOVERS," LIBRARY 27 (1972), 244-51, discusses some unprinted pages of this play which suggest that Ninny was based on Edward Howard.

Several articles, as well as the studies of Shakespeare referred to in Part 1, Section 8.2, concern TIMON. Paul F. Vernon, in "Social Satire in Shadwell's TIMON," SN 35 (1963), 221-26, offers a balanced account of Shadwell's adaptation; Gunnar Sorelius's "Shadwell Deviating into Sense: TIMON OF ATHENS and the Duke of Buckingham," SN 36 (1964), 232-44, shows why Buckingham liked the play and agrees that it is one of the best of the Restoration versions of Shakespeare. John Edmunds, in "Shadwell and the Anonymous TIMON," N&Q 212 (1967), 218-21, argues that this play may have been a source for Shadwell's; in another article, "TIMON OF ATHENS Blended with LE MISANTHROPE: Shadwell's Recipe for Satirical Tragedy," MLR 64 (1969),

Thomas Shadwell

500-507, Edmunds argues that Molière's play influenced TIMON as well as THE SULLEN LOVERS, but his parallels are dubious at times. Don R. Kunz, in "Shadwell's A TRUE WIDOW: 'Promised a Play and Dwindled to a Farce?'" RECTR 10, no. 1 (1971), 43-54, gives a critical analysis of the play.

The treatment of contemporary science in THE VIRTUOSO is the subject of Claude Lloyd's "Shadwell and the Virtuosi, PMLA 44 (1929), 472-94; Everett L. Jones's "Robert Hooke and THE VIRTUOSO," MLN 66 (1951), 180-82 (Hooke took the play as a personal attack on him); and Joseph M. Gilde's "Shadwell and the Royal Society: Satire in THE VIRTUOSO," SEL 10 (1970), 469-90 (a convincing argument that in the play Shadwell attacks false science and Ciceronian style rather than the Royal Society). Two other articles, Gwynne B. Evans's "The Source of Shadwell's Character of Sir Formal Trifle in THE VIRTUOSO," MLR 35 (1940), 211-14, and Florence R. Scott's "NEWS FROM PLYMOUTH and Sir Positive At-All," MLR 39 (1944), 183-85, concern Shadwell's hits at contemporaries. Evans argues that Sir Positive is derived from Sir Solemn Trifle in Davenant's play; Scott, that the character hits at Sir Robert Howard. John H. Smith, in "French Sources for Six English Comedies 1660-1750," JEGP 47 (1948), 390-94, shows the influence of a Montfleury play on Shadwell's THE WOMAN CAPTAIN (1679). Several of Shadwell's plays are indebted to French originals; see the sources cited in Part 1, Section 8.4.

THE TEMPEST has provoked more controversy than any other Shadwell play. The original adaptation by Dryden and William Davenant was produced in 1667 and was quite popular; sixteen performances are recorded prior to April 1674. In that month the play was altered again. It already involved music and dancing, but in the new version it was transformed into a successful dramatic opera by reducing the amount of text and substantially increasing the musical material. The "operatic TEMPEST," as the 1674 version is often styled, remained popular for a century or more. The controversy has been over authorship and began as early as 1904 when William J. Lawrence published his article, "Did Thomas Shadwell Write an Opera on THE TEMPEST?" ANGLIA 27 (1904), 205-17, arguing persuasively that the 1674 version was commissioned of Shadwell by The Duke's Company, which owned the rights to the Dryden-Davenant version. Lawrence continued his argument in "Shadwell's Opera of THE TEMPEST" later in the same volume (pp. 539-41) and revised it for inclusion in LAWRENCE COLLECTION 1, pp. 193-206. In "Purcell's Music for THE TEMPEST," N&Q 110 (1904), 164-65, Lawrence argues that Purcell's music for the play was written for the 1674 production, though the composer was barely sixteen years old. William H. Cummings, whose book on Purcell set a date about 1690 for the music, responded (pp. 270-71), and Lawrence in turn argued that the 1674 TEMPEST published by Herringman was the book of Shadwell's opera (pp. 329-30). William B. Squire discussed the matter in "Purcell's Dramatic Music," SIMG 5 (1904), 489-564, and again in "The Music of Shadwell's TEMPEST," MQ 7 (1921), 565-78. Squire, agreeing with Lawrence, refers to M.L. Pereyra, "La musique écrite sur la TEMPETE d'après Shakespeare par Pelham Humfrey," BSFM 2 (1920), 75-85.

By this time Shadwell's name was firmly associated with the 1674 play, and it

286

was clear that the 1674 and 1690 quartos did not represent the Dryden-Davenant version of the play, as Scott had thought. George Thorn-Drury, "Dryden and the Opera on THE TEMPEST," RES 1 (1925), 327-30, suggested that Shadwell may indeed have had a hand in the piece but argued that the total lack of contemporary reference to him in connection with it suggested it was not his alone. Thorn-Drury believed Dryden must have been involved. Donald M. Walmsley argued against such involvement in "Shadwell and the Operatic TEMPEST," RES 2 (1926), 463-66; Thorn-Drury responded (RES 3 [1927], 204-08), but Walmsley had the better of the resulting exchange (pp. 451-53). Montague Summers accepted Lawrence's position in his edition.

So the matter rested until 1946. In that year, Charles E. Ward published "THE TEMPEST: A Restoration Opera Problem," ELH 13 (1946), 119-30, suggesting that Betterton was involved and raising the issue once again. William M. Milton responded with "TEMPEST in a Teapot," ELH 14 (1947), 207-18, summarizing the history of the argument and concluding (sensibly) that several hands were involved, Shadwell's being the most prominent. James G. McManaway, in the introduction to his edition of "Songs and Masques in THE TEMPEST [c.1674]," THEATRE MISCELLANY . . ., Luttrell Society Reprints, no. 14 (Oxford: Blackwell, 1953), pp. 69-96, agrees with Milton's conclusion. Charles Haywood, in "THE SONGS AND MASQUE IN THE NEW TEMPEST: An Incident in the Battle of the Two Theatres 1674," HLQ 19 (1955), 39-56, presents this piece as an attack on Shadwell's SONGS AND MASQUE, effectively undercutting the argument for Dryden's participation in the 1674 version. Robert E. Moore, in HENRY PURCELL AND THE RESTORATION THEATRE (1961), also accepts the Lawrence-Walmsley-Milton argument, which is further supported by Aline M. Taylor, "Dryden's 'Enchanted Isle' and Shadwell's 'Dominion,'" in ESSAYS . . . PRESENTED TO DOUGALD MACMILLAN, ed. D. W. Patterson and Albrecht B. Strauss (SP, Extra Series 4 [1967], pp. 39-53), and by Maximillian E. Novak, "Elkanah Settle's Attacks on Thomas Shadwell and the Authorship of the 'Operatic TEMPEST,'" N&Q 213 (1968), 263-65. The last word has been that of the California edition of the Dryden-Davenant play, which accepts the multiple-author view of Milton and McManaway but denies to Shadwell and his companions any significant alteration of the Dryden-Davenant text. The controversy, taken as a whole, is redundant but illuminating; its successive stages illustrate not only the gradual unfolding of the evidence but the way in which the interpretation of that evidence has changed with our increasing knowledge of the day-to-day workings of the contemporary stage.

RICHARD BRINSLEY SHERIDAN (1751-1816)

Bibliographies of Sheridan include John P. Anderson's catalog in Lloyd Sanders's biography (see below), upon which that in Walter Sichel's SHERIDAN: FROM NEW AND ORIGINAL MATERIAL, 2 vols. (London: Constable, 1909), is based; George H. Nettleton's in THE MAJOR DRAMAS OF RICHARD BRINSLEY SHERIDAN (Boston: Ginn, 1906); Iolo A. Williams's in SEVEN EIGHTEENTH-CENTURY BIBLIOGRAPHIES (London: Dulau, 1924; first editions only); Raymond C. Rhodes's in THE PLAYS AND POEMS . . ., 3 vols. (Oxford: Blackwell, 1928*). Other valuable bibliographical information is in Cecil Price's THE DRAMATIC WORKS OF RICHARD BRINSLEY SHERIDAN, 2 vols. (Oxford: Clarendon Press, 1974). See also Rhodes's "Sheridan: A Study in Theatrical Bibliography," LM 15 (1927), 381-90, and his "Some Aspects of Sheridan Bibliography," LIBRARY, 3rd ser. 9 (1928), 233-61.

Sheridan's texts present a considerable number of problems, and there have been numerous studies. Frederick W. Bateson's "Notes on the Text of Two Sheridan Plays," RES 16 (1940), 312-17, discusses the texts of THE CAMP (1778) and THE CRITIC (1779); Bateson suggests that Thomas Hull wrote the words to the songs in the former work. Rhodes's "The Early Editions of Sheridan," TLS, 17 and 24 Sept. 1925, pp. 599 and 617, concerns THE DUENNA and THE SCHOOL FOR SCANDAL; Rhodes takes Oxberry's 1820 text as the first authentic edition of the former and (incorrectly) the 1799 Dublin edition as the editio princeps of the latter; see also Cecil Price, "The Text of the First Performance of THE DUENNA," PBSA 53 (1959), 268-70. On THE RIVALS, see (in addition to the comments in the editions of Rhodes and Price) the controversy between Frederick W. Bateson and Rhodes in TLS for 1929 ("The Text of Sheridan," pp. 998 and 1081-82). On the text of THE SCHOOL FOR SCANDAL, see the controversy between M.J. Ryan, Rhodes, and others in TLS (1928, pp. 212, 257, 290, 313-14, 358, 396, 430; 1929, pp. 1029, 1097)--an argument which Rhodes loses to Ryan. See also the following later notes: Bertram Shuttleworth, "Early Editions of THE SCHOOL FOR SCANDAL," TN 6 (1951), 4-7, and 8 (1953), 23; William Van Lennep, "The Chetwynd Manuscript of THE SCHOOL FOR SCANDAL," TN 6 (1951), 10-12; and three articles by Cecil Price, "The Columbia Manuscript of THE SCHOOL FOR SCANDAL," CLC 11 (1961), 25-29; "Another Crewe MS of THE SCHOOL FOR SCANDAL?" PBSA 57 (1963), 79-81; and "The Second Crewe MS of THE SCHOOL FOR SCANDAL," PBSA 61 (1967), 351-56.

Sheridan's plays appeared in many contemporary collections; THE CRITIC (1779), THE RIVALS (1775), and THE SCHOOL FOR SCANDAL (1777) are also frequently included in modern anthologies. The earliest collected edition is THE DRAMATIC WORKS . . . (1797, reissued with a brief biography in 1798). The first authorized edition, with preface by Thomas Moore, was THE WORKS OF THE LATE RIGHT HONORABLE RICHARD BRINSLEY SHERIDAN, 2 vols. (London: Murray, 1821). More than a dozen editions appeared during the next century, including Leigh Hunt's (London: Moxon, 1840), G.G. Sigmond's for Bohn's English Library (London: Bohn, 1848), and especially W. Fraser Rae's SHERIDAN'S PLAYS, NOW PRINTED AS HE WROTE THEM (London: D. Nutt, 1902). Iolo A. Williams's THE PLAYS . . . (London: Jenkins, 1926) was followed immediately by Rhodes's edition (see above). These remained the standard editions until Price's, which is definitive.

Editions of the major comedies are too numerous to list here in full. An excellent text of THE CRITIC is included in the Nettleton, Case and Stone anthology. THE RIVALS has been edited from the Larpent manuscript by Richard L. Purdy (Oxford: Clarendon Press, 1935) and from the 1775 revision by Alan S. Downer (New York: Appleton-Century-Crofts, 1953), Alexander N. Jeffares (London: Macmillan, 1967), and Cecil Price (London: Oxford Univ. Press, 1968); it is available in facsimile from Scolar Press (London, 1973). THE SCHOOL FOR SCANDAL has been edited by Englantyne M. Jebb (Oxford: Clarendon Press, 1928), by R.C. Rhodes (Oxford: Blackwell, 1930), by John C. Loftis (New York: Appleton-Century-Crofts, 1966), by Alexander N. Jeffares (London: Macmillan, 1967), and by Cecil Price (London: Oxford Univ. Press, 1971). It is also available in facsimile from Scolar Press.

THE LETTERS OF RICHARD BRINSLEY SHERIDAN, ed. Cecil Price, 3 vols. (Oxford: Clarendon Press, 1966), is standard. See also R.F., "The Sheridan Papers," BMQ 7 (1932), 38-39; Richard L. Purdy, "A Gift of Sheridan Manuscripts . . .," YLG 22 (1947), 42-43; Ian Donaldson, "New Papers of Henry Holland and R.B. Sheridan," TN 16 (1962), 90-96 and 117-25; and two notes by Price, "Noverre and Sheridan, 1776," TR 7 (1965), 45-46, and "Sheridan-Linley Documents," TN 21 (1967), 165-67.

Early biographies of Sheridan are not particularly trustworthy; the AUTHENTIC MEMOIRS . . . (London: Hone, 1816) falls into this class, as does the unsympathetic MEMOIRS OF THE PUBLIC AND PRIVATE LIFE . . ., 2 parts (London: Colburn, 1817). the MEMOIRS . . . edited by Thomas Moore (London: Longman et al., 1825*), is of first importance, though Moore's account of Sheridan's political career is prejudiced. SHERIDIANA . . . (London: Colburn, 1826) is of little value, but the MEMOIR OF MR. SHERIDAN by William Smyth (Leeds, England: J. Cross, 1840), though quite brief, is unusually good. William Earle's SHERIDAN AND HIS TIMES . . ., 2 vols. (London: J.F. Hope, 1859), is untrustworthy. Margaret Oliphant's SHERIDAN for the English Men of Letters series (London: Macmillan, 1883) is unremarkable, much inferior to Lloyd C. Sanders's LIFE . . . for the Great Writers series (London: W. Scott, 1890). Percy M. Fitzgerald's THE SHERIDANS, 2 vols. (London: Bentley, 1886*), covers a great deal of ground and adds new material but is also biased. W. Fraser Rae's SHERIDAN: A BIOGRAPHY, 2 vols. (London:

Bentley, 1896), was authorized by Sheridan's great-grandson; Rae consequently had access to much new material but was obliged to overlook some of Sheridan's weaknesses. The best of all the early modern lives is Walter Sichel's SHERIDAN: FROM NEW AND ORIGINAL MATERIAL . . ., 2 vols. (London: Constable, 1909), a fully documented, reliable, and objective biography which is unfortunately badly organized and consequently difficult to read.

Recent biographers, with one exception, have added little to their predecessors. Elsie Butler's SHERIDAN: A GHOST STORY (London: Constable, 1931) cannot be recommended. Nor can Kenelm Foss's HERE LIES RICHARD BRINSLEY SHERIDAN (London: M. Secker, 1939), Alice Glasgow's SHERIDAN OF DRURY LANE: A BIOGRAPHY (New York: F.A. Stokes, 1940), or Madeleine Bingham's SHERIDAN: THE TRACK OF A COMET (London: Allen & Unwin, 1972). William A. Darlington's SHERIDAN (New York: Macmillan, 1933) is not much better. Joseph W. Cave [Lewis Gibbs]'s SHERIDAN (London: Dent, 1947*) is undocumented but well organized and capably written. Oscar Sherwin's UNCORKING OLD SHERRY . . . (New York: Twayne, 1960) is popular and overwritten. The best life to date is probably Rhodes's HARLEQUIN SHERIDAN: THE MAN AND THE LEGENDS (Oxford: Blackwell, 1933*), which adds some new material and thoroughly sifts the old.

Most editors and biographers discuss Sheridan's dramatic work as well as his theatrical career. General accounts also include Nettleton's in ENGLISH DRAMA . . . 1642-1800 (1914), Rose Snider's in SATIRE IN THE COMEDIES OF CONGREVE, SHERIDAN, WILDE, AND COWARD (Orono: Univ. of Maine Studies, 1937), Frederick S. Boas's in EIGHTEENTH-CENTURY DRAMA (1953), Arthur Sherbo's in ENGLISH SENTIMENTAL DRAMA (1957), and Arnold N. Kaul's in THE ACTION OF ENGLISH COMEDY (1970). Jean Dulck's LES COMEDIES DE RICHARD BRINSLEY SHERIDAN: ETUDE LITTERAIRE . . . (Paris: Didier, 1962) is a massive study of Sheridan's comedy. Two recent studies are Samuel L. Macey, "Sheridan: The Last of the Great Theatrical Satirists," RECTR 9, no. 2 (1970), 35-45, and Leonard J. Leff, "Sheridan and Sentimentalism," RECTR 12, no. 1 (1973), 36-48. Leff argues persuasively that Faulkland and Julia (THE RIVALS), for example, are seriously rather than satirically conceived and that Sheridan included sentiment in his plays to insure their success.

There are numerous studies of specific plays. Esther K. Sheldon, in "Sheridan's CORIOLANUS: An Eighteenth-Century Compromise," ShQ 14 (1963), 153-61, shows that acts 1 and 2 of Sheridan's production are based on Shakespeare but acts 3 to 5 on Thomson's version. George W. Williams's "A New Source of Evidence for Sheridan's Authorship of THE CAMP and THE WONDERS OF DERBYSHIRE," SP 47 (1950), 619-28, constructs its case on the Drury Lane account books now in the Folger Library, which show surreptitious payments to Sheridan but none to Tickell or Burgoyne (the previously suggested authors or collaborators). Alfred Loewenberg's "The Songs in THE CRITIC," TLS, 28 March 1942, p. 168, concerns the words of the "trios" mentioned in II.ii of the play. Roger Fiske describes his efforts to reconstruct a score for this play in "A Score for THE DUENNA," ML 42 (1961), 132-41.

Arnott and Robinson's ENGLISH THEATRICAL LITERATURE lists a number of
contemporary discussions of PIZARRO; the best modern one is Joseph W. Donohue, Jr.'s in DRAMATIC CHARACTER IN THE ENGLISH ROMANTIC AGE
(1970), pp. 125-56. See also Myron Matlaw, "'This is Tragedy!': The History of PIZARRO," QJS 43 (1957), 288-94 (on the popularity of the play),
and Anthony Oliver and John Saunders, "De Loutherbourg and PIZARRO
(1799)," TN 20 (1965), 30-32. Most of the independent articles on THE RI-
VALS deal with sources or minor matters. Miriam Gabriel and Paul Mueschke,
in "Two Contemporary Sources of Sheridan's THE RIVALS," PMLA 43 (1928),
237-50, suggest that the outline of the main plot comes from Garrick's MISS
IN HER TEENS and the motive of the subplot from Colman's THE DEUCE IS
IN HIM. The latter point is disputed by Tuvia Block in "The Antecedents of
Sheridan's Faulkland," PQ 49 (1970), 266-68; she argues for Beverley in
Murphy's ALL IN THE WRONG. P. Fijn van Draat's "Sheridan's RIVALS and
Ben Jonson's EVERY MAN IN HIS HUMOUR," Np 18 (1933), 44-50, confuses
sources and analogs. Coleman O. Parsons, in "Smollett's Influence on Sheri-
dan's THE RIVALS," N&Q 164 (1933), 39-41, notes a debt to FERDINAND
COUNT FATHOM and a parallel with HUMPHRY CLINKER; see also Sailendra
K. Sen, "Sheridan's Literary Debt: THE RIVALS and HUMPHRY CLINKER,"
MLQ 21 (1960), 291-300. John R. Moore's "Lydia Languish's Library," N&Q
202 (1957), 76, and Elsie E. Phare's "Lydia Languish, Lydia Bennet, and Dr.
Fordyce's Sermons," N&Q 209 (1964), 182-83 (response by Frank W. Brad-
brook, pp. 421-23), concern the catalog in I.ii of the play. Cecil Price, in
"The First Prologue to THE RIVALS," RES 20 (1969), 192-95, notes the dis-
covery of the holograph at Somerville College, Oxford. See also Philip B.
Daghlian, "Sheridan's Minority Waiters," MLQ 6 (1945), 421-22 (a phrase in
II.i), and Jack D. Durant, "Sheridan's 'Royal Sanctuary': A Key to THE
RIVALS," BSF 14 (1973), 23-30.

ROBINSON CRUSOE, a two-act pantomime produced in 1781, is the subject
of an exchange between George H. Nettleton, Frederick S. Boas, and Sybil
M. Rosenfeld in TLS (25 Dec. 1943, p. 624; 1 Jan. 1944, p. 12; 29 Jan.
1944, p. 60; 4 March 1944, p. 120; 15 April 1944, p. 192; 23 and 30 June
1945, pp. 300 and 312). Cecil Price's "The Larpent Manuscript of ST. PAT-
RICK'S DAY," HLQ 29 (1966), 183-89, analyzes this text, comparing it with
the texts of Rae and Rhodes. Price's "The Completion of THE SCHOOL FOR
SCANDAL," TLS, 28 Dec. 1967, p. 1265, dates this in the spring of 1777
and discusses the Moses-Benjamin Hopkins connection. Critical studies of Sheridan's masterpiece include Andrew Schiller, "THE SCHOOL FOR SCANDAL:
The Restoration Unrestored," PMLA 62 (1956), 694-704; J.R. Jackson, "The
Importance of Witty Dialogue in THE SCHOOL FOR SCANDAL," MLN 76
(1961), 601-07; Louis Kronenberger, "THE SCHOOL FOR SCANDAL," in THE
POLISHED SURFACE . . . (New York: Knopf, 1969), pp. 73-84 ("hard candy
with a gooey center"); Christian Deelman, "The Original Cast of THE SCHOOL
FOR SCANDAL," RES 13 (1962), 257-66 (a fine article on the relation between
the text of the play and the actors who created the roles); Arthur C. Sprague,
"In Defense of a Masterpiece: THE SCHOOL FOR SCANDAL Re-examined,"
in ENGLISH STUDIES TODAY, ed. George I. Duthie (Edinburgh: Edinburgh
Univ. Press, 1964), pp. 125-35; Kenneth S. Rothwell, "THE SCHOOL FOR
SCANDAL: The Comic Spirit in Sheridan and Rowlandson," THE SCHOOL FOR
SCANDAL; THOMAS ROWLANDSON'S LONDON (Lawrence: Kansas University

Museum of Art, 1967), pp. 23-45; Leonard J. Leff, "The Disguise Motif in Sheridan's THE SCHOOL FOR SCANDAL," ETJ 22 (1970), 350-60 (this theme and its imagery unifies the two plots); and Jack D. Durant, "The Moral Focus of THE SCHOOL FOR SCANDAL," SAB 37, no. 4 (1972), 44-53, and "Prudence, Providence, and the Direct Road of Wrong: THE SCHOOL FOR SCANDAL and Sheridan's Westminster Hall Speech," SBT 15 (1974), 241-51 (parallels between Joseph Surface and Sheridan's picture of Warren Hastings).

Sheridan's hand in Benjamin Thompson's translation of Kotzebue's THE STRANGER is discussed by Dougald MacMillan in "Sheridan's Share in THE STRANGER," MLN 45 (1930), 85-86; Sheridan made name changes, added two vaudeville scenes, and made numerous cuts. Cecil Price, "Sheridan at Work on THE STRANGER," NM 73 (1972), 315-25, argues that Sheridan also made extensive revisions of phrasing. Myron Matlaw's "Adultery Analyzed: The History of THE STRANGER," QJS 43 (1957), 22-28, discusses the stage history and contemporary reception of the play.

WILLIAM SHIRLEY (fl. 1739-80)

Shirley was originally a merchant in the Portuguese trade. Forced to leave
Portugal in the 1750's, he resided thereafter mostly in London, serving as an
authority on international trade. His first play, THE PARRICIDE (1739), was
not successful; the burlesque KING PEPIN'S CAMPAIGN (1745) did little
better. EDWARD THE BLACK PRINCE (1750), however, was a success; it was
revived during the 1777-78 season and at least twice thereafter. THE ROMAN
SACRIFICE (1777) was again unsuccessful. ELECTRA was prohibited by the
Lord Chamberlain; THE BIRTH OF HERCULES, a masque in rehearsal in 1763,
was put off by the half-price riots and never rescheduled. The two pieces
were published together in 1765. Shirley also left a number of unacted plays
in manuscript. There are no collected or modern editions and only scattered
references (usually to EDWARD as an imitation of Shakespeare's style) in the
secondary literature.

THOMAS SOUTHERNE (1659-1746)

Southerne was born near Dublin, educated at Trinity College, and entered the Middle Temple about 1680. An army career was cut short by the events of 1688; Southerne then turned to the stage on a more-or-less full-time basis. His first plays--THE LOYAL BROTHER (1682) and THE DISAPPOINTMENT (1634)--were not very successful. SIR ANTHONY LOVE (1690) did better, but THE WIVES' EXCUSE (1691) and THE MAID'S LAST PRAYER (1693) were again unsuccessful. In THE FATAL MARRIAGE (1694, from an Aphra Behn story), however, Southerne finally produced a hit; the play remained in the repertory until midcentury, and in David Garrick's adaptation (ISABELLA, 1778) lasted into the next century. OROONOKO (1695, from Aphra Behn's novel) was even more popular, and lasted without significant alteration into the second quarter of the nineteenth century. THE FATE OF CAPUA (1700), THE SPARTAN DAME (1719), and MONEY THE MISTRESS (1726) did not reach this height, and the last, in fact, was a complete failure.

THE WORKS OF MR. THOMAS SOUTHERNE, 2 vols. (1713 and 1721), appears to be made-up; the first collected edition is PLAYS WRITTEN BY THOMAS SOUTHERNE, ESQ. . . ., 3 vols. (1774), which includes all ten plays. THE LOYAL BROTHER was edited by Paul Hamelius (Liège, Belgium: H. Vaillant-Carmanne, 1911). OROONOKO is available from Mnemosyne Publishing Company (Miami 1969, from the 1739 ed.). THE WIVES' EXCUSE, ed. Ralph R. Thornton from the quarto of 1692, is also available (Wynnewood, Pa.: Livingston Publishing Co., 1973).

The standard biography of Southerne is John W. Dodds, THOMAS SOUTHERNE, DRAMATIST (New Haven: Yale Univ. Press, 1933*). The biographical chapter may be supplemented by R.D. Mallery, "Thomas Southerne," TLS, 1 Dec. 1932, p. 923, and Clifford Leech's response, p. 943; see also Leech's "The Political 'Disloyalty' of Thomas Southerne," MLR 28 (1933), 421-30. Dodds devotes a chapter to each of the plays, but his criticism is moralistic, particularly where the comedies are concerned. A better assessment is Kenneth Muir's in THE COMEDY OF MANNERS (1970). Few articles survey Southerne's career; most concern individual plays. A discussion initiated by Clifford Leech's "A Cancel in Southerne's THE DISAPPOINTMENT (1684)," LIBRARY 4th ser. 13 (1933), 395-98, was continued by Ray O. Hummel, Jr.'s "A Further Note on Southerne's THE DISAPPOINTMENT," 5th ser. 1 (1946), 67-69, and Leech's response, "Southerne's THE DISAPPOINTMENT," 5th ser. 2 (1947), 64, and settled by Fredson T. Bowers's "The Supposed Cancel in Southerne's THE DIS-APPOINTMENT Reconsidered," 5th ser. 5 (1950), 140-49. Paul Hamelius, in "The Source of Southerne's FATAL MARRIAGE," MLR 11 4 (1909), 352-56, argued for a Spanish source (Montalvan) for this play. Montague Summers set this account straight in MLR 11 (1916), 149-55*; the correct source is Aphra Behn's story, THE HISTORY OF THE NUN (1689), not her THE NUN; OR, THE PER-JURED BEAUTY (c.1698). There is a good if brief account of this tragedy in John H. Wilson's PREFACE TO RESTORATION DRAMA (1965).

Edward A. Langhans discusses MONEY THE MISTRESS in "Three Early Eighteenth-Century Manuscript Promptbooks," MP 65 (1967), 114-29; Daniel W. Alkofer adds a note on certain symbols in this manuscript in "A Note on the Staging of MONEY THE MISTRESS in 1726," RECTR 11, no. 1 (1972), 31-32. Michael M. Cohen, in "'Mirth and Grief Together': Plot Unity in Southerne's OROONOKO," XUS 11 (Winter 1972), 13-17, argues that the protagonist's stature is emphasized by the play's comic characters. Robert Jordan, "Mrs. Behn and SIR ANTHONY LOVE," RECTR 12, no. 1 (1973), 58-59, argues convincingly that the comedy owes something to Behn's THE LUCKY MISTAKE (1689). Harold Love, in "The Printing of THE WIVES' EXCUSE (1692)," LI-BRARY, 25 (1970), 344-49, responds to John R. Sweney, "The Dedication of Thomas Southerne's THE WIVES' EXCUSE (1692), pp. 154-55; both authors agree that copies of this quarto with Dryden's dedication do in fact exist. A good critical article on this play is Anthony Kaufman's "'This Hard Condition of a Woman's Fate': Southerne's THE WIVES' EXCUSE," MLQ 34 (1973), 36-47, which focuses on Southerne's presentation of the lot of many contemporary wives. Love also notes that an edition of Southerne's plays, edited by himself and R.J. Jordan, is forthcoming from Oxford's Clarendon Press.

SIR RICHARD STEELE (1672-1729)

Bibliographies of Steele's writings were included in George A. Aitken's THE LIFE OF RICHARD STEELE, 2 vols. (London: W. Isbister, 1889*), II, 387-428, and in SELECTIONS FROM THE WORKS OF SIR RICHARD STEELE, ed. George R. Carpenter (Boston: Ginn, 1897); see also Donald F. Bond's listing in the NEW CBEL. The DRAMATIC WORKS . . . (1723) includes THE LYING LOVER (1703) and THE TENDER HUSBAND (1705); THE DRAMATIC WORKS . . . of 1732, a made-up set, also includes THE CONSCIOUS LOVERS (1722). The first modern edition was George A. Aitken's Mermaid edition (London: Unwin, 1894*). The standard edition is THE PLAYS OF RICHARD STEELE, ed. Shirley S. Kenny (Oxford: Clarendon Press, 1971). THE CONSCIOUS LOVERS, ed. Kenny, and THE TENDER HUSBAND, ed. Calhoun Winton, are available in the Regents Restoration Drama series (Lincoln: Univ. of Nebraska Press, 1968 and 1967). THE LETTERS OF RICHARD STEELE . . ., ed. Reginald B. Johnson (London: Lane, 1927), has been superseded by Rae Blanchard's THE CORRESPONDENCE OF RICHARD STEELE (London: Oxford Univ. Press, 1941); see also Pat Rogers, "A New Letter by Steele . . .," ELN 7 (1969), 105-07. THE THEATRE (1720) has been edited by John Loftis (Oxford: Clarendon Press, 1962).

Early biographical accounts like MEMOIRS OF THE LIFE AND WRITINGS . . . (1731) are insubstantial. Macaulay's essay praising Addison at Steele's expense was rebutted by John Forster's review, QR 96 (1855), 509-68, which includes a survey of Steele's life. H.R. Montgomery's MEMOIRS . . ., 2 vols. (Edinburgh: Nimmo, 1865*), is poor; Austin Dobson's RICHARD STEELE (London: Longmans, Green, 1886*) is superior and readable. George A. Aitken's LIFE (noted above) is a first-rate biography and also has excellent materials on each of the plays. See also the supplementary articles by Aitken in the ATHENAEUM (27 Dec. 1890, 6 June and 5 Dec. 1891, and 19 Nov. 1892). After Aitken's work, Willard Connely's SIR RICHARD STEELE (New York: Scribner's, 1934*) seems sketchy, but it is popular and readable. The only biography to compare with Aitken's is Calhoun Winton's CAPTAIN STEELE: THE EARLY CAREER OF RICHARD STEELE and SIR RICHARD STEELE, M.P.: THE LATER CAREER, 2 vols. (Baltimore: Johns Hopkins Univ. Press, 1964 and 1970). Winton's volumes add new material; they stress Steele's social and political environment, especially in Volume 1, and his personal life, especially in Volume 2. Aitken is perhaps fuller on the plays, but Winton is thorough and even more heavily documented from primary materials.

Discussion of Steele's plays begins as early as A COMPARISON BETWEEN THE TWO STAGES (1702). Hazlitt considers them in his LECTURES (1819); Thackeray, in ENGLISH HUMORISTS (1853). Maurice E. Hare, "Steele and the Sentimental Comedy," EIGHTEENTH-CENTURY LITERATURE: AN OXFORD MISCELLANY (Oxford: Clarendon Press, 1909), pp. 5-41, discusses a topic raised by every subsequent historian of sentiment. There are surveys of Steele's plays in Frederick W. Bateson's ENGLISH COMIC DRAMA (1929, laudatory), Frederick S. Boas's EIGHTEENTH-CENTURY DRAMA (1953), and in John C. Loftis's COMEDY AND SOCIETY (1959). Loftis's STEELE AT DRURY LANE (Berkeley and Los Angeles: Univ. of California Press, 1952) studies Steele's theatrical career in its historical, social, and dramatic contexts; it includes the substance of several earlier articles. Articles on more specialized topics include Rae Blanchard's "Steele and the Status of Women," SP 26 (1929), 325-55, and "The Songs in Steele's Plays," in POPE AND HIS CONTEMPORARIES . . ., ed. James L. Clifford and Louis A. Landa (Oxford: Clarendon Press, 1948), pp. 185-200; Elvena M. Green's "Three Aspects of Richard Steele's Theory of Comedy," ETJ 20 (1968), 141-46 (unremarkable); Malcolm M. Kelsall's stimulating discussion "Terence and Steele," RICHARDS COLLECTION, pp. 11-27; and Shirley S. Kenny's "Richard Steele and the 'Pattern of Genteel Comedy,'" MP 70 (1972) 22-37. Kenny offers a good survey of modern scholarship in "Recent Scholarship on Richard Steele," BSM 4, no. 1 (1973), 12-24.

THE CONSCIOUS LOVERS has provoked more discussion than all Steele's other plays together; it is the work usually treated in dramatic histories and surveys. Bibliographical notes on the play include Rodney M. Baine, "The Publication of Steele's CONSCIOUS LOVERS," SB 2 (1950), 169-73, and Shirley S. Kenny, "Eighteenth-Century Editions of Steele's CONSCIOUS LOVERS," SB 21 (1968), 253-61. Attack and defense began early; see A DEFENSE OF SIR FOPLING FLUTTER . . . (1722), an attack attributed to Dennis; Benjamin Victor, AN EPISTLE TO SIR RICHARD STEELE . . . (1722), attacking Dennis; Dennis's REMARKS ON . . . 'THE CONSCIOUS LOVERS' (1723); and a final defense, STEELE AND 'THE CONSCIOUS LOVERS' VINDICATED (1723). John C. Loftis's "The Genesis of Steele's THE CONSCIOUS LOVERS," in ESSAYS CRITICAL AND HISTORICAL DEDICATED TO LILY B. CAMPBELL (Berkeley and Los Angeles: Univ. of California, 1950*), pp. 171-82, is fundamental to any study of the play. Paul E. Parnell, in "A Source for the Duel Scene in THE CONSCIOUS LOVERS," N&Q 207 (1962), 13-15, argues unconvincingly for a debt to Cibber's WOMAN'S WIT. Walt Fisher's "Steele's Great Indian Merchant," LHR no. 6 (1964), pp. 30-35, is a derivative account of Mr. Sealand; David J. Burt's "Rakes, Rogues, and Steele's Servants," BSF 11 (1970), 72-73, a note conjecturing that Tom and Phyllis satirize the love encounter of Restoration comedy. Michael M. Cohen's "Reclamation, Revulsion, and Steele's THE CONSCIOUS LOVERS," RECTR 14, no. 1 (1975), 23-30, argues that Steele fails in the duel scene to support the principle of reclamation through example which is basic to his theme.

The social background of THE FUNERAL is discussed in an excellent article by Robert A. Aubin, "Behind Steele's Satire on Undertakers," PMLA 64 (1949), 1008-26. David F. Foxon, "A Piracy of Steele's THE LYING LOVER," LIBRARY 5th ser. 10 (1955), 127-29, discusses a spurious 1733 edition; Susan

Sir Richard Steele

Staves, "Liars and Lying in Alarcón, Corneille, and Steele," RLC 46 (1972),
514-27, compares the significance of the liar and lying in the three plays
(1621, 1643, 1703).   John H. Smith discusses THE TENDER HUSBAND in
"Tony Lumpkin and the Country Booby Type in Antecedent English Comedy,"
PMLA 58 (1943), 1038-49; he shows that Robert S. Forsythe, in "Shadwell's
Contribution to SHE STOOPS TO CONQUER and to THE TENDER HUSBAND,"
JEGP 11 (1912), 104-11, was wrong in deriving the type directly from Shad-
well.   Paul E. Parnell, in "A New Molière Source for Steele's THE TENDER
HUSBAND," N&Q 204 (1959), 218, makes a good case for a debt to L'AVARE
in V.ii.   Shirley S. Kenny, in "Two Scenes by Addison in Steele's TENDER
HUSBAND," SB 19 (1966), 217-26, attributes parts of III.i and V.i to Addi-
son on both internal and some external evidence; her case has merit.

GEORGE ALEXANDER STEVENS (1710-84)

Stevens, son of a London tradesman, became a strolling actor and later a performer at Covent Garden. He is most famous as an originator of the dramatic
monologue; his "Lecture on Heads" was popular for many years. His dramatic
pieces are mostly farces and entertainments. They include THE FRENCH
FLOGGED (1760, altered as THE TRUE-BORN IRISHMAN, 1777), THE COURT
OF ALEXANDER (1770), THE TRIP TO PORTSMOUTH (1773), and THE CABI-
NET OF FANCY (1780). Avery (NEW CBEL) attributes THE FAIR ORPHAN
(1771) to Stevens; THE LONDON STAGE lists it as anonymous. A novel,
THE HISTORY OF TOM FOOL, 2 vols. (1760), is partly autobiographical,
and there is a life by W.H. Badham in THE WORKS OF THE LATE G.A.
STEVENS, ESQ. . . . (London: for Washbourn & Son, Gloucester, c.1823);
orig. pub. 1807?). See also THE ADVENTURES OF A SPECULIST . . ., 2
vols. (1788), compiled from Stevens's papers and also including a biography.
There are no collected or modern editions of Stevens's plays and only occasional
references in secondary materials subsequent to Baker's BIOGRAPHIA DRA-
MATICA (1812), I, 688-91.

CHARLES STUART (fl. 1780's)

Stuart, born in Scotland, was a journalist as well as a dramatist. His plays are all interludes, entertainments, and farces. They include THE COBBLER OF CASTLEBURY (1779), DAMNATION and RIPE FRUIT (1781), GRETNA GREEN (1783, with O'Keeffe), THE BOX-LOBBY LOUNGERS and THE DISTRESSED BARONET (1787), THE STONE EATER (1788), and THE IRISHMAN IN SPAIN (1791, from the banned play SHE WOULD BE A DUCHESS). THE EXPERIMENT (1777) is sometimes attributed to Stuart. There are no collected or modern editions of his plays and only scattered references in modern secondary materials.

NAHUM TATE (1652-1715)

Tate, son of a Puritan clergyman, was born and educated in Ireland. His plays belong to the early part of his career; after 1688 he was primarily a poet, becoming laureate on the death of Shadwell in 1692 and historiographer royal in 1702. BRUTUS OF ALBA (1678) was his first play, followed in December 1679 or January 1680 by THE LOYAL GENERAL. THE HISTORY OF KING RICHARD THE SECOND was the first of his adaptations of Shakespeare; it was produced about December 1680 as THE SICILIAN USURPER, prohibited after two performances, produced again in January 1681 (as THE TYRANT OF SICILY), and again prohibited. Tate's most famous play, THE HISTORY OF KING LEAR (1681, from Shakespeare), soon became a stock play and was the preferred version of the tragedy for more than a hundred years. THE INGRATITUDE OF A COMMONWEALTH (Dec. 1681 or Jan. 1682, from CORIOLANUS) was less successful. A DUKE AND NO DUKE (1684, from Cokain's TRAPPOLIN SUPPOSED A PRINCE) was another great success; like LEAR, it was a stock piece for a century. Later plays include CUCKOLD'S HAVEN (1685, from EASTWARD HO!), THE ISLAND PRINCESS (1687, from Fletcher), INJURED LOVE (not acted, pub. 1707), and the text for Henry Purcell's great opera DIDO AND AENEAS (c.Dec. 1689).

There is no collected edition of Tate's plays. DIDO AND AENEAS was published by Oxford Univ. Press (London, 1926); a facsimile of the text was printed by Boosey and Hawkes in 1961. It is also included in editions of Purcell's works. A DUKE AND NO DUKE is included in Leo A. Hughes and Arthur H. Scouten's TEN ENGLISH FARCES (1948*). Facsimiles of all four Shakespearean adaptations are available from London's Cornmarket Press. KING LEAR was included in Montague Summers's SHAKESPEARE ADAPTATIONS (1922*), but is better read in Christopher Spencer's FIVE RESTORATION ADAPTATIONS OF SHAKESPEARE (1965); it is also available in the Regents Restoration Drama series (Lincoln: Univ. of Nebraska Press, 1975), ed. James Black.

The best study of the life and work of Tate is Christopher Spencer's NAHUM TATE (New York: Twayne, 1972); chapters 4-6 are devoted to the plays. Histories of the laureateship rarely devote much attention to Tate's dramatic career. Biographical notes (incorporated into Spencer's study) include H.F. Scott-Thomas's "The Date of Nahum Tate's Death," MLN 49 (1934), 161-71, and "Nahum Tate, Laureate: Two Biographical Notes," MLN 56 (1941), 611-12; and Samuel H. Golden's "The Three Faithful Teates," N&Q 200 (1955), 374-80, "Variations in the Name of Nahum Tate," N&Q 201 (1956), 72, and "The Late Seventeenth-Century Writer and the Laureateship," HERMATHENA 89 (1957), 30-38. Arthur H. Scouten shows in "An Italian Source for Nahum Tate's Defence of Farce," ITALICA 27 (1950), 238-40, that much of the preface to A DUKE AND NO DUKE and the essay derived from it (1693) is from A. Mariscotti's DE PERSONIS (1610).

Aside from Spencer's study, there are few general accounts of Tate's work. The best is perhaps H.F. Scott-Thomas's "Nahum Tate and the Seventeenth Century," ELH 1 (1934), 250-75, which concludes that Tate was not a man of his age. Hazelton Spencer's SHAKESPEARE IMPROVED (1927*) is the standard depreciation of the three adaptations; others will be found in the works cited in Part 1, Section 8.2. DIDO AND AENEAS is discussed in Wilfred Mellers's HARMONIOUS MEETING and Robert E. Moore's HENRY PURCELL AND THE RESTORATION THEATRE (1961); see also Eric W. White, "New Light on DIDO AND AENEAS," in HENRY PURCELL 1659-1695: ESSAYS ON HIS MUSIC, ed. Imogen Holst (London: Oxford Univ. Press, 1959), pp. 14-34. The editor's essay in the same collection, "Purcell's Librettist, Nahum Tate," pp. 35-41, argues persuasively that Tate must have his share of credit for the unity and effect of the opera. A DUKE AND NO DUKE is discussed very briefly in Kathleen M. Lea's "Sir Aston Cokayne and the 'Commedia dell' arte,'" MLR 23 (1928), 47-51.

KING LEAR, on which most attention has focused, is treated in the works mentioned above, by Moody E. Prior in THE LANGUAGE OF TRAGEDY (1947), by Kenneth Muir in "Three Shakespeare Adaptations," PLS 8 (1959), 233-40, and by Margareta Braun in "'This Is Not Lear': Die Leargestalt in der Tateschen Fassung," SJ 99 (1963), 30-56. These are primarily depreciations and ignore both theatrical and contemporary values to attack Tate's adaptation as a poem inferior to Shakespeare's. Christopher Spencer's "A Word for Tate's LEAR," SEL 3 (1963), 241-51, is a fine attempt to place the emphasis where it belongs, as is T.D. Duncan Williams's Mr. Nahum Tate's KING LEAR," SN 38 (1966), 290-300. More specialized studies include James Black, "The Influence of Hobbes on Nahum Tate's KING LEAR," SEL 7 (1967), 377-85, and Lawrence D. Green, "'Where's My Fool?': Some Consequences of the Omission of The Fool in Tate's LEAR," SEL 12 (1972), 259-74 (a particularly interesting essay). The stage career of this adaptation is discussed by James Black, "An Augustan Stage-History: Nahum Tate's KING LEAR," RECTR 6, no. 1 (1967), 36-54; by Henry F. Lippincott, "Tate's LEAR in the Nineteenth-Century: The Edwin Forrest Promptbooks," LC 36 (1970), 67-75; by Geoffrey Hodson, "The Nahum Tate LEAR at Richmond," DRAMA, no. 81 (1966), pp. 36-39; and by Peter L. Sharkey, "Performing Nahum Tate's KING LEAR . . .," QJS 54 (1968), 398-403 (a revival at Berkeley, California, in 1967). INJURED LOVE, an adaptation from Webster, is the subject of Hazelton Spencer's "Tate and THE WHITE DEVIL," ELH 1 (1934), 235-49. Spencer also has a brief note on RICHARD II in "A Caveat on Restoration Play Quartos," RES 6 (1930), 315-16.

WILLIAM TAVERNER (d. 1731)

Taverner, the son of a portrait painter, became a civil lawyer and eventually procurator-general of the Canterbury Court of Arches. His plays--all comedies with a persistent interest in intrigue--are THE FAITHFUL BRIDE OF GRANADA (1704), THE MAID'S THE MISTRESS (1708), THE FEMALE ADVOCATES (1713), EVERYBODY MISTAKEN and PRESUMPTUOUS LOVE (1716), THE ARTFUL HUS-BAND and THE ARTFUL WIFE (1717), and 'TIS WELL IF IT TAKES (1719). THE ARTFUL HUSBAND was Taverner's only real success; it was later adapted by Colman senior as THE FEMALE CHEVALIER (1778) and by William Macready as THE BANKNOTE (1795). There are no collected or modern editions of Taverner's plays and only scattered references in modern secondary sources.

LEWIS THEOBALD (1688-1744)

Theobald, son of a Kentish lawyer, also became a lawyer before turning to a literary career. He is best known for his edition of Shakespeare and his controversy with Alexander Pope but in his own day was also recognized as a minor poet, scholarly translator of the classics, and critic, as well as a writer of ineffective tragedies and very successful pantomimes. His tragedies include THE PERSIAN PRINCESS (1708), THE PERFIDIOUS BROTHER (1716), KING RICHARD THE SECOND (1719, from Shakespeare), DOUBLE FALSEHOOD (1727), and THE FATAL SECRET (1733, from THE DUCHESS OF MALFI). PAN AND SYRINX (1718), ORESTES (1731), and THE HAPPY CAPTIVE (1741) are operatic pieces; the masque DECIUS AND PAULINA was included in act 5 of THE LADY'S TRIUMPH (1718), a play usually attributed to Elkanah Settle. Theobald's pantomimes were enormously popular. They include HARLEQUIN A SORCERER (1725), APOLLO AND DAPHNE (1726), THE RAPE OF PROSERPINE (1727), PERSEUS AND ANDROMEDA (1730), MERLIN (1734, with John Galliard), and ORPHEUS AND EURYDICE (1740, listed as anonymous by Arthur H. Scouten in THE LONDON STAGE, but attributed to Theobald by Allardyce Nicoll [HISTORY], Emmett J. Avery [NEW CBEL], and others). Excluding MERLIN, which was not particularly successful, these pieces were performed more than six hundred times between 1747 and 1761 alone; their popularity waned after John Rich's death, but several of them survived to the 1770's. Theobald also published translations of Sophocles's ELECTRA (1714), AJAX (1714), and OEDIPUS (1715), and of Aristophanes's PLUTUS and THE CLOUDS (1715).

There is no collected edition of Theobald's plays. RICHARD II and DOUBLE FALSEHOOD are available in facsimile (London: Cornmaket Press, 1969 and 1970); the latter has also been edited by Walter Graham (WESTERN RESERVE UNIV. BULLETIN, n.s. 23 [1920], 1-89). The only full study is Richard F. Jones's LEWIS THEOBALD: HIS CONTRIBUTION TO ENGLISH SCHOLARSHIP . . . (New York: Columbia Univ. Press, 1919), which includes a bibliography and some discussion of the plays. Edward B. Koster's "Lewis Theobald," ES 4 (1922), 20-31 and 49-60, is merely a synopsis of Jones's book in the guise of a review.

Most of the secondary scholarship on Theobald as dramatist concerns DOUBLE FALSEHOOD. Theobald's claim that the play was Shakespeare's and that he had acquired a manuscript or manuscripts of it was not widely believed at the time and has been disputed ever since. The facts are that no manuscript was ever produced and that Theobald did not include the play in his edition of Shakespeare. The argument is therefore based primarily on the notions that the play, taken as a whole, is beyond Theobald's powers as a dramatist and that it shows traces of more than one hand. Gamaliel Bradford began the modern controversy with "'The History of Cardenio, by Mr. Fletcher and Shakespeare,'" MLN 25 (1910), 51-56, an article connecting DOUBLE FALSE-HOOD and Theobald's manuscript with the 1653 Stationers' Register entry to Moseley for this lost play. Bradford argued that Theobald wrote acts 1-3, but that 4-5 show the hand of Fletcher or a skilled Elizabethan or Elizabethan imitator. Rudolph Schevill, in "Theobald's DOUBLE FALSEHOOD?" MP 9 (1911), 269-85, attacked Bradford's argument on the grounds that the link posited between Theobald and Cervantes was spurious; Schevill was proven wrong by Walter Graham, "The CARDENIO-DOUBLE FALSEHOOD Problem," MP 14 (1916), 269-80. Graham supported Bradford's argument, concluding that the style is not typically Theobald's and that there is evidence of two styles similar to those used in THE TWO NOBLE KINSMEN and HENRY VIII. Ernest C. Oliphant, in "DOUBLE FALSEHOOD: Shakespeare, Fletcher, and Theobald," N&Q 137 (1919), 30-32, 60-62, and 86-88, argued that Theobald had no knowledge of the CARDENIO entry, that there is a sound basis for Fletcher's hand in the play, but not so much evidence for Shakespeare's. He even assumes (in his study of Beaumont and Fletcher, 1927) that the names of Fletcher and Shakespeare were on Theobald's manuscript.

Eduard Castle, in "Theobalds DOUBLE FALSEHOOD und THE HISTORY OF CARDENIO von Fletcher und Shakespeare," ARCHIV 169 (1936), 182-99, looks at analogs of the story in European literature. John Cadwalader's "Theobald's Alleged Shakespeare Manuscript," MLN 55 (1940), 108-09, is negligible, as is Leonard Schwartzstein's "The Text of THE DOUBLE FALSEHOOD," N&Q 199 (1954), 471-72. The main line of argument was renewed by Kenneth Muir in "CARDENIO," EA 11 (1958), 202-09, reprinted in his SHAKESPEARE AS COLLABORATOR (1960); he argues that Theobald probably had an old manu-script, since parts of the play seem beyond his powers, but thinks he did not know of the Register entry; this conclusion was accepted by Walter W. Greg in THE FIRST FOLIO OF SHAKESPEARE: ITS BIBLIOGRAPHICAL AND TEX-TUAL HISTORY (Oxford: Clarendon Press, 1955). Paul B. Bertram, in SHAKESPEARE AND 'THE TWO NOBLE KINSMEN' (New Brunswick, N.J.: Rutgers Univ. Press, 1965), reviews the evidence, agreeing with Muir and Greg that Theobald did not know of the CARDENIO entry and concluding that Shakespeare had no connection with DOUBLE FALSEHOOD. Theobald, Bertram argues, had one or more manuscripts attributing the play to Fletcher and Shakespeare, did not believe the attribution, but pretended to accept it in order to make money.

The next step was taken by Harriet C. Frazier, who in "Theobald's THE DOU-BLE FALSEHOOD: A Revision of Shakespeare's CARDENIO?" CD 1 (1967), 219-33, argues convincingly that Theobald's play was his own. Her argument, perhaps not as well presented as it might have been, is strengthened consider-ably by "The Rifling of Beauty's Stores: Theobald and Shakespeare," NM 69 (1968), 232-56, in which Frazier investigates the pattern of Shakespearean imitation in Theobald's work generally. John Freehafer rejects the Frazier view in "CARDENIO, by Shakespeare and Fletcher," PMLA 84 (1969), 501-13, arguing that Theobald did not tell the truth about his play because his patron believed the Shakespearean attribution. Frazier has countered with "Speculation on the Motives of a Forger: Theobald's THE DOUBLE FALSE-HOOD," NM 72 (1971), 287-96, and there the matter rests.

A few articles and notes concern other plays. William Ingram, in "Theobald, Rowe, Jackson: Whose AJAX?" LC 21 (1965), 91-96, attributes AJAX to Rowe rather than Theobald. Clifford Leech, in JOHN WEBSTER: A CRITICAL STUDY (London: Hogarth Press, 1951*), considers Theobald's version of THE DUCHESS OF MALFI a perversion; R.K. Kaul's "What Theobald Did to Webster," IJES 2 (1961), 138-44, is a much fairer comparison. George W. Whiting discusses THE HAPPY CAPTIVE briefly in "THE TEMPLE OF DULNESS and Other Interludes," RES 10 (1934), 206-11. A 1716 promptbook of THE PER-FIDIOUS BROTHER is discussed by Edward A. Langhans in "Three Early Eighteenth-Century Manuscript Promptbooks," MP 65 (1967), 114-29; RICHARD II is one of the plays treated by Kenneth Muir in "Three Shakespeare Adaptations," PLS 8 (1959), 233-40.

EDWARD THOMPSON (c.1738-86)

Thompson was a naval officer who eventually became a commodore (1783); besides writing some well known contemporary poems and satires, he edited Oldham, Paul Whitehead, and Marvell. His plays include THE HOBBY HORSE (1766), THE FAIR QUAKER (1773, from Charles Shadwell), THE SIRENS (1776), ST. HELENA (1777; Richmond, 1776), and THE SERAGLIO (1776, with Charles Dibdin). In "Garrick and an Unknown Operatic Version of LOVE'S LABORS LOST," RES 15 (1939), 323-28, George W. Stone, Jr., shows that Thompson altered Shakespeare's play at Garrick's request about 1773, but the version was never performed. There are no collected or modern editions of Thompson's plays and few references to him in modern secondary works.

JAMES THOMSON (1700-48)

THE WORKS OF MR. THOMSON, vol. 2 (1736), includes SOPHONISBA (1730); the edition of 1738 adds AGAMEMNON (1738). THE WORKS . . ., 2 vols. (1744), adds EDWARD AND ELEANORA (1739). THE WORKS . . ., ed. George Lyttleton, 4 vols. (1757), also includes ALFRED (1740, with David Mallet), TANCRED AND SIGISMUNDA (1745), and CORIOLANUS (1749, from Shakespeare); the last was reprinted several times and is available in a facsimile of the 1757 Smock Alley edition (London: Cornmarket Press, 1969). JAMES THOMSON 1700-1748: LETTERS AND DOCUMENTS, ed. Alan D. McKillop (Lawrence: Univ. of Kansas Press, 1958), is standard; see also his "Two More Thomson Letters," MP 60 (1962), 128-30.

A good memoir by Patrick Murdock was included in the 1762 edition of the WORKS; Johnson's life in THE LIVES OF THE POETS includes a few remarks on the plays. The first modern study of consequence was Léon Morel's exhaustive JAMES THOMSON: SA VIE ET SES OEUVRES (Paris: Hachette, 1895), which has full discussions of all the plays. William Bayne's JAMES THOMSON (Edinburgh: Oliphant et al., 1898) devotes parts of two chapters to the plays, finding them bombastic; George C. Macaulay's JAMES THOMSON, written for the English Men of Letters series (London: Macmillan, 1908), is a bit more positive, stressing their classical style and declamatory language. The best biography is Douglas Grant's JAMES THOMSON: POET OF 'THE SEASONS' (London: Cresset Press, 1951), which deals with the plays only incidentally; Frederick S. Boas's account of them in EIGHTEENTH-CENTURY DRAMA (1953) may be used to supplement Grant's. Alan D. McKillop's "Thomson and the Licensers of the Stage," PQ 37 (1958), 448-53, is a more specialized treatment of political elements in AGAMEMNON and other plays.

Studies of specific plays are technical in nature. John E. Wells's "Thomson's AGAMEMNON and EDWARD AND ELEANORA--First Printings," RES 18 (1942), 478-86, describes the known editions and issues of both plays. Jean B. Kern, "James Thomson's Revisions of AGAMEMNON," PQ 45 (1966), 289-303, compares revisions in acts 2-5 between June 1737 and April 1738. Alan D. McKillop untangles the complicated stage history of ALFRED in "The Early History of ALFRED," PQ 41 (1962), 311-24, distinguishing the original Thomson-Mallet text from Arne's alteration (Dublin, 1744), Mallet's later opera (1751), and Arne's final version (1753). William B. Todd's bibliographical note, "Unauthorized Readings in the First Edition of Thomson's CORIOLANUS," PBSA 46 (1952), 62–66, deals with changes introduced by Lyttleton after Thomson's death. Jean B. Kern's "The Fate of James Thomson's EDWARD AND ELEANORA," MLN 52 (1937), 500–502, explains why the play was banned; F. Holthausen's "Die Quellen von Thomson's EDWARD AND ELEANORA," BA 51 (1940), 116–18, adds John Speed, Thomas Fuller, and Rapin to the source listed in "Zu James Thomsons EDWARD AND ELEANORA," BA 29 (1918), 71–73. SOPHONISBA was attacked and defended almost immediately after its appearance (A CRITICISM ON THE NEW SOPHONISBA . . . and A DEFENCE OF THE NEW SOPHONISBA . . ., both 1730). Later studies include A. José Axelrad's LE THEME DE SOPHONISBE DANS LES PRINCIPALES TRAGEDIES DE LA LITTERATURE OCCIDENTALE . . . (Lille, France: Bibliothèque Universitaire, 1956); Arthur E. Case's "Aaron Hill and Thomson's SOPHONISBA," MLN 42 (1927), 175–76 (minor); and David F. Foxon's "'Oh! Sophonisba! Sophonisba! Oh!,'" SB 12 (1959), 204–13 (a bibliographical note on the first printing of the play). Recent studies of TANCRED AND SIGISMUNDA are also bibliographical--T.R. Francis's "Some Dublin Editions of Thomson's TANCRED AND SIGISMUNDA," BC 7 (1958), 190; Francis's addenda in "Thomson's TANCRED AND SIGISMUNDA," BC 8 (1959), 181–82; and Carl J. Stratman's further addenda in "TANCRED AND SIGISMUNDA," BC 9 (1960), 188.

JOHN THURMOND THE YOUNGER (fl. 1720's)

The elder Thurmond was a well known actor; his son also acted but was primarily a dancer and pantomime-maker for Drury Lane. His dramatic pieces include THE DUMB FARCE (1719), HARLEQUIN DOCTOR FAUSTUS (1723), HARLEQUIN SHEPHERD (1724), APOLLO AND DAPHNE and THE MISER (1726), and HARLEQUIN'S TRIUMPH (1727). He may also have had a hand in a number of other harlequinades, like THE RISE OF VENICE (1728). HARLEQUIN DOCTOR FAUSTUS was the most popular of his contrivances; THREE ENTERTAINMENTS (1727) included this piece, APOLLO AND DAPHNE, and HARLEQUIN'S TRIUMPH. There are no modern editions and only scattered references to Thurmond in modern secondary materials.

EDWARD TOPHAM (1751-1820)

Topham was the son of a York magistrate; he attended Eton and Cambridge, but left the university without a degree. After traveling in Europe and Scotland, he purchased a commission in the life guards and achieved some reputation for fashionable dress and manners. He was a talented writer of prologues and epilogues and produced as well four two-act farces in the 1780's--DEAF INDEED (1780), THE FOOL (1785), SMALL TALK (1786), and BONDS WITHOUT JUDGMENT (1787). After 1787 he was involved as a journalist with THE WORLD. He retired to Yorkshire early in the 1790's. There are no collected editions of Topham's plays and only infrequent references in modern secondary sources.

CATHARINE TROTTER [COCKBURN] (1679-1749)

Catharine Trotter, daughter of a naval officer who died when she was very young, was born in London in 1679. She was quite precocious; her first play (AGNES DE CASTRO, Dec. 1695 or Jan. 1696) was written when she was about sixteen. FATAL FRIENDSHIP (1698), LOVE AT A LOSS (1700), THE UNHAPPY PENITENT (1701), and THE REVOLUTION OF SWEDEN (1706) are her other plays. None was particularly successful, though the last had six performances. She had early been interested in philosophy; this interest intensified after her marriage in 1708 to Cockburn, a minister, and she produced no more plays. THE WORKS OF MRS. CATHARINE COCKBURN . . ., 2 vols. (1751), was prefaced with a biography by Thomas Birch. There are no modern collections or editions. For surveys of her career, see Edmund W. Gosse, CATHARINE TROTTER: THE PRECURSOR OF THE BLUESTOCKINGS (London: from EDH, 1916), and Herbert Carter, "Three Women Dramatists of the Restoration," BJ 13 (1925), 91-97.

SIR SAMUEL TUKE (c.1620-74)

Tuke was entered in Gray's Inn in 1635 but joined the army of Charles II and rose to a command position before the fall of the royalist forces. He was consequently well treated at the Restoration--knighted in 1664, made a baronet, and sent on several diplomatic missions. His one play, written at the suggestion of Charles II, is THE ADVENTURES OF FIVE HOURS (1663, derived from Coello's LOS EMPEÑOS DE SEIS HORAS); it established the vogue of the cloak-and-dagger intrigue comedy. The play was edited by Adriaan E.H. Swaen (Amsterdam: Swets & Zeitlinger, 1927) and by Bertie van Thal and Montague Summers (London: R. Holden, 1927); Swaen's edition is preferable. The introductions to these editions contain some biographical information; see also Esmond S. deBeer's "Sir Samuel Tuke," N&Q 161 (1931), 345-47. The best account of Tuke's play is Allison Gaw, "Tuke's ADVENTURES OF FIVE HOURS in Relation to the 'Spanish Plot' and to Dryden," in STUDIES IN ENGLISH DRAMA, FIRST SERIES, (Philadelphia: Univ. of Pennsylvania, 1917), pp. 1-61, a very thorough study of the play and its influence. The other major account is that of John C. Loftis in THE SPANISH PLAYS OF NEOCLASSICAL ENGLAND (1973).

SIR JOHN VANBRUGH (1664-1726)

THE PLAYS OF SIR JOHN VANBRUGH, 2 vols. (1719), includes THE RELAPSE
(1696, a "sequel" to Cibber's LOVE'S LAST SHIFT), AESOP (part 1, 1696;
part 2, 1697--from Boursault), THE PROVOKED WIFE (1697), THE FALSE
FRIEND (1702, from Le Sage and Zorrilla), THE CONFEDERACY (1705, from
Dancourt), THE MISTAKE (1705, partly from Molière and Dryden), and A
JOURNEY TO LONDON (unfinished, published 1728). Editions after 1734
also include THE COUNTRY HOUSE (1698, from Dancourt). An afterpiece,
THE CUCKOLD IN CONCEIT (1707, from Molière), was not printed. Vanbrugh also collaborated with Colley Cibber on THE PROVOKED HUSBAND
(1728) and adapted Fletcher's THE PILGRIM (1700). For SQUIRE TRELOOBY,
see under Congreve, above. Most of the plays are included in Leigh Hunt's
collection (1840); the plays were edited by William C. Ward, 2 vols. (London: Lawrence & Bullen, 1893), again omitting THE PILGRIM. The Mermaid
edition, ed. Adriaan E.H. Swaen (London: T.F. Unwin, 1896*) includes
Leigh Hunt's biography. The standard edition is THE COMPLETE WORKS OF
SIR JOHN VANBRUGH, ed. Bonamy Dobrée and Geoffrey Webb, 4 vols.
(London: Nonesuch Press, 1927-28). This edition also includes Vanbrugh's
letters, but see also Howard P. Vincent, "Two Unpublished Letters of Vanbrugh," N&Q 173 (1937), 128-29; John Barnard, "Sir John Vanbrugh: Two
Unpublished Letters," HLQ 29 (1966), 347-52; Albert Rosenberg, "New Light
on Vanbrugh," PQ 45 (1966), 603-13 (also prints the two letters printed by
Barnard); and Arthur R. Huseboe, "Vanbrugh: Additions to the Correspondence,"
PQ 53 (1974), 135-40. Both THE PROVOKED WIFE and THE RELAPSE,
ed. Curt Zimansky, are available in the Regents Restoration Drama series
(Lincoln: Univ. of Nebraska Press, 1969 and 1970), THE PROVOKED WIFE is
also in Alexander N. Jeffares's RESTORATION COMEDY collection; and has
been edited by James L. Smith for the New Mermaid series (London: Benn,
1974). THE RELAPSE is available in facsimile from Scolar Press (London) and
has been edited by Bernard Harris for the New Mermaid Series (London: Benn,
1971).

The standard biography of Vanbrugh has been Laurence Whistler's SIR JOHN
VANBRUGH, ARCHITECT AND DRAMATIST 1664-1726 (London: Cobden-
Sanderson, 1938*). However, a new biography, Madeleine Bingham's MASKS
AND FAÇADES: SIR JOHN VANBRUGH, THE MAN IN HIS SETTING (Lon-
don: Allen & Unwin, 1974), has recently appeared. Briefer surveys include
Kenneth N. Colville's essay in FAME'S TWILIGHT (1923), pp. 185-212;

Bonamy Dobrée's in ESSAYS IN BIOGRAPHY 1680-1726 (1925*); and Bernard Harris's pamphlet for the British Writers series (London: Longman, Green, 1967). Two notes by Herbert S. Vaughan, "Vanbrugh Family" and "Some Vanbrugh Problems," N&Q 155 (1928), 117, and 157 (1929), 62, deal with Vanbrugh's family.

Hazlitt's remarks on Vanbrugh's comedies in A VIEW OF THE ENGLISH STAGE (1818) and LECTURES ON THE ENGLISH COMIC WRITERS (1819) fairly represent early nineteenth-century criticism; see also the preface to Hunt's edition. Contemporary criticism was often on the morality of the plays; Vanbrugh himself entered the Collier controversy with A SHORT VINDICATION OF 'THE RELAPSE' AND 'THE PROVOKED WIFE' FROM IMMORALITY AND PROFANE-NESS . . . (1698*). Modern criticism begins with John L. Palmer's essay in THE COMEDY OF MANNERS (1913*), which after a biographical survey considers only the three original comedies. Palmer's view, popular for a generation, is that Vanbrugh represents insincerity, confusion, and decline; his comedy fails because it harks back to older models and no longer reflects the moral values of contemporary life. Palmer can praise only the dramatist's insight into motive and character, his judgment, and his humor. Bonamy Dobrée gives part of a chapter in RESTORATION COMEDY (1924*) to Vanbrugh, but his picture is as negative as Palmer's; Vanbrugh has no vision and is totally derivative, but can offer broad humor and clever dramaturgy. Henry T.E. Perry, in THE COMIC SPIRIT IN RESTORATION DRAMA (1925*) offers a fuller treatment than Palmer or Dobrée, but the best of the prewar essays is Paul Mueschke and Jeanette Fleisher, "A Re-evaluation of Vanbrugh," PMLA 49 (1934), 848-89, which argues sensibly for seeing Vanbrugh, not as a writer in the comedy of manners tradition or a transitional figure marking a decline from Congreve, but as a vital dramatist presenting unsentimentally the social life of his day. The authors stress Vanbrugh's interest in the problems of the younger brother and the inharmonious marriage and analyze the three original plays in terms of these two themes.

It may be fair to say, as Gerald M. Berkowitz does in "Sir John Vanbrugh and the Conventions of Restoration Comedy," GENRE 6 (1973), 346-61, that the Mueschke-Frazier article is the only significant critical discussion of Vanbrugh in the past century; certainly he is not far wrong. The only other substantial essay one can cite is "Sir John Vanbrugh: THE PROVOKED WIFE," in REPRESENTATIVE ENGLISH COMEDIES, 4 . . ., ed. Charles M. Gayley and Alwin Thaler (New York: Macmillan, 1936), 407-26. Many of the recent books on Restoration comedy stop short of Vanbrugh; studies of eighteenth-century comedy often treat him only in passing. Kenneth Muir's survey in THE COMEDY OF MANNERS is better than most but too brief to be more than suggestive. Berkowitz argues that Vanbrugh deliberately explodes the conventions of Restoration comedy, subverting and modifying such conventions as the duel of wit or the use of clothing as symbols of character and attitude. The argument is interesting, but Berkowitz assumes a "formula" which one doubts ever existed; it is difficult to see Vanbrugh's plays as a conscious departure from previous practice. It is possible that the question of originality troubles critics unduly; surely it is not unreasonable to expect a study of all of Vanbrugh's work which considers both their theatrical and literary merit. That study, however, remains to be written. Two specialized articles may be noted

here: Barry N. Olshen's "The Original and 'Improved' Comedies of Sir John
Vanbrugh: Their Nineteenth-Century London Stage History," RECTR 12, no. 1
(1974), 27-52, and Philip Olleson's "Vanbrugh and Opera at the Queen's
Theatre, Haymarket," TN 26 (1972), 94-101. Laurence Whistler's THE IMAG-
INATION OF VANBRUGH AND HIS FELLOW ARTISTS (London: Art & Tech-
nics, 1954) is focused on its subject's architectural rather than literary gifts.

Articles on THE PROVOKED WIFE include Anthony Coleman's "Five Notes on
THE PROVOKED WIFE," N&Q 214 (1969), 298-300, and "Sir John Brute on
the Eighteenth-Century Stage," RECTR 8, no. 2 (1969), 41-46, and Frank M.
Patterson's "The Revised Scenes of THE PROVOKED WIFE," ELN 4 (1966),
19-23. More attention has been paid to THE RELAPSE, Vanbrugh's best play.
Pieter J. Van Niel, in "THE RELAPSE--into Death and Damnation," ETJ 21
(1969), 318-32, sees the play as Loveless's rejection of Amanda (and a state of
grace) for the devil, and consequently as a victory of the irrational over the
Christian order of love--a thesis which tends to ignore the play as a comedy.
Carl R. Kropf's "THE RELAPSE and the Sentimental Mask," JNT 1 (1971),
193-99, is an interesting discussion of the relation of plot to subplot, but
again in terms of a somewhat exaggerated religious paradigm; Amanda and
Loveless are Christ and sinner, and false worship is a central theme in the
play. Kropf does see the play as anti-sentimental; his insistence on the con-
nections of the two plots is echoed by Irma Z. Sherwood, "Vanbrugh's ROMEO
AND JULIET: A Note on THE RELAPSE," RECTR 12, no. 2 (1973), 41-45.
This article suggests that material from CAIUS MARIUS is yoked with that from
Cibber, distorting the tragic and romantic into the comic and cynical; each
plot alters its original for comic purposes. A similar argument is presented by
Jack D. Durant in "THE RELAPSE, Shakespeare's ROMEO, and Otway's
MARIUS," RECTR 12, no. 2 (1973), 46-49; both writers take hints from the
introduction to Zimansky's edition of the play and develop the notion of inverted parallels or parody as part of Vanbrugh's technique. The argument is
interesting, though not entirely convincing. Perhaps the best discussions of
the play are Arnold N. Kaul's remarks in THE ACTION OF ENGLISH COM-
EDY (1970) and Alan Roper's in "Language and Action in . . . THE RELAPSE,"
ELH 40 (1973), 44-69. Roper handles the religious imagery sensitively, concluding that the play demonstrates the ubiquity of vice without recommending
virtue, and shows the "unresolvable discrepancy" between public and private
life. Roper's emphasis on language is echoed in Bernard Harris's "The Dialect
of Those Fanatic Times," BROWN COLLECTION, pp. 10-40.

FRANCIS GODOLPHIN WALDRON (1733-1818)

Waldron was an actor and also prompter at the Haymarket. His plays include
THE MAID OF KENT (1773, altered as 'TIS A WISE CHILD KNOWS ITS
FATHER in 1795), THE CONTRAST (1775), IMITATION (Richmond 1782, London 1783; altered as HEIGHO FOR A HUSBAND!, 1794), THE PRODIGAL
(1793, an interlude based on THE FATAL EXTRAVAGANCE), LOVE AND MAD-
NESS (1795, from THE TWO NOBLE KINSMEN), THE VIRGIN QUEEN (unacted, published 1797), THE MAN WITH TWO WIVES (1798), and THE MIL-
LER'S MAID (1804). There are no collected or modern editions of Waldron's
plays and only scattered references in modern secondary sources.

WILLIAM WHITEHEAD (1715-85)

Whitehead, the son of a baker, was born in Cambridge and attended Winchester and Cambridge, becoming a fellow of his college in 1742. He came to London about 1745 and achieved some success both in the theatre and the world of letters, becoming laureate upon the death of Colley Cibber. His plays include two tragedies (THE ROMAN FATHER, 1750; CREUSA, QUEEN OF ATHENS, 1754), a comedy (THE SCHOOL FOR LOVERS, 1762), and a farce (A TRIP TO SCOTLAND, 1770). All four pieces were successful; the two tragedies were reprinted in several contemporary collections. To the PLAYS AND POEMS BY WILLIAM WHITEHEAD, ESQ. . . ., 2 vols. (1774), was added a third volume (York, 1788), prefixed by William Mason's memoir. There are no modern editions of Whitehead's plays. Austin Dobson's "Laureate Whitehead," OLD KENSINGTON PALACE AND OTHER PAPERS (London: Chatto & Windus, 1910), pp. 140-72, is a biographical sketch, as is the account in Edmund K. Broadus's THE LAUREATESHIP . . . (Oxford: Clarendon Press, 1921*). The fullest account is August Bitter's WILLIAM WHITEHEAD-- POETA LAUREATUS . . . (Halle, Germany: Niemeyer, 1933), a monograph in German. Chapter 4 of this work takes up each of Whitehead's plays in turn, but the discussion is not rewarding.

JAMES WILD (c.1749-1801)

James Wild, long-time prompter at Covent Garden, was responsible for an adaptation of Fielding's THE MISER (1788) and a group of pantomimes--POLU-SCENICON (1789, usually attributed to Wild), HARLEQUIN'S CHAPLET (1789, a collection of famous pantomime scenes), HARLEQUIN AND FAUSTUS (1793), and HARLEQUIN AND OBERON (1796, with John Follett). There are no collections or modern editions of these pieces and only scattered references to Wild's plays in modern secondary materials.

JOHN WILSON (1627?-96)

Wilson was born in London, the son of a clergyman of Welsh descent. He attended Exeter College but took no degree, was called to the bar in 1649, and eventually became recorder of Londonderry. His plays are THE CHEATS (1663), ANDRONICUS COMENIUS (c.1663), and BELPHEGOR (Dublin before 1675, London 1690). THE PROJECTORS (printed 1665) may also have been acted. ANDRONICUS (printed 1661 and probably acted 1660-61) is attributed to Wilson; it may be an earlier version of ANDRONICUS COMENIUS. See Milton C. Nahm, "John Wilson and His 'Some Few Plays,'" RES 14 (1938), 143-54. THE DRAMATIC WORKS OF JOHN WILSON, ed. James Maidment and William H. Logan (Edinburgh: W. Paterson et al., 1874*), includes the first four plays noted above. THE CHEATS has been edited from the manuscript by Milton C. Nahm (Oxford: Blackwell, 1935). For the Smock Alley performance of BELPHEGOR, see William Van Lennep, "The Smock Alley Players of Dublin," ELH 13 (1946), 216-22. For the banning of THE CHEATS, see Frederick S. Boas, "Stage Censorship under Charles II," TLS 15 April 1920, 238, and "Sir Henry Herbert and THE CHEATS," TLS, 22 April 1920, p. 254. William H. Grattan Flood's "John Wilson (Author of THE CHEATS), Recorder of Londonderry," TLS, 21 July 1921, pp. 483-84, dates Wilson's service in this post 1667/68-82. A German dissertation of 1904, K. Faber's WILSONS DRAMEN, studies sources of the plays.

HENRY WOODWARD (1714-77)

Woodward, son of a tallow chandler, was acting at least as early as 1729.
He became a famous comedian and Harlequin, second only to Garrick in comic
roles and superior in some. His plays, mostly pantomimes and farces, include
TIT FOR TAT (1748), QUEEN MAB (1750), A LICK AT THE TOWN and
HARLEQUIN RANGER (1751), THE GENII (1752), FORTUNATUS (1753),
PROTEUS (1755), MARPLOT IN LISBON (1762, from Centlivre), MERCURY
HARLEQUIN (1756), HARLEQUIN'S JUBILEE (1770), and THE MAN'S THE
MASTER (1775, from Davenant). Several of these pieces were played in
Dublin prior to London production. QUEEN MAB and FORTUNATUS were
Woodward's most popular pantomimes, but HARLEQUIN RANGER, THE GENII,
and MERCURY HARLEQUIN were also very successful. There are no collected
or modern editions of Woodward's pieces and few references to him as a drama-
tist in modern secondary materials.

WILLIAM WYCHERLEY (1641-1716)

THE WORKS OF THE INGENIOUS MR. WILLIAM WYCHERLEY . . . (1713) includes all four of Wycherley's comedies and was several times reprinted. WILLIAM WYCHERLEY, ed. William C. Ward for the Mermaid series (London: Vizetelly, 1888*), superseded Leigh Hunt's THE DRAMATIC WORKS OF WYCHERLEY, CONGREVE, VANBRUGH, AND FARQUHAR (1840). Montague Summers's edition, THE COMPLETE WORKS OF WILLIAM WYCHERLEY, 4 vols. (London: Nonesuch Press, 1924), is not textually reliable but contains extensive notes and commentary. THE COMPLETE PLAYS . . ., ed. Gerald Weales (Garden City, N.Y.: Doubleday Anchor, 1966), is a readable edition which has been reprinted in several formats. Arthur Friedman is at work on a new edition to be published by the Clarendon Press.

THE COUNTRY WIFE and THE PLAIN DEALER were edited together, with a substantial introduction, by George B. Churchill (Boston: Heath, 1924). THE COUNTRY WIFE has been edited by Ursula Todd-Naylor (Northampton, Mass.: Smith College Studies in Modern Languages, Vol. 12, 1931), by G.G. Falls in THREE RESTORATION COMEDIES (New York: St. Martin's Press, 1964), by Thomas H. Fujimura for the Regents Restoration Drama series (Lincoln: Univ. of Nebraska Press, 1965), and by John D. Hunt in the New Mermaid series (London: Benn, 1973). A facsimile is also available (London: Scolar Press, 1969). Both this play and THE PLAIN DEALER have been widely anthologized; the latter is also available in the Regents series, ed. Leo Hughes (1967), and in facsimile from Scolar (1971).

Early biographies include the MEMOIRS OF THE LIFE OF WILLIAM WYCHERLEY . . . (1718), usually attributed to Charles Gildon, and Major Pack's brief memoir prefixed to Volume 1 of the POSTHUMOUS WORKS . . . (1728). Charles Perromat's WILLIAM WYCHERLEY: SA VIE, SON OEUVRE (Paris: Alcan, 1921) includes both a biography (pp. 11-108) and a bibliography (pp. 444-68), as well as a now somewhat dated study of the plays. Willard Connely's BRAWNY WYCHERLEY . . . (New York: Scribner's, 1930*) adds some new material, but is rather impressionistic and anecdotal. The biographical chapter in Katharine M. Rogers's WILLIAM WYCHERLEY (New York: Twayne, 1972) is accurate but often presents the dramatist's life too rosily. Biographical notes include W.G. Hargest, "Wycherley and the Countess of Drogheda," TLS, 21 Nov. 1929, p. 960, which should be supplemented with Eleanore Boswell's response, pp. 1001-02, and her later note in MLR 26 (1931), 345. Howard P. Vincent, in "The Date of Wycherley's Birth," TLS, 3 March 1932, p. 155, suggested 1641 rather than the traditional 1640; see the correspondence which followed, p. 202, confirming 1641. Vincent's "The Death of William Wycherley," HSN 15 (1933), 219-42, gives an excellent account of Wycherley's deathbed marriage; W.R. Chadwick's "Wycherley: The Seven Lean Years," N&Q 216 (1971), 30-34, presents a convincing argument that Wycherley may have been imprisoned in the Fleet for less than a year (and certainly less than four years) rather than the seven years heretofore assumed. See also B. Eugene McCarthy, "Biographical Data on William Wycherley and His Father," N&Q 216 (1971), 34-36. Robert J. Allen printed two letters by Wycherley in TLS, 18 April 1935, p. 257.

Wycherley is discussed in William Hazlitt's LECTURES ON THE ENGLISH COMIC WRITERS and in Leigh Hunt's edition, cited above; neither account is remarkable. Macaulay's review of Hunt's work, ER 72 (1841), 490-528, stresses the playwright's immorality--but also his ability. The most important of the early modern accounts is John L. Palmer's in THE COMEDY OF MANNERS (1913). Palmer spends much of his time refuting Macaulay's estimate of Wycherley's character; in discussing the plays, he takes the view that Wycherley's moral fury often intrudes upon and spoils his later plays. THE PLAIN DEALER exposes vice for our disgust, but THE COUNTRY WIFE is the better of the two plays. Palmer's treatment of the moral issue is exceptional for his time, and his essay is still worth reading. Bonamy Dobrée, in RESTORATION COMEDY (1924), takes a view similar to Palmer's: "the virulence [of THE PLAIN DEALER] is absolutely ruthless"; THE COUNTRY WIFE is a masterpiece. Henry T.E. Perry's account in THE COMIC SPIRIT (1925) is inferior, as is Harley Granville-Barker's essay "Wycherley and Dryden," ON DRAMATIC METHOD . . . (London: Sidgwick & Jackson, 1931), pp. 113-55. Elisabeth L. Mignon gives considerable attention to the youth-age opposition in Wycherley's plays in her book CRABBED AGE AND YOUTH (1947).

The postwar emphasis on close reading is clearly evident in Fujimura's chapter on Wycherley in THE RESTORATION COMEDY OF WIT (1952). Fujimura sees that the praise of Wycherley's moral purpose in what the nineteenth-century critics saw as an age of vice was based on their identification of Manly with his creator and argues that this identification is wrong. Wycherley's life shows him to be something of a libertine with a strong satiric and ironic bent; his naturalistic temper, Fujimura thinks, is clearly reflected in his plays, though not necessarily in the character of Manly. Norman Holland gives a chapter in THE FIRST MODERN COMEDIES (1959) to each of the four plays, seeing them largely in terms of their opposition of social convention to natural instinct, and analyzing imagery and structural elements in support of this approach. T.W. Craik, in "Some Aspects of Satire in Wycherley's Plays," ES 41 (1960), 168-79, stresses the truewit-false wit contrast and the lack of structural and thematic unity in the plays; he argues that their author was more interested in theatrical effectiveness than in the serious moral purposes critics have attributed to him. The opposite view is taken by J. Auffret in "Wycherley et ses maîtres les moralistes," EA 15 (1962), 375-88, looking at Wycherley in terms of contemporary French moralists. John S. Bowman's "Dance, Chant, and Mask in the Plays of Wycherley," DS 3 (1963), 181-205, is impressionistic but suggestive of the visual and aural means used to project ideas in the plays.

Anne Righter, in "William Wycherley," BROWN COLLECTION (1965), pp. 70-91, agrees with Holland that the later plays divorce cleverness from goodness; she emphasizes Wycherley's interest in excess, his "astringency," and his nihilism. Rose A. Zimbardo's WYCHERLEY'S DRAMA: A LINK IN THE DEVELOPMENT OF ENGLISH SATIRE (New Haven: Yale Univ. Press, 1965)--the first full-length study of Wycherley's plays in the century--argues a new thesis. Wycherley, as she presents his work, becomes the link between Elizabethan and Augustan formal satire; his plays are less comedies than satires skeptically testing different perceptions of reality and focusing on the vice which satire lashes in order to correct. The "heroes" in the plays are satyr-satirists, and each play presents some sort of thesis addressed by a satiric spokesman and an adversary.

One major weakness common to the approaches taken by Fujimura, Holland, Righter, and Zimbardo--as different in some respects as these approaches are--is that the plays become shadowy battlegrounds for new-critical wars. One has to remind oneself that these works have traditionally been considered comedies, not illustrations of Hobbes, philosophical essays on the appearance-reality problem, or Juvenalian satires. Dramatic effect and theatrical context simply cannot be ignored if one's account of a play is to be convincing. Whatever the weaknesses of Virginia O. Birdsall's WILD CIVILITY (1970), her argument that the protagonists of contemporary comedies are usually actors, showmen, manipulators, and mischief-makers at least accords with some basic comic values. Wycherley, however, presents difficulties in applying her thesis which are not really overcome in the three chapters devoted to him.

If Kenneth Muir's essay on Wycherley in THE COMEDY OF MANNERS (1970) is the best brief survey of the plays, Katharine M. Rogers's book (noted above) is perhaps the best of the extended accounts. Both give sensible discussions of the plays, taking into account the major modern scholarship but avoiding its excesses. Cynthia Matlack's "Parody and Burlesque of Heroic Ideals in Wycherley's Comedies: A Critical Reinterpretation of Contemporary Evidence," PLL 8 (1972), 273-86, argues for the deliberate inclusion of Christina, Alithea, and Fidelia in their respective plays as heroic characters whose function is to question the effectiveness of heroic ideals and sentiments in contemporary society. Gerald Weales, "William Wycherley," MQR 12 (1973), 45-58, emphasizes theatrical artifice in the plays. More specialized articles include Emmett L. Avery, "The Reputation of Wycherley's Comedies as Stage Plays in the Eighteenth Century," RSW 12 (1944), 131-54; Richard C. Blakeslee, "Wycherley's Use of the Aside," WS 28 (1964), 212-17; Sujit Mukherjee, "Marriage as Punishment in the Plays of Wycherley," REL 7, no. 4 (1966), 61-64 (marriage as poetic justice in the plays); and Archer Taylor, "Proverbs in the Plays of William Wycherley," SFQ 21 (1957), 213-17.

Several articles and notes consider Wycherley's sources, including a number of German dissertations. The debt to Molière is explored by John Wilcox in THE RELATION OF MOLIERE TO RESTORATION COMEDY (1938), pp. 82-104, and in several other of the studies listed in Part 1, Section 8.4. George B.

Churchill, "The Originality of William Wycherley," in SCHILLING ANNIVER-
SARY PAPERS, ed. Arthur H. Quinn (New York: Century, 1923*), pp. 65-
85, discusses the borrowings in some detail, noting that Wycherley replaces
Molière's value system with satire. Debts to Furetière's LE ROMAN BOUR-
GEOIS are explored by Edwin E. Williams in "Furetière and Wycherley: LE
ROMAN BOURGEOIS in Restoration Comedy," MLN 53 (1938), 98-104, and
M.J. O'Regan in "Furetière and Wycherley," MLR 53 (1958), 77-81 (espe-
cially Oldfox in THE PLAIN DEALER).

Fujimura considers LOVE IN A WOOD naturalistic, but he follows standard
opinion in denying it any structural unity. Holland stresses the oppositions in
plot, imagery, and theme; he sees more unity in the play than Fujimura does.
Zimbardo, agreeing with Holland that the play owes much to Fletcher's GEN-
TLE SHEPHERDESS, goes on to exaggerate the pastoral element in it; her thesis, suggestive but Procrustean, is attacked by Virginia O. Birdsall in WILD
CIVILITY as ignoring the heavy, coarse elements in the play which distinguish
it from the pastoral romance. Katharine M. Rogers (1972) treats the play as
a conventional comedy of the period, funny and spirited. Eric S. Rump's
"Theme and Structure in Wycherley's LOVE IN A WOOD," ES 54 (1973),
326-33, studies the thematic connections between the three plots, particularly
in terms of light (knowledge) versus dark (ignorance) images. Source studies
include James U. Rundle's "Wycherley and Calderón: A Source for LOVE IN
A WOOD," PMLA 64 (1949), 701-07, which notes that the Ranger-Christina
plot comes from Calderón's MAÑANAS DE ABRIL Y MAYO (1632). Paul F.
Vernon, "Wycherley's First Comedy and Its Spanish Source," CL 18 (1966),
132-44, argues that Rundle unfairly depreciates Wycherley's workmanlike use
of the Calderón material. John C. Loftis's SPANISH PLAYS OF NEOCLASSI-
CAL ENGLAND (1973) gives a good summary of the extent of Wycherley's
debt.

THE GENTLEMAN DANCING-MASTER will not fit Fujimura's thesis very well
and is, therefore, considered too farcical and uneven to be a good play. Holland's analysis is more impressive; he stresses the thematic significance of
dancing in the action and fits the play neatly into his appearance-versus-reality thesis. Katharine M. Rogers disparages the play in relation to LOVE IN
A WOOD; Virginia O. Birdsall agrees with Holland that it is more unified
than Wycherley's first play but with Fujimura that it is also too farcical and
repetitious. Rose A. Zimbardo treats the play as Wycherley's only formal
comedy; since it therefore does not fit her scheme, her treatment of it is
sketchy and unconvincing. Notes on the play include R.F.'s "William Wycherley," N&Q (1924), 70, and T.W. Tyrrell's response, p. 103--both concerned
with an allusion to Mustard Alley, and D. Biggins's "Source Notes for Dryden,
Wycherley, and Otway," N&Q 201 (1956), 298-301 (a debt to Jonson's THE
DEVIL IS AN ASS).

The two major plays have provoked much more discussion. John L. Palmer
(1913) considered THE COUNTRY WIFE the best farce in English literature, "a
whirlwind of inspired buffoonery." Norman N. Holland values the play equally
highly; whereas Palmer saw Horner as reflecting the contemporary code of the
rake, Holland treats him as the reflection of READER'S DIGEST morality. The

Pinchwife plot shows one wrong way of life, the Horner plot another; Harcourt and Alithea represent the right way, so that this action becomes "the education of Alithea." The analysis which follows, if oversubtle, is provocative and detailed. In Zimbardo's discussion, Horner becomes the parasite-malcontent of a formal satire--the public satirist in him screens the private satyr. Her analysis is interesting but not finally convincing, since it ignores the play's dramatic structure. Birdsall stresses the influence of Jonson, especially VOLPONE; Rogers, the themes of selfishness pervading human social relationships. To Anne Righter's notion of Horner as a sexual monomaniac, and the conceptions of his character just noted, Rogers opposes a view related to Palmer's: Horner is a truewit, but with "comically sordid aspects."

Independent studies of the play include "THE COUNTRY WIFE: No Place to Hide," N&Q 203 (1958), 250-51, an article on the disguise theme in the play attributed by Avery in the NEW CBEL to R.E. Hughes; Carl Wooten, "THE COUNTRY WIFE and Contemporary Comedy: A World Apart," DS 2 (1963), 333-43, comparing the play's moral attitudes with those of three modern plays; and Vivian Mercier, "From Myth to Idea and Back," in IDEAS IN THE DRAMA . . ., ed. John Gassner (New York: Columbia Univ. Press, 1964), pp. 42-70, arguing that the play does not present any meaningful confrontation of ideas or ideals. David M. Wilkinson, in THE COMEDY OF HABIT (1964), provides the best depreciation of the play, emphasizing and objecting to its stylization, patterning, stereotyped characters, and substitution of statement for demonstration. David M. Vieth, in "Wycherley's THE COUNTRY WIFE: An Anatomy of Masculinity," PLL 2 (1966), 335-50, analyzes the interrelation of the three plots in terms of their treatment of what constitutes true masculinity; his essay is perceptive and stimulating. Ronald Berman's "The Ethic of THE COUNTRY WIFE," TSLL 9 (1967), 47-55, treats Horner as often the voice of good sense in the play, a representative of the new materialism who masks himself to remove the masks worn by others. Roy S. Wolper's "The Temper of THE COUNTRY WIFE," HAB 18, no. 1 (1967), 69-74, attacks those who see the play as a satire, noting that the play is far too ambiguous and complex to imply a clear moral norm--"The wenchers and the married both are victorious and undefeated." LeRoy J. Morrissey stresses the stylized and dance-like movement of the play in "Wycherley's Country Dance," SEL 8 (1968), 415-29. Peter Malekin, "Wycherley's Dramatic Skills and the Interpretation of THE COUNTRY WIFE," DUJ 31 (1969), 32-40, and Fernand Lagarde, "L'art de Wycherley: créateur des personages dans THE COUNTRY WIFE," CALIBAN 7 (1970), 3-21, are less impressive than William Freedman's "Impotence and Self-Destruction in THE COUNTRY WIFE," ES 53 (1972), 421-31, which looks at male inadequacy in the play's three plots as Wycherley's symbol of the defects of contemporary society. Charles A. Hallett, in "The Hobbesian Substructure of THE COUNTRY WIFE," PLL 9 (1973), 380-95, argues that the three questions basic to the play are posed and resolved as an attack on Hobbes's theory that the best society is founded on enlightened self-interest.

More specialized articles include Emmett L. Avery, "THE COUNTRY WIFE in the Eighteenth Century," RSW 10 (1942), 141-72; Robert Megaw, "The Two 1695 Editions of Wycherley's COUNTRY WIFE," SB 3 (1950-51), 252-53 (reversing the order in Woodward and McManaway's CHECKLIST); and Fernand Lagarde, "Wycherley et Webster," CALIBAN 1 (1965), 33-45 (stressing debts to Webster and other earlier playwrights).

The central problem of THE COUNTRY WIFE is how to interpret Horner; that of THE PLAIN DEALER, how to interpret Manly both as a character and as a figure central to the tone and structure of the play. John L. Palmer objected to the play's nihilism, not its supposed indecency; a more balanced account is given by Herbert E. Cory, "William Wycherley: THE PLAIN DEALER," in REPRESENTATIVE ENGLISH COMEDIES, 4 . . ., ed. Charles M. Gayley and Alwin Thaler (New York: Macmillan, 1936), pp. 257-71. Thomas A. Fujimura stresses the notion of Manly as a comic butt, despite the tag "manly Wycherley" applied to the dramatist by contemporaries. Norman N. Holland, analyzing the play according to his appearance-reality scheme, notes that in THE PLAIN DEALER the "right way" becomes unreal; Fidelia upsets the realism of the play. Holland ranks the play with LE MISANTHROPE, but his analysis is often difficult to follow and at times seems contradictory. Alexander H. Chorney, in "Wycherley's Manly Reinterpreted," in ESSAYS DEDICATED TO LILY B. CAMPBELL (Berkeley and Los Angeles: Univ. of California, 1950*), pp. 159-69, follows Fujimura in seeing Manly as the object of satire but adds the notion that he is a humorous character--the stereotype of the bull in the china shop.

Katharine M. Rogers's "Fatal Inconsistency: Wycherley and THE PLAIN DEALER," ELH 28 (1961), 148-62, reviews the Fujimura-Holland-Chorney view, noting that those who make Manly merely a comic figure or a satiric butt cannot adequately explain the last act of the play, which rewards Manly with Fidelia and clearly presents him as admirable. Her view, repeated in her book (1972), is that the play finally lacks unity, an opinion also sensibly presented by Anne Righter's essay in BROWN COLLECTION (noted above). Rose A. Zimbardo, in "The Satiric Design in THE PLAIN DEALER," SEL 1 (1961), 1-18, first presented her view of the play as "a perfect rendition of formal satire in the dramatic mode." Manly is the satyr-satirist, Freeman his adversary; the play attacks vice and recommends virtue (Fidelia). Ian Donaldson's "The 'Tables Turned': THE PLAIN DEALER," EC 17 (1967), 304-21, follows Righter and Rogers in analyzing Manly's character but makes a virtue of the play's paradoxes and complexities. Its contradictory nature, Donaldson argues, is the source of its energy and brilliance; its weaknesses are the ending, in which Manly is rewarded without developing moral insight, and the wit, which is overplayed and "suicidal." Anthony M. Friedson, in "Wycherley and Molière: Satirical Point of View in THE PLAIN DEALER," MP 64 (1967), 189-97, returns unconvincingly to the notion of Manly as a comically honest and naive man used to attack a corrupt society. B. Eugene McCarthy, in "Wycherley's THE PLAIN DEALER and the Limits of Wit," ENGLISH MISCELLANY 22 (1971), 47-92, discusses the language of the play

More specialized articles include Percy G. Adams's "What Happened in Olivia's Bedroom? Or, Ambiguilty [sic] in THE PLAIN DEALER," in ESSAYS IN HONOR OF ESMOND LINWORTH MARILLA, ed. Thomas A. Kirby and William J. Olive (Baton Rouge: Louisiana State Univ. Press, 1970), pp. 174-87 (does Manly rape Olivia or not?), and Emmett L. Avery, "THE PLAIN DEALER in the Eighteenth Century," RSW 11 (1943), 234-56 (stage history). Source studies include James L. Shepherd, "Molière and Wycherley's PLAIN DEALER: Further Observation," SCBS 23 (1963), 37-40 (influence of L'ECOLE DES FEMMES); Norman Suckling, "Molière and English Restoration Comedy," BROWN COLLECTION, pp. 92-107; and Peter J. Dorman, "Wycherley's Adaptation of LE MISANTHROPE," RECTR 8, no. 2 (1969), 54-59 and 62 (Wycherley transforms a plotless comedy of character into a complex plotted comedy of situation). J.M. Auffret, in "THE MAN OF MODE and THE PLAIN DEALER: Common Origin and Parallels," EA 19 (1966), 209-22, argues that Manly--despite Molière's Alceste--is an idealized portrait of John Sheffield. Howard Mumford Jones, in "Wycherley, Montaigne, Tertullian, and Mr. Summers," MLN 47 (1932), 244-45, suggests that Wycherley was indebted to Montaigne's essay on Vergil for his scabrous handling of sexuality in the play.

EDWARD YOUNG (1683-1765)

Young is best known as the author of NIGHT THOUGHTS, but he wrote three tragedies spanning more than a quarter of the eighteenth century. They are BUSIRIS (1719), THE REVENGE (1721), and THE BROTHERS (1753). The first two had successful runs, but THE REVENGE was easily the more popular, remaining in the repertory into the nineteenth century. A bibliography is included in Walter Thomas's LE POETE EDWARD YOUNG . . . (Paris: Hachette, 1901); see also Francesco Cordasco, EDWARD YOUNG: A HANDLIST OF CRITICAL NOTICES AND STUDIES (New York: for Long Island Univ. Press, 1950). Both THE WORKS OF THE AUTHOR OF NIGHT THOUGHTS, 4 vols. (1757), and THE DRAMATIC WORKS OF EDWARD YOUNG (1778) include the plays, as does THE COMPLETE WORKS OF EDWARD YOUNG, ed. James Nichols, 2 vols. (London: Nichols, 1854*). Young's correspondence has been edited by Henry Pettit (Oxford: Clarendon Press, 1970).

Samuel Johnson's life of Young was written by Herbert Croft, though Johnson gives a brief paragraph to the plays in his concluding comment. Thomas's study, noted above, is exhaustive both biographically and critically; see also Henry C. Shelley, THE LIFE AND LETTERS OF EDWARD YOUNG (London: Pitman, 1914). Frederick S. Boas, in "A Manuscript Copy of Edward Young's BUSIRIS," TLS, 22 May 1930, p. 434, compares a manuscript copy with the first edition of the play.

INDEXES

Index of Names

Index of Play Titles

INDEX OF NAMES

This index is alphabetized letter-by-letter; numbers refer to page numbers and underlined numbers to main entries. All names mentioned in the text are indexed except names of dramatic characters, some names mentioned only in the titles of books or articles, and names of publishers. Organizations and associations are indexed when they serve as the author of a publication.

Index of Names

Index of Names

Behn, Aphra 52, <u>99-100</u>, 131, 294, 295
Belden, Mary M. 179
Beljame, Alexandre 60
Bell, Hamilton 23
Bellen, E.C. van 244
Benjamin, Lewis 33, 36, 189
Benn, T. Vincent 208
Bennett, Gilbert 78
Bensley, Edward 233
Benson, George 29
Bentley, Eric 10, 44, 63, 73, 85
Berger, Arthur V. 191
Bergmann, Fredrick 186, 187
Bergquist, G. William 4
Berkeley, David S. 60, 66, 67, 133
Berkowitz, Gerald M. 183, 184, 285, 315
Berman, Ronald 170, 173, 260, 285, 326
Bernard, William B. 35
Bernbaum, Ernest 72, 73, 99, 100, 235
Bernhardt, W.W. 162
Bertram, Paul B. 305
Berveiller, Michel 180
Besterman, Theodore 1
Bettany, William A.L. 223
Betterton, Thomas 48, 78, <u>101-02</u>, 287
Bevan, Bryan 36
Bevan, Ian 31
Bevis, Richard W. 15
Bickerstaffe, Isaac 75, <u>103</u>, 187, 228
Bicknell, Alexander 35
Biggins, D. 161, 259, 325
Bingham, Frederick 28
Bingham, Madeleine 290
Birch, Samuel 104
Birch, Thomas <u>91</u>, 312
Birdsall, Virginia O. 65, 67, 125, 128, 169, 170, 324, 325, 326
Birley, Robert 233
Birrell, Augustine 189
Bissell, Benjamin H. 57
Biswanger, Raymond A., Jr. 167
Bitter, August 318
Black, James 302
Blair, Thomas M.H. 98
Blake, William 180

Blakeslee, Richard C. 324
Blakiston, Noel 258
Blanchard, Rae 296, 297
Blashfield, Evangeline W. 99
Block, Tuvia 291
Blow, John 74
Boaden, James 37, 38, <u>105</u>, 220, 228
Board, M.E. 27
Boas, Frederick S. 28, 54, 58, 73, 91, 103, 111, 112, 115, 120, 135, 141, 173, 176, 179, 189, 195, 211, 215, 226, 235, 250, 265, 279, 290, 291, 297, 308, 320, 329
Bogorad, Samuel N. 179, 257
Bohn, William E. 68
Boissy, Louis de 180
Bolton, Margaret 184
Bond, Donald F. 3, 7, 46, 50, 296
Bondurant, Alexander L. 157
Bonner, Charles 255
Booth, Michael R. 15, 54, 73, 123
Borgman, Albert S. 248, 284
Bossuet, Jacques 44
Boswell, Eleanore 18, 133, 322
Boswell, James 43, 180, 195, 240
Bouilly, Jean Nicolas 123
Boursault, Edmé 274, 275, 314
Boutet de Monvel, Jacques M. 104, 277
Bowers, Fredson T. 7, 9, 98, 101, 127, 150, 151, 159, 162, 163, 167, 233, 246, 269, 295
Bowman, John S. 323
Bowyer, John W. 112
Boyce, William 186
Boyette, Purvis E. 170
Boyle, Roger. See Orrery, Roger Boyle, Earl of
Boys, Richard C. 224
Bracegirdle, Anne 248
Bracher, Frederick 168
Brack, O.M., Jr. 175
Bradbrook, Frank W. 291
Bradford, Gamaliel 305
Braganza, Catherine of 242
Braham, George C. 83, 185
Braun, Margareta 302
Brayley, Edward W. 21
Brecht, Bertold 191

Index of Names

Index of Names

Cossel, Louise von 49
Cotton, William 27
Courthope, William J. 91
Coward, Noel 126
Cowley, Hannah (Parkhouse) 131
Cox, R.S., Jr. 171
Craig, Hardin 50, 72, 161
Craik, T.W. 323
Crawford, Bartholow V. 63, 107
Crawford, James P.W. 127
Crean, P.J. 19, 59, 118
Crinò, Anna M. 152
Croft, Herbert 329
Croft-Murray, Edward 34, 36
Croissant, DeWitt C. 72, 114
Crosby, Benjamin 33
Cross, Gustav 233
Cross, John Cartwright 132
Cross, Richard 22, 24
Cross, Wilbur L. 175, 176
Crowhurst, G.W. 261
Crowne, John 78, 133-34, 265
Cudworth, Charles 75
Cumberland, John 14
Cumberland, Richard 58, 72, 135-
  36, 208, 211
Cummings, William H. 76, 286
Cunningham, John E. 26, 53
Cunningham, Peter 36
Cunningham, Robert N. 246
Cunnington, Cecil W. 19
Cunnington, Phyllis 19
Curll, Edmund 37, 38, 48, 188
Cushing, Helen 2

D

Dacier, André 69
Daghlian, Philip B. 291
Daiches, David 50
Daland, Will 11
Daly, Augustin 39
Dance, George 137
Dance, James 137
Danchin, Pierre 30, 86
Dancourt, L.H. 314
Darlington, William A. 78, 290
Dasent, Arthur I. 36
Davenant, Sir William 22, 68, 101,
  138-39, 154, 159, 162, 286, 287,
  321

Davies, Godfrey 6
Davies, H. Neville 157
Davies, Paul C. 170
Davies, Thomas 37, 55, 125, 184,
  195, 235, 258
Davis, Herbert 124, 141
Davison, Dennis 15
Day, Cyrus L. 10, 151, 166, 167
Day, Robert A. 99
Dean, Winton 76, 83
Deane, Cecil V. 68, 257
Dearing, Vinton A. 150, 200
deBeer, Esmond S. 160, 216, 220,
  313
De Castro, Paul 184
Deelman, Christian 82, 185, 291
Defoe, Daniel 291
Dejaure, Jean E.B. 228
Delap, John 140
Delius, Nicholas 138
DeLoutherbourg, Philippe. See
  Loutherbourg, Philippe de
de Mandach, André. See Mandach,
  André de
Dennis, John 42, 44, 55, 91, 141-
  42, 153, 297
Dent, Edward J. 76, 160, 188
Dent, John 143
Derrick, Samuel 260
Destouches. See Néricault-Destouches,
  Philippe
des Vivetières. See Marsollier des
  Vivetières
Detisch, Robert J. 136
Deutsch, Otto E. 76
Devenish, Anne 278
Devine, Mary E. 8
Devlin, James J. 98
Dias, Dary 224
Dibdin, Edward R. 144
Dibdin, Charles, the Elder 48, 52,
  144-45, 146, 307
Dibdin, James C. 29
Dibdin, Thomas John 137, 146
Dick, Hugh G. 10
Dilke, Thomas 147
DiLorenzo, Ronald E. 165
Dircks, P.T. 75, 254
Dircks, Richard J. 78, 135, 186
Disher, Maurice W. 57, 73
Dix, E.R. 194

338

Index of Names

Fuller, John 115, 189
Fuller, Thomas 309
Furetière, Antoine 325
Fussell, Paul, Jr. 229
Fyvie, John 33, 164, 179

G

Gabriel, Miriam (later Mueschke)
 291
Gagen, Jean E. 58, 128, 154
Gagey, Edmond McAdoo 77, 177,
 190
Galliard, John E. 217, 267, 304
Galt, John 33
Gamble, William B. 2
Gardner, William B. 151
Garnett, Richard 50
Garrick, David 20, 31, 74, 78, 82,
 83, 103, 106, 121, 177, 183-87,
 201, 202, 206, 228, 250, 275,
 291, 294, 307, 321
Gassman, Byron 196
Gassner, John 45, 64, 326
Gaw, Allison 153, 313
Gay, John 49, 54, 70, 74, 77,
 115, 122, 177, 188-91
Gaye, Phoebe F. 189
Gayley, Charles M. 15, 63, 174,
 315, 327
Geisinger, Marion 49
Gemmingen, Otto H. von 209
Genest, John 47, 51, 86
Gentleman, Francis 33, 55, 127,
 186, 192
George I 278
Gerber, Helmut E. 186
Gerould, Gordon H. 261
Gerritsen, Johan 9
Ghosh, Jyotish C. 258
Gibbon, Brian 125, 126
Gibbs, A.M. 138
Gibbs, J.W.M. 194
Gibbs, Lewis. See Cave, Joseph W.
Gilde, Joseph M. 286
Gilder, Rosamond 2, 34
Gildon, Charles 47, 99, 101, 193,
 279, 322
Gillespie, Gerald 70, 261
Gillet, Joseph E. 86

Gilliand, Thomas 48
Gilmore, Thomas B., Jr. 114
Gipson, Alice E. 211
Giteau, Cécile 2
Glasgow, Alice 290
Glick, Claris 84
Glicksman, Harry 115
Glover, Richard 195
Goberman, Max 188
Godden, Gertrude M. 176
Godwin, William 208
Goethe, Johann Wolfgang von 196,
 209, 276
Goggin, L.P. 156, 176, 178
Goldberg, Homer 259
Golden, Samuel A. 57
Golden, Samuel H. 302
Goldgar, Bertrand A. 177
Golding, William 233
Goldoni, Carlo 121, 148, 199
Goldsmith, Oliver 49, 55, 70, 72,
 73, 194-96
Goldstein, Malcolm 278, 279
Gordan, John D. 121
Gore-Brown, Robert 37
Gosse, Anthony 127
Gosse, Edmund W. 15, 62, 99, 125,
 168, 259, 312
Gottesman, Lillian 76, 186
Graham, Cary B. 85, 141, 166
Graham, Walter 304, 305
Grant, Douglas 151, 308
Granville, George. See Lansdowne,
 George Granville, Lord
Granville-Barker, Harley 158, 323
Graves, Richard 148
Graves, Thornton S. 20, 35, 77
Gravitt, Garland J. 173
Gray, Charles H. 41, 55
Gray, Philip J., Jr. 61
Green, Clarence C. 46
Green, Elvena M. 74, 297
Green, Lawrence D. 302
Greene, Graham 233
Greg, Walter W. 9, 305
Grice, F. 29
Grieder, Josephine 87
Grieder, Theodore 9, 87
Griffin, Benjamin 190, 198
Griffin, William 195
Griffith, Benjamin W., Jr. 188

341

Index of Names

Griffith, Elizabeth 199
Griffith, Reginald H. 115, 236
Grimaldi, Joseph 146
Guffey, George R. 150, 162, 165
Guiet, René 103
Guthke, Karl S. 234
Guthkelch, Adolph C. 91
Guthrie, William 43

H

Habbema, D.M.E. 115
Hafter, Ronald 184
Hagstrum, Jean H. 152, 156
Hahn, Emily 99
Hainsworth, J.D. 187
Hall, Lillian A. 1
Hallett, Charles A. 326
Halliday, Frank E. 82
Halsband, Robert 91
Ham, Roswell G. 159, 161, 232, 258, 281
Hamelius, Paul 294, 295
Hamilton, Marion H. 162
Hampden, John 15
Handasyde, Elizabeth 197
Handel, George Frederick 56, 74, 76, 177, 188
Hands, Terry 170
Hannah, Robert 58
Haraszti, Zoltán 124, 150
Harbage, Alfred C. 4, 7, 8, 53, 60, 138, 154, 162
Harbeson, William P. 235
Harcourt, Bosworth 28
Harding, W.N.H. 10
Hare, Arnold 29, 36
Hare, Maurice E. 297
Hargest, W.G. 322
Hargreaves, Henry A. 100
Harley, Graham D. 129
Harris, Arthur J. 121
Harris, Bernard 68, 161, 314, 315, 316
Harris, Joseph 200
Harris, Thomas 23
Harrison, Thomas P., Jr. 157
Harrison, William 225
Hart, Sophie C. 278
Harth, Philip 152, 155

Hartmann, Cyril H. 35
Hartnoll, Phyllis 1, 5, 59
Hartsock, Mildred E. 153
Harvey-Jellie, Wallace R. 85
Hassall, Anthony J. 176, 177
Hastings, Warren 292
Hatchett, William 203
Hatfield, Glenn W. 176
Hathaway, Baxter 41, 46
Haun, Eugene 76, 141
Hauser, Arnold 73
Hauser, David R. 260
Hauteroche. See Le Breton, Noel, Sieur d'Hauteroche
Havard, William 201
Havens, P.S. 161
Havens, Raymond D. 236
Haviland, Thomas P. 282
Hawkins, Harriett 66, 127, 128, 170
Hawkins, Sir John 49, 195
Haycraft, Howard 34
Hayley, William 202
Hayman, John G. 170
Haywood, Charles 165, 186, 287
Haywood, Eliza 203
Hazlitt, William 62, 125, 189, 208, 297, 315, 323
Hedbaeck, Ann-Mari 139
Hedgcock, Frank A. 184
Heffner, Hubert C. 25, 123
Heilman, Lee W. 92
Heilman, Robert B. 45, 73, 128, 195, 236
Heisch, Elisabeth 10
Heldt, W. 59
Hell, Thomas 123
Heltzel, Virgil B. 92
Hemmings, William 280, 281
Henderson, John 56
Henley, William E. 175
Henn, Thomas R. 45
Hennig, John 196
Henshaw, Nancy W. 77
Herbert, Sir Henry 8
Herrick, Marvin T. 62
Heuston, Edward 190
Heywood, Thomas 139
Hibbard, George R. 196
Hiffernan, Paul 204
Highfill, Philip H. 8, 20, 34, 38, 75

342

Index of Names

Index of Names

Lelyveld, Toby B. 84
Lenanton. See Oman, Carola
Lennep, William Van. See Van
  Lennep, William
Le Sage, René 314
Lessing, Gotthold E. 87
Levine, George R. 176
LeViness, William T. 202
Lewes, John 37
Lewis, Matthew G. 81, <u>234</u>
Lewis, Paul 109
Lewis, Peter E. 107, 165, 189, 190
Ley, William 9
Lillo, George 122, 235-36
Lincoln, Stoddard 1<u>29, 197</u>
Link, Frederick M. 99, 100, 151,
  152
Linley, Thomas 289
Lippincott, Henry F. 302
Lisle de la Drévetière, Louis F. de
  227
Lissner, Max 280
Little, David M. 183
Littlewood, Samuel R. 220
Litto, Fredric M. 5
Lloyd, Claude 286
Lloyd, Robert 94
Locke, John 174, 285
Lockman, John 49
Lockwood, Thomas 176
Loewenberg, Alfred 4, 26, 290
Loftis, John C. 41, 55, 59, 60, 71,
  87, 91, 100, 112, 115, 150, 153,
  155, 157, 159, 161, 176, 195,
  232, 233, 289, 296, 297, 313,
  325
Logan, Terence P. 141
Logan, William H. 14, 133, 138,
  231, 320
Lohenstein, Daniel von 232
Lonsdale, Mark 264
Lonsdale, Roger 50, 75
Lord, Phillip 76
Lorimer, Emily O. 60
Lourdet de Santerre, Jean B. 144
Loutherbourg, Philippe de 19, 74,
  291
Love, Harold 30, 46, 60, 155, 295
Love, James. See Dance, James
Lowe, Robert W. 4, 33. 52, 101,
  114

Lucan 278
Lucchini, Antonio M. 218
Lucey, Janet C. 39
Lumiansky, Robert M. 98
Lundeberg, Olav K. 148
Luttrell, Narcissus 100
Lyles, Albert M. 124
Lynch, James J. 17, 30
Lynch, Kathleen M. 63, 68, 121,
  125, 128, 154, 155, 166, 257
Lyons, Charles R. 127, 128
Lyttleton, George 308, 309

M

McBurney, William H. 235, 260
McCamic, Frances S. 169
McCarthy, B. Eugene 196, 323
Macaulay, George C. 308
Macaulay, Thomas B. 62, 63, 91,
  125, 152, 296, 323
Macaulay, Thomas C. 86
McClumpha, Charles F. 258
McCredie, Andrew D. 75
McDonald, Charles O. 66
Macdonald, Hugh 150, 163
McElderry, Bruce R., Jr. 58
McElroy, Davis D. 5
McElroy, L.A. 5
Macey, Samuel L. 111, 165, 178,
  290
McFadden, George 161
Machiavelli, Nicolo 266
Mackenzie, Aline (later Taylor) 261
Mckenzie, Henry 211, 236
McKenzie, Jack 29
MacKenzie, John H. 112
Mackenzie, Kathleen 38
McKillop, Alan D. 50, 60, 112,
  205, 240, 308
McKinnon, Dana G. 85
Mackintosh, Donald T. 18, 20
Macklin, Charles 20, 43, 78, <u>237-38</u>
McKusker, Honor 229
McLeod, Alan L. 232, 233
McManaway, James G. 9, 11, 15,
  19, 84, 85, 150, 167, 185, 222,
  259, 274, 287, 326
MacMillan, Dougald 9, 11, 14, 71,
  115, 116, 159, 185, 211, 237,
  272, 292

Index of Names

Paul, Harry G. 141
Paul, Henry N. 101, 139
Paulson, Ronald 176
Payne, Frank W. 154, 257
Payne, Henry N. 263
Payne, Rhoda 20
Peake, Charles H. 244
Peake, Richard B. 121
Pearce, Charles E. 36, 37, 190
Pearce, Ethel 9
Pearce, William 264
Pearlman, E. 79
Peavy, Charles D. 36, 114
Peck, Louis F. 234
Pedicord, Harry W. 22, 24, 30, 31, 278
Pemberton, Thomas E. 26
Pendlebury, Bevin J. 154
Penley, Belville S. 26
Pentzell, Raymond J. 20
Pepys, Samuel 173, 251
Percy, Thomas 195
Pereyra, M.L. 286
Pérez de Montalbán, Juan 295
Pergolesi, Giovanni B. 103
Perkin, Richard 285
Perkins, Merle L. 159
Perkinson, Richard H. 61, 85, 163
Perrin, Michael P. 6
Perromat, Charles 322
Perry, Henry T.E. 62, 169, 173, 284, 315, 323
Peterson, Martin S. 222
Peterson, William M. 19, 71, 114, 116, 133, 174, 188, 198, 232, 233
Petit, Herbert H. 156
Pettit, Henry 329
Phare, Elsie E. 291
Philips, Ambrose 265
Philips, William 266
Phillips, Edward 267
Pickering, Roger 43
Pilon, Frederick 56, 83, 268
Pinto, Vivian de Sola 6, 280
Pix, Mary 269
Platt, Harrison G., Jr. 100
Plautus 157, 177
Plutarch 259
Pogson, Rex 27

Pointer, John 101
Pollard, Alfred W. 82
Pont-de-Veyle. See Ferriol, Antoine de, Count of Pont-de-Veyle
Pool, E. Millicent 128
Pope, Alexander 72, 114, 176, 188, 189, 304
Popkin, Henry 4, 41
Popple, William 55
Porter, Endymion 270
Porter, Henry C. 27
Porter, Thomas 270
Poston, Mervyn L. 68
Potter, Elmer B. 127
Pottle, Frederick A. 240
Poullain de Saint-Foix, Germain F. 144, 255
Powell, George 271
Powell, George R. 27
Powell, J. 104
Powell, Jocelyn 170
Powell, William 21
Preston, John 191
Prévost d'Exiles, Antoine F. (Abbé) 87
Price, Cecil 17, 23, 25, 26, 30, 74, 76, 78, 288, 289, 291, 292
Price, Joseph G. 83, 84
Price, Lawrence M. 123, 236
Price, Martin 59, 69, 70, 128, 154, 156, 191
Prior, James 194, 195
Prior, Matthew 158
Prior, Moody 69, 70, 156, 157, 158, 260, 302
Pritchard, William 178
Proffitt, Bessie 260
Protopopesco, Dragosh 125
Prouty, Charles T. 184
Purcell, Daniel 246, 281
Purcell, Henry 11, 74, 101, 151, 160, 281, 301
Purdy, Richard L. 289
Purvis, A. 100

Q

Queensberry, Anna M. Larpent, Duchess of 189
Queensberry, James Douglas, Duke of 278

Index of Names

353

Index of Names

Index of Names

Wallace, John M. 153
Wallace, Leonard 159
Wallerstein, Ruth 156
Walmsley, D.M. 76, 203, 284, 287
Walpole, Horace 43, 73, 222
Walpole, Sir Robert 59, 177, 191
Walsh, Martin W. 248
Walsh, William 129, 272
Walwyn, B. 43
Wann, Louis 61
Ward, Adolphus W. 53, 133, 235
Ward, Charles E. 101, 151, 157,
    161, 163, 287
Ward, W.C. 314, 322
Wardle, Ralph 195
Wasserman, Earl R. 46, 78
Waterhouse, Osborn 72
Waterhouse, Robert 170
Watson, George 3, 42, 151
Watson, Harold F. 58
Watts, Guy T. 27
Watts, John 177
Weales, Gerald 322, 324
Weatherly, Edward H. 180, 184
Weaver, John 49
Webb, Geoffrey 314
Webb, John 23
Webster, John 101, 200, 206, 233,
    302, 304, 327
Weinbrot, Howard D. 156
Weisinger, Herbert 45
Weisstein, Ulrich 19'
Welby, Alfred 25
Welle, J. van der. See Van der
    Welle, J.A.
Wellek, René 42, 45
Wells, James M. 8
Wells, John E. 177, 308
Wells, Mitchell P. 19, 74
Wells, Staring B. 55
Wellwarth, George E. 235
Welwood, James 278
Wenther, Fritz 260
Wermuth, Paul C. 100
Wertheim, Albert 21, 174
West, Michael 153
Westbrook, Jean E. 7
Wewitzer, Ralph 268
Wharton, Robert V. 179
Wheatley, Katherine E. 86, 265

Whetstone, George 139
Whibley, Charles 49
Whicher, George F. 203
Whincop, Thomas 47
Whistler, Laurence 314, 316
White, Arthur F. 133
White, Arthur P. 59
White, Eric W. 11, 75, 302
White, Frederic C. 115
Whitehall, Harold 285
Whitehead, Paul 307
Whitehead, William 318
Whiting, George W. $\overline{22}$, 61, 162,
    174, 306
Whitmore, Charles E. 56
Whitty, John C. 31
Wickham, Glynne 50
Wikelund, P.R. 244
Wilcox, John 57, 86, 169, 324
Wild, James 319
Wilde, Oscar $\overline{126}$
Wiles, Roy M. 25
Wiley, Autrey N. 16, 58, 151
Wilkes, Thomas 48, 55
Wilkins, A.N. 141
Wilkinson, David R.M. 64, 170,
    326
Wilkinson, Tate 29, 38
Wilks, Robert 79
Willard, Helen D. 2
Willcocks, Mary P. 176
Williams, Aubrey 126, 127
Williams, Edwin E. 325
Williams, George W. 290
Williams, Gordon 260
Williams, Iolo A. 189, 194, 288,
    289
Williams, John 33
Williams, Stanley T. 72, 84, 135,
    136
Williams, T.D. Duncan 302
Williamson, G.C. 184
Williamson, Jane 37
Willoughby, L.A. 88
Wilmeth, Don B. 36
Wilson, Albert E. 57
Wilson, James 60
Wilson, John 320
Wilson, John H. $\overline{}$ 9, 15, 25, 34, 35,
    36, 53, 60, 84, 100, 107, 128,
    133, 159, 165, 169, 197, 260,
    280, 295

INDEX OF PLAY TITLES

This index is alphabetized letter-by-letter; numbers refer to page numbers. Only titles of English plays 1660-1800 mentioned in the work are listed; for foreign plays and plays in English earlier than the period covered, consult the appropriate entry in the author index. Adaptations and alterations are listed under the title given the play by the adaptor. If the original title was retained, no attempt is made in the index to distinguish that original from later alterations or adaptations; such distinctions are made in the text. In a few cases an indexed title refers to two different plays; consult the text at the appropriate page references.

Index of Play Titles

Index of Play Titles

Index of Play Titles

Index of Play Titles

Index of Play Titles